Find It Online

The Complete Guide to Online Research

©1999 By Facts on Demand Press
4653 South Lakeshore Drive, Suite 3
Tempe, AZ 85282
(800) 929-3811
www.brbpub.com

Find It Online

The Complete Guide to Online Research

©1999 By Facts on Demand Press and Alan M Schlein
4653 South Lakeshore Drive, Suite 3
Tempe, AZ 85282
(800) 929-3811

ISBN 1-88915006-1
Cover Design by Robin Fox & Associates
Edited by James R. Flowers, Shirley Kwan Kisaichi, Peter J. Weber

Cataloging-in-Publication Data

025.04	**Schlein, Alan**
SCH	Find it online : the complete guide to online research / Alan M. Schlein – 1st ed.

480 p. ; 7 x 10 in. – (Online ease)

Includes bibliographical references and index.

ISBN: 1-889150-06-1

1. Internet addresses—Directories. 2. Web sites—Directories. 3. Internet addresses—Directories. 4. Street addresses—Directories. 5. Database searching. I. Title

ZA4375.S35 1999   025.04
                                    QBI98-1600

Acknowledgments

I owe a lot of people a great deal of thanks for their help and inspiration in getting this book done.

First to my contributors, listed on the back cover and in the indexes section, whose insights have helped teach me and hopefully the readers. You have all been the best mentors and friends anyone could have. You are tops in your fields, and I thank you for sharing your knowledge with me and contributing to the book. Special thanks to Sue Feldman, Greg Notess, Nora Paul and Barbara Quint.

To my speaking and writing partners, Carole Lane and Don Ray, I can't thank you enough for all your help, guidance and support. Thanks for loaning me your expertise and for keeping me on track. I could not have done it without you.

I also want to thank all my friends from the Association of Independent Information Professionals (AIIP) who have been a great support network, particularly Alex Kramer, Mary Ellen Bates, Reva Basch, Richard McEachin, Jan Davis Tudor and my colleagues from Investigative Reporters and Editors. All of you have let me vacuum up your knowledge, and I appreciate your efforts.

To Owen Thompson, Victoria Vanson, Katherine Fee and Ginny McNair for helping me with the administrative support to get this finished.

I also could not have learned the online tools without the help of my colleagues at the online providers like LEXIS-NEXIS, Dow Jones, DIALOG, DBT and the many other companies who have helped me out with access to their services. Same goes for the great folks at PSI-Net, my web provider and my colleagues at the National Press Club for unyielding support.

Thanks also to my publisher, Michael Sankey, for having the faith in me and to my multi-faceted editor, Shirley Kwan Kisaichi, without whom I would never have gotten this done well and on deadline. Thanks for this chunk of your life. And to Jimmy Flowers, Peter J. Weber and the rest of the BRB team for getting the book done well.

On the personal front, thanks to my family for their constant support, particularly my sister Carol as well as my wonderful stress-relief team (you know who you are), for getting me through the rough periods, and my A-team (Kathryn Scott, Kelli Emerick, Holly Klotz, Angela Rollings, Christopher Fotos, J. J. Newby, Lisa Day, Julie Montgomery, Keri McClain, Cynthia Hunter, Mitch Gerber) and my many other friends whose ears I bent in the course of this book. You know how important you are to me.

To Lora Ware, thanks for being the calm in my storm. And of course to my two cats – Moose and Murph – whose endless affection and habit of crawling on top of me at just the right moment was constantly inspiring.

Alan Schlein
February 1999

Contents

Foreword 7

Before You Start 9
Some Basic Terminology.. 9
How to Read an Internet Address 9

Chapter 1 - The Megabusiness of Gathering & Selling Data 11
Data Mining... 11
Online Technology: Picking Up Where Direct Marketing Leaves Off........................ 12
How Much Is Too Much, & When? 13
You Can Level the Playing Field! 18

Chapter 2 - Framing Your Search Strategy 21
Creating Your Own Roadmaps of the Information Superhighway............................... 21
What is a Search Strategy? 22
Other Search Strategy Considerations 26
Sources, Friends & Enemies 26
Boolean Operators & Keywords 26

Chapter 3 - General Search Tools.. 29
Searching & Search Tools: An Introduction.. 29
Search Engines 30
How a Search Engine Works 31
Best Search Engines 33
AltaVista... 33
Excite.. 35
HotBot.. 36
Infoseek 37
Lycos 37
Northern Light 38
Natural Language Search Engines 39
Subject Directories 39
When to Use a Subject Directory: 40
Best Subject Directories 42
General Subject Directories.. 42
Specialized Subject Directories 44
Topic-Specific Subject Directories.. 45
Portals: Enhanced Search Tools 46
Meta-Tools: The Second Generation... 47

    Advantages & Disadvantages of Meta-Tools 47
  Best Meta-Tools 48
  Which Tool to Use? 50
  Search Engine Comparison 50
    Features of Internet Subject Directories 51
    Features of Online Multi-Search Engines 52
  The Hidden Internet: What Search Tools Can't Access 52
    Accessing Hidden Content 53
  Search Tools & HTML 53

Chapter 4 - Specialized Tools 57

  Micro Tools 57
    People Finders 57
    Best People Finders 59
    Specialty People Finders 60
  E-Mail Finders 63
  Expert Finders 63
  Mapping Tools 64
  Document Finders 65
  Macro Tools 69
    Ready Reference Tools 69
  Yellow Page Finders 71
  Quotation Finders 72
  Backgrounding Tools & FAQs 73
  The Human Element 73
  Types of Discussion Groups 73
    Newsgroups 73
    Mailing Lists 74
    Chat Rooms 75
    Conferencing 76
    Searching Newsgroups 78
    Participating in Newsgroup Discussions 80
  Fee-Based Tools for Finding Specialized Information 82
    Using Fee-Based Services 82
  Best Commercial Vendors 83
    Comparing the Giants 86

Chapter 5 - Saving & Downloading Your Results 87

  Identifying File Types 88
  A Field Guide to File Formats 89
  Saving Files 90
    Saving Programs 90
    Saving Documents & Text 90
    Saving Images & Sounds 92
    Web Pages & Screen Captures 92
    Saving Web Links 93
  Compressing & Decompressing Files 93
  Sending or Transferring Files 100
    Via E-Mail 100
    Via Telnet 101

Contents

Via FTP — File Transfer Protocol 102

Chapter 6 - Government Sources Online 105
Government Gateways.. 106
   Best Government Gateways.. 106
Best Online Government Resources 108
State & Regional Resources 112
Best Sites for Government Statistics.. 115
Best International Resources 117
Legal/Legislative Resources 121
Free Legal Resources on the Internet.. 122

Chapter 7 - Public Records 125
Government Records Versus Public Records 126
Types of Public Records... 126
   Voter Records... 126
   Property Records 127
   Grantor/Grantee Indexes.. 128
   Vital Records.. 128
   Court Records... 129
   Bankruptcy Court Records 130
   The Uniform Commercial Code & Tax Liens 131
   Corporate Records 131
   Fictitious Business Name Statements 132
   Other Kinds of Records 132
Document Access & Retrieval.. 136

Chapter 8 - News Resources Online 143
News in General 144
Best News Collections: Print & Broadcast... 145
News Wires.. 146
Top Online News Wires 147
Newspapers.. 148
Top Online Newspapers 148
Magazines & Newsletters 150
Best Magazine & Newsletter Web Sites 151
Television & Radio... 152
E-Zines & Online Publications 153
   Top Online Publications Collections 154
   Foreign News Sources 154
Archives & Transcripts.. 155
Favorite Journalism Collection Sites 156

Chapter 9 - Business Tools 159
Business Resources in General 159
Company & Industry Research... 159
   Backgrounding a Company 159
   Where Do You Start? 160
Company Directories: How to Find Basic Information 161
SEC & Related Resources 162

Should You Pay for SEC Documents? 164
Company Information from News Sources 164
Market Research 165
   Free Sources of Market Research Data... 166
   Market Research Data Vendors 167
   The Giant Databases... 168
Sales Prospecting... 170
Competitive Intelligence.. 171
   CI Example 171
Best Competitive Intelligence Sites 172
Patents & Trademarks.. 177
Personal Financial Information... 178
Investment Research 180

Chapter 10 - Managing & Filtering Information 181

Managing Incoming Information.. 181
   Managing E-Mail... 181
   Managing Web Sites (Bookmark Folders) 182
   Managing Downloads... 183
   Managing Your "Twinkie Time"... 183
Managing Your Offline Life... 183
   Some Helpful Hard Drive Organizers... 184
Filtering: Controlling the Deluge.. 184
Filtering for Kids 185
Best Filtering Tools 186
   Commercial Filtering Tools Recommendations 188
Intelligence Agents 188
Personalized "Opening Pages" 189
   High-Tech Personalization Tools 190
Bots: Personal Search Tools 191
Best Bots... 191
Push Technology 192
   Push: The Downside... 193

Chapter 11 - Evaluating Accuracy, Credibility & Authority 195

Credibility... 196
Authority... 196
   How to Use InterNIC/ICANN to Trace Web Authorship............ 198
Timeliness... 202
Coverage & Objectivity.. 203
   Evaluating Web Site Information 204
   The Quick Link Credibility Test... 205
Useful Evaluative Tools 206
Accuracy: A Pop Quiz.. 207

Chapter 12 - Sample Searches 209

Sample Search 1: People Finder 210
   The Assignment.. 210
   So What Do You Do?... 210
   Can I Go Online Now?... 210

Before Going Online – Q & A...211
   People Finder Search Plan..214
   Postscript to the Tesh Search...222
Sample Search 2: Business Profile..223
   The Assignment:...223
Business Finder Search Plan...224
   Postscript to the Veterinarian's Best Business Profile 230
Sample 3: Problem Solving 231
   My Assignment...231
   Your Assignment 231
   So What Do You Do?..231
   Can I Go Online Now? 232
   Did You Find Enough "Right Information?"...235
Final Thoughts on Search Strategies...235

Chapter 13 - Privacy & Protection...245
Online Interactions: A Reality Check 245
   Privacy & E-mail 247
The Ultimate Gold Mine: You...248
   The Golden Trail of Cookie Crumbs 248
   Get to Know Your Cache 248
Privacy Threats..249
   1. Identity Fraud: A Devastating Epidemic 249
   2. Medical Records: A Privacy Meltdown Waiting to Happen................................250
   3. Children: Prime Targets for Data-Miners 250
   4. Workplace Privacy...251
Your Data & Industry Concerns 252
More Ways to Protect Your Privacy..255
The State of the Law..258
   Some Perspectives on the Larger Debate...259

THE INDEXES

Government Public Records by State...262

Private Online Sources of Public Records 355
Application Indexes..357
Vendor Profiles..364

Web Site Profiles 419
Accuracy..420
Business...424
Employment..436
Filters & Filtering..438
Government & Government Records 444
Miscellaneous 453
News 455
People Finders 464

Privacy 466

Public Records 468

Saving & Downloading 470

Search Engines 471

Specialized Tools 475

Subject Directories 483

Contributors 485

Glossary 487

Page Index 491

Foreword

by James R. Flowers Jr.

The Internet is among the great achievements of the 20th Century, empowering nearly everyone with access to information as never before. As we rush to get online, Internet use is staggering. Some say it is a mess. Others say it has growing pains.

Most agree, however, that the Internet is disorganized. Individuals and organizations launch web sites filled with spelling errors, poor indexing and in some cases, useless content. There is no class required to start a web page, no set of standards to follow when making one, and no "Internet police" around to make sure what appears on the Web is designed to be useful. In addition, web sites that are here today may be gone or in a different location tomorrow. Therefore, it can be very difficult to find what you are looking for.

So, how *do* you find what you care about?

This book is your solution. *Find It Online* enables you to get the information you want as quickly and easily as a professional researcher. It is a practical, how-to guide written by a non-techno geek and developed for real people. *Find It Online* is designed for you – no matter how much computer experience you have.

With *Find It Online*, you get more than 400 pages of valuable information and tips from some of the top online researchers, including exhaustive amounts of *useful* web sites and commercial databases.

The Internet & Online Resources Have . . .

. . . made vast amounts of information available to the masses. Within these pages, you'll learn the difference between search engines and subject directories – plus, you'll discover tricks for using both. *Find It Online* also teaches you how to develop a "search strategy," so that you do not waste time viewing pages that have nothing to do with what you are looking for.

. . . brought people closer together. *Find It Online* gives you the tools necessary to find people online. For instance, you can use the people finders discussed in Chapter 4 to find friends, relatives, colleagues and more.

. . . revolutionized government operations. You can use *Find It Online* to cut through government red tape. The best online government resources are examined in detail in Chapters 6 and 7. Plus, extensive profiles of government agencies online are included in the indexes of this book, making it easy to get what you want from the government directly *and* online.

. . . resulted in the creation of new words and new technologies. By using this book, you will become familiar with newsgroups, FTP, filtering, Telnet, chat rooms, cookies, conferencing and many other emerging technologies and terms.

. . . become sources of news. A great deal of magazines, newspapers and other publications are now available online, and Chapter 8 is your guide to these resources. You'll learn what the top news sites are, how to access archives and where to go for news information about foreign countries.

. . . invaded our privacy. Data is collected about online users and utilized to target advertising. Confidential information may be shared online, and children may be exposed to harmful material. Chapter 13 of *Find It Online* examines the privacy issues raised by the Internet and explains how you can protect yourself online.

. . . changed the way the world does business. Stocks are traded online. Meetings are conducted online. Chapter 9 shows you how to find information on companies, access annual reports, conduct market research and perform competitive intelligence.

. . . produced some questionable content. How can you tell if what you read on the Web is true? Chapter 11 addresses this issue. It illustrates how to find out who owns a particular web site, confirm its credibility and trace its authorship.

Essentially, the Internet has changed our society dramatically. *Find It Online* teaches you how to process and adapt to all of these changes. More than that, *Find It Online* shows you how to find what you want. *Find It Online* is your Internet consultant-on-a-shelf!

Before You Start . . .

Some Basic Terminology

To help those who are new to the foreign language known as "cybergeek speak," here are a few key definitions. For those of you who are comfortable in this language, here's a simple review:

The **World Wide Web** is a vast collection of interconnected computers that offers text, graphics, sounds and video images. Using a **web browser**, which enables you to visit the web sites and see pictures and images, you can click your mouse and connect to a virtual world of endless proportions. You can also use your browser as a communication tool – to send electronic mail or to participate in conferences with others, or group discussions. Netscape Navigator and Microsoft Internet Explorer are the two primary browsers. Both have versions available for Macintosh and Windows operating systems. Both offer similar features. The choice between them is mostly one of personal preference.

One common feature of web pages is **hypertext links** or **hyperlinks**. These are spots (on a web page) on which you can click to move from one page to another. Click on a link button and it will bring up a screen or more information related to that link.

E-mail is the most common Internet function and, perhaps, the most powerful one. It allows you to send and receive individual messages with anyone who has an Internet address anywhere in the world. E-mail also lets you put a human face on the Internet, making contacts with people you know, people you don't know, people you might want to know and some that you wish you didn't know (once you know them, of course).

URL stands for Uniform Resource Locator, which is the address of a web page.

For more definitions, see the Glossary.

How to Read an Internet Address

Let's say we're looking at the following address:
`http://www.whitehouse.gov`

The letters before the ":://" describe the way a browser can get to the resource. The "http://" stands for "Hypertext Transfer Protocol," which is the way the Web moves data around. Following the colon are two slashes (always forward slashes, never backward slashes) and the name of the host computer on which the resource exists — in this case, the "White House." Later in the book we will discuss the importance of .gov, .com and the other three-letter codes used as identifying suffixes. However, to summarize:

> .com   refers to a commercial site.
>
> .org   refers to a non-profit organization's site.
>
> .gov   refers to a government site.
>
> .mil   refers to a military site.

When you see an address like www.voxpop.org:80/jefferson, which is a great collection of political sites, the ":80" part of an address is a port number, which specifies which of the programs running on the host should handle your request.

Within These Pages

Throughout *Find It Online*, you will find sidebars written by contributing experts. The sidebars are comprised of the tips and techniques of many professionals making these pieces well worth reading. A list of the contributors has been included in the Indexes section.

You'll see a lot of tips throughout the book. These practical suggestions are meant to make your online work more efficient.

Chapter 1

The Megabusiness of Gathering & Selling Data

Before getting into the specifics of how to find what you want online, it is important to understand the power of the Internet. Reading this chapter will open your eyes to the Internet and how it affects your life and your privacy.

The Internet is an amazing resource. The doors to virtually unlimited information have swung wide open, and anyone who has computer access has an opportunity to use the Internet's ever-growing resources. But the future is also closing in on us. It is a future in which every detail of our lives is noted, stored and, more often than not, sold to marketers and advertisers, conscientious service-providers and con-artists alike.

If you feel monitored and manipulated – you're right. If you feel vulnerable – well, you should.

For better or worse, online technology is making it easier than ever for personal information to be accessed – and for that information to be collected and disseminated – by a mind-boggling array of people and entities. Even if you don't use a computer, your privacy is being violated on a daily basis. If you think you can avoid the online world, you are sadly mistaken. Like it or not, the online world has already found you.

Data Mining

The process of harvesting information, referred to as "data mining," is a huge, booming business. When you register your pet, your house or your car, pay your taxes, use a credit card, send in a warranty, subscribe to a magazine or conduct any of the hundreds of activities that comprise normal life in America, you leave behind information about yourself. In recent years, the quantity and detail of information about our lives has skyrocketed.

In the old days – called "B.C." for before computers – credit card bureaus and junk mailers collected information about people from the purchases they made and the warranty cards they mailed in. But the companies had to record the information by hand and cross-referencing of the material was an inaccurate and unwieldy process.

They were able to target-market groups by gender, age, ethnicity, neighborhood and so on, but with nowhere near the precision they do now.

Today, every time you use a supermarket's discount card, the store tracks your purchases, builds a profile on you and, most likely, sells that profile to marketing companies – for a surprisingly hefty price. This is a component of "direct marketing." Many companies offer incentives to stores in order to be able to buy this data from them.

Magazines sell their subscription lists to direct marketers, too. Increasingly, so do other institutions such as schools, churches, banks, insurance companies, mail order companies, chain stores, etc. They do it mostly without our knowledge and, in some cases, contrary to our consent. To these companies, information about their customers belongs to them, not you. They consider the money they make from selling the information to be part of their profit stream.

Businesses are not immune to the same kind of targeting. There is such interest in business profiles that many companies build extensive databases, company profiles and reports on industries and competitors. In addition, companies target specific businesses and follow their every movement to get new sales leads, and scour publications and all kinds of information to get a jump on a trend or to stay a step ahead of their competition.

Three of the leading US data-mining companies – Metromail, First Data Corp and Acxiom – each control databases comprising more than 90 million households apiece – or about 140 million people. Information stored in them include our birth dates, how often we travel, what we buy, prescriptions we use and whom we telephone. Some companies also gather, store and sell our Social Security Numbers. The major credit bureaus – Experian, Equifax and Trans Union – maintain databases with information about people's jobs, income, bank accounts, credit limits and *most significantly*, credit card transactions.

Direct marketers who buy wholesale or custom-made databases from credit card companies and other sources use the information to develop more product marketing and targeting strategies. You know those telemarketing calls that keep your home phone ringing off the hook? Guess how they got your name, number and buying habits? Right. Read on.

Online Technology: Picking Up Where Direct Marketing Leaves Off

There is one big difference between traditional direct mail and the Internet. Internet target marketing starts where direct mail ends. Online technology enables *almost anyone* to access information contained in one or more databases and combine them in a nanosecond. This allows the marketers (and their clients) to zero in on your specific interests.

In fact, some of the largest commercial sites on the World Wide Web have agreed to feed information about their customers' reading, shopping and entertainment habits into a system developed by Engage Technologies of Massachusetts. Engage is already tracking the moves of more than 30 million Internet users, recording where they go and what they read — often without the users' knowledge.

This enables webmasters to track users so that advertisements can target the likeliest consumers of goods and services.

Not surprisingly, this technology disturbs privacy-rights advocates who worry about the increasing ability of online companies to collect and store personal data.

> **EXAMPLE:** A cat food company wants to introduce a new line of gourmet food products. Using traditional direct marketing techniques, they could contact a data-miner and purchase lists of people that precisely fit their target profiles. The data would include home addresses, phone numbers, the names of their pets and the contact information for the nearest pet store to their homes.
>
> They could also purchase lists of cat owners and people who buy cat products from supermarkets and pet store companies. Using the Internet, they could purchase lists of e-mail addresses of people who visit cat-related web sites or those who use cat-related newsgroups and mailing lists. Such discussion groups are in abundance on the Internet. The cat-related groups include `alt.animals.felines`, `alt.cats` and `rec.pet.cats.misc`. Discussion groups are discussed further in Chapter 4.

In addition, there are other discussion groups, called mailing lists, where people subscribe to receive correspondence about specific subjects. One cat-related group is called the PURRS listserv. Also, chat groups might be utilized, including #kittens and cats, which dubs itself "a purrfect place for all cats and kittens to chat."

Marketers are only beginning to tap into the resources of these groups. The use of these groups for marketing purposes is expected to increase.

How Much Is Too Much, & When?

Some companies advertise their ability to obtain the past and current addresses, phone numbers, birth dates, driving records, bankruptcy history and other information of just about anyone in the United States. You've seen them on late-night television advertising help in finding lost relatives, men dodging child support obligations, or a certain someone from those hazy high school days.

You could be a customer; you could also be a target. You could be both at the same time without knowing it. That's because the Internet relays information from one computer to the next until it reaches its destination computer. Anyone who can view your data can grab it, copy it and keep it. They can do anything they want with it: alter it, sell it, pass it off as someone else's personal history, you name it.

Most people don't realize that what you thought was a private e-mail between you and a friend could actually be seen by others along the route. At every step along the way your information footprint passes across the screens of numerous online handlers whose staff (permanent, temporary, subcontracted, ex-convicts, whoever) can read your data — information that you never intended for unauthorized viewing.

One example where information considered private surfaced is the e-mail messages of Monica Lewinsky. She may have eliminated them from her computer, but her "friend" Linda Tripp kept copies of Monica's correspondence with President Bill Clinton. Tripp's copies were used by prosecutor Ken Starr as evidence.

Unauthorized collection and abuse of personal data happens all the time. What follows is a humorous letter that illustrates the depth of data collection:

The Letter You'll Never Get

by Don Ray

Don Ray is a multi-media investigative reporter/producer/author and frequent lecturer. His books include *The California Investigator's Handbook*, *Checking Out Lawyers*, *Diggin' Up Gold on the Old Paper Trail: a Guide for Investigatin' Folks* and *Don Ray's 104 Privacy Tips*. Don Ray's web site is www.donray.com/donray, and his e-mail is donray@donray.com.

Dear Mr. Average Consumer:

Just a long-overdue note to say thanks for all the information you gave us yesterday—information we computerized and are making available to hundreds of other marketers like us. You're our prime source of income – and information.

In case you weren't paying attention, here's where you dropped loose "information change" into our little "information piggy bank":

When you turned on your cellular phone this morning, we noted that you got a late start to work. We didn't sell the information, but we're working on it.

You stopped to get gas and used your electronic credit card to pay for the gas and a quart of oil. I see you bought that new synthetic oil. We sold that information to the manufacturer. They said they may send you a coupon for the next one before they sell your address to someone else. You might want to drop them a thank you note.

Did you miss breakfast again? You stopped at that chain fast-food place and used your ATM card. You actually had them put mayonnaise on your potato nuggets? We'll alert the condiment manufacturers. They may want to track the rest of your eating habits.

We were wondering if you were running low on cash. Sure enough, you stopped at the ATM for a $60 withdrawal. Oh, I hope you don't mind — we noticed from the security camera there that you're a bit overweight. Too much mayonnaise and potatoes? Just kidding. We sent the information from your bank account to a couple of weight-reduction clinics. We do our best to keep you in good health.

Hey, thanks for dropping your business card into that fishbowl at the restaurant at lunch. Listen, don't count on getting a free lunch, but we were able to see from your card that you work in retail sales. At your age, you should be doing better. We took it upon ourselves to give your name and address to a couple of trade schools. For a minute we thought you might want to go to the truck driving school, but with your driving record, you might be better off as a dental hygienist.

While you were at work we received that warranty card you mailed last week when you bought the new VCR. Thanks for letting us know that you like to play tennis, you enjoy gardening, and you and the Mrs. have a combined income of $72,000. We'll let the appropriate people know. There are some telemarketers who'll call you tonight to tell you about some promising stock options.

Oh, wait. Tonight's your bowling night. We just got the list from the bowling center. Is your wife going to go to her creative writing class at the community college tonight? After using her credit card to buy $115 worth of textbooks, she'd better.

You went to the supermarket on your way home from work last night. You saved $3.80 by using your Handy Preferred Customer Card, and we were able to learn a lot about your family. You've been buying disposable diapers for two years. You were buying the pink brand, with the protection at the bottom. Now you're buying the blue brand with the protection in front. A baby boy, eh? I confess, we checked the birth certificates to learn the little tyke's name. Brandon, eh? Named after your mother's father. How nice.

You know, we really value all the wonderful marketing information you're giving us. We have visions of tracking you for the next 20 years.

Again, thanks so much to you, your wife Martha, your three kids and Rascal for all you've done for us.

Sincerely,

Your Neighborhood Marketing Folks

P.S.: Forgot to mention that Rascal needs his rabies vaccination before the end of the month.

Believe it or not, some people don't mind marketing. In fact, the following piece illuminates the bright side to advertising on the Internet:

Personal Information from a Marketer's Point of View

by Robbin Zeff, Ph.D.

Robbin Zeff is president of The Zeff Group, a research and training firm specializing Internet advertising and marketing. She wrote the best-selling *Advertising on the Internet* and *The Nonprofit Guide to the Internet*. Address: robbin@zeff.com or www.zeff.com

Before you get all worked up and conclude that the use of personal information by marketers is a bad thing and has no direct benefit to you, consider this:

♦   When is a quarter-page print ad in a magazine not just filler on a page?

♦   When is a billboard not just scenic junk?

♦   When is an ad on the radio not just noise on the airwaves?

♦   The answer is: when it's information you want!

Having someone know what you like and how you like it can simplify the buying process. I like it when I go to my favorite coffee shop and Bill behind the counter knows just how I like my latté and has it ready for me when I get to the front of the line. Bill can do this because I've been there before, and he remembers how I like my latté. Bill also knows that I like scones, and his recommendation of the day's choice of scones will often result in a sale. This personalized service makes me feel at home and results in my returning again and again. In short, it's good business.

Targeting and personalization in advertising on the Internet has the same effect. Through the sophisticated technological capabilities of the Internet, an advertiser can deliver the right ad to the right person at the right time. In the example above, when Bill recommends a scone as he hands me my coffee, he knows that is the right time to hit me up for an additional purchase. This strategy works just as well in selling books or CDs. If you are purchasing the latest murder mystery novel by John Grisham, you might be interested in an ad for a similar page-turner by a different author. In which case, the ad becomes a source of information.

This is precisely the strategy behind targeting and personalization in Internet advertising: put the right ad in front of the right person at the right time to increase the relevancy of the ads to the individual. For the marketer, personal information allows the advertiser to maximize the efficiency of the ad and make each ad a piece of relevant information to the consumer. Targeting like this has been the age-old dream of advertisers. What the Internet brings to the forefront is the ability to deliver on this promise.

Targeting Based on Content & Context

The first level of targeting in marketing is based on content and context. For example, when you read a fashion magazine like *Vogue* or *Glamour*, you expect to see fashion ads for clothing and cosmetics. The content of the magazine is about fashion and the ads are also about fashion. When you read the *Los Angeles Times*, you expect to find ads for businesses in the Los Angeles area. Moreover, the ads in the *Los Angeles Times* not only represent business in that geographic area, but also narrow in on specific interests, so that in the automotive section, you find ads directly relating to cars: car dealers, automotive repairs, car washes, etc. Likewise, when you watch a football game on TV, the commercials reflect the audience demographics so that you see beer and car ads instead of ads for diapers or back-to-school sales.

Targeting based on content and context is easily achieved on the web by placing ads on specific web sites and on particular pages within those sites. Search engines do this through keyword ad placement. For example, an advertiser can buy a specific keyword like "allergy" and every time that keyword is requested, an ad for its allergy relief medicine appears on the page. But this is only the beginning of the targeting capabilities for Internet advertising.

Targeting Based on Analyzing, Web Site Log Files

The next level of targeting information comes from analyzing the log files of web sites. Log files hold all the on-site activity records: who entered the site, what browser was employed, the user's entrance and exit pages, etc. This information is useful for understanding the traffic and usage patterns on a site, but it doesn't provide *demographic* information. Why? The log file identifies *only* the Internet address of the computer that visited the site, *not* the individual behind the computer.

The only real way to get demographic data on the Web is to ask the user for this information. Sites gather data through registration forms, subscription forms, contest registration forms and the like. The strategy works.

> **EXAMPLE:** When the *New York Times* went online, it chose to make access free to all registered users. The value of the demographic information provided by the viewers was deemed to be more valuable than the potential income from subscription fees. Information about the demographic profile of its readership enabled the *New York Times* to charge a premium for its ad space. But online targeting can do even more.

The backbone of direct mail is using databases to target consumers with specific interests and then exposing them to products that their profile might find of interest. These databases are built on previous buying patterns, magazine subscriptions and even ZIP Code analysis. Marketers rent these lists and then send their material to the targeted lists. Internet marketers compile their own lists in addition to overlaying existing database information. The result is that soon Internet marketers will be able to do everything online that traditional direct marketers do through the mail. But online targeting can go even further.

The next level of targeting is unique to the technological capabilities of the Internet. Through a technique called "collaborative filtering," companies are learning the buying preferences of consenting surfers and then using this information to recommend books, music and even movies. The result is that an enabled site can function as an old and trusted sales clerk who knows your taste in music and movies and, consequently, knows just what to recommend.

Then there is a method of Internet targeting based on actual behavior, in which special software analyzes a user's behavior on the site and then presents ads to that user based on analysis of the user's behavior during that particular online session. In other words, the software does not keep the data. Each user session is treated as unique. For example, a surfer who behaves like a thirteen-year-old girl will receive ads that appeal to 13-year-old girls. Likewise if that person comes to the site another day and acts more like an adult, different ads will be shown.

So, is it a bad thing to have an advertiser know what you like and how you like it?

When the issue of access to personal information is put in this light, the answer for most consumers is "No." Targeting in advertising is actually a service to the consumer. One way or another, ads will be shown on web sites. Personally, I appreciate the fact that when I visit my favorite web sites, I'm only shown ads for products and services of interest to me. Likewise, I like the fact that when I walk into my favorite coffee shop, Bill behind the counter knows just how I like my latté. My only hope is that someday my computer will be able to brew up a great latté while I surf the Web.

You Can Level the Playing Field!

You can protect yourself by using the same technology that people are using to find information about you. Later in Chapter 13, we'll show you how to protect yourself and how you can use the information collected about you or someone else to your advantage.

It's a matter of understanding the kind of access that you have in a given situation. Here are some examples:

EXAMPLE 1: You work for a company that solicited and received bids for a large contract. The lowest bid looks good ...too good. So you go online and discover some interesting facts: the low-bidding company was incorporated just two years ago, and its CEO's previous companies were tangled in numerous lawsuits, liens and bankruptcies. Clearly, the CEO had a habit of changing companies every time he ran into trouble – and he ran into trouble regularly.

EXAMPLE 2: You're a divorcee and your alimony checks have been shrinking. You're due a specified percentage of your ex's income, and something seems amiss. So you start digging online and discover that he has remarried and is in the process of transferring his assets to his new wife. Clearly, his strategy is to reduce his assets and reduce his alimony payments. You, however, have a right to file a court appeal – and let's say you do. You are also able to ask the court to recalculate the earlier alimony award, based on an extra business he hadn't revealed the first time around. All of this was accomplished using public records, which cost you almost nothing to access.

The list of everyday applications is endless.

Before you can regain control of how people may be using your information, you must understand the online landscape.

As you read this — whenever you use this book — you will become familiar with tools and concepts that enable you to move freely and effectively online. This final chapter also lays out a number of specific ways for protecting your privacy.

Chapter 2

Framing Your Search Strategy

The Crucial First Step to Staying Afloat in a Sea of Data

Searcher Magazine editor Barbara Quint likens computers to dogs: "faithful, friendly but not very bright." She also thinks they're like children at the "one joke" age in which the punch line is always the same. No matter how many times you complain about something they didn't do, the response is, "Because you didn't ask me" (meaning: "because you didn't ask me *right*!")

If you've ever gone looking for information about a specific subject on the Internet, you probably went to a search engine, input your subject and received a zillion results, called hits. "Wow!" you might have thought. "The Internet is great. Look how much information I found!" A closer look at the results made you think, "Oh, no – I need *useful* information within the next ten minutes!"

How do you reduce the number of hits to a manageable and relevant number of twenty sites? That's the goal of this chapter. Anyone can come up with a zillion hits. The real goal of research is quality information. For that, there are tools – lots of them – each with its own strengths, shortcomings and peculiarities.

Creating Your Own Roadmaps of the Information Superhighway

You're reading this book because you want to burn rubber on the Information Superhighway. Well, the highway exists, all right, but it has potholes that can swallow huge amounts of time, if you let it.

The Internet gained mass appeal in 1994 or thereabouts, when the World Wide Web was established. The Web added graphical capabilities and search engines to Internet documents. Also, the Web made it much easier to navigate between the four million or so web pages available at that time.

Now, there are more than 320 million web pages and counting. None of the 1200-plus search tools in existence can keep up with the mushrooming number of pages. At best, the top five search tools index only about 40% of the sites out there.[*] As it now stands, no one search tool will come close to indexing even half of the Web

---

[*] *Science*, April 3, 1998

anytime soon. Some search engines index only keywords, while others index complete content, graphics, video, audio etc.; still others assign their own keywords based on reviewed content. What does this mean to you? The results of each search engine are different, so you need to become familiar with *several* search tools in order to find your search items. No two search tools provide *identical* results.

This overwhelming, exponential growth is the source of a lot of frustration for would-be researchers. By the time you've devised your own methods for getting around the Internet, it will have changed. Keeping up is, in itself, a full-time job. But there are rules of thumb that will stand you in good stead.

While online research can be frustrating, it can also be fascinating. As we all know, there's usually more than one way to reach an intended destination. If you're stymied in one direction, the trick is to devise another way to get there.

What is a Search Strategy?

People speak often of "surfing the net." Online searching is, essentially, the opposite of online surfing. When surfing the Internet, you have little control over where you go and how you get there. It is akin to TV "channel surfing," where one navigates aimlessly through whatever the media has to offer, looking for something "entertaining" rather than something specific. You simply hitch a ride on a wave of information and go where it takes you.

Searching, on the other hand, is more like being at the helm of a boat. The idea is to go to the destination of your choice directly as possible.

Most good researchers have developed their own ways to focus their searches. The habit dates back to the early days when access was far more restricted and searches cost more because only fee-based tools were available. Consequently, researchers developed the habit of thinking things through before placing an order that would set the dollar meter ticking.

Today so much data is available that, without a plan, you can easily find yourself swimming in an ocean of information. The trick is to stay clearly focused on your goal, and at the same time to be flexible and creative enough to revise your approach, depending on the results you encounter during your online travels.

One of the best approaches is the one devised by Nora Paul of The Poynter Institute, a non-profit foundation for the continuing education of professional journalists. She has taken the "five W's and H" (who – what – when – where – why – how) of reporting and devised a simple checklist that will help you formulate a search strategy by providing many avenues that can take you to the answer you're seeking. Framing your research strategy is critical to finding what you are looking for. A good, clear question will save you hours of work.

Framing Your Question

by Nora Paul

> Nora Paul is the Library Director of The Poynter Institute, a former *Miami Herald* librarian, a nationally-recognized lecturer and co-author, with Margot Williams, of the upcoming *Great Scouts! Cyberguides for Subject Searching on the Web*.

First and foremost, frame your question. Putting your question into words forces you to think about what you want. By taking the time to identify the key phrases and visualize the ideal answer, you'll be more likely to recognize that answer when you find it online.

The following checklist will help you think through the details of your information quest.

Who:

- Who is the research about: a politician, a businessperson, a scientist, a criminal?

- Who is key to the topic you are researching? Are there any recognized experts or spokespersons you should know about?

- Who do you need to talk to: someone who has experienced something, someone who knows someone, someone who is an expert?

- Who have you already talked to? Who do they know who might help you?

What:

- What kind of information do you need: statistics, sources, background?

- What kind of research are you doing: an analysis, a backgrounding report, a follow-up?

- What type of information will be useful: full-text articles or reports, specific facts, referrals to a person, public records?

- What are you trying to do: confirm a fact you've been given, find someone to interview, get up to speed on a topic, background somebody, narrow a broad topic, fill in a hole in your knowledge?

- What would be the best source of the information: an association, a government agency, a research center, a company?

- What information do you already have: what do you already know about the topic or person?

- What would the ideal answer look like? Envisioning the perfect answer will help you recognize it when you find it!

When:

♦ When did the event being researched take place? This will help determine the source to use, particularly, which information source has resources dating far enough back.

♦ When did the event being researched end?

♦ When will you know you should stop searching? (When you have the answer!)

Where:

♦ Where did the event you're researching take place?

♦ Where are you in your research: just starting (looking for background), in the middle (looking for verification of information found), towards the end (looking to tie up loose ends).

♦ Where have you already looked for information?

♦ Where is the biggest collection of the type of information you're looking for likely to be: university research center, association files, a specialty database?

♦ Where did the person you're backgrounding come from?

♦ Where might there have been previous coverage: newspapers, broadcasts, trade publications, court proceedings, discussions?

Why:

♦ Why do you need the research: seeking a source to interview, surveying a broad topic, pinpointing a fact?

♦ Why must you have the research: to make a decision, to corroborate a premise?

How:

♦ How much information do you need: a few good articles for background, everything in existence on the topic, just the specific fact?

♦ How are you going to use the information: for an anecdote, for publication?

♦ How far back do you need to research: the current year, last two years, 10 years ago?

Once you know what you're looking for, it then becomes a matter of determining where to find it.

Determining Your Information Resources

by Nora Paul

Once a question has been formulated clearly, then you can select the information resources you need to answer the question. Those resources may include online resources (Internet, commercial data services, etc.) as well as conventional tools (phone calls, books, interviews, etc.).

Every project requires a different combination of resources. Sometimes you'll have more than a library at your disposal. Sometimes you'll have a hefty research budget but a tight deadline, and so forth. All of these factors come into play when you examine your information resources. This checklist will help you determine which information resource can best be of service.

Who:

♦ Who might have the kind of information I'm seeking?

♦ Who has the data I need? Does the database I'm considering include information from the time period I want?

What:

♦ What kind of database should I use: am I looking for full-text articles, public records, statistics?

♦ What services are available to me?

♦ What does each offer? At what cost?

When:

♦ When are the services available: will they be accessible when I need them?

♦ When should I use another service: at which point does it make sense to try a different one?

Why:

♦ Why might I choose one service option over another? Determining factors include cost, range of material, ease of use.

Where:

♦ Where am I most comfortable searching: which service is most familiar to me?

♦ Where do I have the best deal? Database services offer varying options at varying prices.

♦ Where can I get the search support I need?

How:

♦   How can I select the most logical resource? Sometimes the best way is to consult a specialist who is familiar with the range of choices and their features.

Other Search Strategy Considerations

Sources, Friends & Enemies

Information comes from people. If you're looking for information that really matters to you, the ultimate source is other people.

Generally, people can be classified as friends, observers or enemies. If you can't get information directly from one person, talk with someone who knows that person well, such as a friend. Or, try someone who spends a significant amount of time observing that person – perhaps a work colleague. Another potential information source is someone who dislikes the person. If someone doesn't want to talk to you, ask yourself who else might have the information you seek.

Translating this idea to the Internet, if you want to know more about your company's new president, you can go online and research the companies where he or she used to work. You can also talk to people he or she has worked with previously – both friends and enemies. Former employees often know a company's secrets and have no inhibitions about sharing them, if asked. Online research can help you locate sources, but it's no substitute for actually talking to real people.

Boolean Operators & Keywords
The Bloodhounds of Online Searching

At the beginning of this chapter, editor Barbara Quint said that computers were like dogs, "friendly, but not very bright." Like dogs, computers obey specific commands.

Here are the commands. They are simple. It's unfortunate that such simple commands were given a name straight from outer space – Boolean. But if you can get through the next two paragraphs, you'll be well on your way to online proficiency.

There are three major Boolean operators:

NOT

AND

   and

OR

Say you are interested in the rose industry, and you want to focus on thornless roses. Your primary search word would be "roses." If you submit "roses" as your primary search term on the search engine HotBot, you would get 147,940 hits, and on Infoseek (another search engine), you would receive about 1.4 million hits. The number of hits is too large to be manageable. That's where the Boolean operators AND and OR come into play.

If you submit "roses" OR "thornless," you'll get even more hits. In fact, you will get a list of every available reference that mentions *either* of those two words. However, if you submit "roses AND thorns," you'll get *only* the hits that contain both of those words. Can you see the difference one little word can make?

Engine	Roses	Thornless	Roses OR Thornless	Roses AND Thornless
HotBot	147,940 hits	784 hits	93,105 hits	202 hits
Infoseek	1,880,037 hits	586 hits	1,880,038 hits	63 hits

Some search engines also use + and - instead of or in addition to AND (+) and NOT (-).

The next chapter will introduce you to basic search tools – all of which accept Boolean operators and keywords to help you search.

Chapter 3

General Search Tools

Search Engines, Subject Directories, Portals & Meta-Tools

Each day, vast numbers of new web sites are created. The numbers are so large that they are incomprehensible, and the growth rate is so explosive that some companies spend all their time simply tracking Internet development. When searching in this furiously expanding universe of information, first prepare by following these three steps—

First step: Define the data you want.

Second step: Figure out where it's likely to be found.

Third step: Select the search tool most likely to provide it.

In this chapter, we'll introduce the general search tools and discuss easy strategies for applying these steps.

The two most basic and commonly used search tools are search engines and subject directories. If you understand these two tools, you'll be ahead of most non-professional Internet users and certainly a far more effective researcher. Unless you're a veteran or specialty researcher, you should try these tools first, once you've developed your question, framed your research strategy and determined your search terms.

Other search tools are portals and meta-tools. Portals are enhanced search engines with subject directories. Meta-tools enable you to query multiple search tools simultaneously. This chapter will introduce you to all four types.

Searching & Search Tools: An Introduction

In pre-computer days, a library's card catalog was a chest of drawers that contained a card for each book. On each card was listed the book's name, author, publisher and other information. In other words, a card catalog was a database; each card was a record and each piece of information (name, author and so on) was a field.

Every search tool is made up of one or more databases that contain records and fields. With electronic databases, you can isolate the information you want by specifying the fields you want to search. For example, you can search through all the books by Tom Clancy and then specify (or limit) the result to books published in 1995, or only those from a certain publisher. You can do this because you're searching through information (fields) common to each card (record) – in this case, the fields containing the author's name, the books' publication dates and the publishers.

As Cheryl Gould suggests in her excellent book *Searching Smart on the World Wide Web*, "the database of a search tool can be visualized as a gigantic, never-ending three-dimensional tic-tac-toe board with unlimited boxes. Each box contains a piece of information that relates to information in other boxes. The relationships built between the pieces of information are created by the database provider and serve as one of the ways the search tools differentiate themselves."

Use help screens. Before you begin using a search tool, consult the Help, How-To or Tips Page linked to its front page. Each search tool has one.

Search Engines

A search engine is an enormous database of web sites compiled by a software robot that seeks out and indexes web sites (and sometimes other Internet resources as well). There are more than 1200 search engines, and they vary in speed, skill, depth of indexing, size of database, advanced search features and presentation of results. Every search engine's method of searching is proprietary; the depth and breadth and realm of its database is unique, and each search engine possesses its particular strengths and idiosyncrasies.

Data is collected according to a unique mix of criteria. These criteria – also called variables – are weighted and trigger tradeoffs that make each database dramatically different from its counterparts. For example, when you use HotBot, you're using another database that was organized in a specific way, and when you use Excite, you're using another database, which was organized differently. Consequently, you may get wildly different results. This is true for the many different search engines.

An eye-popping number of search engines claim to be the best, the largest or most thorough. Several even claim to be comprehensive. You can ignore all those claims because every search engine database is woefully incomplete. According to a recent study, the top search engines index less than 40% of the material available on the Web. HotBot ranked first in thoroughness because it was able to retrieve 34% of existing web pages on a given subject. Other search engines' indexing reliability was even less impressive (28% for AltaVista, 20% for Northern Light, 14% for Excite, 10% for Infoseek, and only 3% for Lycos). The study also found that search engines were able to locate individual pages within a web site, but not necessarily the entire web site nor even the web site's home page.

The hype extends to subject directories and meta-tools. The largest subject directory, Yahoo!, was examined in the same study and was found to have indexed less than 5% of the Web. None of the meta-tools have been studied. It's too difficult to calculate their indexing ability because they offer many search engine selection options.

Never do just one search. Always do the same search using several different search tools because every search tool uses different retrieval criteria.

How a Search Engine Works

Search engines consist of three major elements.

1. Spider: A spider – also known as a crawler, robot or worm. A spider is an automated tool that visits a web page, reads it and then follows links to other pages within that site. From the web site designer's perspective, the process is known as being "spidered" or "crawled."

2. Index: The spider returns to the site periodically, usually every month or two, to look for changes. Everything the spider finds goes into the second part of the search engine: the index. The index, sometimes called the catalog, contains a copy of every web page that the spider finds. Sometimes there's a time lag, so that a web page may have been spidered but not yet indexed.

Until it is indexed, it's unavailable to search engine users. If a spider finds changes on a web page, then it updates the index to include the new information. The word "index" implies categorization and classification – activities that require human assessment and interpretation. In reality, the indexing for a search engine is done by computer (software, actually), and the rankings of the responses, or hits, are calculated by mathematical formulas as well.

3. Software: The third part of a search engine is its software (i.e. indexing) program, which sifts through the millions of pages recorded in the index to find matches to a search. The software program then ranks the matches by what it perceives as their relevance.

Receiving too many hits? If your initial search returns an overwhelming number of hits, visually scan the results for keywords that can narrow the returns from your second search.

Get maximum returns. Most search engines will let you determine the number of hits returned on your screen. Set the Display Option (which you'll find almost always under the Advanced Search feature) to the maximum number, which usually varies from 10-100 at a time, depending on the search tool.

Search engines differ in the way they work. Say you want more information about chocolate-flavored peanut butter. One search engine or subject directory might search its database first for "chocolate." Then it takes *those* results and searches them for the additional word "peanut." Then it takes those results and scans for the word "butter," and presents you with the results.

Another search tool might require you to submit a term using a + sign, so your search term would be "chocolate+peanut+butter." Another might require you to submit "chocolate and peanut and butter." And a fourth search engine might conduct three simultaneous searches – one for each word – and extract only the documents that the three sets have in common. Other search tools might utilize a combination of these approaches.

All of this isn't very important until you're clear about what you want. For now, it's enough to understand that every one of these search engines works differently. Consider them different tools for different purposes. For example, AltaVista is especially good for finding foreign sites and information in foreign languages because it has a built-in translation component. HotBot allows you to opt for image-only and graphics-only hits. Northern Light customizes your results into folders – essentially an automatic grouping feature that makes for easier searching.

Use Phrase Searching to narrow or expand a search on a Search Engine. If you're interested in the puffer fish and search the word "puffer," you'll get thousands of hits, most of them irrelevant. But if you search the phrase "puffer fish," you'll get more relevant hits. You can phrase search in AltaVista, Infoseek, and Excite by putting your phrase within double-quotations, "like this," and do the same in HotBot through a dropdown menu. And, when you search for the puffer fish's scientific name, tetradon, your hits will be far more specific. Also, on many engines, a + sign can denote a phrase (puffer+fish).

Search engines also vary in their presentation of results. Some search engines list their results alphabetically, others by relevance ranking and some use a combination of both criteria, or different criteria altogether. Search engines are programmed to rank results according to many factors, including the location and frequency of keywords on a page.

For example, pages with keywords appearing in the title are assumed to be more relevant, and pages with keywords located higher up on a web page – in a headline or the first few paragraphs of text – are ranked higher than pages where the keywords appear lower on the page. Also, the more frequently a keyword is mentioned, the more relevant a web page is considered to be. We'll go into more detail about relevancy rankings later on in this chapter.

Search engines treat numbers and other non-alphabet characters such as a forward slash (/), a numeral or a hyphen in differing ways. If a search term includes special or non-alphabet characters, try incorporating it into a search phrase. If that doesn't work, try

using a "wildcard" character in place of the special character. Consult the search tool's help screen to identify that search tool's wildcard character. For example, on AltaVista, submit `wish*` to find **wish, wishes, wishful, wishbone** and **wishy-washy**. The `*` in this example is considered a wildcard character.

The Link Search feature of some search engines (namely AltaVista, HotBot and Northern Light) can also serve as a quick credibility check because the links identify other sites that consider this site to be credible. For example, a site linked to universities and government agencies is more credible than a site linked to the Beavis and Butthead home page. Credibility checking is discussed in Chapter 11.

Best Search Engines

(listed alphabetically)

AltaVista
www.altavista.com

This easy-to-use search engine is one of the best. It pulls material from an estimated 150 million pages, making it one of the Internet's largest databases. Its crawlers index about ten million pages a day and large parts of the AltaVista site are refreshed nightly. But, its database is so large that revisions can take as long as six weeks.

What It Does Best	AltaVista is very good at retrieving specific phrases. It digs down into the page and finds actual words and phrases from within the full-text of the web sites. As a result, if you can pin your search down to one word or a unique phrase, you can find it quickly.
Search Options	Two Search options are offered: Simple and Advanced. To do a Simple Search, you must submit +, - or " " signs to narrow and focus the search. The Advanced Search option requires you to type the actual Boolean operators (AND/OR/NOT). Don't forget to utilize the ranking capability in the Advanced Search mode, as well.
Search Tips	AltaVista has terrific field searching ability. You can search for title and/or URL in both the Simple Search and Advanced Search modes. Restricting by URL will allow you to limit your hits to government or education sites and focus your hits' overall

credibility. To use this tool, simply write Title:<subject>; example: Title:tree, and you will get sites that have "tree" in their titles.

Media Specific Searches

AltaVista's Title and/or URL searching feature is a particularly valuable technique for finding images or locating links to other sites, and if you search for .jpg or .gif within the titles you want, or on the URLs you are looking for, you'll bring up pages containing images within your search results. AltaVista is also capable of searching newsgroup postings.

Special Features

AltaVista was the first search engine to offer a Link Search feature that allows you to find any web pages linked to a particular site. It's a valuable way of conducting competitive intelligence on rival companies. In Chapter 9, AltaVista's Link feature is discussed in the context of competitive intelligence.

AltaVista recently introduced a few new features, including a Photo-finding tool using Corbis' extensive photo library, and a Family-friendly Version so that you can bar access to pornographic sites.

Another useful new feature is called "Ask AltaVista," which consists of thousands of commonly-asked questions and answers, catalogued by subject and designed to help new users.

AltaVista also allows you to set up a Translation account, allowing you to access its sophisticated simultaneous translation capability for reading documents that are in foreign languages.

Excite

www.excite.com

Excite is one of the larger search engines on the Internet. It now offers "channels," which are subject directories with pre-selected and reviewed material.

What It Does Best

If you search for a company, Excite automatically ranks that company's site at the top of your list of search results. Therefore, Excite is a speedy tool when backgrounding a business.

Search Options

Excite is capable of Concept Searching. You'll get a lot of bad hits using concept searching, but also interesting ones that may not have occurred to you. For example, search for "baseball." Not only do you get the results that match that word, but you also get a results page that is topped by current scores, links to stats and other key information. It also offers news articles and recent photos.

Excite has added Phrase Searching, however, it doesn't always result in an exact match, even if you submit the phrase in quotes. And, there's no field searching capability.

One innovative feature offers real-time data. For example, searching "Washington, DC" automatically brings up the current temperature, a five-day forecast, latest local sports scores, maps and news.

Search Tips

Use + and - signs to narrow your searches, and use quotes for Phrase Searches in the Regular Search mode. In Advanced Search mode, you can't type in Boolean operators. Instead, terms must be chosen from drop-down menus.

Special Features

Excite offers a News section, which provides access to web versions of newspapers and magazines. It also provides a thesaurus to help you refine your search terms.

HotBot

www.hotbot.com

HotBot uses lots of pop-down menus to give the searcher multiple options.

What It Does Best

HotBot's power lies in its "More Search Options" function, formerly known as SuperSearch. More Search Options allows all kinds of field searching, including Link Searches. Many professional searchers prefer HotBot because they needn't go to a different page to do an Advanced Search, as with AltaVista. HotBot's "Exact Phrase" and "Must Have" combination is especially effective to narrow and focus a search.

Search Tips

One unique and very helpful feature is HotBot's automatic searches for names as first name followed by last name. You can also limit results by date, which can be helpful when you are looking for time-specific material.

Media Specific Searches

For media specific searching, HotBot is great for pulling up images and graphics. Its indexing feature will retrieve only images, if you wish.

Special Features

HotBot's newest features include a Family-content Filter, Site Clustering (to find sites similar to those you like) and a "Direct Hit" list of the most popular web sites on a given subject. The last is a new technology that other search engines are expected to emulate.

Infoseek

www.infoseek.com

Infoseek has grown from just a search engine to a combined engine-and-directory.

What It Does Best	Having partnered with Hoover's, a business research company, Infoseek does a good job of providing company information on the web site.
Search Options	Infoseek allows you to narrow your searches to links, titles and URLs.
Search Tips	One unique and terrific feature lets you narrow and focus a search by "refining further" from your pool of initial results. You can Refine Further the subsequent results as many times as desired.
Special Features	Infoseek provides reviews of some of the sites in its database.

Lycos

www.lycos.com

Lycos offers a search engine as well as two subject directories called Sites by Subject (formerly "a2z") and Top 5% Sites (formerly "Point").

What It Does Best	The web guides on the main page point to its Top 5% Sites section, which are Lycos' recommendations for best links/web sites about the subject for which you're searching.
Search Options	Lycos completely revamped its search system and added full Boolean searching. The Advanced Search mode offers more search options and many advanced features.
Search Tips	Lycos allows you to add Related Terms to your search words, so that if you submit "medicine," the results will include "medicinal," "medical" and so forth.
Media Specific Searches	Like HotBot, Lycos can do image-only and sound-only file searches.
Special Features	Early in its development, Lycos began reviewing the content of the web sites it indexes.

Northern Light
www.northernlight.com

A newcomer to the Web, Northern Light prefers to do things differently. It hires librarians to design and organize its site. Rather than rely on advertising dollars to support the free search engine, it sells full-text articles from a database of newspaper and magazine stories for $1.00 to $4.00 each. This feature, along with its news filtering technology, is certain to be copied by Northern Light's rivals.

What It Does Best	The company's Special Collections database goes back to 1995, and Northern Light expects to add date coverage information soon. This database makes Northern Light a hybrid between a search engine and a clipping service – and an extraordinarily valuable tool for quick backgrounding.
Search Options	Northern Light has added full Boolean fields, limits, and a helpful Power Search function.
Search Tips	Northern Light is innovative in another way: search results are put into customized folders so you can see the results *by category* instead of *by relevancy*. This enables you to target material much quicker, and allows you to view your hits from different perspectives — by subject, date and/or groupings. It also returns 25 hits at a time, while most search engines return only ten at a time.
Special Features	At an estimated 95 million pages, its database is second only to AltaVista in size, and, like AltaVista, it now offers Link Searches. Not advertising supported. Also unique to Northern Light is a money-back guarantee if you are not satisfied with the clippings that you purchase.
	In addition, Northern Light allows you to do industry specific, publication specific and news specific searches.

Natural Language Search Engines

One of the hottest trends is the development of so-called "natural language search engines" that allow users to submit search terms in normal English rather than using Boolean operators, quotes, + signs and other search terminology. Many search engines claim natural language processing when what they actually mean is that Boolean operators aren't required.

According to Dr. Elizabeth Liddy, developer of **Manning & Napier's Information Services Dr-Link** natural language search engine www.mnis.com, a true natural language search engine extracts the meaning of the document by re-processing it and pulling out relevant terms. Then it compares potentially relevant documents and finds similarities.

The pages are isolated. Then, the engine provides summarization and analysis across potentially relevant documents. Then it finds commonality among documents.

> **EXAMPLE:** if you submitted "Robert," a natural language search engine might look for "Bob" as well. Natural language searches evaluate proximity of terms, phrase recognition, capitalization and keyword occurrence in titles, subheads and text. If you wanted to know where Winston Churchill delivered the Iron Curtain speech, a natural language search engine would search for items containing the following words: winston, churchill, iron, curtain and speech.

AltaVista and many other search tools use portions of natural language technology as part of advanced searching options. So, when you get a list of results in AltaVista, you can press the Refine button to find what the retrieved searches have in common. You can then choose from a list of related words and specify that should be included and/or excluded.

Another site on the Internet using some natural language is the *Encyclopedia Britannica* site, www.eblast.com.

Subject Directories

A subject directory is a database of titles, citations and web sites organized by category – similar to a filing cabinet containing folders with files in them. Categorization and indexing are performed by human beings, not machines or software. Users travel down a series of menus, though you can usually select keywords from a pre-defined list, as well.

Unlike search engines, where a computer attempts to rank the most relevant results first, subject directories present results in categories, usually alphabetically, and the category titles vary from one subject directory to the next. The information is organized, evaluated and catalogued by a person – not software – who ranks the material using pre-determined criteria. The entire process of collecting, arranging, HTML coding and annotating requires a great deal of human effort. As a result, subject directory databases tend to be much smaller than those of search engines. Subject directories are designed for ease of browsing.

The largest and most well-known subject directory is **Yahoo!**, (www.yahoo.com) which categorizes subjects into fourteen topics and hundreds of subtopics.

> **EXAMPLE:** If you want to know more about Caribbean vacations, searching for the phrase "Caribbean vacation" won't work. You must look under Travel, Vacations and then by region of the world before you will find information.

Most subject directories are organized in similar ways. It is important to note that you cannot always "search" a directory (i.e. using a search mechanism). Oftentimes, you must select a category and "browse."

Other examples of subject directories include:

INFOMINE: Scholarly Internet Resources Collection

http://lib-www.ucr.edu/Main.html

eBLAST: Britannica's Internet Guide

www.eblast.com

When to Use a Subject Directory:

Subject directories are useful when you want to know more about broad-based subjects, such as:

General topics

Popular topics

Specialty databases

Product information

Current events.

Let's consider each of these in turn.

General Topics

Say, for example, you're thinking about a beach vacation and want to evaluate some choices. On Yahoo!, for instance, you would choose the travel category and browse away, finding beaches all over the world. But, if you start out in search of a specific black-sand beach on Grenada, you'll have to go down many multiple-choice paths before concluding that a particular subject directory does or doesn't have information about it. If you're set on going to Grenada, you'd be better off submitting "Grenada" to a search engine.

Popular Topics

Let's say you're looking for information about baseball's home run king, Mark McGwire. You would start looking under baseball. Due to a subject directory's file-within-a-file system, you'd have to start at recreation, then go to sports, then baseball, then major league baseball, then players, then McGwire, Mark. Using a keyword search of either a subject directory or a search engine in this case would quickly get you to pages about the St. Louis Cardinal superstar. When comparing search directories and search engines, here's the difference: in a search directory tool like Yahoo! you'll find, for example, 31 categories in which McGwire pops up, all pre-sorted and indexed by a human being. A similar search on the Excite search engine for "mcgwire, mark" would retrieve more than 1000 hits, including several personal home pages about McGwire's 1998 home run record chase.

Specialty Databases

There are thousands of searchable databases on the Internet. Finding and searching them can be cumbersome.

The Internet Sleuth (www.isleuth.com) is a particularly good search tool to locate subject directories on specific topics. The Sleuth maintains an index of 3,000 searchable databases, most of which can be searched directly from The Sleuth. It's organized like a subject directory. Say, for example, that you're looking for a recipe for chicken Marsala. Using The Sleuth's search engine, if you entered "chicken Marsala," you would get no results since there is no chicken Marsala database on the Internet. However, if you entered the search term "recipe," you'd receive a list of several searchable Internet databases, including the *Usenet Cookbook* and *The Epicurious Gourmet Online Cookbook*, and you could hunt for a chicken Marsala recipe from within these databases.

If you know exactly what you want, a search engine is the place to go. But, if you're looking for information about types of products or specific product information and had no luck at manufacturer web sites, try a subject directory.

Using a subject directory works especially well if:

♦ You're hunting for information about a group of products

♦ You don't know the name of the manufacturer

♦ You suspect the product information is on the web site of the manufacturer's corporate parent, parent's parent, and so forth.

Current Events

Most subject directories have pre-set categories for news topics of general interest that link related information and recent news stories. News resources are also available in other places (*see* Chapter 8, News Resources Online).

Subject directories are especially valuable when you're trying to determine the key players in a specific industry or locate specific kinds of information. Chances are that a subject directory – because it's organized by people – will bring you to the best one-stop site for that industry. If you were looking for aviation information, for example, you could look at specific airlines' web sites. Subject directories would point you to a specialized subject directory like **LANDINGS** at www.landings.com, which focuses solely on aviation-related sites.

Should you use a subject directory or a search engine? If you're just beginning to research a subject, use a subject directory to find search words, phrases and keywords that you can submit to other search tools. If you're trying to find the most current information on a subject that's already familiar to you, try a search engine. Search engines, since computers update them, tend to be more current than subject directories, which are updated by hand.

BEST SUBJECT DIRECTORIES

General Subject Directories

Argus Clearinghouse
www.clearinghouse.net

You can browse by category or submit search terms. This subject directory breaks its material into fourteen categories and hundreds of subcategories. Argus is particularly strong because its guides are maintained by people with some expertise in each field, yet, some lists are excellent while others aren't.

The guides are rated from one to five, based on several criteria. This site is very strong in pop culture, politics, other general subjects and in academic resources.

eBLAST: Britannica's Internet Guide
www.eblast.com

Encyclopedia Britannica's first web effort is an extensive subject directory based on its encyclopedias, which date back to 1768.

Also on the site are other resources from the company, including the Merriam-Webster's Dictionary, Thesaurus and Britannica Online, a great reference resource.

LookSmart

www.looksmart.com

This relatively new subject directory shows great promise. It is already second in size to Yahoo! and is being used by AltaVista and HotBot when subject access is needed. It doesn't provide web site ratings, but offers twelve main categories and more than 18,000 subcategories.

Magellan Internet Guide

www.mckinley.com

Both a search directory and a search engine, Magellan is owned by the Excite company. You can browse information in major categories or submit search terms. The directory includes web sites that are both reviewed and rated.

Some sites are reviewed as "Green Light" sites, meaning they're safe for kids. Searches can be limited to these sites only.

The Mining Company

www.miningcompany.com

A relative newcomer, this site is terrific for its excellent, evaluative guides on more than 500 subject areas. What makes the Mining Company site so valuable is that it has designated a person to maintain the links in each category, providing you, the interested researcher, with a personal guide for the specific subject in which you are interested. Several of them to be wonderfully helpful. This site continues to delight because of the high quality of the links it recommends.

WebCrawler

www.webcrawler.com

Magellan's sister site and also part of the Excite search family. WebCrawler's guides are set up in channels. All sites have been reviewed, but you can also search unreviewed web sites using keywords.

Yahoo!

www.yahoo.com

Yahoo!, the largest and most comprehensive of all navigational guides, is very good at providing information for the masses. It offers current news, sports scores, stock quotes, and has subject directories in fourteen major categories as well as many thousands of sub-categories.

If a Yahoo! search fails to return any hits, the search is automatically shifted onto Inktomi, the same database used by HotBot. While handy, this feature is rarely as effective as a well-structured search run directly on AltaVista.

To refine a search on Yahoo!, use + and - signs as well as " " marks. In other words, put a + before the keywords you want, a - to eliminate words and " " to denote a phrase. For example, if you want movies about Bruce Lee and/or pythons, but hate Monty Python, you could phrase your search this way: movies+Bruce+Lee or python-monty.

Specialized Subject Directories

The hottest trend on the Internet is development of specialized and topic-specific subject directories. There are some good compilation sites and several, excellent topic-specific sites. Here are few of the best:

AlphaSearch - Gateway to the "Academic" Web
www.calvin.edu/library/as

Calvin College's AlphaSearch provides instant access to hundreds of sites through a single gateway. The sites are all related to an academic discipline, subject or idea.

Direct Search
http://gwis2.circ.gwu.edu/~gprice/direct.htm

Direct Search is a list of lists – a directory of the best subject-oriented directories, developed by Gary Price, MLIS at George Washington University. Direct Search often provides information that can't be found anywhere else.

INFOMINE: Scholarly Internet Resource Collections
http://lib-www.ucr.edu

This site contains scholarly Internet resources pulled together by librarians for the University of California and Stanford University campuses. INFOMINE is terrific for academic and scholarly resources, but isn't designed for other purposes. It is searchable by keyword and category.

Librarians' Index to the Internet
http://sunsite.berkeley.edu/internetindex

This site is geared to academic resources. It is collected and categorized by public librarians for the purpose of answering reference questions. The database is relatively small, so use search terms that are broad in scope. All materials are evaluated, annotated and selected for content and reliability.

━━ Topic-Specific Subject Directories

AVIATION:
LANDINGS
www.landings.com

The LANDINGS directory is a great starting place for aviation-related information.

BUSINESS:
Dow Jones Business Directory
www.bd.dowjones.com

Dow Jones, owners of *The Wall Street Journal*, has created a tremendous business subject directory.

ENVIRONMENT:
Best Environmental Resources Directory
www.ulb.ac.be/ceese/meta/cds.html

This excellent site was established by the Belgian government's Office of Scientific, Technical and Cultural Affairs.

Another good environmental site is

Argus Clearinghouse: Environmental
www.clearinghouse.net/cgi-bin/chadmin/viewcat/Environment?kywd++

GENEALOGY:
Cyndi's List of Genealogical Sites on the Internet
www.www.Cyndislist.com

Cyndi's List is very good starting point for genealogy research.

LEGAL:
FindLaw
www.findlaw.com

FindLaw is an excellent subject-specific meta-tool. The site is more than just a well-organized directory of law sites; it also has a search engine for law-oriented web pages, a terrific free database of full-text US Supreme Court cases, a directory of online law reviews, a collection of state codes, and continuing discussions about education as well as law. The core of the directory is the Legal Subject Index, which includes 36 general legal topics.

University Law Review Project
www.lawreview.org

Offers information on law journals, some in full text.

STATISTICS:
Statistical Resources on the Web
www.lib.umich.edu/libhome/Documents.center/stats.html

This extensive resource contains valuable statistics, mostly from federal government sources. It also lists other resources and other subject directories of value.

Portals:
Enhanced Search Tools

To differentiate themselves – and make more money – many search engine and search directory companies have enhanced their offerings by adding other services. Portal sites combine specialized content, free e-mail, chat services and a variety of retail and consumer offers to entice you into making the site your starting point *as well as* their principal destination on the Web. Some of the new offerings include e-mail capability, maps, yellow page listings, news headlines, city search guides and access to chat discussions and newsgroups. Like a Swiss army knife, you select the tools you want to use.

Portals make money from advertisers who pay according to user "ratings" that are tallied each time you click on a linked web page. The busiest sites on the Internet are portals.

For example, Yahoo! is now a portal site. It allows you to customize its opening page, get your e-mail there, bid on and sell things auction-style, check local movie and weather listings and trade stocks. It even has a special area geared to kids, **Yahooligans**. Likewise, Excite has transformed itself from a mere search engine into a portal with e-mail boxes, personalized news, weather, sports and a local event finder.

Meta-Tools:
The Second Generation

You can access multiple search engines and subject directories simultaneously through meta-search tools – meta-tools, for short.

Meta-tool examples are **SavvySearch** (www.savvysearch.com/search) and **MetaCrawler** (www.metacrawler.com).

Meta-tools don't create their own databases, rather they rely on databases gathered by other Internet search engines. Essentially, meta-tools are a window or an interface for submitting queries to multiple finding aids.

Not all the meta-tools operate in the same way.

The all-in-one approach used by **Beaucoup!** (www.beaucoup.com) lets you use various search engines but keeps you on the meta-tool's search page. You can conduct only initial, simple searches, meaning you can't further refine, or limit, your search. It also sharply limits the number of hits retrieved to no more than, say, thirty. That means if the search tool ranks its results and your desired item doesn't show up among them, you won't see it at all.

However, if you consult the actual search tool directly, you will get many more hits. The multi-dimensional approach allows you to search many search engines and subject directories simultaneously, resulting in quicker, shallower and more broad-based searches. Along the way, you can stumble on new search engines and subject directories that you may not have tried before.

Yet another type, exemplified by **ProFusion** (www.profusion.com) and **Dogpile** (www.dogpile.com), lets you select the search tools through pop-down menus. Some will even select the search features for you.

Advantages & Disadvantages of Meta-Tools

The biggest advantage of meta-searching is, of course, the ability to simultaneously access multiple search engines. Another advantage is that by using meta-tools, you can cover more ground and a more complete picture of what is available on the Internet. Some meta-tools, like Dogpile, even remove duplicate hits and sort the remaining results by host, keyword, date or search engine.

Meta-tools have weaknesses, too. In many cases, they're programmed to use the simplest search mechanism offered by most search engines. In order to use a search engine's more advanced features, you must visit the search engine itself — not through a meta-tool. Also, meta-tools are unable to use field searching and other advanced features. You are limited to making a single request, and some can't accommodate Boolean terms.

When you click the Search button on your browser — especially Netscape Navigator and Internet Explorer — you'll go to special miniature versions of selected search tools. These mini-versions

aren't as powerful or as comprehensive as the real search engines. Search results from the browser versions aren't the same as results from the original, full-size search engines. The same thing happens when a subject directory, America Online or a portal kicks you through a button to a search engine. For example, the Lycos access via a browser is a limited version of the full-size Lycos engine.

Best Meta-Tools

All-in-One
www.albany.net/allinone

All-in-One presents dozens of search tools and is unique because of its Other Interesting Searches/Services feature, which is a wonderful collection of specialized search engines, many geared to specific topics. All are searchable from the All-in-One search form. Many are highly specialized and the list is constantly growing. Examples include **Astronet**, an astronomy and astrophysics-specific search engine, and **StreetEYE Index**, which searches resources of interest to investors and investment professionals.

Beaucoup!
www.beaucoup.com

This site contains links to the most thorough collection of search engines, directories, finding aids and indexes on the Internet so far – 1200+ at last count. You can browse from broad categories or via specialized search tools. Beaucoup! also provides great summaries of difficult-to-locate resources on topics like arts, politics, education and music.

Actually, Beaucoup! isn't really a meta-tool because it doesn't run searches through multiple search engines. Technically, it's a one-stop shopping site to a plethora of other search tools.

Dogpile
www.dogpile.com

The most complex, but by far the most thorough of all the meta-tools, Dogpile is extremely flexible. It permits searches of up to 25 search tools simultaneously You can even designate which ones. For some reason, however, it doesn't include Northern Light (it may by the time you read this). You can also query newsgroups using Deja News, or use its File Transfer Protocol (FTP) file-finding tools to locate and download huge files (for example, software programs).

Regardless, keep your Dogpile queries as simple as possible in order to accommodate the query standards of the various search tools being accessed.

Inference Find
www.infind.com

One of the easiest search tools to use, it goes out to a half-dozen search engines and subject directories, submits your request and brings back the results, removing the duplicates (something all search tools should do but don't) and groups the items by site of origin. It's great for overview searches and helps make sense of large groups of results.

The Internet Sleuth
www.isleuth.com

Internet Sleuth is a very good tool. You can choose up to six of the top search engines and directories together and run selected searches for "top," "reviewed," "new," and "best of the Web" sites, allowing you to find reviewed quality sites quicker. If you're looking for authorities on a specified subject, or a good set of sites on a particular subject, it's a great place to start.

Also, Internet Sleuth has built an excellent chart (at www.isleuth.com/hts-chart.html) showing how the different search engines use Boolean logic and other features.

ProFusion
www.profusion.com

Another excellent meta-tool, ProFusion works with most of the major search engines, and can notify you of new information weekly, bi-weekly or monthly.

SavvySearch
www.savvysearch.com/search

SavvySearch is particularly good for searching international sites because it permits searching in many languages. Searches can be limited to people finders, reference tools or images. You can also request the presentation of results as one continuous list or as separate lists according to search engine. Leaving the Integrate Results box unchecked allows you to see which search engine is helping most so that you can then query that search engine directly for more effective results.

Which Tool to Use?

The more specific you are, the less likely you'll find what you're looking for in a subject directory. While many novices will reach for a search engine first, many veteran searchers will start with a subject directory to obtain the right phrases and keywords. Some subject directories don't have search capabilities; in those cases, your only choice is to browse through the categories and subcategories offered. With search engines, the approach is reversed: use keywords that are as unusual as possible. Narrow your search even further by using combinations of unusual words and by using advanced features. Make lists of words that you think may help you narrow your query. Submit unique keywords first, since some tools rank the order of words submitted.

Search engines tend to be more effective than subject directories for searches with unusual keywords, for combining keywords, for using advanced features like field searching, and for finding pages buried inside a web site.

For details on how to use search tools and how search tools rank pages, two sites are worth visiting: Danny Sullivan's *Search Engine Watch* **Search Engines Features Comparison Chart at** http://searchenginewatch.com/webmasters/features.html **and Greg Notess'** *Search Engine Showdown* **at** http://imt.com/~notess/search. **Both sites compare meta-tools;** *Search Engine Showdown* **considers subject directories, as well.**

Meta-tools are especially valuable when you're on a deadline and need information quickly, or want an overview of coverage in general. A subject directory is a better bet if you think someone somewhere has developed a collection of quality links on a specific subject.

When narrowing a subject, try putting the rarest or most unusual keyword first. For example, if you're looking up the Dow Corning Company, you'll get fewer misses if you submit it as: corning dow. When juggling word order, however, be sure not to use quotation marks or + signs, which would require the search tool to return hits that contain words only in the exact order they're submitted.

Search Engine Comparison

These charts summarize the primary search features of web search engines. For more detailed reviews, visit **Search Engine Showdown** http://imt.net/~notess/search. The search engines here are grouped according to size, as measured by statistical comparisons published on Search Engine Showdown.

Three Largest Search Engines

Engine	Boolean	Proximity	Truncation	Fields	Limits	Sorting
AltaVista	Full + - system	Phrase, Near	Yes	Title, URL, link, more	Language, date, more	Relevance
Northern Light	Full + - system	Phrase	Yes %, auto plurals	Title, URL, more	Doc type date, more	Custom Folders
HotBot	Full + - system	Phrase	Yes	Title, more	Language, date, more	Relevance, site

Smaller Search Engines

Engine	Boolean	Proximity	Truncation	Fields	Limits	Sorting
Infoseek	+ - system[†]	Phrase	No, auto plurals	Title, URL, link, site	No	Relevance, site
Excite	Full + - system	Phrase	No	No	No	Relevance, site
Lycos	Full + - system	Phrase, adj, more	No	Title, URL	Language, domain	Relevance
Magellan	Full + - system	Phrase	No	No	No	Relevance
WebCrawler	Full	Phrase, near, adj	No	No	No	Relevance

Features of Internet Subject Directories

Engine	Selection[‡]	Size	Boolean	Truncation	Fields	Sorting
Yahoo!	User Submitted	730,000	+ - system	Automatic, except in phrase	t:title u:url	Categories, sites, then Inktomi
Look-Smart	Selected	250,000+	Automatic AND	Automatic stemming	None	Random sites, then AltaVista
eBLAST	Selected	125,000	Full	Automatic stemming	Title, creator, description	Relevance, then AltaVista

---

[†] Infoseek only allows the use of "+" and "-." Others allow for "and" and "or" in addition to "+" and "-."

[‡] "Selection" refers to whether you may type in your own search string ("user-submitted") or whether you must make a choice from a menu ("selected").

Features of Online Multi-Search Engines

*(Note that none search Northern Light and only a few get Yahoo! results from Inktomi.
It is often far more effective to search the search engines directly.)*

Service	Basic Boolean?	Includes
Cyber 411	Yes	AltaVista, Excite, Lycos, WebCrawler, Yahoo!, Magellan, Thunderstone
Inference Find	Some	AltaVista, Excite, Lycos, Infoseek, WebCrawler, Yahoo!
Dogpile	Yes	AltaVista, Excite, Lycos, Infoseek, WebCrawler, Yahoo!, Magellan, Thunderstone
MetaFind	Yes	AltaVista, Excite, Infoseek, WebCrawler, PlanetSearch
SavvySearch	No	AltaVista, Excite, Lycos, Infoseek, WebCrawler, Yahoo!, Magellan
MetaCrawler	Yes	AltaVista, Excite, Lycos, Infoseek, WebCrawler, Yahoo!, Thunderstone

The Hidden Internet: What Search Tools Can't Access

Spiders cannot index pages that are "gated" – in other words, that are attached to web sites that require log-in, a password or registration. **The *New York Times* on the Web** (www.nytimes.com) is a good example. The site is free, but registration is required. Most of the great value on the web site isn't indexed simply because spiders can't get behind the registration form.

The same problem exists with data sets. One of the best sites for regional economic data, http://govinfo.kerr.orst.edu (the **Government Information Sharing Project**), contains great local statistics, but that data isn't directly browsable or accessible to spiders. Users access information by selecting desired variables that produce the requested data. Since the spiders can't fill out forms, only the top-level pages of the site are indexed.

Most search tools do not search FTP (see Glossary), and few index FTP, Telnet, newsgroups and mailing lists. While some of these resources can be found in some subject directories, the vast majority cannot.

Commercial online databases are also ignored by standard subject directories and search engines, again because of password restrictions. (Some companies are now building databases of hidden resources in an attempt to compensate.)

Many web sites – especially proprietary ones – create pages on the fly specifically in response to your question. As a result, the contents of those databases aren't found by the search engine's robots because they don't exist until you search for the information. To see an example, go to the Labor Department's **Bureau of**

Labor Statistics web site (http://stats.bls.gov) and request the unemployment statistics for your hometown.

Formatted file pages are scanned images of pages that don't get indexed by search engines, which catalog by keywords (i.e., text, not images). For example, pages that exist as Adobe .pdf files (see the chart of file extensions in Chapter 5 for more information on .pdf) would be indexed by the words that link to the .pdf file. If the only words linked are something like "volume 1, issue 5," spiders and crawlers won't index keywords describing the pages' subject matter.

Accessing Hidden Content

Some professional searchers have developed strategies to access some hidden content. They combine knowledge of commercial online tools and registration processes to locate the information, and then they search within that resource.

Take the Thomas Register of American Manufacturers as an example. A search engine might not be able to find a direct link to information about a specific product, but you could go to a subject directory like Yahoo!, select "Manufacturing" and find a link to the **Thomas Register of American Manufacturers** — www.thomasregister.com. Once you fill out its registration form at the site, you could probably get the information you need – information that is unavailable to search engines because their spiders can't access the individual Thomas Register records.

Yet another promising way to search the hidden Internet comes from Excite's News Tracker, a database of major US newspapers. Excite can program its spider to sign into the appropriate resource and index its content. Greg Notess, a Montana State University reference librarian and search engines expert, believes this technology is the harbinger of a "Readers' Guide" for the hidden Internet.

■■■ Search Tools & HTML

The primary language used to format documents on the Internet is called "HTML" — or Hypertext Markup Language. In the background of a web page there are a series of HTML "tags" – instructional coding – that tell the computer browser how to display the document on your screen – its layout, typeface, colors, etc. HTML coding also "links" one page to another. Most text links are shown on-screen in a different color, often, blue. However, you can always tell if your cursor is "on" a link because the pointer on your screen will change from an arrow to a finger-pointing hand. Also, the destination page's address will appear in the status bar at the bottom of your browser.

Search tools use the hypertext links to identify important parts of the document, including the main body of text, other links, titles, major headings and images. They also use the HTML coding to help track some of the things that are contained on a web site. This kind of coding is called a "meta-tag" – an invisible tag on the web page that allows the author to highlight important phrases and terms — i.e., keywords — that may not appear in the title, text or headings but are still relevant to the page.

For example, the web site for *The Late Show with David Letterman* may list tomorrow's guests or tonight's Top Ten List, but may never use the phrase "comedy." But the site may be categorized as comedy in its meta-tags.

On some search engines, terms are given more weight if they have meta-tags. Certain pages are ranked higher among search results than others. Knowing how to maneuver these meta-tags has allowed people to scam the system. If you do a search on Bill Clinton, for example, you'll find several pornography sites high up on your list of hits. That's because many web site programmers try to divert web traffic from other sites to theirs by covering their pages with meta-tags like "Bill Clinton," "President" and "White House."

Two search engines – HotBot and Infoseek – do give a boost to pages with keywords in their meta-tags, according to Danny Sullivan, whose **Search Engine Watch** (www.searchenginewatch.com) is a well-respected newsletter and web site. But, he also notes that Excite doesn't read the tags at all, and that there are many examples of pages without meta-tags that are highly ranked.

Many of the major search engine companies have revamped their ranking formulas to make meta-tag stacking less important. Some search engines are so sophisticated that they penalize or exclude pages if they detect spamming (see Glossary for more information on spamming). Also, some of the better search engines permit searches restricted to specific fields, such as within URLs, headers, titles and author names.

Tips from a Search Engine Guru

by Greg R. Notess

Greg R. Notess is author of *Government Information on the Internet* (2nd edition available from the publisher at www.bernan.com), a reference librarian at Montana State University and a columnist for *Online* and *Database* magazines. Address: notess@imt.net and http://imt.net/~notess.

1. Learn What You Can Expect to Find on the Internet – & What Isn't Likely to be Posted

What kind of information do organizations typically make available on the Web? Product information, public relations material, collaborative scientific project reports, staff directories, mission statements, library catalogs, current news, government information, selected article reprints and press releases are just some of what is commonly accessible on the Web. Trade secrets, strategic plans, commercial databases and most copyrighted published material (except some news and magazine articles) are not readily accessible.

2. Go Straight to the Source

Consider what organization is most likely to provide the kind of information being sought. Then go directly to that organization's web site.

For example, rather than searching all over the Web for the population of a US town, go straight to the web site for the US Census Bureau. Or, for detailed information on one side of the gun control debate, check out the National Rifle Association web site.

3. Locate a URL the Easiest Way

Doing some simple URL guesswork before trying subject directories and the larger search engines can save you time. Guessing the unofficial standard address (www.nameofcompany.com) can, as often as not, take you directly to a company's main web page where you can see what information is available at the site and how it is organized.

Both Netscape Navigator and Microsoft's Internet Explorer automatically take a host address and add the common http:// at the beginning. Sometimes an address will not work without the http://, usually it is because there is no www in the address. So to save typing a few strokes, just leave that part of the URL off. Since www is the most common way to begin a host address, start with that when guessing. After the www, try the organization's name, acronym, or abbreviated name, and then add the appropriate top-level domain. While most commercial sites now have the .com domain, don't forget the other common US endings: .edu for educational institutions, .gov for US government, .mil for US military and .org for other organizations. Using these, it becomes relatively easy to guess that the **US Census Bureau** is at www.census.gov and that the **National Rifle Association** is at www.nra.org.

4. Slice — or Truncate — a URL to Find a Page's New Location within a Web Site

Since web sites are being reorganized continuously, the dead-end message "file not found" pops up frequently. One strategy is to use the site's own organization to find a page's new location. Slice off parts of the URL, starting on the right hand side and stopping at every slash. A page formerly located at www.yourco.com/products/sales/needthis.html may have been renamed, moved to another directory, or completely removed. If it is still available, try www.yourco.com/products/sales to see if any files are still available in that directory. If you still get an error message, next try www.yourco.com/products. If the page pointed to a product on sale, it may still be available under the regular section now. If all else fails, try the root URL at www.yourco.com as your tracking base. Web sites are altered continuously, but relatively few pages are deleted altogether.

5. Use a Subject Directory for Difficult-to-Find URLs

Some associations and companies have names that overlap with the names or acronyms of other companies, making it harder to track their URL. For example, the **American**

Marketing Association was the first to claim www.ama.org, so the **American Medical Association** decided to go with www.ama_assn.org. For URLs that are more difficult to guess, try a quick search in a subject directory such as **Yahoo, Snap**, or **LookSmart**. Where are they located? At www.yahoo.com and www.snap.com and www.looksmart.com, of course! Most subject directories link to the top-level pages of web sites, rather than to all the pages at the site.

6. Use a Subject Directory for Product Information Searches

Subject directories should also be the first step in a product information search. While the strategy of going to the company's web site may work, searching a directory for product information is especially helpful when searching for a group of products, or for products where the company's name isn't known.

7. Run a Phrase Search on a Search Engine

The best search engines have enormous databases that index not only main pages but also lower-level or subsidiary pages. For example, AltaVista has well over 150 million individual web pages fully indexed in its database. With a database this size, a single word search will often result in far too many hits to be useful, unless the word is infrequently used. Chemical names, taxonomic categories, unique small business names or personal names may be unusual, but not unusual enough to limit the returns to a manageable number.

All the major search engines support phrase searching to some degree. Surround the search phrase in double quote marks (" "). By running a phrase search, the search engine is looking for the exact term in exactly the word order specified. If you can express information needs with a phrase (at least two words are required), try the search with the phrase first, before broadening out to other strategies. For example, submitting the phrase "digital frequency hopping" can get far more precise results than searching it without the double quotes, which will elicit thousands of additional pages that don't contain that exact phrase but rather contain only one or more of those words.

Chapter 4

Specialized Tools

Micro & Macro Tools, Human Resources, Fee-Based Tools, Maps

There are thousands of specialized web tools. As with everything else on the Internet, they are in a state of continuous improvement in scope, depth and targeting ability.

This is an overview of the most commonly used kinds of tools, and an introduction to the tools we find most useful. When backgrounding an individual or business, don't confine yourself to the specialized tools described in this chapter. And, once again, thanks go to Nora Paul at the Poynter Institute, who developed the categories used in this chapter (i.e. people finders, subject finders, etc.) for her book *Computer Assisted Reporting*.

Always insist on original documentation. Never assume that online content is correct, since all online materials are by definition secondary source material that could have been input in error by a software program or by a human being.

MICRO TOOLS

People Finders

There are literally hundreds of telephone books, people locators, reverse phone directories, e-mail address finders and professional directories. Most are advertiser-sponsored and free to users. Others are available only through pay services.

For the most part, people finders provide publicly-listed telephone numbers. Through them, you can do a national search in a matter of seconds. They also work well as e-mail address finders. They vary considerably in accuracy and consistency. Skilled researchers generally use a combination of free and commercial tools, since the fee-based services usually offer more extensive people directories.

The real question is, *how often are these tools updated?* The answer can vary widely. Test them by submitting your own name or the name of someone with a *listed* phone number. All people finder databases originate from other vendors, so their information is at best third-hand. There's no clearinghouse for processing e-mail address changes, so e-mail addresses are less reliable than phone numbers.

To test a people finding tool, submit your own name or the name of someone you know, then judge the tool by the results.

The commercial people finders – sometimes called skip-tracing tools – tend to be more accurate than the free people finders. Some of them – like **DBT Autotrack** and **DCS** – restrict access to professionals who can demonstrate a need, such as lawyers, insurance company employees, law enforcement agencies, journalists and others. However, the information is still available from other companies and can be found for a price. These tools use a combination of different information resources to build profiles of individuals. They're not restricted to listed phone numbers, and, using other resources, gather unpublished phone numbers along the way.

According to their web sites, the following companies will sell you . . .

. . . unlisted phone numbers (www.discreetdatasystems.com).

. . . driving record histories (www.discreetdata.com).

. . . banking account records (http://A1Trace.com).

Nearly all the free phone books online gather their information from the same databases used by the regional phone companies as well as from public directories. Fee-based services like **CDB Infotek**, **Information America** and DBT Autotrack also use other resources, like credit headers. A header is the information reported to credit agencies. For the most part, only the "identifying information" about a person is easily obtainable online from fee-based companies. Identifying information generally includes the consumer's name, address, age, year and date of birth, home telephone number, and previous address.

As with most web tools, phone finders generally cover only a portion of existing telephone numbers. Don't forget to try several phone books.

Also, portals like **AOL** offer members the opportunity to view profiles of other members, which can be a great resource for locating people.

Best People Finders

AnyWho
www.anywho.com

This newcomer from AT&T is one of the best. It is thorough (claiming more than ninety million listings) and easy to use. It's divided into several categories, including people and businesses, and includes an excellent reverse directory to help you trace the name that belongs to a phone number.

AnyWho also has brought a new component to free web search, something many of the fee-based tools have provided for a fee for years: the ability to search for neighbors online. This feature allows you to find anyone with a listed phone number on a specified block anywhere in the country. Reporters use this feature to locate and contact neighbors of people in the news. You can use it to locate the neighbor of someone you can't reach. AnyWho will also help you get a map and directions to the neighborhood. Again, test its accuracy by submitting your own name. Only listed numbers are made available, and anyone can opt to be deleted.

Yahoo! People Search
http://people.yahoo.com

Yahoo! People Search is a good phone book but a much better e-mail directory. **Four11** (www.four11.com) was recently purchased by Yahoo, but the information you could find on Four11 remains and has added options because of the new alliance. It gathers profile information and links to that data when possible, which is very useful when you're trying to find one particular John Smith.

InfoSpace.com
www.infospace.com

Like some others, InfoSpace.com offers maps, reverse directories and other tools. But its listings of government numbers (using the excellent Carroll's Directories) makes InfoSpace.com a must-use tool. InfoSpace.com also features the phone books of several countries, including Canada and the UK. In addition, the mapping feature gives user-friendly directions like "take a right" instead of "go northwest for three blocks."

Switchboard
www.switchboard.com

Has deep resources for phone directories as well as for e-mail addresses.

WhoWhere?
www.whowhere.com

WhoWhere? offers a powerful e-mail address finder that works in English, French and Spanish. This Lycos-owned company also includes valuable business resources like resume finders and a mortgage finder.

Ultimate White Pages
www.theultimates.com/white

The Ultimate White Pages includes easy access to a centralized common interface to five of the previously mentioned people finders, which you can run simultaneously. It also offers access to other valuable tools, like a reverse directory from **PC411** (www.pc411.com/search).

WorldPages Global Find
www.worldpages.com/global

This international phone book provides access to phone books for more than 60 countries from Afghanistan to Zimbabwe.

Try Phrase Searching names. Try submitting a person's name as a Phrase Search in a Search Engine — especially if the name is an uncommon one. You can also submit distinguishing details as keywords.

Specialty People Finders

For Fraternity & Sorority Lists
Greek.Com
www.greek.com

For University Students, Teachers & Employees:
American Universities
www.clas.ufl.edu/CLAS/american-universities.html

World Alumni Net
www.infophil.com/World/Alumni

This has especially good international listings.

Colleges & Universities Web Site Links
www.mit.edu

From the MIT main site you can access Christina DeMello's alphabetical listings of 3000 colleges and universities. Navigating this site is very difficult, however.

UCSD Science & Engineering Library: People & Organizations
http://scilib.ucsd.edu/people-org/people.html#university

Universities.com
www.universities.com

This lists more than 4500 colleges and universities around the world.

University Alumni and Development Offices
http://weber.u.washington.edu/~dev/others.html

Phonebook – Server Lookup
www.uiuc.edu/cgi-bin/ph/lookup

When you get to the lookup site, click on the 342 (and now probably more) campus phone books maintained by Northwestern University.

For University Administration Staff:
Peterson's
www.petersons.com

The home of Peterson's, which publishes *The Register of Higher Education*. An online version may be available, with a promised listing of faculty members. Great sites for access to schools.

For 23,000 High Schools in the US & Canada:
ClassMates Online
www.classmates.com

For Overseas Listings:
InfoSpace.com
www.infospace.com

(described previously in Best People Finders Section)

For Foreign Residences:

WorldPages
www.worldpages.com

> For white pages, government and business listings in more than 150 countries including the US. World Pages isn't always thorough, but it deserves credit for taking on this daunting project.

For Professional Listings:

American Medical Association Physician Select
www.ama-assn.org/aps/amahg.htm

> This gives you the American Medical Association's Physician Select listing of licensed doctors. For their addresses and credentials, click on AMA Health Insight.

Martindale-Hubbell Lawyer Locator
www.martindale.com/maps/../locator/home.html

> For lawyers and their bios, put up by long-time legal directory publisher Martindale-Hubbell.

West Legal Directory
www.wld.com/ldsearch.htm

> Another excellent directory of lawyers put up by West Publishing of Westlaw Publications fame.

Biographical Dictionary
www.s9.com/biography

> For a collection of biographies of well-known people.

Teeth.com
www.catalog.com/cgibin/var/dale/index2.html

> For a list of dentists, who have registered themselves with this site, in most states.

militarycity.com Databases
www.militarycity.com/newsroom/databases.html

> For active duty personnel and members of the reserve and National Guard.

VetSearch
www.vetsearch.com

For veterinarians, but you must search by ZIP Code.

E-Mail Finders

While most of the online phone books have reverse directories, many also include e-mail finders. One tool that specializes in e-mail addresses is:

Internet Address Finder
www.iaf.net

Can't find someone and think they might have a web presence? Try using a search tool to sniff out a personal home page. Home pages — even of relatives — often contain a surprising amount of personal information.

Expert Finders

There are hundreds of lists of experts and methods of reaching and querying them. One way is to use specialized subject directories like **Argus Clearinghouse** www.clearinghouse.com and **The Internet Sleuth,** www.isleuth.com. Another is to use filtering and search tools. Two of the better ones are:

FACSNET: Sources Online
http://facsnet.org/sources_online/main.htm

This list of valuable sources — think tanks, advocacy groups, special interest organizations as well as government, academic and private sector experts — was developed by Foundation for American Communications, a journalism group.

Sources & Experts
http://metalab.unc.edu/slanews/internet/experts.html

A Directory of Directories was compiled by researcher Kitty Bennett and is maintained by the Special Libraries Association's News Division. An invaluable resource.

Once you identify a good source or expert, you can use Deja News' Power Search feature (discussed in the Newsgroup section that follows) to retrieve other postings by that person, or about that person.

Mapping Tools

It's one thing to find a person; it's another to find a location. That's where mapping tools come in. The Internet accommodates graphics easily and maps in general especially well. Many map sites exist on the Web. There are maps that give you directions, others that tell you how to find biking routes in Algeria and still others that provide a view of the earth from outer space. Some companies are so taken with these maps, that they have developed special software allowing you to build your own map, while others offer such features as notations of famous places.

Nearly all of the people finding tools have a free mapping feature, which provide maps of and to the location of the person or business that you're seeking.

Some of the best mapping tools are:

DeLorme
www.delorme.com

By the creator of *The Street Atlas* software maps, this site generates door-to-door address routing.

ETAK SkyMap
www.etak.com/skymap

ETAK's SkyMap attaches a small homing device to your laptop, uses global positioning satellites and helps guide you home if you're lost. Other companies have developed similar technology. The high technology approach makes this kind of service costly.

MapQuest
www.mapquest.com

Allows you to view an atlas, zoom in and out of a locality, locate specific addresses, get city-to-city or street-to-street driving information and locate convenience stories and automatic teller machines.

Maps On Us
www.mapsonus.com

A map, route and yellow pages service. When you enter a street address, a map of the area appears onscreen. Registration is required for some free customized services.

MapBlast!
www.mapblast.com

Offers interactive mapping service using US road maps. You can create maps of any vicinity and e-mail them, too.

National Atlas of the United States of America
www-atlas.usgs.gov

Offers official US government maps, atlas-style.

Odden's Bookmarks:
The Fascinating World of Maps and Mapping
http://kartoserver.frw.ruu.nl/html/staff/oddens/oddens.htm

Another extensive collection of links to maps, geographical societies and things cartographic.

Perry-Castaneda Library Map Collection
www.lib.utexas.edu/Libs/PCL/Map_collection/Map_collection
.html

Another great collection of more than 230,000 maps.

US Census Bureau: Thematic Mapping
www.census.gov

The Census Bureau has an incredible collection of maps. See the Chapter 6 for more information on the Census Bureau's site.

USGS National Mapping Information
http://mapping.usgs.gov

The US Geological Survey's site. In addition to mapping data, you can order maps.

Document Finders

The Internet is particularly good for finding current documents, but if you are looking for a comprehensive view, you still must turn to fee-based services for the encyclopedic view. Fee-based services will give you a more thorough and focused historical perspective. In addition, using fee-based services will enable you do conduct a more sophisticated, comprehensive and current search.

The key to document finding is, as suggested in Chapter 2, getting as much information as possible about the actual documents – even specific phrases or statements that might be found in their texts – because many of the resources for document location can be searched by keyword. Therefore, submitting a specific phrase can help retrieve the document you're targeting.

However, if you're in search of government documents, please consult the government and public records chapters of this book.

Health & Medicine Information Tools

by Susan M. Detwiler and John E. Levis

Susan M. Detwiler is president of The Detwiler Group, an information consulting firm that has long specialized in the business side of medicine and health. Since 1992, she has produced *Detwiler 's Directory of Health and Medical Resources*. Address: sdetwiler@detwiler.com or www.detwiler.com.

John E. Levis is president of John E. Levis Associates, a longtime specialist in primary and secondary market research in healthcare and medicine, and a past president of the Association of Independent Information Professionals (AIIP). Address: john@jelevisassoc.com or www.jelevisassoc.com.

When you're sick, everyone has advice to offer. Your Aunt Tillie knows someone with your condition who ended up in the hospital; your friend's mother developed a severe rash all over her body because of it; your grandmother called to say she was sending over a "sure cure" — a pot of chicken soup made from her secret recipe. It's a fact of life that when you're sick, you're fair game for self-proclaimed experts.

The Internet has made your grandmother's secret chicken soup recipe available to everyone. Technology has made it possible for anyone with a few dollars and some spare time to set up a web sites hyping this cure and that, or offering up "what worked for me."

At the same time, the Internet has become a rich tapestry of scientific and medical truth, woven by truly knowledgeable people, cross-linked to each other by meta-sites and specialty search engines.

Avoid the personal web sites by avoiding the general search engines, and start instead with a good site specializing in health matters. You'll find that most of them offer access or a link to Medline, the unparalleled repository of citations to clinical medical articles, sorted, categorized, abstracted, and indexed by our own US government's National Library of Medicine (NLM). After decades of requiring the public to use a commercial vendor or dial direct for electronic access to this database (and its sister databases Toxline, Aidsline, Cancerlit, and Physicians Data Query, to name just a few), the government now makes Medline available everywhere. It is offered, free of charge, to the public through the PubMed search tool at www.ncbi.nlm.nih.gov/PubMed. And, when you've found the citation you're looking for, you can order the full text online for a fee.

Good Places to Start

If your query is personal, or you're looking for information in layperson's terms, there are a number of good places to begin.

One of our favorites is Healthgate at www.healthgate.com. This site has Medline for free, as well as a number of other well-respected sources including patient education, nursing information and the Wellness Center. Add a low-cost subscription to its MedGate access plan, and you have access to DIH: Drug Information, Reuters Medical News, MDX Health Digest and much more. An extensive list of wellness topics provides consumer information written in everyday language. If you find the article you need through the many available links, a full text document delivery service is available.

Another site offering a wide variety of credible links for both consumers and health care professionals is Medscape at www.medscape.com. You'll need to register to access many of Medscape's functions, but it's free. The requisite link to Medline is there along with a drug database, a medical dictionary, practice guidelines, and much, much more. Medscape's topics are divided into individual home pages. That makes navigation easier. Just click on the subject index, and then pick your topic. The site also offers extensive links to published medical literature.

Another way to begin your quest is to find a professional association devoted to coverage of your disease interest and the people who treat it. The American Cancer Society, found at www.cancer.org, is a good example. This site offers extensive information to cancer patients and their families. It offers advice on finding a doctor, alternative treatments and links to other resources. The American Medical Association, at www.ama-assn.org, keeps a database of more than 650,000 US-licensed physicians. It has current and archived articles from the *Journal of the American Medical Association* (*JAMA*) and several other peer-reviewed journals. AMA Health Insight, a link within the AMA web site, has consumer-oriented information.

The American Dental Association is another favorite site. You'll find it at www.ada.org. If you want to know about fluoridation, crowns, tooth brighteners or sealants, here's the place to start. For professionals, the Research & Clinical Issues area provides a link to Medline, along with access to the *Journal of the American Dental Association* (*JADA*). The link to *JADA* provides major articles from the current issue and a searchable archive.

The NIH Sites: A Vast Resource

The US government has made a lot more than just Medline available as a dependable information source. One of the best sites for health care is the National Institutes of Health (NIH) at www.nih.gov. If you're not sure where to begin, use the search engine. Enter a few keywords, and you can search across this vast resource. Along with Medline and Cancerlit, there's AIDS Information, The Women's Health Initiative and more. If you're a research scientist, you can find out how to apply for NIH grants and/or open job postings.

One of the best sources for information on conventional cancer treatment is the National Cancer Institute (NCI) at www.nci.nih.gov. There you'll find cancer information written from the perspectives of patients, the media, health care professionals and basic researchers. There is access to the Cancerlit database, the Journal of the National Cancer Institute, clinical trial information, and NCI's extensive cancer statistics. If your interest lies in communicable diseases, then the Centers for Disease Control and Prevention (CDC) at www.cdc.gov will be of interest. Click on Health Information and up comes a laundry list of communicable diseases. You can use this site to find out what inoculations you'll need before your next vacation and what precautions you'll need to take once you get there. Like most government sites, you'll find excellent statistics. If you're doing basic research, there's information on CDC-funded grants.

Drug-Related Information

There are many credible sources for drug-related information. When drug companies test drugs, they go through clinical trials. Centerwatch at www.centerwatch.com is a reliable resource for finding trials. It's divided into two sections, Patient Resources and Industry Resources. The patient section has a listing of available trials by therapeutic category, and an e-mail notification system that lets you know when new trials begin. There's also information about new Food & Drug Administration (FDA) approvals and a primer on clinical research. The industry information section profiles clinical research centers, companies that provide contract services to the clinical trials industry and industry news. Both sections have relevant links to other sites of interest to patients, their advocates and health care professionals.

Then there is the extensive FDA web sites at www.fda.gov, which accesses information about drugs for human use, biologics, medical devices and radiology, toxicology, medical products reporting and more. In addition to a search engine, there are links to other government agencies and access to the Code of Federal Regulations.

Yet another comprehensive source of drug information is the Pharmaceutical Information Network web sites at www.pharminfo.com. Besides providing current news about the industry there are linked disease centers with information about conditions, articles, and links to other reliable sources of information. The site has a drug database that is searchable by either trade or generic name, a drug FAQ, and a file of press releases about drugs and pharmaceutical companies.

Other Resources

Another place to look for credible information on scientific, medical and health care topics is on the meta-sites produced by universities and medical centers. One of our favorite places is the University of Michigan's Document Center located at www.lib.umich.edu/libhome/Documents.center/stats.html.   This meta-site has quite an extensive set of links to statistics from a variety of disciplines including health, demographics, environment and science. There are links to a significant number of government resources, as well.

More specific to medicine are The University of Texas M. D. Anderson Cancer Center at www.mdacc.tmc.edu and The Johns Hopkins University web sites at http://hopkins.med.jhu.edu/top.html. M. D. Anderson is an excellent resource for cancer patients. It provides basic information on understanding cancer, treatment research, cancer prevention and information on becoming a patient at M. D.

Anderson. Johns Hopkins provides information for patients, health care professionals, business, and the media. Here, consumers and patients can visit the InteliHealth site, with information on picking a physician or a hospital. There are links to the American Medical Association, the National Cancer Institute, the National Health Council and National Institutes of Health. From the Johns Hopkins Health Resource page, you can link to the US Pharmacopoeia, Medline and the USDA nutrition database. InfoFinder lets you select a specific medical condition and get reliable information.

Most of the sites mentioned above are accessible without charge. There are, however, a couple of services that offer extensive health care and medical information on a subscription basis. Both America Online and CompuServe have "chat rooms" or "forums" devoted to a host of health care topics. They've achieved a measure of credibility because they're mediated by a system operator, or "sysop." In addition, many of them attract health care professionals, officials from associations and other knowledgeable individuals — all of whom serve to filter postings. Another benefit found on these fee-based services is that they provide messages archives through their libraries. And if you're not comfortable surfing the Internet for health information, America Online and/or CompuServe are good ways to get your feet wet. AOL has links to several of the resources we've talked about, all in its handy health center.

Finally, if you have doubts about any given web site's credibility or the advice it gives you, check out QuackWatch at www.quackwatch.com. This site has a doctor for a webmaster and offers reviews of conventional, alternative, and unproven therapies. It also offers links to proven sources of medical information both traditional and alternative as well as to other sites offering consumer protection information.

With all of the above available, it's wise to remember that when it comes to your own medical care, your best source of information is your personal physician. And, unless your doctor advises otherwise, you can still have that bowl of chicken soup while seeking out more information.

Macro Tools

Ready Reference Tools

When they need a quick fact or two, librarians reach over to a shelf of "ready reference" materials that include almanacs, encyclopedias, dictionaries, a thesaurus or two, and quotation sources. Not surprisingly, many of these have begun popping up on the Web.

There are also virtual libraries on the Internet – dozens of them, many of which are tied to universities. Plus, you can always try the enormous caverns of the virtual Library of Congress (www.loc.gov). Few, if any, libraries put complete texts online. But, many have made their catalogs searchable over the Internet and others are developing digital archives. Online listings tells you what library resources are available, and many web sites have Frequently Asked Question (FAQ) summaries available on all kinds of subjects.

Internet Public Library Ready Reference Collection
http://ipl.si.umich.edu/ref/RR

Extremely thorough and wonderfully put together. IPL has twelve categories to choose from, including Genealogy and Quotations.

The IPL is set up like a real building with a reading room and a reference center. The reference center is of particular value to researchers because of the well-organized way in which it has been constructed.

eBLAST: Britannica's Internet Guide
www.eblast.com

eBLAST is from Encyclopedia Britannica Company. The full encyclopedia is for sale on a CD, but eBLAST, its first entry on the web, is free and invaluable — very deep, very impressive. The company's literature calls it the "thinking man's guide to the Web" because of its evaluations of web sites on a variety of subjects.

Encyclopedia.Com
www.encyclopedia.com

Based on *The Concise Columbia Electronic Encyclopedia*, Encyclopedia.com provides current information available in all major fields of knowledge – from politics, law, art, and history to sports, literature, geography, science and medicine. More than 17,000 articles provide free, quick and useful information on almost any topic. Like many of the library sites, it does not provide full-text resources, but rather, short article summaries. Encyclopedia.Com also provides links to a fee-based service, Electric Library, where users can find extensive full-text materials.

Encyclopedia Smithsonian FAQs
www.si.edu/resource/faq/start.htm

The Smithsonian Institution receives a great many public inquiries covering a wide range of topics. As a result, they have compiled FAQs on many topics from aeronautics to zoology.

Ready Reference Using the Internet
http://k12.oit.umass.edu/rref.html

An extensive collection from the UMassK12: Electric Library, organized by reference librarians at the Winsor School in Boston.

Research-It!
WWW.iTools.COM/research-it

A very useful collection of reference material, including full-text dictionaries and thesauruses as well as translations, acronyms, biographies and maps.

Virtual Reference Desk
http://thorplus.lib.purdue.edu/reference/index.html

This collection is a model for a well-organized, well researched web site, courtesy of the librarians at Purdue University. It includes dictionaries, phone books, maps, science information, and other reference materials.

CIA World Factbook
www.cia.gov/cia/publications/factbook/index.html

The CIA compiles a thorough country-by-country index with details on governmental structure and geo-political impact regionally and globally. It also includes geographic and demographic detail.

Best Information on the Internet –
Statistical Sources & Calculation Tools on the Net
www.sau.edu/cwis/internet/wild/Refdesk/Stats/staindex.htm

Best Information on the Internet is a wonderful collection from the librarians at St. Ambrose University in Iowa links great collections of statistics from the census, political polling data, demographic information, universal currency converters and personal finance calculators. Add #useful to the URL to get to Useful Data and Formulas.

US Census Bureau
www.census.gov

The census is also a great resource for reference material. See the Government Section for detailed descriptions.

Yellow Page Finders

There are many yellow pages phone books online, but a few of the better ones include:

BigBook
www.bigbook.com

More than just the yellow pages of a phone book because of two features. One, called The Nearest, (within its Detailed Search option) allows you to search for businesses by category and name simultaneously. The other, Search Nearby, retrieves addresses within a specified radius of the business or address for which you're searching. You should have no trouble finding the 24-hour pharmacy closest to your mother's house. If you're contemplating a new business, you can also use it to find competitor locations.

BigYellow

www.bigyellow.com

Similar to BigBook, BigYellow allows you to search by category and nearby locations.

Infobel: International Directories

www.infobel.be/infobel/infobelworld.html

This is an international yellow pages.

Quotation Finders

Bartlett's Familiar Quotations

www.cc.columbia.edu/acis/bartleby/bartlett

In Columbia University's Project Bartleby Archive, you'll find the 1901 Bartlett version, which, obviously, excludes the twentieth century. Great for older quotes: ancient, biblical and Shakespeare.

Commonplace Book, The

http://metalab.unc.edu/ibic/Commonplace-Book.html

Includes current submissions of Quotable Quotes. An interesting site with unusual quote material.

Yahoo! Reference: Quotations

www.yahoo.com/reference/quotations

Backgrounding Tools & FAQs

Backgrounding is a process of general research or getting yourself "up to speed" on a given topic. Many tools discussed elsewhere in this book can be used for backgrounding, as well.

One effective method is to consult a FAQ (Frequently Asked Questions) document. There are several good FAQ indexes on the Internet. Among the best ones are **USENET FAQs** at <u>www.faqs.org/usenet</u> and **FAQ Finder** at <u>http://ps.superb.net/FAQ</u>.

If you want to find a FAQ, try this search on a good search engine:

    +title:topic +faq

Substitute a one-word description of your interest in place of the word "topic." For example, +title:hepatitis +faq

The Human Element

You may need to identify people who've undergone certain experiences, or who possess a range of opinions. You can find them in the various types of interactive discussion forums. They all share one thing – opinions. Lots and lots of opinions – and experiences – about every subject imaginable.

The Internet is an ideal medium for accommodating and storing personal opinions. But don't forget that people can and do lie, especially online where it's easy and convenient to create new online identities. And, this is especially true in chat rooms and newsgroups. It is not easy to ascertain if an online identity is genuine.

To find a virtual community that interests you, try Forum One at <u>www.forumone.com</u>. **It's not comprehensive, but it's a relatively complete list (260,000 web forum discussions) and a good place to start.**

Types of Discussion Groups

There are several types of discussion groups online. Many of them accommodate unconventional points of view and personal accounts. While you can find experts and knowledgeable people in all of them, you can also go on wild goose chases, so be skeptical until a "source" proves itself.

Newsgroups

Newsgroups are online discussion groups that have nothing to do with news. The beauty of newsgroups is that they accommodate everyone – *everyone*. Militia members, pornographers, cultists of every stripe – they're all out there. So are, as

Dave Barry likes to say, teenagers, poets, cat lovers, religious people, gays, gay teens who read religious poetry to cats and, of course, guys who have pointless arguments about sports. You can also find eyewitnesses to every experience imaginable. Newsgroup members talk to each other in groups, and you can read and respond, since newsgroups are public forums. You can "eavesdrop" on the discussion without participating, or respond privately to messages that interest you via e-mail. All newsgroups comprise what is called the "Usenet" portion of the Internet.

Consider the life span of newsgroup postings. Assume that anything you post to a newsgroup will be there forever unless you delete it using Deja News (<u>www.dejanews.com</u>). This goes for some mailing lists, too.

Mailing Lists

One of the most powerful ways of finding people with a particular interest (as opposed to finding an individual) is via electronic mailing lists. Mailing lists are, like newsgroups, large online discussion groups. There are more than 90,000 of them, each about a different subject, comprising every topic imaginable.

Unlike newsgroups, you must subscribe to a list in order to receive the postings. All the messages on a subject are sent to a listserv computer or majordomo computer and are forward to all the members of the subscribed group via e-mail. None of the messages are private, but they are not readable outside of the subscribed membership.

These lists give you access to people who care about a subject, sometimes passionately. Some have expertise and others don't, but to a researcher they offer access to a community of knowledge and a way to tap into great resources of information.

Mailing lists vary widely.

- ◆ Some are open to anyone who's interested.

- ◆ Some are restricted to members of a specified organization.

- ◆ Some are moderated.

- ◆ They are wide-ranging and freewheeling in their content.

Moderators often use a screening mechanism to keep the postings on topic. With certain topics, moderators may have to calm emotions and ask participants to be civil.

To subscribe to a list, simply follow the instructions provided by the list administrator. These instructions usually state that you should send a subscription request to the mailing list. Make sure you send it to the right place. Most mailing lists have two addresses:

- ◆ An administrative one that handles the subscribing/unsubscribing.

♦   Another administrator who routes all the postings.

To get on or off a list, send a note to the administrator, not the entire list. If you happen to err, you'll doubtless get a stack of angry e-mail, called "flames". Your message should follow a standardized format, in which you leave the subject line blank and, in the body of the text, write "subscribe" followed by your first name and then last name with no punctuation. The server will automatically send you a confirmation and a welcome note of rules and guidelines. Save and consult it if and when you decide to unsubscribe. This method works for most but not all mailing lists.

Free discussion being what it is, some mailing lists generate avalanches of postings daily. Be prepared.

The best list of web mailing lists, **Liszt** (www.liszt.com), is a comprehensive searchable directory of more than 90,000 live mailing lists worldwide. You can also use one of Liszt's subject categories as a subject directory.

Chat Rooms

Chat rooms are essentially free-for-alls in which large numbers of people monitor and converse in real time.

The word "chat" may be somewhat misleading because you are not really *talking* to anyone, just typing and reading text messages that other chat participants write. Once you enter a chat room, which is really just a web page, you can choose to only read the exchanges (that's known as *lurking*) or you can join in by typing – called posting – your own messages.

Like the incredible proliferation of newsgroups, chat rooms focus on specific topics as well as general ones. They are more likely to be a waste of time than a valuable use of your resources.

You get what you pay for – and chatting is free, most of the time.

Chat room postings aren't officially archived, but people can and do freely copy and forward postings, and there is no assumption of privacy or ownership of your words.

The largest chat company in the world, which provides AOL's chat services as well as its own, known as ICQ, is **Mirabilis** (www.mirabilis.com).

Chat software can be used on the web with your browser to conduct online discussions with one or as many as a thousand users simultaneously.

Many companies offer this kind of software and the best versions allow you to add in images, video and audio to the discussions. One company, **Webchat** (http://wbs.net/wcc.html), uses the Internet browser with no added software to let businesses do marketing, sales and educating consumers while chatting. Chat discussions also are now used online to provide classes and technical support for web users.

America Online (AOL) has made its mark offering chat rooms of all kinds to its users. If you subscribe to AOL, all the software needed to participate in chat rooms comes with the AOL program.

Examples of other online chat rooms include:
www.2meta.com/chats *and*
www.all-links.com/webchat

WebChat Broadcasting System features all sorts of subject-oriented rooms, with thousands of participants. You can find news chats, like Nando Times, or age-related rooms (the thirty-something room), geographic and ethnic rooms and more general interest ones.

For a more extensive list of chat rooms, try searching the term "web chat" using
Yahoo! Computers & Internet: Internet: World Wide Web: Chat

http://dir.yahoo.com/Computers_and_Internet/Internet/
World_Wide_Web/Chat

There are a few chatting safety information sites that teach you how to protect yourself. They include:

WorldKids Network Internet Safety Tips
www.worldkids.net/school/safety/internet/internet.htm

Conferencing

Using the Internet, we are able to communicate inexpensively around the world through the computer in real time. The technology has moved so quickly that conferencing is now an affordable way of doing business.

Conferencing can take many different forms, such as videoconferencing, audioconferencing, multimedia conferencing, screen-sharing, and to a lesser extent, chat discussion sessions.

Videoconferencing

The most popular form of Internet conferencing is a video program called CU-SeeMe, which allows people to use the Internet to see each other's faces in small windows on your computer screen and to hear their voices through computer speakers using digital cameras that now costs as little as $100. The software is free at **Cornell's CU-SeeMe** at http://rocketcharged.com/mac/cu-seeme.html and many other places.

For more details on CU-SeeMe, consult its Frequently Asked Questions (FAQ) on the **CU-SeeMe FAQ Page** at http://support.wpine.com/cuseeme

Videoconferencing allows people in different locations to address educational, personal and business issues more quickly, productively and economically. It can be done one-on-one or one-on-many. It has great potential for reducing the costs of doing business and making small companies competitive.

For more information, a good starting point is: **Videoconferencing**
http://disc.cba.uh.edu/~rhirsch/spring97/rappold1.htm

Online Audio Conferencing

Internet teleconferencing allows you to make calls around the world through the Internet for the cost of a local call. While the audio quality still leaves something to be desired, this technology is improving rapidly.

The software needed depends on your computer. **Speak Freely for Windows** (www.fourmilab.ch/speakfree/windows) for example, offers audio-conferencing as well as voice mail — and it can be downloaded free. Macintosh users can use **DigiPhone** software at www.digiphone.com.

Software programs like **Virtual Meeting** (www.rtz.com/demoLicesneMac.html) and **Net Meeting** (www.microsoft.com) enable meetings and presentations in many locations simultaneously. You electronically raise your hands and when the moderator gives you the floor, you speak. Other software types allow you to conduct round-table meetings without a moderator.

Document conferencing software also exists allowing people in remote locations to share work on projects via the Web.

To see how electronic conferencing is used in academia, see the **Directory of Scholarly & Professional E-Conferences** at http://hplus.harvard.edu/alpha/dir_schol_conf.html.

Also, the **HotBot** search engine allows you to connect to a Discussion Groups feature that includes Usenet newsgroups, discussion lists, mailing lists and some chat groups.

A new trend is 3D chatting, which allows people to talk to others while moving around in an imaginary three-dimensional world using special software. An example is **Cybertown, the 3DVR Community of the Future** at www.cybertown.com. The research value of this is questionable unless you are checking out the virtual worlds.

A Newsgroup Primer

A newsgroup's address is its identity. alt.backrubs for example, is an address and a clear indication of topic. Newgroups belong to one of a growing number of subject categories, according to their address. Here's a primer:

rec stands for recreation. For example, rec.music.acapella is one of more than forty other rec groups.

comp means computer-related.

sci describes science-related categories.

newusers is for Usenet beginners. Lots of valuable tips and suggestions tend to appear here.

soc describes discussions of social and cultural topics, including country-by-country discussions at `soc.culture`.

talk Here is where you'll find opinions on any subject. Unsubstantiated rumors, absolute falsehoods and idle conjecture are here as well.

biz harbors mostly business-related discussions. A good place for company announcements and job leads. It is especially good for checking out competitors.

news is a misnomer. This is about updates and announcements concerning the newsgroups themselves, not about current news events.

bionet is for biology and environmental-related newsgroups.

bit is an odd collection of mailing list groups that want to be cross-indexed within newsgroups. Runs the gamut from blues and bluegrass music to travel and transplants.

k12 is geared to teachers and kids from kindergarten through high school.

misc is short for miscellaneous. This is a collection of things that don't fit elsewhere. "misc" is wide-ranging.

alt is about alternative subjects and views, non-mainstream and is much looser than the ones listed above.

There are few newsgroup rules to begin with and virtually anyone can start a newsgroup. Some come and go quickly. "Alts" represent the widest cross-section of the Internet. When Tonya Harding and Nancy Kerrigan had their famous skating clash, overnight popped up the newsgroup `alt.kill.tonyaharding, die, die, die`. Currently, there's a similarly titled newsgroup about pre-school icon Barney.

More than thirty-five countries have their own newsgroups. Nearly every state has developed its own newsgroups, as have private companies. While the actual discussions may appear largely trivial, some groups, like `sci.med.diseases.cancer` and `alt.support.cancer` are great ways to find someone who has faced or is facing a disease you or a loved one may be confronting.

Searching Newsgroups

The golden key to searching newsgroups is **Deja News** at www.dejanews.com. It is a free tool that catalogs the entire Usenet (or newsgroup) portion of the Internet. At last count it consisted of more than 100 million postings, accounting for more than 175 gigabytes of disk space (the equivalent of about 120,000 400-page novels). Deja News officials say they receive 500 megabytes of new messages in 15,000+ newsgroups every single day. And, the volume is skyrocketing.

There are also several search engines that will hunt through newsgroups and retrieve postings – AltaVista and HotBot, for example. But Deja News is unquestionably the most thorough tool that monitors postings.

Using Deja News is fairly simple. There's a Basic Search, in which you submit a key term and wait. It will retrieve the most recent postings on that subject. To find a newsgroup about a subject of interest, click on the Interest Finder. If you've already decided on a particular newsgroup, enter it through the Browse Groups option.

There are also several more sophisticated search methods. By clicking on Power Search, you can limit the number of postings by date; you can also isolate a particular posting. Say, for example, you wanted to locate someone who wasn't happy with Viagra. First you would use the Interest Finder to locate groups discussing Viagra. Most probably, your choice would be `alt.support.impotence`. Then click on Power Search and type `alt.support.impotence` into the space for Forum Name. Then submit the word "failure" in the subject field and run the query (see below). You'll get several postings.

Search Options <u>help</u>

Limit Search
these options help to further narrow your search

Organize Results
these options help to organize your search results

Match ⦿ all ◯ any keywords

Language | any ▾ |

Example: FAQ or (frequently asked questions)

Subject | failure |

Example: alt.tv.x-files or "x-files"

Forum | alt.support.impotence |

Example: demos@dejanews.com

Author | |

Example: Apr 1 1997   Example: Apr 5 1997

Date | | | |
from   to

Results format
| tabular ▾ |

Sort by
| confidence ▾ |

Results per page
| 25 ▾ |

You can also click on Author Profile to find other postings by that person. Smart users of Deja News use the author profile to get background information on people who have written about subjects of interest.

You can take a poster's e-mail address and put it through one or more people finder tools to come up with a name and address for that person – and other information, as well. Of course, the reverse is also true. Keep that in mind before posting a message yourself.

Reference.Com at www.reference.com is another free tool that, like Deja News, searches newsgroups by key phrase. But it goes a step further: in its Advanced Mode, you can also search for postings by organization. It's wonderful for locating people. The catch is that the database goes back only to May, 1998. But, it searches newsgroups, mailing lists and web forums.

Web forums are a relatively new way to collaborate on the Internet. They are, in essence, a highly centralized bulletin board system, navigated with a web browser. Users must visit a particular web site for each web forum to read messages from others and post their own. While no authoritative statistics are available, Reference.Com estimates more than 25,000 web forums are in operation today, though most are sparsely trafficked. Another Reference.Com features: if you fill out a customized query form, you'll be able to run any specific search you want every time you come back to the site. Even better, you can search Reference.Com by e-mail request, and set up and store your requests via e-mail.

Participating in Newsgroup Discussions

If you want to participate in newsgroups, your web browser contains a tool called a News Reader. Both Netscape Navigator and Microsoft Internet Explorer browsers come with built-in news readers. Also, Deja News has developed its own free web-based news reader, **My Deja News**, available at the Deja News site at www.dejanews.com. Another company, Forte, makes a terrific and free news reader that's recommended if you're intending serious usage of newsgroups. It's called **Forté Free Agent Newsreader** and can be found at www.forteinc.com/agent/index.htm. You can use Free Agent to set up screening mechanisms so that you can manage a large volume of Usenet traffic.

Each newsgroup has a particular custom and culture. Before contributing to the online discussion, you should "lurk" silently for a while to take its temperature. It's also considered common courtesy, or netiquette, to do so.

Learn web manners from a netiquette primer maintained by Florida Atlantic University at www.fau.edu/rinaldi/netiquette.html **.**

Proper "netiquette" insists that before you post any kind of question, see if the subject has already been discussed in its FAQs archives. You can search the Deja News web site for a FAQ by inputting your subject of interest.

Case Study: Uncovering Federal Abuse

by Dave Wickham,

Dave Wickham is creator of the Public Servant's Internet Abuse Page.
Address: davew@inlandnet.com

I am an electrician, and I often monitor Usenet newsgroups in search of timely information to include in a web page that I maintain covering fly fishing on the Yakima River in Washington state. While browsing a fly-fishing newsgroup, an article caught my attention — not because of its content, but because the author used the same small local Internet provider I was using. The article, an offer to sell fishing tackle, asked respondents to contact an e-mail address that was on a Washington state government server. He had posted this article from his home but was using his work account to receive requests for information.

I responded and the next day received three phone messages, as well as two e-mails originating from the Washington State Department of Social and Health Services. I began trying to track this person's activity on Usenet. The problem was that news servers usually only maintain postings for a few days. Deja News (`www.dejanews.com`), however, has archived Usenet articles for several years and provides search capabilities within this archive. I was able to retrieve all of this person's posts and discovered that, by using wildcards in the search string, I could retrieve Usenet posts originating from all Washington state government servers. For example, I could search for an individual at the Department of Social and Health Services (`user@dshs.wa.gov`) or I could use the asterisk wildcard to search for anyone posting from a Washington State government domain (`*.wa.gov`).

Browsing these retrieved postings, it was apparent that there were many state employees using the state system for personal use and pleasure at their offices. I compiled a portfolio of the worst examples of misuse and e-mailed a summary to every newspaper and television station in Washington that had an e-mail address. I was sure that this information could lead to a great investigative story. The story would show government employees wasting time and would be easily verifiable.

But only one media organization responded, and its reporter failed to follow up on a story. I was left with only one way to publicize the issue: the Internet. With help from my Internet Service Provider — which was willing to risk hosting a controversial and potentially high-volume site — the **Public Servants' Internet Abuse Page** was established at `www.adsnet.net/states.htm`. This page cites many of the examples I found, as well as a description of the method I used to acquire them.

The web page came to the attention of an Associated Press reporter in nearby Yakima, who used the web page and her own research to write an article about government employee Internet abuse that ran on the front pages of major newspapers in Washington state and across the country. Since the article appeared, I have been contacted by hundreds of reporters, many of whom have used Deja News and similar archives to monitor Usenet activity by government employees on national, state, county and local levels. Subsequently, stories uncovering similar abuses have appeared in the *Detroit News*, *Cleveland Plain Dealer*, *Portland Oregonian*, *Miami Herald* and several smaller papers. The web page was also described in *Editor and Publisher* magazine.

It's ironic that when I first placed the page on the Internet, I was trying to publicize an issue for which I'd been unable to get media coverage. These days, by far the majority of queries I receive is from reporters asking how to research a specific area or government agency. It's gratifying that these reporters then go on to write stories that are influencing how government employees are permitted to use the Internet during their working hours.

Fee-Based Tools for Finding Specialized Information

There are hundreds of fee-based services, and most of them are extremely good. Using them, you can find extensive background information about a person – name, Social Security Number, last five addresses, relatives' names, value of property owned or rented, all kinds of business records (Chapter 9 of this book will provide more detail), information about neighbors, vital records (see the chapter on public records), and so forth.

The big information supermarkets (DIALOG, LEXIS-NEXIS, Dow Jones, Information America and others) maintain virtual warehouses of information — extensive libraries of published information on a myriad of subjects, including full-text periodicals. Other fee-based tools contain public records derived from government entities, publishers' mailing lists, mail forwarding orders, real estate information, registered voter files, tax assessor and county recorder records, bankruptcy courts, and many other places. Through services like CDB Infotek, DBT Autotrack, Merlin Data Systems, KnowX, Information America and others, you can "people search" by name using white pages, publishers' mailing lists, voter registration files, credit header files and property data.

Many of the proprietary services like LEXIS-NEXIS, DIALOG and Dow Jones have developed easy-to-use point and click systems on the web to expand their base market beyond librarians and professional researchers. Be warned, however, that there is so much content available that it still takes time to learn how to use each company's system effectively. But what you will find remains the most sophisticated and thorough information available, far exceeding most web sites.

Also, all the supermarket databases claim to house more useable information than the entire Web. DIALOG alone claims it has more than six billion pages of text in more than nine-hundred databases.

Using Fee-Based Services

Most of these companies charge you for everything you download. Most of them have dropped the charges for your time online, charging a flat fee instead. DIALOG is the exception with something called Dial Units. For every document you look at and for every one you download, you are charged.

Where you get a significant advantage is that the search engines on these tools are extremely robust and powerful. They allow you to conduct more precision searching. They also help you focus your results through refining techniques. They often offer material that is unique and not found on the Web, things like market studies, doctoral theses and scholarly journals.

Fee-based services also allow you much more flexibility in defining your search. They provide a quality screening mechanism, determining on your behalf where the valuable resources might be found, centralizing them and letting you know where the resources come from. Fee-based services allow you to scour large numbers of resources simultaneously and run your search in one shot.

The tradeoff, as always, is time versus money. You spend more money to get an answer with a fee-based service, but save time in the process.

On fee-based services in particular, the structure of each database can be different, so if you are searching more than one database at a time, be careful to switch rules of operation when you switch databases. Even if you are searching all on the same fee-based service, this happens.

So, how do you choose between DIALOG, Dow Jones and LEXIS-NEXIS or the thousands of other proprietary services online? Refer back to the questions from Chapter 2 – Framing Your Search, and ask yourself:

◆ How much money do I need to spend?

◆ How much time do I have?

◆ Is what I need available when I need it?

◆ How comfortable am I with each of the different services?

◆ Most importantly, does a particular service have what I need?

Sign up for a free introductory trial with any fee-based service that interests you and sit at the controls and test drive it.

Best Commercial Vendors

Here's a quick run down of the three industry giants:

Dialog Corporation
www.dialogweb.com

Users view **DIALOG Web** as a supermarket because it has so many aisles with so many different varieties of products. The Dialog databases include key categories such as news and media, medicine, pharmaceuticals, chemicals, reference, social sciences, business and finance, food and agriculture, intellectual property, government and regulations, science and technology, and energy and environment. Within each category are extensive collections of articles, journals and other written material.

The key to using and understanding DIALOG's depth is to read its **BlueSheets**, a detailed guide as to what is contained in the files, how best to search them and how far back they go.

As part of its move to the Web, Dialog Corporation has posted the BlueSheets to DIALOG Web. Using the non-web version of DIALOG involves an extensive learning curve of search command language, which allows you to combine different sets of search results. DIALOG also eliminates the duplicates from the search results, allows you to link different terms and rank the concepts you think will be most appropriate in doing your search.

DIALOG Web has a unique Guided Search Option that allows you to search the system without being familiar with the DIALOG command structure at all.

DIALOG Web also gives you access to DIALOG Classic for those who are more comfortable with the DIALOG command language, the way librarians have searched DIALOG for many years. Plus, DIALOG offers the **Dial Index**, which is the master database of all the different DIALOG databases. Using the index often points out resources you may have forgotten about or don't know about on your search subject.

Dialog now owns and offers **Responsive Database Services**' Business and Industry, TableBase and Business and Management Practices — three excellent business databases geared to tables and charts.

Dialog recently overhauled its pricing structure (formerly based on connect charges and hit charges) to a "Dial Unit" pricing structure, based on the types of search commands issued during a search session, with prices varying from database to database.

Limited access to some DIALOG databases is also available through some fee-based services, including CompuServe.

Dow Jones Interactive

www.dowjones.com

Dow Jones', crown jewel is *The Wall Street Journal*, but Dow Jones owns an empire of media resources. There is a difference between the **Wall Street Journal Interactive Edition** (www.wsj.com) and **Dow Jones Interactive**. The WSJ Interactive Edition provides an online version of the newspaper and access to the rest of Dow Jones for a monthly subscription fee. However, Dow Jones Interactive (DJI) has significant other resources. In addition to archives from *The Journal* and many other newspapers including *The New York Times, LA Times* and *The Washington Post*, DJI offers other information services, in-depth market research reports, company profiles, securities, dividend and exchange rate information. DJI also has an extensive clippings file that is said to contain eighty million articles from more than 5500 full-text publications. Its Company and Industry Center is quite extensive, allowing you to compare one industry's performance to another and get analysts reports by region of the country. DJI also allows you to search by company, person and industry.

You can also customize DJI to get the clips and stories you want as well as receive specific subject-requested articles by e-mail.

DJI is especially valuable because it lets you use pull-down menus to limit your search to lead paragraphs. This allows you to get the who, what, when, where, why and how of a news story without searching the entire story.

LEXIS-NEXIS
`www.lexis-nexis.com`

LEXIS-NEXIS started as an online service for the legal community, expanded to include case law from other countries, state law and public records, and then added the NEXIS collection of full-text and abstracts of magazines, newspapers, newsletters. It also added financial information, market research reports and country and personality profiles. For years, LEXIS-NEXIS had exclusive deals, giving it sole access to back files of the *New York Times*. That has now changed, however, and you can get the *New York Times* on other services.

LEXIS-NEXIS is moving more and more of its holdings to the Web. The most flexible, thorough research can still only be done through the direct dial-in, non-web version of the service. The web version offers sign up on a transaction-based fee schedule, meaning you're charged per search. However, you get access to the extensive NEXIS resources at a fraction of the cost of the full service by using a service called **reQUESTer**.

reQUESTer provides web access on a per-search basis to more than 7000 NEXIS sources, including newspapers, trade journals, company financial information and market studies. It allows you to use keywords, people's names, or company or industry names to search this database. But, be forewarned: searching a group like AllNews, CompanyNews or People in the News, will cost you more than searching an individual file.

Other LEXIS-NEXIS services on the web are:

News QuickCheck lets you check the extensive news media archive for published reports in newspapers, television and radio broadcasts, newsletters and magazines. You can search by key name (which is great as a people finder), company/industry name or topic.

SalesSmart can pinpoint prospective clients in thousands of industries, research companies, and build a contact database. This can help organize researchers trying to learn specific industries.

Xchange provides access to the LEXIS database, which includes court decisions, legal statutes, and limited access to news resources and market information. Xchange is designed for lawyers and legal researchers.

Company QuickCheck lets you access the extensive news clipping archive dating back twenty years, study SEC filings, monitor business news, research company management, and evaluate rival companies within an industry. It is a good business tool. It can also be used as a people finder to check employment history details about a person.

InfoTailor is an electronic clipping service. The LEXIS side allows access to property records and other public records, including assets, bankruptcies, civil court filings, corporate filings, jury verdicts and settlements.

Comparing the Giants

Many researchers use all three — LEXIS-NEXIS, DIALOG and DJI — the way they use several search engines and other online search tools. On science and medicine, no doubt DIALOG is tops. On news and breaking information, many find it is a toss-up between LEXIS-NEXIS and Dow Jones. Some prefer Dow Jones if the subject is business-related, but lean to LEXIS-NEXIS if it is more political.

See Chapter 7 for a similar discussion of public record fee-based companies and skip-tracing tools.

Chapter 5

Saving & Downloading Your Results

Do you want to save data from a web site or store a radio or television broadcast so that you can listen to it again or share it with someone else? Using your computer, you can find and save all kinds of files – text, transcripts, photos, radio broadcasts and TV news reports. You can also display them, or play them back from your computer, or send them to other people. This chapter will show you how.

Typically, downloading is the process of accessing and saving files to your computer from another computer. If you wanted to send something from your computer to another computer, the process would be referred to as "uploading." Most of the time, though, you'll be on the receiving end, downloading.

For instance, when you access a web page, you're actually downloading the page of text and all the associated graphics from a server. In fact, when you receive electronic mail that contains an attachment, you have actually downloaded both the e-mail message and the attachment. The files you download can be documents or programs that let you

◆ Update your computer's software

◆ See graphics

◆ Hear sounds, music

◆ See video pictures

◆ Read text

Downloading is the process that creates your own copy of a file by copying it from another computer to yours. Once a file is downloaded, it's a simple matter to use it or change it.

But first, you must identify the file type (also called its format).

Identifying File Types

In the Windows environment, the file extension lets your computer know which program opens that file. It is the piece of text at the end of a filename, preceded by a period, that identifies the file type.

For example, the .txt extension means the file is a plain text file. It is also sometimes referred to as an ASCII file. Any program that can read ASCII text can open this file and read it.

Most file extensions are three or four characters long. On some operating systems, such as UNIX, they are four characters. Normally, each file has only one file extension, but some operating systems like UNIX and Windows '98, allow multiple extensions as well as extensions with more than three characters.

For the most part, on the Internet, every file has a three or four character extension. Macintosh files don't require a file extension and instead have an identifier built into the file that is visible only to the computer. Mac files on the Internet, however, do have extensions, like .sea.

Most image files end with .jpeg and .gif. The former stands for JPEG which is a popular compression standard for photos and other still images. The latter extension stands for Graphics Interchange Format, a standard that was developed by CompuServe in the late 1980s. Both these graphics formats can be used on PCs, Macs or UNIX machines as long as viewing software has been installed. Also, your word processor can work with these files using the Insert Picture from a file option in Microsoft Word or Insert Graphics from file in WordPerfect.

Popular extensions for video files are .avi for the PC, .mpg (short for MPEG), .mov and .qt for QuickTime movies.

Sound files come in .aiff for Macintosh; .au for Mac and UNIX; .wav for the PC; and .ra for Real Audio, which is a proprietary system for delivering and playing real-time audio on the Web.

A Field Guide to File Formats

The software needed to read these files comes with most standard browsers. The "File Formats" are also called file extensions.

File Format	Type of File It Identifies
.avi	Video for Windows
.bmp, .pcx	Common bitmap graphics formats
.doc	Microsoft Word files from Word for Macintosh, Word for Windows and Windows WordPad
.exe	A program file or a self-extracting archive file
.gif	Graphic Interchange Format files often found in web pages
.hlp	Windows help files
.html, .htm	The language which web documents are authored and saved in.
.jpg .jpeg, .jpe	JPEG graphics files often found in web pages
.mpeg, .mpg, mpe, .m1v	MPEG (Motion Pictures Expert Group) video formats
.pdf	Portable Document Format, an Adobe Acrobat hypertext file. This format is becoming very popular means of distributing electronic documents
.ram, .ra	Real Audio. This sound format plays while it's being transmitted
.rtf	Rich Text Format. These word processing files are readable by a variety of word processors
.sea	A Macintosh self-extracting archive
.tif	A common graphics format
.txt, .text	A text or ASCII file, readable by most word processing programs
.wav	The standard Windows "wave" sound format
.wpd	A WordPerfect document file
.xls	A Microsoft Excel spreadsheet file
.zip	A PKZIP archive file (a DOS and Windows compressions file) used by many Windows (and some Macintosh) compression utilities

Saving Files

A web page may look like a seamless unit, but actually it's a compilation of several files and several types of files. The words are either `.text` or `.html`. The photos are image files such as `.gif` or `.jpg`. That flashing banner or dancing baby may be a Java file or something similar. A video file is often an `.mpeg` and an audio file can be a `.wav` or another type of file.

How you download a file depends both on its size, format and your reason for downloading it. Generally, you can choose where to store the file (i.e. on a floppy disc, zip drive or hard drive), what to name it and what type to save it as.

Today's browsers are intuitive and will often walk you through the process.

Saving Programs

The first type of file most people download is a program file. Perhaps it's a software "patch" to fix a bug or glitch found after the original product was shipped, or maybe it is a program that allows you to view other types of files. Web pages that download software usually ask you to click to start the process. At this point, your browser will ask you if you want to "save to disk." Tell it where you want to store the file, and note the location so you can retrieve the file later. The computer will then automatically begin the download process.

What you will have downloaded is usually an "executable" file, such as `.exe`, which you can double-click on to install. For some files you may have to use the "Run" feature instead of double-clicking. When the program file is comprised of several files or is compressed (such as a `.zip` file), you will need another software program to open it before it can be downloaded (*see* the Compressing and Decompressing Files section later in this chapter).

Saving Documents & Text

Maybe you have found an information-loaded web site and you want to download some of its material. While bookmarking is always a good idea, a web site may disappear without notice, so it's best to grab (and save) material when you can.

For this example, let's assume the information you want to download is some form of text. The text could be imbedded in the web page itself, or it could be a separate file that can be downloaded in its entirety.

If the text is part of the overall web page, you can simply Save the page. In actuality, when you go to your browser and choose "Save" you will only be getting a portion of the page. Remember: all those banners, dancing dogs and other eye-catching graphics are separate image files. If you "Save As" `.html`, you can re-open the file while offline using your browser, and usually the page will look like it did online, except sections with graphics will become little boxes. If you "Save As" `.txt`, you will have a plain text file which can be opened in your computer's most basic text editor, such as Windows Notepad. Depending on your computer's configuration, you can later convert this.

Now, you can revert to the old "cut and paste" method to manipulate text information as you can with any text file. If you have inadvertently copied some of the document's HTML code, then you may see some strange symbols. After you've pasted the text into your document, simply delete any extraneous characters.

Sometimes the text is stored as a separate file that can be downloaded in its entirety. One of the most popular formats for this is .pdf (portable document format) which uses Adobe Acrobat software. Acrobat is a popular format for several reasons:

♦ It is a quick way to put information on the web rather than converting existing files to HTML

♦ It is a convenient way to preserve formatting that is important either for integrity or aesthetics

♦ It is a good way to store very large files.

You must have an Adobe Acrobat Reader to view these files. The Federal Government has endorsed using Acrobat Readers, and its usage is widespread.

Downloading documents such as .pdf files is very similar to downloading a program. Again, you may actually be downloading from an FTP site. Usually there will be a link that you can click on that will make your browser do most of the work.

Incidentally, downloading the software necessary to read .pdf files won't cost you anything. It's free for the asking, and you can download it from Adobe Systems at www.adobe.com/productindex/acrobat/readstep.html

Let's say you want to send something. First you must highlight — select —what you want to send. There are several ways to do that.

If you want the entire text of the document on the screen,

you can hit "Select All" under Edit on your browser, you will be able to highlight all the text you want to send.

or, you could press Ctrl+A to select *all* of the text.

If you want *only a portion* of the entire text:

you can click the mouse at the beginning of a section and drag the mouse to the end of the selection

or, you can also click at the beginning of a section — anywhere, actually —and hold down the Shift key on the keyboard, and use the arrow keys to select the text you want to copy.

Once you have the text highlighted, you can choose the "Copy" command from the Edit menu. Alternatively, you can use Ctrl+C to copy the selected text into the Windows clipboard.

Once the text is in the clipboard, you can switch to another program and use the "Paste" function to incorporate the text (or graphic) into that program. If the program doesn't have an icon or menu option for "Paste," you can use CTRL+P to paste from the Windows clipboard. This technique of copying from a web page and pasting into a word processing document is a very effective way to enhance your documents and avoid re-typing information that is already available on your computer.

Saving Images & Sounds

To save an image, move your mouse directly over the image itself then press the right click button on your mouse. You will be presented with a menu of options. Choose "Save Image As" or "Save Picture As" from the menu that appears. If it is a JPEG file, you will probably want to save it as a .jpg. You can change the File Name — the part before the extension — to a name you can better recognize. The suggested names for image files are usually pretty cryptic, like "x32yT.jpg." You could rename this "charlie.jpg" and you'll know from the extension .jpg that it's an image of Charlie.

If changing the names is too much work, just keep a list somewhere of what the file is called and where you put it. Some people keep a running log of the files they download and where they saved them.

Most sound files feature a link that initiates the download process. Again, you will probably want to preserve the format and file extension as you would an image file, as explained above.

To open image and sound files, your computer must be configured with the right programs to do so. Usually, when you double-click on a file, the appropriate program will probably launch, opening the file onto the screen

Web Pages & Screen Captures

There are several reasons you may want to save an entire web page. Perhaps you want to be able to read it while you are offline. Maybe you're giving a presentation and would like to show the page as an example of something. Again, the intended use determines the format in which you should save the file. Always be aware of the copyrights associated with web pages — and use web material accordingly. (See the Stephanie Ardito's sidebar "Your Rights & Copyrights Online" on the following pages.)

If you copy the entire page to your computer, you must save each file on that page separately, using the techniques outlined above. Usually, you begin by using the "Save" function of your browser — saving to .html. Then you have to individually save each of the image and sound files. All of them must be stored in the same folder and must maintain their original names. If you do this properly, you will be able to double-click on the "main" file (the one you saved as .html) and the other files will load automatically.

If you merely want to save the "look" of a web site, it may be easier to do a screen capture. To capture a screen, press Alt+Prt Sc (Print Screen) which copies the active window, then paste it into the application of your choice (perhaps a paint or graphics program). To paste, press Ctrl+V or go to the Edit button and hit Paste. Then Save the file as a bitmap or .bmp file.

If you want to get fancier and be able to copy parts of a page including their graphics, so you can play with the images size and shapes, you will need special software to do what's known as screen capturing of a page. There are dozens of companies that provide free, low cost or high cost capturing software. If you need a more sophisticated program, try a program like **Jasc's Paintshop Pro** www.jasc.com. These programs allow you to control what part of the screen you want to capture and also let you edit the image or convert it to a large number of formats.

Saving Web Links

Once you get comfortable with downloading, you may want to make a connection to the actual page without actually being online. A hyper-text link connects your computer to a site on the Internet through HTML coding.

You can save a linked page without going to the link itself. Put your pointer over the link and click your right mouse (or hold down the mouse button if you are a Mac user). From the pop up menu that appears, select "Save Link As." That will give you the "Save As" dialog box where you can select a folder and drive for the page.

▬▬▬ Compressing & Decompressing Files

Program files on the Internet can be very big. If you couldn't shrink files, you'd waste time sending and receiving huge files. Compressed files do just that, reducing files to as little as 2% of their normal size, depending on the type of file and the program you are using. Normally, compression reduces files between 40% to 75% of their size. If you want to transfer a file or group of files across the Internet, it's a lot faster to transfer a compressed file than an uncompressed one.

How does it work? It gets kind of techno-geekish, but all compression programs rely on the fact that there are many instances of lengthy, repeated information in program code. They can all be abbreviated as they are being sent, and then restored when the item is decompressed.

Most compressed DOS and Windows files are in .zip format, which were created by a program called PKZIP. There are other compressed formats as well. If it is a UNIX program, .z, .gz, and .tar are common archive formats. On the Macintosh, they are called .sit (Stuffit) and .pit (Packit).

One thing that makes zipped files valuable is that you can package many files inside one .zip file. If a program, for example, needs ten files in order to run, it's convenient to compress them as a single file rather than transfer each of the ten files individually.

PKZIP programs can also create files that can run themselves automatically. These are called self-extracting files and usually end with .exe instead of .zip. They are very useful for sending a compressed file to someone who you are not sure has the capability to decompress the file. So, if you receive a PKZIP file with an .exe extension, you can run that file directly from the DOS prompt or from the Run prompt in the Start menu, just by typing its folder and filename then pressing Enter or by double-clicking in the Windows Explorer File Management program. When you do these tasks, all the compressed files pop out. If you know there are going to be several files inside the main .zip file, it's a good idea to create a temporary folder and copy the .zip file into it before unzipping or expanding it into its separate component pieces. On a Mac, the .sea (self-extracting archives) do the same thing.

If you use a .zip file, you must have a program that can read the .zip file and extract the archived files from within. You may already have such a program. Some Windows File Management programs, for instance, can work with .zip files. Otherwise you'll need a decompression program.

There are many places where you can download freeware and shareware that will unzip files. Among the most popular programs are PKZIP/UNZIP and WINZIP.

Your Rights & Copyrights Online

by Stephanie C. Ardito

Stephanie C. Ardito is President of Ardito Information & Research, Inc., an information firm specializing in pharmaceutical, medical and business information research, as well as intellectual property and copyright matters. She is a past president of the Association of Independent Information Professionals. Contact: sardito@ardito.com

In the US, the Copyright Act of 1976, and its revision in 1978, govern the use of copyrighted works. Works are protected from the moment of their creation and remain in effect during the author's life plus fifty additional years after the author's death (essentially the same terms as England's 1719 Statute of Anne, considered to be the world's first copyright law).

In 1989, the US joined the Berne Convention, which guarantees copyright protection for authors in all member nations (more than 130 countries) and guards against copyright infringement of foreign members' works in the US. The Berne Convention does not require registration, a copyright symbol or notification of any kind on authors' publications. In other words, one should assume that *all* Internet works are copyrighted and protected by the Berne Convention.

To determine what can be legally downloaded, copied and printed from the web, users should look for terms and conditions and/or links detailing the site owner's permission for reproducing content. Generally, commercial sites (those ending in `.com` and including content from companies, databases, newspapers, newswires and magazines) permit reproduction for personal use or for nonprofit educational purposes. Commercial sites do not permit the making of multiple copies to be distributed to individuals other than one user. Copyright violations potentially exist if web content is passed on within a user's organization for commercial reasons. It is best to seek the site owner's permission for such reproduction. A second option is to forward the web site's address, also known as a URL, to other users so each viewer's use will be legal.

US federal government web sites are not protected by copyright and can be copied freely. The contents of these sites are considered to be in the public domain. Content of state government web sites may be protected by copyright laws; as with commercial sites, users should be careful about making more than one copy. Content from US patent documents and federal legal documents can also be copied without fear of copyright violation; however, any proprietary information from private parties that is attached to federal documents is protected by copyright law.

Other countries' copyright laws are more restrictive. Canada and the UK, for example, *do* protect their government publications, so users should observe copyright and terms and conditions before making multiple copies of non-US government documents.

The US Supreme Court has ruled that telephone directory information is not protected by copyright law, but users should be cautious about what they download and reuse. One can copy directory listings, but not "value-added" information such as indexing terms, descriptors, abstracts and formats.

Non-profit groups, such as associations, also copyright their materials. Seek permission before distributing multiple copies, especially if the material may be used for commercial purposes.

There isn't yet a clear-cut legal decision on whether linking is protected by international copyright laws. Many industry experts believe that the Internet was established to link individuals and organizations with common interests, and that to copyright links would severely restrict the Internet's great strength. On the other hand, many organizations don't want indiscriminate linking of their web sites and are threatening lawsuits and/or requiring periodic royalty or licensing payments in order to control their content.

The practice of placing the content of other people's web sites into your own web page is called "framing" or "inlaying," and can also be a copyright infringement. When in doubt, seek permission from the content owner.

In searching the Web and sites furnished by online service providers, I recommend the following:

> **Look for and read copyright notices** (keeping in mind that content does not have to have a copyright notice to be protected), terms and conditions, and vendor licensing agreements (generally, a commercial online provider's fees include copyright permission to type, print and view each document as a one-time use).

There are three things you can do when in doubt about what can and cannot done: **contact the web site owner**, contact the US **Copyright Clearance Center Online** (www.copyright.com), or contact the relevant licensing agency in your country. In the US, it is still safe to download or print content if for personal use – i.e., one copy for your own non-commercial purpose.

Refer other users within your organization to Internet URLs to retrieve information. If each individual logs on and downloads his or her own version of web pages, then reproduction may be viewed as personal use copying.

Know that **you are agreeing to a contract** that is probably enforceable when you click on a terms and conditions agreement in order to access an Internet document. Violations could result in lawsuits.

Don't frame web sites that you don't personally own.

Information brokers, librarians or other intermediaries conducting research on behalf of another individual or company should search commercial databases for full-text articles or use a document supplier who pays royalties to the **US Copyright Clearance Center** or other international licensing agency. Content is not free; however, signed terms and conditions are quite clear about reproduction rights. Unlike terms and conditions agreements on web sites, many commercial online vendors furnish special clauses that clearly explain the rights of librarians and independent information professionals.

When downloading online search results, **keep all copyright notices** with each record. In other words, don't delete copyright notices when post-processing search results. The notices will serve as reminders to users that the content is copyrighted and any further reproduction is forbidden unless permission has been received from the copyright holder.

For the more adventurous data mavens, Drew Sullivan shows you how to handle the nuances of downloading databases and spreadsheets.

Downloading Databases & Spreadsheets: A Practical Introduction

by Drew Sullivan

Drew Sullivan is a reporter for the *Nashville Tennessean* and former systems director for the National Institute for Computer Assisted Reporting.

Address: drew@nicar.org and www.nicar.org/~drew

Simply defined, a database is information structured in a particular way. A good example of database output is your phone book. The first line is always the name sorted alphabetically by the last name. The second piece of information is the address and the third piece is the phone number.

Database programs are tools used to manipulate the data in a way that makes it easy to recall individual pieces we may want to use – say, the phone number of your favorite pizza parlor.

A spreadsheet is a specialized kind of database program. It's an electronic ledger sheet that makes it easy to manipulate rows and columns of numbers. Like a database program, a spreadsheet program lets you sort, filter and graph data.

The Web is the world's richest source of easy-to-use databases and spreadsheets. Using the Web, an interested person could find out how many workplace safety violations a local company has been cited for, the amount contributed by a celebrity to a gubernatorial candidate in Florida, the relative cleanliness of a restaurant in Nashville, the number of accidents a particular railroad company has experienced or the owner of a particular airplane.

What these seemingly disparate pieces of information all have in common is they are all stored in databases on the Web. Sometimes the information is easy to get to; sometimes it requires a bit of work. It all depends on how the information is stored and the means provided to retrieve it. In general, we can define three ways in which information is stored and retrieved:

> As a searchable database with a front-end – or tool – designed to help you search the data

> As a set of structured data that can be downloaded from the web into a database or spreadsheet program

> As a set of data that can be downloaded and converted into a form usable by a database or spreadsheet program

Searchable Databases

You've probably seen dozens of searchable databases with front-ends so far in this book. For example, Yahoo!'s People Search database lets you look up the name and address of millions of people in much the same way you would use directory assistance to look up a name in the phonebook. Here are some other examples:

Establishment Search in the Occupational Safety & Health Administration
www.osha.gov/cgi-bin/est/est1

OSHA's database of workplace safety inspections. Enter the name of an establishment and click on the "Submit" button.

National Traffic Safety Board Aviation Accident/Incident Database
http://nasdac.faa.gov/asp/asy_ntsb.asp

On the Federal Aviation Administration's web site. Enter an airline's name under the operator-airline field and click "Submit" to find all the accidents in which that airline was involved.

EPA's Toxic Release Inventory

www.epa.gov/enviro/html/tris/tris_query_java.html

Using the TRI Query Form, enter a name of a chemical company or facility to find the planned and actual releases by the company into the environment.

Federal Deposit Insurance Corporation Institutions

http://www2.fdic.gov/structur/search

In this database of Bank Ownership, enter the link to search a company's holdings. For example, enter a name of a holding company to learn which banks that company owns.

Try playing with these sites. Each time you find one of these sites on the Web, you'll have to learn how its search screen works. Some of this data is very complicated and is designed for use by experts in their respective fields.

Always be careful when using searchable databases because data is often not standardized – or "clean," as database people call it. For instance, if you wanted to find all the inspections of IBM's facilities in the US, you can go to the OSHA site and search by the term "IBM". But what happens if the person entering the data typed the company's name as "I.B.M.", "International Business Machines", "I B M" or even incorrectly as "IMB." You don't want to miss those records – they could be very important to you.

An important thing to remember when using these databases: you are not searching for web pages as you are with HotBot, AltaVista or other search engines. With these database search screens you are searching information that is stored someplace else, usually in a file readable by a database program. When you search the database, the web server temporarily creates a web page with the search results and presents it to you.

Structured Data Sets

The second type of database is a set of structured data that can be downloaded from the web and into a database program. Unlike web-based searchable databases, which use a front-end to search the data in the same way we would use directory assistance, downloading this type of database is akin to downloading a phonebook from the Web.

Data in this format are usually stored in a File Transfer Protocol (FTP) format. FTP is a standard (also called a "protocol") that we use for copying files between machines on the Internet. An FTP site is a site on the web that serves files much the same way a web server serves web pages.

What's important to you when downloading data from an FTP site is determining the format of the file. A file can be stored in dozens of different formats. The most common are as ASCII text, as a spreadsheet file (either Excel, Lotus 1-2-3 or other), or as a database file (FoxPro, Access or other). Often the extension on the file will tell you its format. The table below gives you some common extensions.

.xl* or .xls Excel Spreadsheet

`.wk*`	Lotus 1-2-3 Spreadsheet
`.wq*`	Quattro Pro Spreadsheet
`.txt` or `.asc`	ASCII text files
`.csv`	ASCII comma separated text file (fields are separated by commas)
`.dbf`	FoxPro Database
`.mdb`	Microsoft Access Database
`.db`	Paradox Database

Once you determine the format, the file can be downloaded and saved on your computer and imported into the spreadsheet or database program of your choice.

Below are some examples of government sites where you can download complete files. In each case, the procedure is a little different. What you see when you try to download a file from the Web often depends on how you have your browser configured. When a browser sees a file, it looks at its extension and tries to determine what you want to do with it, based on your browser settings. For instance, if you try to download a file named "`file.xls`", your browser can do one of three things.

- It may try to display the file – in which case you will get garbage on your screen. That's because the text editors and most web browsers can't read an Excel Spreadsheet file.

- It may ask you to save it to your computer

- It may launch Excel automatically and show you the file.

You can configure your browser by looking in the preferences or options setting of your browser and then looking for the applications tab. Each browser is a little different, but each supports these options in some way.

Follow the directions at the sites below and download the data. I prefer to download the data, because data changes rapidly on the Web. What's there today may be gone tomorrow.

Emergency Response Notification System Data & Documentation
www.epa.gov/ERNS/docs/data.html

From this EPA database, follow the simple directions to download a file. Pick a small one.

FAA Office of System Safety, Safety Data
http://nasdac.faa.gov/safety_data

Enter the site and look for Bureau of Transportation statistics and the link that says "Excel."

Endangered Species Database: US Fish & Wildlife Service
www.fws.gov/r9endspp/listdata.html

Select a text file and not a .pdf file.

Data that Is Downloadable and/or Convertible into a Spreadsheet or Database

The final method for downloading data from the Web is to import data from tables or charts into a spreadsheet or database. Before you begin, you'll need familiarize yourself with basic data structures and the import features on a spreadsheet or database program.

There are two formats that a table can take on the Web: an **HTML table** or a **text table**. A table's format may be hidden but can be easily determined by looking at the language that makes up a web page, which is called Hypertext Markup Language (HTML). An HTML table uses the table tag to format the table for your browser.

A text file is simply text entered onto the web page without any special HTML tags. To find out whether your page has HTML tags, from your browser select the "View" and "Page Source" options on your browser menu.

For example, if you go to the US Census Bureau page on **State Poverty Rates** at www.census.gov/hhes/poverty/poverty96/pv96state.html and look at the page source, you'll find it's made up of a series of <TR> and <TD> tags. That means it's an **HTML table**. These can be imported into Excel or other newer spreadsheets by selecting an HTML format as the import format.

Text file example: Census Bureau's **Monthly Estimates of the US Population** at www.census.gov/population/estimates/nation/intfile1-1.txt. If you look at the page source here, you won't see the HTML tags but, rather, the neat rows and columns of a text file. This information can be cut and pasted or saved and imported into a spreadsheet easily.

You can select, or specify, the data that you want to download – meaning that you don't have to download everything the web site has to offer. Once you have finished downloading, be sure to save your new database or spreadsheet file before closing it.

🖳   🖳   🖳

▬▬▬ Sending or Transferring Files

Via E-Mail

Sooner or later, you will want to send a file to a friend or receive a file from a friend. That means you must learn to attach files to your e-mails and receive files attached to incoming e-mails.

When you talk about attaching things, you're talking about using special file formats and systems that can read them. Sometimes the entire message is in a special format (like MIME) and sometimes people attach things to their e-mail.

Basically, all attachments come in three formats:

♦ MIME – which stands for "Multipurpose Internet Mail Extensions."

♦ Uuencoding – which is a method of including information in e-mail. It was invented in the days of UNIX to UNIX e-mail — hence the strange spelling.

♦ BinHex – which stands for Binary To Hexadecimal.

You'll never need to know all the technical details on these programs. But your e-mail program *must* be capable of attaching files to your e-mails, and it also must be capable of detaching incoming files that other people send you.

For the most part, you can send a file as an attachment by composing your message, attaching the file and then sending out the e-mail.

When you receive a file that is attached to an e-mail message, your mail program will tell you that something is attached. Usually, your program saves the attached file as a separate file in the folder or directory you specify. After it has been saved, you can read and use it like any other file. The key is in saving the attachment with the proper extension. If it is a picture or image, chances are it is a `.jpg` file or a `.gif` file. See the Field Guide to File Formats on page 89.

If you receive an unknown attachment, it will appear as a large message in your mailbox. If it contains text, it may be garbled but still readable. In this case, you can try saving the message as a file and then extracting the contents of it through a separate program. However, if the garbled text represents a botched attempt at sending a sound or picture, you will not be able to recover the information.

Via Telnet

Telnet is a software program that lets you use the resources of a distant computer somewhere else in the world – meaning that you can tap into your computer from anywhere. You can log onto a "host" computer, issue commands as if you were on your own computer and gain access to all of the computer's resources. How Telnet works is you run a piece of software on your own home computer to use the resources of a distant computer. That other computer is called the host.

The host computer allows many different computers to simultaneously access its resources. To use Telnet, though, you will need to know the address of the Internet host whose resources you want to access.

When you use Telnet, you must log in and then you "take over" the host computer. Usually, host systems will let you sign in as "guest," but some require a user name and password.

You can Telnet into many different computers and computer systems. Each one works differently. When you contact the host computer, the distant computer and your computer negotiate how they will talk with each other. To make things easier to use, many hosts use a menu system allowing you to mimic the hosts computer. This is called terminal emulation.

Via FTP — File Transfer Protocol

FTP is particularly good for transferring very large files. Many software companies incorporate FTP into their web sites to enable you to download program files and software patches more quickly and easily. You probably won't even realize that you are using FTP to get these files. If you want to have your own web site, you will want to get one of the FTP programs to let you transfer the files you create on your own computer to your ISP's server. You can do this through a stand-alone program that is free.

When you connect to the other computer (using an FTP program), you get a split screen, with the files on your computer's hard drive on the left side and the files of the computer you dialed into on the right. In the middle of the screen are arrows. Highlight the file you want to transfer and then click on the arrow – the left one if you want to download or receive something, the right arrow if you want to upload or send a file from your computer.

FTP can transfer enormous quantities of data. It is used to transfer computer software and upgrades, anti-virus utilities, games, graphics and so forth.

If, for example, you wanted to download a copy of either *Alice in Wonderland* or *The Adventures of Tom Sawyer* from the Internet, both (and more) are available at www.gotubs.com/alice.html, an ESC Marketing Group site.

You would likely use FTP to download it. Simply saving it from a web page directly without FTP would take much longer.

There are many places to get shareware FTP programs. WS_FTP and Breeze FTP are two easy to use Windows FTP programs. Below are places with free versions of FTP programs or inexpensive shareware versions.

SHAREWARE.COM www.shareware.com
Jumbo! Download Network www.jumbo.com
CNETSoftware Library www.cnet.com
ZDNet Software Library www.hotfiles.com
FilePile www.filepile.com

As with most files you download, there will be a text file accompanying the FTP program that explains how to use it.

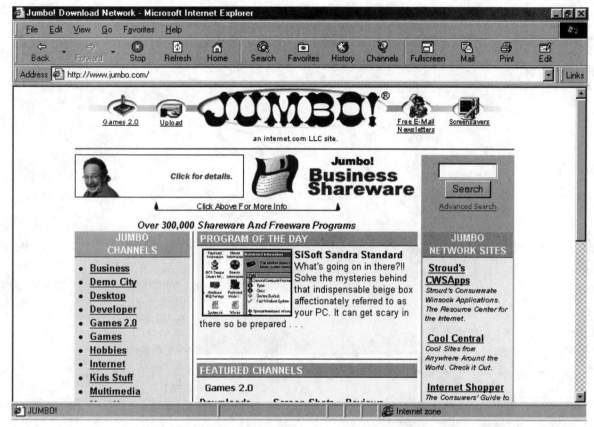

This is the opening screen to Jumbo! Download Network (www.jumbo.com), which offers many downloadable files.

Chapter 6

Government Sources Online

You can use the vast government archives to research a subject, track government actions and/or find data about specific persons, companies and organizations. In this chapter, we'll discuss researching general subjects and tracking government activities; the following chapter on public records will discuss researching of specific entities using a myriad of public records databases.

The Federal government determined very early that the Internet solved a big democratic predicament by providing open and easy access to governmental information resources. And, it saved on printing costs – especially since government documents are copyright-free.

As the Internet has developed, federal, state and local governments moved online and since then, their presence has matured. Most federal agencies have progressed from simply posting mission statements and public relations materials to organizing and archiving valuable resources. The Electronic Freedom of Information Act (EFOIA) of 1998 requires all federal agencies to put all their forms, documents and data online by December 1999 so that this evolution will continue.

Most importantly, all online federal government resources are available to anyone with Internet access. Millions of people use government web sites (federal, state and local), and government resources rank high among the most popular web sites. Much like the Web itself, government's online presence is great in some places, good in others and poor elsewhere. State and local governments generally have a strong presence on the Internet – almost always for free – and many states, especially California and Florida, provide excellent public access to records and information.

But the government is also the biggest wholesaler of private information. Federal and state government agencies routinely sell databases to marketing companies and other interested buyers. Many states sell their motor vehicle information in bulk – for a profit. Doing so probably keeps down the cost of your driver's license and car registration. It also means that your government is in the business of gathering and selling information about you.

However, some states have started to prohibit the government from making a profit from selling public records, and more than thirty states have legislation pending to limit access to motor vehicle records and driving information. California and several other states already forbid the sale of driver-related information.

Government Gateways

Almost every federal government agency is online. There's a nationwide network of depository libraries, including the enormous resources of the National Archives (www.nara.gov), the twelve presidential libraries, and four national libraries (the Library of Congress, the National Agricultural Library, the National Library of Education and the National Library of Medicine). A 1997 government survey counted 4,300 web sites and 215 computer bulletin boards at 42 departments and agencies, and those numbers keep growing. State and city government web sites are mushrooming, too.

While the material is easily accessible, finding it sometimes requires professional researching skills. In response, the government has been developing government resource gateways and finding aids. Many of them are quite good. Among them:

Commonly Requested Federal Services
www.whitehouse.gov/WH/services

This is the White House's collection of top federal government sites.

Fedstats
www.fedstats.gov

A terrific collection of statistical sites from the federal government.

Healthfinder
www.healthfinder.org

This is a great starting point for health-related government information. See the Susan Detwiler sidebar in Chapter 4.

Best Government Gateways

In addition, there are hundreds of web sites, called government gateways, that organize and link government sites. Some are simply collections of links. Others provide access to bulletin boards of specific government agencies so that you find and contact employees with specific knowledge. Guides are becoming increasingly important in light of the growing number of reports and publications that aren't printed any more, but simply posted online.

Here are some of the best government gateway sites:

Documents Center

www.lib.umich.edu/libhome/Documents.center/index.html

Documents Center is a clearinghouse for local, state, federal, foreign, and international government information. It is one of the more comprehensive online searching aids for all kinds of government information on the Internet. It's especially useful as a meta-site of meta-sites.

FedLaw

http://fedlaw.gsa.gov

FedLaw is an extremely broad resource for federal legal and regulatory research containing 1600+ links to law-related information. It has very good topical and title indexes that group web links into hundreds of subjects. It is operated by the General Services Administration (GSA).

FedWorld Information Network

www.fedworld.gov

FedWorld is a massive collection of 14,000 files and databases of government sites, including bulletin boards that can help you identify government employees with expertise in a broad range of subjects. A surprising number of these experts will take the time to discuss questions from the general public.

US Federal Government Agencies Directory

www.lib.lsu.edu/gov/fedgov.html

This directory of federal agencies is maintained by Louisiana State University and links to hundreds of federal government Internet sites. It's divided by branch and agency and is very thorough, but focus on your target because it's easy to lose your way or become overwhelmed en route.

GOVBOT – Government Search Engine

http://ciir2.cs.umass.edu/Govbot

Developed by the Center For Intelligent Information Retrieval, GOVBOT's searchable keyword index of government web sites is limited to sites with a top-level domain name ending in .gov or .mil.

US Government Information

www-libraries.colorado.edu/ps/gov/us/federal.htm

This is a gem of a site and a good starting point. From the University of Colorado, it's not as thorough as the LSU site above, but still very valuable.

INFOMINE: Scholarly Internet Resource Collections
`http://lib-www.ucr.edu`

INFOMINE provides collections of scholarly Internet resources, best for academics. Its government portion — Government INFOMINE — is easily searchable by subject. It has detailed headings and its resource listings are very specific. Since it's run by a university, some of its references are to limited to student use only.

Speech & Transcript Center
`http://qwis2.circ.qwu.edu/~gprice/speech.htm`

This site links directly to web sites containing transcripts of speeches. Pulled together by George Washington University professor Gary Price, it encompasses government resources, business leaders, and real audio. A large section is devoted to US and international government speech transcripts – including Congressional hearings, testimony and transcripts.

Federal Web Locator
`www.law.vill.edu/Fed-Agency/fedwebloc.html`

`www.law.vill.edu/Fed-Ct/fedcourt.html`

This web locator is really two sites in one: a federal government web site and a separate site that tracks federal courts – both of which are browsable by category or by keywords. Together they provide links to thousands of government agencies and departments. In addition, this site has an excellent **State Web Locator** at `www.law.vill.edu/State-Agency/index.html` and a **State Court Locator** at `www.law.vill.edu/State-Ct`. All four are top-notch resources.

Best Online Government Resources

Your tax dollars are put to good and visible use here. A few of the government's web pages are excellent. Some can be used in lieu of commercial tools, but only if you have the time to invest.

A few of the top government sites – the Census and the Securities and Exchange Commission – are models of content and presentation. They are very deep, very thorough and easy to use. If only the rest of the federal government would follow suit. Unfortunately, the best of the federal government is just that: *the best*. Not all agencies maintain such detailed and relevant resources.

Following are the crown jewels of the government's collection, in ranked order:

US Census Bureau
www.census.gov

Without question, this is the US government's top site. It's saturated with information and census publications – at times overwhelmingly so – but worth every minute of your time. A few hours spent here is a worthwhile investment for almost anyone seeking to background a community, learn about business or find any kind of demographic information. You can search several ways: alphabetically by subject, by word, by location, and by geographic map. The only problem is the sheer volume of data.

One feature, the **Thematic Mapping System**, allows users to extract data from Census CD-ROMs and display them in maps by state or county. You can create maps on all kinds of subjects – for example, tracking violent crime to farm income by region. The site also features the **Statistical Abstract of the US** in full text, with a searchable version at www.census.gov:80/stat_abstract.

The potential uses of census data are infinite. Marketers use it to find community information. Reporters search out trends by block, neighborhood or region. Educators conduct research. Businesses evaluate new business prospects. Genealogists trace family trees though full census data isn't available for 72 years from the date the census was taken. You can even use it to identify ideal communities in which to raise a family. The *San Jose Mercury News*' Jennifer LaFleur used it to find eligible bachelors in specific areas of San Jose for an article on which she was working.

US Securities & Exchange Commission (SEC)
www.sec.gov

Only the Census site is better than the SEC site, which is first-rate, must-stop place for information shopping on US companies. Its **EDGAR** database search site www.sec.gov/edaux/searches.htm is easy to use and provides access to documents that companies and corporations are required to file under regulatory laws.

The SEC site is a great starting point for information about specific companies and industry trends. The SEC requires all publicly-held corporations and some large privately-held corporations to disclose detailed financial information about their activities, plans, holdings, executives' salaries and stakes, legal problems and so forth. For more details, see the Chapter 9.

Library of Congress (LOC)
www.loc.gov

This site is an extraordinary collection of documents. **Thomas**, the Library's Congressional online center site (http://thomas.loc.gov/home/ thomas2.html) provides an exhaustive collection of congressional documents, including bill summaries, voting records and the full Congressional Record, which is the official record of Congressional action. This LOC site also links to many international, federal, state and local government sites. You can also access the library's 4.8 million records online, some versions in full-text and some in abstract form. Though the Library's entire 27 million-item collection is not yet available online, the amount increases daily. In addition to books and papers, it includes an extensive images collection ranging from Frank Lloyd Wright's designs to the Dead Sea Scrolls to the world's largest online collection of baseball cards.

Superintendent of Documents Home Page (GPO)
www.access.gpo.gov/su_docs

The GPO is the federal government's primary information printer and distributor. All federally funded information from every agency is sent here, which makes the GPO's holdings priceless. Luckily, the GPO site is well-constructed and easy to use. For example, it has the full-text of the Federal Register, which lists all federal regulations and proposals, and full-text access to the Congressional Record. The GPO also produces an online version of the Congressional Directory, providing details on every congressional district, profiles of members, staff profiles, maps of every district and historical documents about Congress. With EFOIA requiring all federal government resources to be computerized and available online by the end of 1999, this site will expand exponentially over the next few years, as the number of materials go out of print and online.

National Technical Information Service (NTIS)
www.ntis.gov

The best place to find federal government reports related to technology and science. NTIS is the nation's clearinghouse for unclassified technical reports of government-sponsored research. NTIS collects, indexes, abstracts and sells US and foreign research – mostly in science and technology – as well as behavioral and social science data.

IGnet: Internet. . . . for the Federal IG Community
www.ignet.gov

This is a truly marvelous collection of reports and information from the Inspector Generals of about sixty federal agency departments. Well worth checking when starting research on government-related matters.

White House
www.whitehouse.gov

This site wouldn't make this list if not for two features. One, a terrific list of federal government links called **Commonly Requested Federal Services** and two, a transcript of every official action the US President takes. Unfortunately, as with many government sites, its primary focus is in promoting itself.

Defense LINK – US Department of Defense (DOD)
www.defenselink.mil

This is the brand-name site for Pentagon-related information. There's a tremendous amount of data here, categorized by branch of service – including US troop deployments worldwide. But the really valuable information is on the DTIC site below.

Defense Technical Information Center (DTIC)
www.dtic.mil

The DTIC site is loaded with links and defense information – everything from contractors to weapon systems. It even includes recently de-classified information about the Gulf War. It is the best place to start for defense information. You can even find a list of all military-related contracts, including beneficiary communities and the kinds of contracts awarded.

Bureau of Transportation Statistics
www.bts.gov

The US Department of Transportation's enormous collection of information about every facet of transportation. There's a lot of valuable material here including the Transportation Statistics Annual Report. It also holds financial data for airlines and searchable databases containing information about fatal accidents and on-time statistics for airlines, which can be narrowed to your local airport.

National Archives & Records Administration
www.nara.gov

A breathtaking collection of research online. The National Archives has descriptions of more than 170,000 documents related to the Kennedy assassination, for example. It also contains a world-class database holding descriptions of more than 95,000 records held by the Still Picture and Motion Picture, Sound and Video Branches. This site also links to the twelve Presidential Archives with their records of every person ever mentioned in Executive Branch correspondence. You can view an image of the original document.

State & Regional Resources

The federal government isn't the only government entity with valuable information online. Each of the fifty state governments and the US territories have a web presence. Some are top quality, like Texas and Florida. Others aren't as good. Here are some of the better regional compilation sites:

NASIRE - National Association of State Information Resource Executives

www.nasire.org

This site provides state-specific information on state-government innovations and is a companion to the NASIRE State Search site mentioned by Greg Notess in his sidebar "Finding Government Web Sites," which appears later in this chapter.

Government Information Sharing Project

http://govinfo.kerr.orst.edu

This site, from the Oregon State University Library, is a great collection of online databases about everything from economics to demographics. It's particularly valuable because it has regional information on the economy and demographic breakdowns all the way down to the county level. Its content is sometimes outdated. Still, it's worthwhile for finding how federal money trickles down to localities and where state and local agencies spend tax dollars.

USADATA

www.usadata.com/usadata/market

This is an innovative site for finding information about a particular region or part of the country. Data is not only sorted by region, but also by twenty subjects within each region.

Global Computing

www.globalcomputing.com/states.html

A solid collection of links on a variety of topics. This site is especially strong on state and local government topics.

Finding State Governmental Web Sites

by Greg R. Notess

State governments have been quite active in putting state-level government information on the Internet, and now each state has an Internet presence. In most states, each of its three branches – executive, judicial and legislative – has a central web site.

The following sites are selected from *Government Information on the Internet*. The first two are finding aids for state government information. State and Local Government on the 'Net features an excellent hierarchical classification of state and local government sites. State Law focuses more on legislative and judicial sites, and its classification by function sets it apart from the others. The other sites listed supplement the first two. Occasionally, they turn up sites that either aren't listed in the others or offer a more precise focus.

State & Local Government on the 'Net

www.piperinfo.com/state/states.html

Each state's resources are categorized by State Home Page, Statewide Offices, Legislative Branch, Judicial Branch, Executive Branch, Boards and Commissions, Counties and Cities. In addition, the site features some other state-oriented categories such as Multi-State Sites, Federal Resources, National Organizations and Other Links.

It's an excellent finding aid for state and local government resources. The categorizations of each state's listings enable quick identification of pertinent web sites.

StateLaw: State & Local Government –
Executive, Legislative & Judicial Information

http://lawlib.wuacc.edu/washlaw/uslaw/statelaw.html

Organized by state, this site lists Internet resources from or about state governments, state legislative information, state legal information, and more. Under each state, the sites are categorized under Home Page, Legislative Information, Courts, Rules of Court, Statutes, Bills, State Agencies, Local Government, and Miscellaneous. Information is available for all fifty states, although not all categories are used for each state. Another section adds links to sites of interest related to all states.

The various state sites are grouped by function, making it an easy-to-use finding aid for state Internet resources. Since the developers take a broad view of legal resources, it is useful for those interested in legislative information and in general state and local governmental information.

StateSearch
www.nasire.org/ss

NASIRE (National Association of State Information Resource Executives) represents chief information officers and managers from the 50 states, six US territories, and the District of Columbia. This web site, introduced by NASIRE in 1995, provides a directory for state government information by subject areas such as Education, Revenue, Treasurers and State Legislatures.

It can be used to find state agencies and administrative departments grouped by function, rather than just listed by state. While not completely comprehensive, it's updated frequently and appears fairly accurate.

State Court Locator
www.law.vill.edu/State-Ct

The State Court Locator provides links to the sites of state and local courts. It includes sites with state court opinions, rules of court, and county court links. The page is arranged alphabetically by state.

State Web Locator
www.law.vill.edu/State-Agency/index.html

Broader in scope than The State Court Locator, The State Web Locator is another finding aid for state government sites on the Internet. It includes links for all fifty states and a few territories and possessions. Under each state, the sites are categorized by headings such as State Home Page, Executive Branch, Legislative Branch, Departments, Agencies and Judicial Branch.

While not quite as detailed or as up-to-date as State Law or State and Local Government on the 'Net, this site is a useful adjunct to those two and the other state finding aids.

US House of Representatives – Internet Law Library – US State & Territorial Laws
http://law.house.gov/17.htm

This site presents a basic alphabetical list of states with a separate page for any state-related legal material. On the top-level page, it also has a section about model acts and interstate compacts and Indian nations and tribes. Under each state, items are listed such as state constitutions, codes, cases, legislative information, individual acts and local regulations. The lists are a straight alphabetical listings, but links to major sites for the constitutions, codes and cases are put first.

At first look, this site may seem disorganized; however, it can be helpful for finding state legal information that may not be easily found elsewhere. On the other hand, some of the links lead to dead ends. It could use more frequent updating and verification checking.

WWW Virtual Library:
Law: State Government

http://www.law.indiana.edu/law/v-lib/states.html

This listing, part of the World Wide Web Consortium 's Virtual Library, is a list of links to state government sites arranged alphabetically by state. Within each state section, there is no obvious order to the listed links. It links primarily but not exclusively to state legal web sites.

This site is not as useful as the State Law or State and Local Governments sites because it doesn't categorize by function the links under each state heading. However, it can supplement the other two sites.

Yahoo! Government: US Government: US States

www.yahoo.com/Government/U_S_Government/
U_S_States

This section of the well-known Yahoo! directory includes links to governmental sites in all fifty states. It also features some multi-state categories such as Organizations and State Government Jobs. Within each state's section, it lists the main government page first, then any subcategories that might be available and then an alphabetical list of other government sites.

This site has much broader coverage of state government than some of the other finding aids, but it is not categorized as neatly as the State Law site.

💻   💻   💻

Best Sites for Government Statistics

For many people, the federal government is most useful at providing current and reliable statistics on trade, the economy or immigration. Here are some of the best sites for that purpose.

Bureau of Economic Analysis (BEA)

www.bea.doc.gov

As part of the Commerce Department, BEA covers national, regional, and international topics such as gross domestic product, personal income, population, employment, balance of payments, investment abroad and foreign investments in the US.

Bureau of Justice Statistics (BJS)

www.ojp.usdoj.gov

A terrific US Department of Justice site for statistics on crimes, victims, drugs, criminal offenders, law enforcement prosecution, courts and sentencing.

Bureau of Labor Statistics (BLS)

http://stats.bls.gov

The Labor Department's statistical shop, BLS houses information on everything about US labor, employment, earnings, prices, the economy in general and even foreign labor statistics.

CIA World Factbook

www.odci.gov/cia/publications/factbook/index.html

The Central Intelligence Agency's publication resource about international statistics and reliable background information about other countries.

Best Information on the Internet - Statistical Sources

www.sau.edu/cwis/internet/wild/refdesk/stats/staindex.htm#useful

This meta-site, by Iowa's St. Ambrose University, contains some good information in useful categories – including Business and Economic Statistics, Social and Demographic Data, Public Opinion Data, and Useful Data and Formulas, which includes personal finance calculators and mortgage relocation cost estimators.

White House - Economic Statistics Briefing Room

www.whitehouse.gov/fsbr/esbr.html

This White House site is one of the most valuable clearinghouses of government statistical resources.

Fedstats

www.fedstats.gov

This site is the central locator for US government statistics supplied by more than seventy federal agencies.

STAT-USA Internet

www.stat-usa.gov

STAT-USA is a US Census Bureau-sponsored site with great statistics and good regional information. However, be aware that STAT-USA is a fee-based service.

Statistical Resources on the Web

www.lib.umich.edu/libhome/Documents.center/stats.html

This is a phenomenal collection of statistical information by subject, including much regional information.

In addition, Paula Berinstein's *Finding Statistics Online* from Pemberton Press is an excellent book on how to locate the elusive numbers you need.

Best International Resources

Regions & Countries Information

www.ita.doc.gov/ita_home/itacnreg.html

The Commerce Department's International Trade Administration site has some excellent background information on trade issues organized by world region.

US State Department: Regions

www.state.gov/www/regions.html

This web site provides good country descriptions accompanied by geopolitical, contextual analysis.

TradStat

www.dialogweb.com

TradStat, available on DIALOG, a commercial service, provides detailed numbers, statistics and industry-by-industry breakdowns, including tables and charts.

Foreign Governments & Intergovernmental Organizations

by Greg R. Notess

Information on foreign governments and intergovernmental organizations varies widely in quantity and quality. The primary international finding aids aren't comprehensive and international sites tend to be more transient presences (often far more transient) than federal US resources.

For Finding Foreign Government Sites:

Governments on the Web

www.gksoft.com/gov

This is quite an extensive list of international, national, regional, and local governmental and government-related web servers. Its database covers many governmental institutions – including parliaments, ministries, offices, law courts, embassies, city councils, public broadcasting corporations, central banks, multi-national organizations and political parties. More than 9700 entries from 205 countries and territories were listed. Available in English and German, it is arranged in a hierarchical index organized by continent, country and then by smaller divisions. It also provides thematic groupings by categories such as head of state, parliament, political parties, elections and currency.

Yahoo! Government: Countries

www.yahoo.com/Government/Countries

This section of the well-known Yahoo! Directory of Internet Resources covers government sites from over 130 other countries. Under a country's name, the links may include sections such as Agencies, Elected Officials, Embassies and Consulates, Executive Branch, Law, Legislative Branch, Military, Ministries and Politics.

While this site is not as comprehensive as Governments on the Web, it is a useful adjunct that occasionally has links not found on Governments on the Web.

Foreign Government Resources on the Web

www.lib.umich.edu/libhome/Documents.center/frames/forfr.html

The frames version of this web site is easier to navigate than the no-frames version, but both are available. The site features links to the web sites of governments worldwide. The primary frame includes access by region. The index frame provides additional access via continent, country, and subject.

Finding International & Intergovernmental Agencies:

Geneva International Forum

http://geneva.intl.ch/geneva-intl/gi/egimain/edir.htm

Geneva International focuses on international organizations located in Geneva. This site is a directory of international institutions, missions, consulates and foreign companies. It covers hundreds of international institutions, permanent missions, and companies. You can access the database by theme, keyword, and geography as well as by type of organization (for example, UN agency intergovernmental organization, non-governmental organization, and permanent mission). The institutions listed here cover a wide range of social, technical and scientific themes.

International Documents Task Force (IDTF)

www.library.nwu.edu/govpub/idtf/home.html

While this site is primarily designed for the International Documents Task Force and its members, its listings of Internet resources from other governments and for intergovernmental organizations are one of the best starting points for international governmental sites. Links to the Selected International Organizations Section are well organized. Includes Links to a wide variety of intergovernmental organizations, as well as direct links to the press releases, documents and publications for each organization when available. The Links to National Governments section lists central and some subsidiary government sites for other countries.

This IDTF web site is sparse in terms of design, yet it excels in information content both as a finding aid for intergovernmental organization sites and for sites of other countries.

International Agencies & Information

www.lib.umich.edu/libhome/Documents.center/frames/
intlfr.html

This frames version (see the Glossary for more information on frames) of the University of Michigan Document Center web site is easier to navigate than the No-frames version. It directs the user to many other lists of international and inter-governmental web site via pointers. The Frames version provides access via agencies, related sites and subject. The Agencies section is an alphabetical listing by acronym in the frame or by Agency in the full window version of the site.

United Nations System

www.unsystem.org

This site is the official web site locator for the UN System of Organizations. It includes an Alphabetic Index of all United Nations Organizations (UNOs) with their abbreviations as well as the city where the headquarters is located. The other option is the Official Classification of the United Nations System of Organizations with its explanation of the various categories of UNOs including program, specialized agencies, autonomous organizations and inter-agency bodies. Under Frequently Requested Information, the site gives a listing of UNOs that provide online information for frequently requested items. System-wide searching is available across all the UN web sites.

This site should be your first stop if you are looking for web sites of component UN organizations. The listings are easy to browse, and they clearly indicate agencies that have Internet presence.

Finding Foreign Parliamentary Bodies

Inter-Parliamentary Union
www.ipu.org

The IPU is an international organization of parliaments. The IPU web site features two databases and links to parliamentary web sites around the world. The two databases are PARLINE and PARLIT. For all countries with a national legislature, the PARLINE database provides general information on each parliament's chambers, a description of the electoral system, the results of the most recent elections, and information on the working of the presidency of each chamber. PARLIT is a bibliographical database covering parliamentary law and legislative elections throughout the world from 1992. Other sections include Functioning and Documents, Main Areas of Activity, Publications, Women in Parliaments, and Press Releases.

This is an information-rich site, and the two databases are especially valuable.

Web Sites on National Parliaments
www.soc.umn.edu/~sssmith/Parliaments.html

This page presents a simple list of links to web sites by or about parliamentary bodies from different countries. The entries range from the Estonian Riigikogu to the Nicaraguan National Assembly and the Israeli Knesset. Toward the bottom of the page is a short list of international and regional parliamentary institutions.

This is an excellent searching aid. Though simple in design, it is an effective tool for locating parliamentary web pages.

Finding Other International Legal Information:

LawRunner: Global Index
www.ilrg.com/nations

LawRunner functions as an international finding aid in a number of ways. It links to central government, legislative, judicial, and other legal web sites of a long list of countries. In addition, it provides a scripted interface to AltaVista that limits the search to results from top-level domain web sites.

Legal/Legislative Resources

Legal research involves figuring out how a judge in a court of law would deal with a given issue. Can you use the Web to do traditional legal research? Not really. Many of the valuable primary law materials necessary for legal research include recent federal and state court opinions, state statutes (for most, but not all, states), federal statutes, federal regulations and, in some states, administrative regulations.

In legal research, finding information is only the beginning. You must also find out how courts have interpreted existing facts, whether the opinion still stands or has been over-ruled by a higher court, and what legal scholars think of the issue(s).

Many of the great legal tools are just starting to come to the Web, and the tools for analyzing the law and accuracy are online – it's just that they aren't available at no cost. However, that's changing. There are some fine legal sites on the Internet. If you're going to court, though, you'll want complete reliability, which means comprehensive research.

First, let's discuss where you can do proper legal research: on two expensive fee-based tools.

LEXIS-NEXIS

www.lexis-nexis.com

LEXIS-NEXIS is part of the European publishing conglomerate Reed Elsevier. See the Fee-Based Tools for Specialized Information section in Chapter 4 for more information on LEXIS-NEXIS.

Westlaw

www.westgroup.com

Westlaw is a division of another giant, West Group.

In their collections, Westlaw and LEXIS-NEXIS have large sections of primary law sources – including statutes, court cases, secondary sources and opinions, legal encyclopedias, periodicals and law journals. They are, in effect, a law library online and almost as thorough as an actual law library. Both database vendors have added natural language search features, and both provide variable pricing structures, but there's no way around the fact that they are expensive.

Two other online commercial services are also worth mentioning here: **CourtLink** and **PACER**.

CourtLink

www.courtlink.com

CourtLink offers data from federal circuit courts of appeal, bankruptcy courts and US District Courts, in addition to a small collection of state documents. Most of the online services begin keeping files only after lawyers have filed paperwork, but CourtLink gets in a step earlier. CourtLink includes charges made against someone. While the coverage is limited to Washington State, parts of Oregon, New York and Texas, it's a unique offering. See the Chapter 7 for more details.

PACER

www.uscourts.gov/PubAccess.html

PACER is an electronic bulletin board providing docket numbers, thorough case summaries and texts of opinions from most of the country's federal courts. It is the federal government's central courts system made available to the public. It's searchable by case number, defendant and plaintiff, and you can download, even print, the indexes and summaries. It is inexpensive (relative to LEXIS and Westlaw) – well under a dollar a minute. Register for PACER at 1-800-676-6856.

Free Legal Resources on the Internet

There are some very valuable primary resources on the Internet. At the federal level, online materials include: complete collections of federal statutes, known as the US Code, federal court rulings, many state rulings, collections of federal and state laws as well as historical documents like the *Constitution* and the *Declaration of Independence*.

Congressional Quarterly

www.cq.com

Congressional Quarterly (CQ), the best news magazine covering Congress, offers some content for free and the rest by subscription. Two free *Congressional Quarterly* sites are listed below.

Free CQ Sites:
American Voter

www.cq.com/FreeSites/freesites.htm

An acclaimed site that offers Congressional member profiles. "Rate-Your-Rep" lets you compare your position on key issues to those of Congressional Representatives. American Voter also features Congressional floor speeches, selected Congressional committee votes and bill introductions, plus daily Congressional news highlights.

Congressional Quarterly's VoteWatch

http://pathfinder.com/CQ

A web-based feature on Time-Warner's **Pathfinder** site, VoteWatch provides timely news stories on key Congressional votes and a searchable database of members' individual votes.

Legal Information Institute

www.law.cornell.edu

One of the best legal libraries online, this has an extensive online legal database, which includes Supreme Court decisions going back to the 1930s and the US Code, among other things. It also has a terrific collection of secondary sources, such as lists and biographies of legal experts as well as lists of law journals.

Counsel Connect

www.counsel.com/lawlinks/lawlinks.html

Counsel Connect offers links to many good legal resource collections. It also has a subscription service for lawyers and a great collection of legal resources.

FindLaw

www.findlaw.com

FindLaw is the top free web site for legal resources. It includes statutes, laws, law schools, judicial opinions, law journals and reviews and a vast array of other searchable resources.

Law Library of Congress

http://lcweb2.loc.gov/glin/lawhome.html

See the Library of Congress description earlier in this chapter.

Thomas – US Congress on the Internet

http://thomas.loc.gov

If you're tracking a bill that's moving through Congress, visit this site for official Congressional information, including voting history, and committee membership. It also has full-text versions of the *Congressional Record* and the *Federal Register*.

Meta-Index for US Legal Research

http://gsulaw.gsu.edu/metaindex

This site, built by the Georgia State University College of Law, provides a simple searchable database of federal legal information. From it, you can access Supreme Court opinions all the way back to 1937, every federal court of appeals decision and the *Congressional Record*.

In addition to the features mentioned at the top of this section, **Congressional Quarterly** has two online fee-based publications on the web. *Governing* is one of the top sites for state and local campaign information, at www.governing.com. *Campaigns & Elections* is a political insiders' magazine about the nuts and bolts of campaign tactics and strategies at www.camelect.com.

Cloakroom, at www.cloakroom.com, owned by *National Journal*, offers deep coverage of congressional, political and governmental actions, as well as a pay tool component. It's the only rival to CQ's top-flight information.

Chapter 7

Public Records

Public records are public treasures. They oil the wheels of democracy.

♦ They tell us whether the guy living next door, who happens to be the tax assessor's brother, is assessed at the same rate as we are and is paying his taxes.

♦ They reveal whether the poor folks in town are getting the same treatment in court as the rich folks.

♦ They disclose when the mayor's received big campaign contributions from the contractor who's chosen to build the new city hall.

♦ They enable us to make certain everyone's voted only once.

♦ They assure us that the company selling public stocks has an adequate financial base; and that the man you're marrying isn't already married to three other women.

But only if you check. It's not overstating matters to say that democracy depends on public access to public records. You have the right to use them, and you can use them for any reason you wish.

♦ Journalists, private investigators, reunion organizers and skip tracers use them to locate people.

♦ Realtors use them to price property, and then they hunt for buyers by combining change of address forms and marriage notices.

♦ Diaper-makers use them to locate and market to parents of newborns.

♦ Political activists use them to profile potential voters.

♦ Investors use them to research a corporation's board of directors.

♦ Employers and lenders use them to verify applications.

♦ Attorneys and paralegals use them to identify the assets of a company or a person before they decide to sue.

Lists of people, lists of companies, assets, transgressions, lists of things – nearly everything the government regulates, licenses, inspects or taxes – are available.

What are the differences between government records and public records?

Government Records Versus Public Records

Government information is information the government keeps, compiles and generates. Technically, every piece of paper in every government agency is government information – everything typed, computerized, recorded, photographed, filmed, videotaped, etched in stone or even encrypted. Not all of it is available to us, however. For example, the Internal Revenue Service collects your tax return, but federal law forbids its disclosure. Thus, your tax return isn't made public and isn't a public record. Rather, *a public record is government information that we, the public, have a right to access, view and copy* as a result of the federal Freedom of Information Act (FOIA). You can read the FOIA for yourself at the US Department of Justice's **Office of Information & Privacy** under Significant New Decisions `www.usdoj.gov/oip/foia_updates/ Vol_XVIII_4/page2.htm`.

Government entities can wear multiple hats. Take the time to ascertain an agency's mission and its agency functions; you'll have a clear perspective of what data exists and the agency's goals in obtaining the information. It will put you ahead of others who don't get some public records because their requests aren't specific.

Types of Public Records

Voter Records

If you're trying to locate someone, the most useful public record is a voter registration record. Most adults register to vote, and the records are almost always public. Voter registration affidavits and indexes can include: name, date of birth, address, political affiliation, place of birth, prior address and, sometimes, Social Security Number. There may even be descriptions and reference to other voters in the household.

Depending on the state, the registrar can be a town clerk, a city clerk, a county recorder or even the Secretary of State.

Officials in many state and local government agencies are permitted to give or sell voter registration records to commercial marketers, while other states restrict access to these lists to people using the information for political purposes only. One company, ARISTOTLE, offers nationwide voter information as a fee-based service that can be purchased on a state-by-state basis.

Property Records

You'll find some of the best information about people in property records – if the person you are investigating is a property owner.

Property records are divided into two major categories:

♦ Records related to property taxes, usually found at the assessor's office

♦ Records related to property ownership, usually found at the recorder's office.

Both types of records can now be found online. Most likely you'll find them at the county or city level. The assessor will have fairly current information about the physical property, buildings on the property, its value and the billing name and address of the taxpayer, usually the owner, but not always.

It's important to know where you find the actual records because there are subtle but important distinctions to note if you ever have to check the actual record rather than the online version.

The assessor's records are updated annually and generally searchable up to five different ways – by name, property address, legal description, file number issued or physical location (point to it on the assessor's map). The file will likely refer to the property deed on file over at the recorder's office, so it makes sense to visit the assessor first.

The recorder has a completely different job: to keep copies of important documents so that no one will alter them. It's important to understand this distinction. The recorder doesn't care about the contents of the document or, for that matter, whether the seller even owned the property in the first place as long as the signature is real. The assessor, on the other hand, doesn't care who owns the property as long as someone receives the tax bill.

Online commercial services index assessor information for nearly the whole country. Companies like **Acxiom DataQuick** at www.dataquick.com and **IQ DATA Systems** at www.iqdata.com sell real estate information online. Some companies, such as **KnowX** (www.knowx.com) provide real estate assessor and recorder information on the Web for a fee. Many other companies are starting to move toward web-based access to this information.

Two other good resources – free ones – for finding property information on the Internet are the IAAO and Amrex. The **IAAO is The International Association of Assessing Officers** – www.iaao.org – the trade organization and education arm for the various tax assessors across the world. While it doesn't offer property records, you can find someone who might be able to help you locate a particular record quickly if you can't find it online.

AMREX – the American Real Estate Exchange – www.amrex.com – licenses data from a variety of sources, archives articles and has an easy search system for records filed with the federal government. The records include property listings, market demographics, building start activity and environmental risk assessment reports. You must join the association, which is free to guests, in order to get access.

For a list of links to tax assessor web sites, go to the **IAAO Index** www.iaao.org/1234.htm.

Grantor/Grantee Indexes

Grantor-grantee records, usually maintained by local county governments, tend to be a catch-all for a wide assortment of public records. You can find judgments, property transfers, financing statements, liens, notices of defaults, powers of attorney and hundreds of other documents.

If you can find them free online, it'll be at the county level. Commercial services harvest this information and sell it. **Superior Information Services**, for example, a company that specializes in records for the mid-Atlantic area, has recently put up most of New York City's real property, deed/mortgage and other property records. Many of the larger data providers, such as LEXIS-NEXIS, have much of this grantor-grantee information as well.

Vital Records

Birth, death, marriage and divorce documents are all vital records. They are required documents, but, in many states, access is restricted.

Birth Certificates are loaded with information. You'll find names of parents, mother's maiden name and previous births, place of birth, address, profession, place of employment and obstetrician. They're a great way to find the parents' places of employment and their birthplaces, as well.

Marriage Certificates are also filled with information. They give the bride's maiden name, home and work addresses of both parties involved and the witnesses at the time. Most states require two witnesses at a wedding (typically, the best man and the maid of honor), who are usually great leads for tracking information about a divorce or good background about the husband or wife.

Divorce Records can be found in the civil court indexes or sometimes contained in separate databases. The actual records often include much detail about the divorcing couple – everything from assets to pet custody.

Death Certificates lead you to the existence of possible probate court filings. Probate court records, in turn, might provide the names of relatives and other family members, as well as lists of liabilities and assets.

Are these records online? Yes, but usually it costs money to access them. The Internet is particularly weak for public records like birth and marriage. Kentucky offers online indexes of marriage, divorce and death records, and is the first state to do so. One company, **VitalChek**, has a voice and fax network program through which, for a fee, they'll find certified copies of vital records. Its web site www.vitalchek.com lists accessible vital records. Indexes to state vital records can also be found through **Vital Records Information, United States** at http://vitalrec.com/index.html. Both indexes are free, but record orders cost money.

A genealogy company, **Ancestry.com** at www.ancestry.com offers the Social Security Death Index for free on the Web. Other services offer that same database, but at a cost.

Online death record indexes can include the deceased's name and date of death, date of birth, destination of Social Security benefits, Social Security Number, location of the SSN issuance, and last residence. But only the actual death certificate – available at the county level and not yet online – includes cause of death, place of death, and next of kin.

Other vital records are available from fee-based vendors. DCS, a Texas-based company, offers many states' birth records, Merlin Data Systems offers marriage records for California. Legal database companies, like LEXIS-NEXIS, Westlaw and CourtLink offer death records and indexes to many of these records, but not death certificates.

Court Records

Court records are loaded with good information. Few of them are free on the Web, and for the most part, they're available only in index form online. But they're invaluable for backgrounding individuals and companies. You can find valuable data in criminal court, civil court, family court, bankruptcy court, probate court and US district courts, which are discussed, in turn, below. Naturalization court, tax court and most other court and hearing boards are also valuable resources for information, though they're just starting to come online.

Criminal Court Records show convictions ranging from felonies such as murder, rape, robbery and kidnapping all the way down to misdemeanors such as minor traffic violations, petty theft, city code violations, drunk driving, and drug possession/use. Just about every court should have a name index. Little of this is currently online. You can find an index indicating that a particular criminal court record exists, but that's about it. But if you can't look it up yourself, a friendly clerk should be able to help you view at least part of the case file without charge. A friendly telephone manner never hurts. In a criminal court case, the key is to find the document called the complaint, which usually indicates the charge(s) against the defendant. It'll often include the arrest report, with identifying information about the defendant and the reason for the arrest.

Civil Court Records arise when someone – a person, a company, an association or a government agency – sues another person or entity. The suing party claims damage and seeks financial restitution. Civil cases can be a treasure trove because they're prompted by anger – the same anger that prompts the airing of dirty laundry. That's why divorce cases are such a valuable source of personal information.

The type of court depends on the amount of damages requested. Investigative reporter Don Ray notes that, interestingly, anger levels and court levels tend to be proportionately reversed, so that **small claims court** should be your first destination. In small claims court, the plaintiff might win, but learns that the defendant can hide and protect his assets, which can make actual collection impossible. The result is a victorious, but angry, plaintiff. Find that person and find an oft-times juicy source of information.

Divorce cases and **child custody cases** can be great sources of personal information. In a divorce proceeding, much of what's written is fiction created to get money from the opposing side. Figure that about half of what is said is true, in the manner of mud flung against a wall in hopes it sticks.

Depending on the state, **Probate Court** is sometimes part of county superior court and sometimes on its own. Probate court exists to resolve disputes over who gets what when someone with assets dies. As Don Ray likes to say, "Where there's a will, there's a family. And, when there's a will, there's a fight – because where there's a will, there's someone who feels cheated. And, when there's someone who feels cheated, there's a probate judge who'll settle the dispute and make certain things are fairly distributed."

Probate court is a good place to check asset distributions to relatives. Remember the friends and enemies rule and look for someone who may have been slighted and is willing to talk about it.

Tax Court Records, as with divorce records, sometimes involve proceedings that cause individual tax filings to be made public. Tax cases are heard primarily in Washington, DC, but the court travels to regional offices around the country every year and conducts field hearings. Few, if any, tax court records are available online, though occasionally, news stories about significant tax cases are available.

Naturalization Court Records result from the process of petitioning for citizenship. Every applicant must fill out a lengthy questionnaire about his or her life in both countries and provide character references. These records are not yet online, but efforts are being made to computerize them in California and Texas. You can expect to see them online in the near future.

Other Court-Related Records – including those of labor boards, workers compensation appeals boards and state bar reviews – may also have valuable records on individuals. Most aren't yet online. To find the names of existing boards try the State Government section of phone books or their online versions. Two particularly good ones are the **Carroll's Government Directories & Charts** at www.carrollpub.com and the Government section of **InfoSpace.com** at www.infospace.com, which uses data from Carroll.

Bankruptcy Court Records

Here you'll find the names and addresses of all the creditors owed by the debtor, as well as the amounts claimed. In addition, you'll find a listing of the assets the person had at the time the case was filed and how much each creditor might actually get.

These records contain lots of detail – sometimes down to numbers of T-shirts owned. Bankruptcy proceedings can tip you off to other court records for details like alimony and child support.

Nearly every bankruptcy court is now online, through PACER, a government-sanctioned fee-based service. A few bankruptcy courts are moving online for free. One example is in the Western District of North Carolina, where entire bankruptcy proceedings – not just the index – are online at www.ncbankruptcy.org.

Several companies which offer nationwide bankruptcy indexes – IRSC, CDB Infotek and Merlin Data Systems – are particularly strong for California records while DBT Autotrack is strongest for Florida. Superior Online has extensive records for New Jersey, New York and other mid-Atlantic states. Besides the legal companies, two smaller companies, Banko and CourtLink, which used to be known as Data West, offer bankruptcy listings for most of the nation, and CourtLink also offers civil and criminal indexes for some western states. PACER, a commercial online service, offers nation-wide access to federal criminal and civil indexes as well as bankruptcy records. The actual case record content varies by district.

See the Private Online Sources of Public Records Index for additional companies.

The Uniform Commercial Code & Tax Liens

The Uniform Commercial Code (UCC) is used to regulate businesses by states, counties and cities, which means you can find companies' UCC filings at all three levels.

The most useful part of the filing is the section on loans. Lenders usually receive some kind of collateral when they loan money, and UCC filings can help identify both parties and their assets.

Liens can be found at the state level and at the county recorder's office. Mortgages and UCC liens are voluntarily accepted by a borrower in order to obtain financing. Involuntary liens arise from legal action against a person or business whose debt would otherwise lack collateral. The federal and state governments file tax liens when there's a failure to pay income or withholding taxes. A contractor might file a mechanics lien to be first in line to receive payment for materials used on a job.

States that offer online access to corporation records generally put the lien records online as well. There's less likelihood of finding this information online at the local government level, where private companies compete to obtain and offer access. There are several nationwide commercial databases available, like Information America, LEXIS-NEXIS and CDB Infotek, as well strong regionally-focused companies like Superior Online and Commercial Information Systems.

Other business records can also be found at the Secretary of State's office – including corporation records listing companies' owners, officers and locations.

Corporate Records

To do business in your state, a corporation must register with the Secretary of State's office that, in most states, collects and maintains extensive collections of corporation information. Partnership records and some political contribution records are kept at Secretary of State's offices, depending on the state. Most offices have some sort of an online presence, but actual availability varies by state. Commercial vendors like Merlin Data in California, for example, offer much easier access and indexing of the information than does the state government. Many state offices will tell you over the phone if a commercial provider exists.

In addition, two kinds of partnership records can prove valuable: limited liability company (LLC) or limited liability partnerships (LLP).

♦ LLCs provide the benefits of a corporation but also some of the legal protections of a limited partnership. In many states, the papers are open for inspection.

♦ LLPs provide varying amounts of detail.

Both kinds of documents will identify the company's officers and locations. Some states have family limited liability companies, which help families reduce their tax burdens when a business is transferred to offspring. Few of these records are free on the Internet, but many fee-based services offer indexes of partnership records.

Fictitious Business Name Statements

In many states, fictitious business name statements are called "doing business as (d/b/a or dba)" or "assumed names" filings. When a person, partnership, corporation or some legal entity uses another name, it's required to publish the names of the true owners. These records can usually be found for free at the Secretary of State's office, or at local government offices or courts. Some states put them on the Web for free. They are usually available from fee-based services as well.

Other Kinds of Records

Some records make their way into the public view because they become part of news stories, are published in phone books or other ways. These are technically not public records, as the public has no rights to this information. But they become public anyway. Drivers license records, motor vehicle records and licensing records all fit into this category and are useful resources in this context.

Arrest Records have been openly available for decades from most local police stations in the form of the "booking log." They're usually not available from public record vendors (perhaps because arrests don't always result in convictions), but some communities and community newspapers have begun to post arrest records.

Sexual Predator Databases (of people convicted of sex crimes who've since been released) have been made available for California, Alaska, Florida, Indiana, Kansas and other states. An example of California's can be found at www.sexoffenders.net. Search tools will readily turn up other such lists.

Missing Children Information is readily available on the Internet. Search under "missing children."

Driver & Motor Vehicle Records

If available, driver's license and motor vehicle information are a goldmine of data. The operative words are "if available." While many driver and vehicle databases are online, most are restricted to "permissible users" such as insurance underwriters and law enforcement officials. The amount of information available and accessible varies widely from state to state. In some states you can obtain a person's complete driving record, including details of every speeding ticket and accident. *Driver records aren't available anywhere on the Internet for free* (though they may be for sale). However, there's a clear trend to restrict access to personal information (as many as thirty states have law changes in the works).

The best identifying information is on the driver's license:

- Name
- Prior Names
- Address
- Prior Address
- Date of Birth
- Good Physical Descriptions — eye color, hair color, corrective lenses if required, height, weight.

Some states provide the ultimate in data: the photograph.

Vehicle Registration records have an edge over driver's license records because they're updated yearly. They can provide you with the owner's name (sometimes both husband's and wife's), address, bank name and address, or title holder, usually a credit union or finance company. Of course, there's also the make, model and year of the car, its license number and even its vehicle identification number (VIN). Some registration data is available from fee-based services. At this writing, none is freely accessible on the Internet.

Consumer Affairs Records & Licenses

Most states license, certify, or register professionals such as contractors, hair dressers, doctors, psychologists, private investigators, automobile repairers, accountants, electricians, funeral directors and so forth.

The information available, however, is likely to be limited. Usually you can find out the date of licensing, a work address, date of birth and, in some cases, pertinent education. Few listings are online for free, though fee-based services offer licensing information for many states. Some states do post professional license lists – for example, **Utah Department of Commerce Division of Occupational & Professional Licensing** www.commerce.state.ut.us/web/DOPL/current.htm and the **New York State Education Department Online License Verification** at www.nysed.gov/dpls/opnme.html.

Complaints against licensed professionals and businesses are also worth checking. Commercial vendors provide regionally focused information on licensing boards.

Merlin specializes in California and KnowX focuses on Georgia. Therefore, they are particularly good sources for this kind of information.

Don't Forget Source Documents

by Don Ray

By now you're aware that there are a growing number of public records indexes available for free or for a fee on the Internet. Today, an eight-year-old in Sydney can zero in on a hefty amount of information about someone in Cedar Falls, Iowa without having to lose sight of her Barbie collection.

This at-your-finger-tips technology is a blessing to researchers but also a curse. If you've never laid eyes on the source documents to which the indexes refer, you'll never know you're missing.

Here's an example: Suppose you were investigating some guy named O. J. Simpson. You could go on line and learn a lot of information about him. But the online data will never tell you how much more is screaming out to you in the source documents. It so happens I've run just about every computerized index for O. J. Simpson documents. But . . . I also pulled the source documents. So you can see for yourselves. Hold onto your hats.

- ◆ You can learn online that there's a 1977 deed on file indicating Simpson bought a house. But you have to see the deed to know he and his first wife paid $650,000 for it and that the tax bill was to go to his attorney, Robert Kardashian.

- ◆ You can learn online that there's a deed of trust recorded the same day between the Simpsons and Brentwood Savings and Loan. But you have to see the document to know that it's for the purchase of the famous Rockingham Avenue estate even though they use their prior residence to secure the loan.

- ◆ You can learn online that there's yet another deed of trust recorded that day between the Simpsons and a couple named Easton. But you have to see the document to know that it's a second deed of trust in the amount of $125,000 that the sellers are carrying.

- ◆ You can learn online that there are two reconveyances on file in 1978 involving the Simpsons. But you have to see the documents to learn that they somehow paid off the two loans mentioned above in less than seven months.

- ◆ You can learn online that there's a power of attorney recorded in 1978 between O. J. Simpson and a Leroy B. Tate. But you have to see the document to learn that Tate is another of Simpson's attorneys and that he's getting the power to handle real estate transactions involving two specific properties.

- ◆ You can learn online that O. J. Simpson filed for divorce against his first wife, Marguerite, in 1979. But you have to see the case file to learn the names, birth and addresses of their children and to see that O. J. accused Marguerite of threatening him with bodily harm.

♦ It's possible for some people to access O. J. Simpson's voter registration affidavit online. But they would have to see the actual affidavit to learn that he was born in California and calls himself an actor.

♦ You can learn online that O. J. Simpson married Nicole Brown on February 2, 1985. But you have to see the marriage certificate to learn that his son and her sister stood up for them before a Presbyterian minister in Brentwood . . . and to see the names and birthplaces of the couple's parents.

♦ You can learn online that there's a quitclaim deed recorded in 1985 between Nicole Brown Simpson and O. J. Simpson. But you have to see the source document to learn that she was releasing all of her interest – that's what a quitclaim deed does – in the Rockingham property to her husband.

♦ You can learn online that there was a deed of trust recorded the same day between O. J. and a bank. But you have to see the document to learn that O. J. is using the Rockingham estate as collateral for a $725,000 line of credit. When you put the two documents together, you get a hint as to why Nicole signed away her interest in the property. We normally see such quitclaim deeds used as a pre-nuptial agreement before the wedding or as a settlement after a divorce. This one shows up, however, while they're married. Juxtaposed with the deed of trust, we can surmise that O. J. could not qualify for the loan if Nicole jointly owned the property. Sometimes this happens when one spouse earns little income, has bad credit or otherwise presents a risk to a lender. (The right to half the property in the event of divorce could conceivably be considered such a risk, but there are some things even the source documents can't tell us.)

♦ You can learn online that A. L. L. Roofing and Building Materials Corp. recorded a mechanics lien against O. J. Simpson in 1985. But you have to see the lien to know it was to secure payment of $1,507.07 for a roofing job started nearly two months earlier by a neighborhood contractor.

♦ You can learn online that Nicole Brown Simpson filed for divorce against O. J. on October 5, 1992. But you have to see the case file to know she claimed O. J. was hiding money he may have borrowed from his own Honey Baked Ham stores.

♦ You can learn online that the Internal Revenue Service recorded a federal tax lien against O. J. Simpson. But you have to see the lien to know that it's in the amount of $685,249.69 for the tax period ending December 31, 1994.

♦ You can learn online that O. J. Simpson filed two UCC financing statements in 1996 indicating he owed money to a man. But you have to see the documents to learn he used a Tiffany lamp and an Andy Warhol portrait of himself (combined value: nearly $50,000) to secure money he owed. These were two of the items the Los Angeles sheriffs were trying to find pending the outcome of the civil suit against Simpson.

▬ Document Access & Retrieval

Most commercial services providing online public record access have a regional focus. Superior Online, for example, focuses on the mid-Atlantic states, and Merlin Data focuses primarily on California. Some companies offer "national" access, but that access is still limited to what they can obtain, and most of them will tell you what records they have and don't have.

Many companies provide document retrieval services. These services search the indexes of records available around the country and then, on receiving an order, send someone to the courthouse to fetch the actual records. An excellent source to find record retrieval companies can be found at the **Public Record Retriever Network** www.brbpub.com/prrn.

Data Sources for Asset Searches

by Lynn Peterson

Lynn Peterson, President of PFC Information Services Inc in Oakland, CA, is a well-known expert in public record research and retrieval. Address: lpeterson@pfcinformation.com or www.pfcinformation.com.

Asset searches are conducted by potential lenders, business partners and people considering initiating a lawsuit, among others. Components of an asset search include:

Liabilities

If there are no significant liabilities then the way is cleared for a full asset investigation. One good way to assess liabilities is to search for bankruptcies, liens, judgments and notices of default or foreclosures – generally through commercial vendors. Also, bankruptcy case files contain detailed records of both assets and liabilities, as do pending civil litigation.

Real Property

A home is usually a person's largest single asset. Most public record vendors offer statewide databases searchable by owner name. Don't forget that ownership may be recorded under someone else's name (often a relative) or as a family trust.

Vehicles, Boats & Aircraft

Motor vehicle records, searchable via many vendors, include cars, trailers, buses, RVs and motorcycles. In some states, such as California, it's not possible to search the whole state by name of individual; rather, vehicles are registered by address. Smaller boats can be found via DMV searches in several states. (Boat registrations in some states may be handled by the Department of Fish and Game, the Department of Natural Resources,

Parks and Wildlife, or a myriad of other state agencies and are not available online.) Larger vessels (those over 27 feet) are registered with the Coast Guard, and can be searched through commercial vendors. Similarly, the Federal Aviation Administration's aircraft ownership records are also commercially available. You can also check state governments also what's publicly available.

Credit Reports

Credit reports can provide clues to real property held in someone else's name – for example, when no property is found, yet the credit report lists a mortgage or a car loan. They can also point to hidden assets by indicating many credit cards or large credit card balances. Non-header credit report information is accessible only with the written consent of the creditee, or when the creditor possesses a judgment against the creditee. And, as noted elsewhere in this chapter, credit reports are error-prone and unreliable as sole sources of data.

Business Records

Look for businesses in which the subject is an owner or financial participant. Numerous online databases of company affiliations are available. Also, search for corporations, partnerships and fictitious name filings (such as DBAs). Uniform Commercial Code (UCC) filings may also indicate assets. Sales Tax Permits can point to retail businesses owned by an individual. CDB Infotek offers sales tax information from Texas and California.

Court Records & Judgments

Court records can contain detailed financial data. Please consult this book's sections on court records – especially divorce, probate and small claims – for more detail.

Stocks

Stock ownership is available online for individuals who own more than 5% of a publicly-held company through the SEC's EDGAR database and other free and commercial sources. The same is true of stock ownership data of officers, directors, and shareholders that own 10% of the stock of a public company and those who intend to sell a specified amount of a restricted stock. For more detail, consult Chapter 9.

Bank Accounts & Insurance Policies

Although public records, such as court cases, can point to the existence of bank accounts and insurance policies, the information isn't usually searchable online. (It's usually obtained by telephone, using pretexts). Private investigators sometimes provide bank account or insurance information, but old-fashioned phone work involving the use of pretexts is how this information is usually obtained. Bank loans listed on credit reports can indicate an individual's relationship with a particular bank; however, credit reports don't contain bank account information (though UCC filings may).

Pre-Employment Background Checks

by Lynn Peterson

Pre-employment background screenings can be conducted only with written permission from the applicant. They vary widely, depending on the nature of the job. If the employment is denied due to information discovered with the background check, the applicant is entitled to a copy of the report. Here are some common data sources.

Understanding Credit Reports

Credit reports are divided into three sections. The first, known as the header, includes formal names, former names, addresses, former addresses and, sometimes, employment history. Thus, credit reports are a good way to verify the information provided on the application or resume. Also, this information may point to other geographic areas or previous names that should be checked.

The next section contains public records, such as bankruptcies, tax liens and judgments – and, sometime, collection accounts.

The third section is about the applicant's accounts and payment history – of interest if the job entails money-handling, or if amounts owed are disproportionate to salary level. Also listed: creditors that report data, such as amounts owed, monthly payments due and payment histories.

While credit reports can be obtained online, they are restricted. Small employers usually obtain this information through a smaller credit reporting agency or broker.

Keep in mind, however, that credit reports are notoriously unreliable. About 70% contained some type of error, and 29% contained errors serious enough to result in a denial of credit, according to a March, 1998 study by the **Public Interest Research Groups**. For detail, see www.pirg.org/reports/consumer/credit.htm.

Social Security Number

Social Security Numbers (SSNs) can be verified via direct access to credit bureau databases or through most of the large commercial public record vendors. The information available from Social Security verification is essentially the credit header and nothing else. Input the Social Security Number and out comes verification, as well as header information for any names associated with that SSN as reported by creditors to the credit bureaus.

For example, a potential employer might seek to verify a Social Security Number provided by applicant Susie Smith, born in 1972 – only to find that the Social Security Number was issued in 1965, under the name of Gordon Jones. It could be that the Social Security Number itself was mistakenly transcribed, or perhaps the actual card has been altered in some way. Many illegal immigrants use Social Security Numbers of people who are dead.

Criminal Records

There's no national criminal records database. except for the FBI's NCIC (National Crime Information Center) database, which isn't public and is accessible only by criminal justice agencies. There are literally thousands of separate criminal indexes maintained at the counties, parishes, townships and cities nationwide, and most are unavailable online.

At the state level, 27 states have designated their statewide criminal records repositories as public records, but only a handful allow online access (including Alabama, Colorado, Florida, Hawaii, Maryland, Mississippi, Oregon, Texas and Washington), often at a cost. But the records may not be complete. For example, Maryland's records include state district court records from all counties, but only three circuit courts – even though all felonies are tried at the circuit levels.

The **Texas Department of Public Safety Criminal Records** database at `http://records.txdps.state.tx.us/dps/default.htm` allows its subscribers to search statewide for criminal histories and sex offender information – the first state to allow Internet access to criminal data. However, the courts and agencies don't always report their data in a timely fashion, and don't always include dates, locations and other details. Similarly, Ohio and Michigan offer online access to statewide arrest (not conviction) records via a subscriber-based service called OPEN - Online Professional Electronic Network. Bear in mind also that criminal records are indexed by defendant name, not Social Security Number.

Commercial vendors offer online criminal court records for parts of California, Arizona and Texas – but the information is usually limited to defendant name, case number and date. The actual documents must be retrieved. Numerous vendors will retrieve criminal records (with a delay of up to ten days) – including Adrem Profiles and AVERT.

Through PACER (the source for Federal Court and Bankruptcy records described previously in this chapter), many federal courts are searchable online by defendant name, with no other data available online. Many of the federal courts allow access to criminal cases. However, records are searched by name of defendant and no identifying information pertaining to the subject is available online.

One more note about criminal records checks. Numerous services on the Internet advertise "nationwide criminal records checks." The adage that "if something sounds too good to good to be true, it usually is" clearly applies. These so-called "national criminal records" usually consist of a search of online newspapers and magazines. The gaps are obvious since usually only the most serious and bizarre crimes are reported in the newspaper, and online searches of newspapers don't include every newspaper in the country.

Civil Court Records

In general, civil court records are more widely available online than criminal court records. In fact, PACER provides online access to civil records from most US District Courts. However, as with online criminal records, once an applicant's name is matched, the actual records must be pulled. Some of the larger vendors that provide immediate access to civil court records are Information America, KnowX, CDB Infotek, LEXIS-NEXIS and Superior Online.

DMV Reports

As noted elsewhere in this chapter, DMV information access is restricted, though many states sell the data to large "middle man" firms that, in turn, sell the data to third-party vendors. Large commercial vendors such as CDB Infotek allow for delayed retrieval of DMV information in most states. Among notable gateways, TML stands out because it provides immediate online access to DMV data from approximately thirty states. Other DMV gateways include CDB Infotek (New York), DBT (Florida) and DCS in several states.

For more information about DMV data restrictions, consult the Driver's Privacy Protection Act and the Federal Fair Credit Reporting Act.

Bankruptcies, Liens & Judgments

Information about bankruptcies, liens, and judgments is included in credit reports, which are notoriously inaccurate. For example, judgment data may not be listed if, say, a Social Security Number isn't listed when the judgment is recorded (at the county), or if the address doesn't match. All of the major online commercial public records vendors offer a combined index of bankruptcies, liens and judgments, but availability varies from state to state. Bankruptcies can also be searched online via PACER.

Professional Licenses

Professional license information is just beginning to appear on the Internet. Commercial vendors offer online data for the following states: Arizona, California, Connecticut, Florida, Georgia, Illinois, Indiana, Louisiana, Massachusetts, Michigan, New Jersey, Ohio, Pennsylvania, South Carolina, Texas, Virginia and Wisconsin. Utah offers online searches on the Internet, and Nebraska provides Internet access to private investigators and collection agency licenses. The American Board of Medical Specialties (ABMS) Public Education Program's physician locator and information service offers Internet access to physicians' specialty certification records. (For more information about specialty people finders, please consult the specialized tools chapter of this book)

Academic Records

University registrars can verify academic credentials over the telephone. Also, many alumni associations have web sites that include biographical information about alumni. For a list of alumni associations, try **University Alumni & Development Offices** at `http://weber.u.washington.edu/~dev/others.html`). Other resources are listed in the Specialized Tools Chapter 4 of this book.

Workers' Compensation Records

These records are public in some states, but are obtainable only via subpoena in others. The Americans with Disabilities Act (ADA), which specifies access, states that employers (with fifteen or more employees) can access Workers' Comp claims only in cases of a clear, conditional offer of employment.

Most frequently, Worker's Comp records are obtained from employment screening firms and third party commercial vendors that maintain proprietary databases, such as Avert, US Datalink and Informus. California allows public access to EDEX, its database of adjudicated claims. Information about California's Workers' Compensation EDEX is available via **CompData** at www.compdatagovtedi.com. Other states are expected to follow suit.

Chapter 8

News Resources Online

It first arrived in an e-mail in mid-August 1997. Then, it appeared at least a dozen times within a four-hour period on the same day. Everyone was talking about it – the most candid, honest, refreshing graduation speech they'd ever heard. It was allegedly an 850-word commencement address given by author Kurt Vonnegut to the graduating class of 1997 at the Massachusetts Institute of Technology in June of that year. The speech was spiced with pithy advice such as "Wear sunscreen," and "Be kind to your knees. You'll miss them when they're gone."

In journalism, there is an expression – "If your mother tells you she loves you, check it out." Perhaps this e-mail was fictitious. What could be done to check it?

You could check the MIT web site to see if there was a published commencement address or a mention of Vonnegut as the speaker. You could attempt to contact Vonnegut. You could look for newspapers from the alleged day of the speech and see what had been written about it.

Using LEXIS-NEXIS and DIALOG, a check of the *Boston Globe* and *Boston Herald* reveals nothing. Typing "be kind to your knees" on a search engine results in no hits. In addition, the MIT web site claims that UN General Secretary Kofi Annan gave the commencement address for the 1997 graduating class.

Here's what really happened:

The "Sunscreen" speech was never given. It had actually been part of a column by Mary Schmich, a self-deprecating *Chicago Tribune* columnist, best known as the text writer of the cartoon *Brenda Starr*. As a result of the e-mail, she was interviewed on ABC's *Nightline* and by *People Magazine*. Vonnegut heard about the "Sunscreen" speech from his wife after someone sent her a copy of the e-mail.

At MIT, an editorial assistant started getting a lot of phone calls from journalists about the "speech." After checking a copy of Annan's speech, the assistant got an e-mail suggesting that the "speech" sounded remarkably similar to a column in the *Chicago Tribune*. She searched the *Tribune*'s web site and found Schmich's "Sunscreen" column. To confirm her findings, she visited MIT's library and viewed a two-month old paper copy of the issue of the *Tribune* that contained the column. That day, she told a reporter, "You can't believe everything you read on the Internet."

What started as a rumor and mushroomed overnight into an "e-mail classic" was able to be disproved quickly and efficiently using online resources. As evidenced by this anecdote, the Internet is powerful. Using the Internet, rumor and innuendo can spread like a brush fire. At the same time, the Internet can be used to uncover the truth.

To view the full text of the fictitious "Sunscreen" speech, visit either `wee.mastersforum.com/renewal-e3.htm` or `www2.magmacom.com/~mwarburt/advice.html`.

You don't have to be as prominent as Vonnegut to have been mentioned in the newspaper and for those references to show up on the Internet. When were you last in the newspaper? Maybe it was when you were asked about the top Chinese restaurant in your community or when you scored 20 points in a high school basketball game. The reasons are numerous.

If your name was mentioned in a newspaper, it can be found – either on the Internet or through fee-based databases with large archives.

So how can you use newspaper clippings to your advantage? They can help you find an expert, learn about a medical condition, locate someone you once knew or provide background information on a particular topic. Whether you are following an election, checking on the political climate in the Middle East, searching for information on a recent school board meeting or trying to find a weather forecast for a city you are going to visit, you can find the latest information online through news sources.

The Web has dramatically increased the pace of daily journalism. Distribution online has turned once-a-day newspapers into 24-hour operations, increasing the pressure on television and radio broadcast news operations to meet continuously rolling deadlines. The Web has also enabled just about anyone to be a reporter and a publisher. With the capability for frequent updates and unlimited archive space, there's enough free news coverage available on the Web to satisfy any news junkie.

News in General

Television stations have started to provide video clips and archives of video and text materials for free or inexpensively. Public Broadcasting's *News Hour with Jim Lehrer* (`www.pbs.org/newshour`) goes so far as giving you audio and text transcripts of the nightly news program. Search engines AltaVista and Lycos offer video clips that are searchable by keyword. Most transcripts are searchable by keyword.

Many newspapers provide free access, but force you to register so they can gather marketing information about you and/or for you. Others require passwords or payment. Some newspapers and magazines provide access to one or two stories to encourage you to purchase the hard copy of the magazine, and still others provide free access to that day's news, but make money by selling copies of archived material for a fee.

Perhaps the best advice in finding the most reliable and valuable source of information for you is to go with the brand you trust. The Web gives you an opportunity to experience other news options.

The free online tools do offer considerable access to media outlets. If you're looking for something current, the free Web is *quite* reliable and useful. Archive fees for news materials are very reasonable – remember, however, there are copyright issues to consider.

Generally speaking, the free news resources don't come anywhere close to replacing commercial online news databases. The fee-based services offer unmatched depth of coverage. At best, the Internet's leading free resources offer a two weeks' worth of coverage or a few dozen stories about a subject; the commercial services add thousands of new articles every day and maintain deep archives that are available on demand. In addition, the commercial services offer a full range of searching options, like field searching and Boolean capabilities.

Online news resources are so extensive, that I've divided them into eleven sections with top recommendations of sites for each.

Best News Collections: Print & Broadcast

AJR/Newslink
www.newslink.org

This site is the home of *American Journalism Magazine* and also a clearinghouse for the most comprehensive online list of domestic and international newspapers — more than 4,200. It also links to broadcast sites, magazines and surveys. The site is carefully organized and easily maneuverable.

BiblioData's Full Text Sources Online (FTSO)
www.bibliodata.com

Directs users to full-text magazines, newspapers, newsletters, wires and broadcast transcripts. Unlike the other entries in this list, FTSO, based on a book of the same name, is a pay service that's accurate, invaluable and updated twice yearly. Buy the book, and you get free online access to the password-restricted portions of the web site.

Editor & Publisher Interactive
www.mediainfo.com

Editor & Publisher magazine's outstanding collection of links to about 3,000 newspapers, as well as TV stations, radio stations and magazines. Consult the site index by clicking on "Past Archives Search" unless your interest is that day's top headline. This is another great place to start.

Yahoo! News Collection

www.yahoo.com

Go to the site and click on News & Media.

This collection is especially strong because you can search by subject or region. It is also a great starting place for finding a quick overview because you can search by media outlet's name, by municipality name or by geographic region.

Newspapers Online

www.newspapers.com

An aspiring mega-site developing links to newspaper sites inside and outside the US, this site is especially deep and offers links to local weekly shoppers, *Pennysavers* and small community papers. It has a nice collection of overseas links, as well. You can find resources here that you won't find anywhere else.

News Wires

While news wire services have always been crucial information sources in newsrooms, they've become more influential as the Internet has expanded. The Internet's strength is its ability to accommodate immediacy of breaking news – which the news wires deliver. One example is the relaying of Federal Reserve Board announcements that influence the world markets. News wires are staples of online news services and key components of news filtering tools.

There are five types of wire services:

International news wires all operate differently and have varying standards of editorial quality, journalistic integrity and credibility. The two dominant international wire services – The Associated Press (AP) and Reuters – are credible, reliable, journalistically-independent operations with thousands of bureaus worldwide. They cover everything from general interest to politics to business to crime for their local, national and international services. The AP is dominant in the US, but Reuters is more well-known around the world and has a much bigger online presence. That's because AP is a cooperative organization available to member organizations only, while Reuters offers its menu of wire service products to any interested consumer.

National news wires represent their home countries but are largely unknown elsewhere. Examples include Notimex in Mexico, Xinhua of China, Jiji and

Kyodo in Japan, and PA in England. Some are credible news organizations and still others are publicity vehicles for their governments. Notimex, the Mexican news service, for example, is a reliable, largely credible news service covering issues related to Mexico, but it is funded by the Mexican government and its coverage must be regarded with reservations.

Specialty wires are geared to specific topics, like business, telecommunications or health care. Examples include Dow Jones and Bloomberg Business News, both of which offer business-focused coverage that is journalistically strong and credible.

Re-packagers are wire services that are efforts by existing news organizations to sell their coverage to other news outlets. *The Washington Post* and *The Los Angeles Times* sell their combined products as one wire service. Another, the Knight-Ridder-Tribune wire, consists of news from papers owned by the Knight-Ridder newspaper group (including the *Philadelphia Inquirer* and *Miami Herald*) and the Tribune papers (which include the *Chicago Tribune* and the Orlando Sentinel). The repackaged products are considered as credible as the newspapers they represent.

The fifth category is **corporate press release services**. PR Newswire and Business Wire are publicity machines for companies. They aren't objective news tools, but rather, relayers of company press releases and corporate messages with no editorial or journalistic credibility. That said, they're still valuable for information that issuing companies want you to have – but you must not mistake them for unbiased sources.

Top Online News Wires

The Associated Press
http://wire.ap.org

From this web site, you can access the AP's regional and national wires.

Nando Times
http://www2.nando.net/nt/nando.cgi

You can also find the Associated Press, Reuters and other wires posted by news organizations all over the Internet. Nando Times, for example, published by the Raleigh (N.C.) *News and Observer,* contains that city's newspaper and access to many of the AP, Reuters and Cox News Service wire stories.

Reuters
www.yahoo.com/text/headlines/newsw/summary.html

For the Reuters wire, you can get key headlines and the top stories at **Yahoo!**. Many other companies offer access to wires. America Online, CompuServe and

Prodigy all offer varying clusters of wire services. AOL offers the strongest collection of wires of those three. Nearly all of the portal sites now also offer news wires of some form or another.

United Press International
www.upi.com

United Press International, another wire service, recently moved to the Web.

Newspapers

According to Eric Meyer, who runs *Newslink*, one of the top collections of newspapers online, (www.newslink.org), there are 4,925 newspapers online. Not all provide full-text and even fewer provide archives of past issues. Interestingly, more than 40% of all online newspapers are now based outside the US. Many sites make their money from advertising and provide the online versions of the newspapers for free as publicity and a public service. Some make money by providing interview transcripts and other reports for a fee. Still others charge only for access to content that's older than a few days.

The best online newspapers are taking full and creative advantage of the Internet's unlimited storage space and interactivity. For example, you may be able to input your ZIP Code and find out how your local schools rank statewide, your lawmaker's Congressional voting record or the local crime rate relative to similar neighborhoods.

Archive holdings vary. Some newspapers – such as the *LA Times* and the *San Jose Mercury News* – charge readers per story read or downloaded. Some newspapers archive only their web site postings; others, only the print publication; still others archive both. For example, you can search the *Washington Post*'s two-week web archive for free, and its full-text newspaper archive (dating back to the 1980s) from commercial vendors.

Most online newspapers do not offer access to their archives at all.

Top Online Newspapers

Here are a few examples of some of the better and bigger online newspapers, in alphabetical order.

Chicago Tribune
www.chicago.tribune.com

This award-winning site is cleanly designed and easy to use: the home page connects you to splash screens that rotate new content every twenty seconds. Click on items of interest; then click on the *Tribune* logo to return to the main page. Because the *Tribune* is a multi-media company, it often offers multi-media content that includes video clips, sound clips and photo images. The archives, however, aren't free.

Los Angeles Times
www.latimes.com

The *Los Angeles Times* has put its stellar newspaper online with a fee-based archive and a free retrieval feature. The *Los Angeles Times* site is deep and offers extra features to online users. Incorporated into the online stories are links; for example, a business story from the print version may contain links to current stock quotes and corporate profiles of companies mentioned in the article. Its archive is relatively inexpensive and easy to use.

New York Times
www.nytimes.com

The *New York Times* site is, like the newspaper, almost in a class by itself.

Posted is most (but not all) of the national edition (the Sunday magazine, for example, isn't online). There are a few online-only sections like *CyberTimes*, which has terrific, state-of-the-art articles about cyberspace news. You can also contact reporters, debate with fellow readers and obtain details that didn't make it into the edited versions of the stories.

The *Times* site requires registration, and they sell their subscriber lists to advertisers. They also sell their archives to subscribers at a substantial discount to non-subscribers.

Perhaps the most valuable part of the *Times* online is the Book Review Section and the Books on the Web Section, which provide books reviews going back to 1980. In her Chapter 11 sidebar, contributor Kitty Bennett suggests using these *Times* sections to find expert sources.

Wall Street Journal
www.wsj.com

The *Journal* Interactive edition costs $29 a year if you subscribe to the print version and $49 if you don't – a real bargain.

It contains nearly everything printed in the *Journal*, plus special online reports, a sports section and access to the Personal Finance Library — which includes the **Dow Jones Business Directory**, a guide with reviews and links to more than 350 useful business web sites.

You also get access to the extensive Dow Jones Publications Library. Searching the more than 3500 newspapers, magazines and newsletters costs nothing; headline viewing is also free. The first 10 articles are free; subsequent ones are about $3.00 each.

Washington Post
www.washingtonpost.com

One of the most exhaustive news web sites. Not only are two weeks' worth of the entire newspaper there, easily searchable, but also most of the Associated Press wire for that same two week period. *The Washington Post* does a good job of regularly updating its news site, especially when major news is breaking. It also offers all kinds of special databases, including access to the **Hoover's Corporate Directory** of more than 10,000 companies in more than 36 countries (see Chapter 9 for more about Hoover's), news links and reference material for more than 200 countries and news wires about all 50 states.

USA Today
www.usatoday.com

Another terrific web site, loaded with much of the newspaper's contents and much more developed just for the web site. It's interactive with chat groups and shopping deals. Unfortunately, it does not include much of the reporting of its sister, the Gannett News Service, which carries local reporting from many newspapers around the country.

Its best feature is the technology section, which includes "Hot Sites: What's New, Cool and Notable on the Web," a not-to-be-missed column once you are hooked on searching online. The rest of the technology section is also excellent.

Magazines & Newsletters

The magazine world has jumped onto the Internet as a way to disseminate information for current and potential subscribers, to offer corporate information and advertise other products.

The Internet makes niche publications easily accessible. For a publisher, the problem is finding the appropriate balance between giving enough and too much information for free on the Internet. Publishers want to provide enough online material to gather interest, but they don't want to provide so much that a print subscription becomes unnecessary. Some see the online access as a way to *supplement* print subscriptions and other see it as an *alternative* to print subscriptions. As a result, there are all kinds of resources, ranging from bibliographic information like tables of contents, abstracts, some full-text articles as well as some entire magazines and newsletters.

Many magazine sites also require user registration even if there is no access fee. Few magazines post the full contents of their publications. Most simply offer a few articles from the current issue and selected "hot articles" from the issue in full text.

Magazines, like *Advertising Age*, when posting key articles on their sites, change the titles and often omit other citation information for the web site editions, making research difficult. On the other hand, *Advertising Age* does put additional supporting information on the web site (www.adage.com) that does not find its way into the print addition.

A different approach is taken by the excellent Time-Warner's Pathfinder site (http://pathfinder.com), which offers a large portion of the material it publishes in its print publications. (See below.)

Best Magazine & Newsletter Web Sites

Some of the better magazine sites on the Internet include the following, as well as those listed in Chapter 9.

Electronic Library
www.elibrary.com

This is a collection of more than a million newspaper articles and hundreds of thousands of magazine articles and book chapters. It also includes TV and radio transcripts. The first 30 days are free.

Media Finder
www.mediafinder.com

This site has a phenomenally deep collection of newsletter listings, which are keyword searchable. It has a national directory of magazines and another of directories and catalogs.

Time-Warner
www.pathfinder.com

Time-Warner's publications include *Time Magazine, Money, People, Sports Illustrated* and *Money, Fortune* and *Entertainment Weekly* among others. The company offers the publication and then posts subscriber extra services like chats, bulletin boards, transcripts of key interviews and interactive feedback sections. These special features allows subscribers to get added value online.

Time-Warner and others also make tough-to-find international editions available online. However, images, photos and charts from the print editions are often omitted.

Its on-site search engine leaves a lot to be desired. It's often easier and faster to use a commercial online service.

One of the site's better features is a daily news service that upgrades and updates its site to the equivalent of a daily national newspaper with current stories written by the in-house editorial staff.

US News Online
www.usnews.com

US News & World Report offers its contents online and features several additional services: a college and careers section, an e-mail newsletter and discussion forums.

Television & Radio

As brands and known commodities, the networks are trying to be bold and innovative on the Internet, but also maintain the look and feel that appeals to their TV viewers. ABC, NBC, CBS, CNN and FOX all have a creative and visible presence on the Web.

ABC News
www.abcnews.com

Like the other networks, ABC offers breaking news headlines, and in-depth features at its site. It is rich with content and lets you search for video clips from the multi-media archives. In addition, ABC has put considerable effort into discussion groups about breaking news. It is one of the stronger news sites online.

ABC Radio, working with Real Audio technology, regularly puts breaking news online at www.realaudio.com/contentp/abc.html.

CBS News
www.cbs.com

The CBS site asks you to type in your ZIP Code and then provides local news for you every time you visit the main page. (NBC does the same.)

This site offers many features. You can get video and sound clips, if your browser is configured properly. CBS's Sportsline and Market Watch are excellent resources. Need a quirky chuckle? David Jackson's weekly feature "Untold Stories" features items you may have missed that week.

CBS Radio, partnered with the Westwood One Radio Network, also offers a full complement of news stories at www.cbsradio.com

CNN Interactive
www.cnn.com

CNN Interactive offers breaking stories, as well as easy-to-download video clips including sound. CNN does graphics well, and most coverage is graphics-rich, so when a new story breaks in a distant part of the world, you'll get maps and background as well as the news. They also use hotlinks very well, so when you get *Billboard's* Top Ten List of music sales (a standard feature) you also get links to sound files of each of the songs mentioned. Current coverage is cross-referenced with previous stories.

The CNN site maintains about a month's worth of content on the site as a searchable database, which is much more extensive than other news sites.

National Public Radio (NPR)
www.npr.org

If you are a fan of *Morning Edition*, *All Things Considered* or other wonderful programs, you can now go to NPR's web site and find the programs you missed. Regional programming is also available.

MSNBC News
www.msnbcnews.com/news

MSNBC is the web outlet for the resources of NBC, MSNBC and sister network, CNBC. NBC was the first TV network to launch a major presence on the web, and it is a very strong site. NBC has intelligently tied all its local affiliates to the web site, enabling you to choose a region from a country map on the site and allow you to get local news as well.

E-Zines & Online Publications

One of the Internet's most unusual creations is E-Zines – magazines developed online that do *not* have companion printed versions. They tend to be opinionated, hip, irreverent and sometimes bizarre publications, often produced by one person or a small group of people. Many are done for fun or personal reasons. Most don't contain advertisements and are not really geared for a mass audience.

The other extreme is online publications that are versions of print magazines. Some are hybrids of both, like *Slate* at www.slate.com, which offers a free trial subscription, but then charges $19.95 as do many traditional magazines.

E-Zines and online publications appear, disappear and reappear as quickly as mouse clicks, but here is a list of good starting places.

Top Online Publications Collections

E-Journal

www.edoc.com/ejournal

E-Journal is another great collection of magazines. This is a branch of the WWW Virtual Library discussed among the ready reference tools.

It has very deep subject area. You could look up the music magazines list and locate *ROCKRGRL Magazine - Information & Inspiration for Women in the Music Business*. The keyword search option isn't always effective, so use it as a subject directory and drill into the lists.

Kiosk

www.online-journalist.com/resources2.html#Online

Doug Millison's Kiosk of web publications is a great starting place for finding out about the unique world of online-only publishing.

E-Zine List

www.meer.net/~johnl/e-zine-list

This is a great collection of E-Zines from John Labovitz.

Foreign News Sources

Megasources

www.ryerson.ca/journal/megasources.html

A truly staggering collection of online resources compiled by Ryerson Polytech professor Dean Tudor. Though it has especially good Canadian resources, it's valuable to anyone.

Journalism Net

www.journalismnet.com

This is Julian Sher's list for investigative reporters with special sites for Canadian journalists. Both this site and Megasources, while serving Canadian journalists well, extend deeply into international sources and resources as well.

Mario Profaci's Cyberspace Station
http://mprofaca.cro.net

This site, by a Croatian journalist, is loaded with more than 400 pages of materials and links. His privacy page has links to some of the best people-finding tools online.

NewsTrawler
www.newstrawler.com

One of the best collections of foreign newspapers anywhere.

Archives & Transcripts

Most journalism sites keep material online for only one to three days. For news older than, say, a week or two, you'll have to refer to an archive and that's where the charges start to add up because most of these cost money.

To date, very few newspaper archives have developed a successful business model for making money on the Web. But other fee-based services have long archived news stories and have been quite successful in housing and storing huge amounts of news information.

On the Web, storage space (a hard drive) costs money to maintain and demand for the past is low. On the free web, few news archives date back several years. Some small and regional newspapers around the country have free news archives, including *The Denver Post, The Detroit News* and *The San Francisco Chronicle* and *Examiner*.

Christian Science Monitor
www.csmonitor.com

The only national newspaper with a *free* archive online is the *Christian Science Monitor*.

Newshunt
www.newshunt.com

Newshunt has links to more than 75 free archive sites on the Internet.

SLA News Division
Main Archives
http://sunsite.unc.edu/slanews/internet/archives.html

Foreign Archives

http://sunsite.unc.edu/slanews/internet/
ForArchives.html

The best collection belongs to the Special Libraries Association's News Division, which are a group of news librarians from media companies. Originally it was compiled by Margot Williams of *The Washington Post*. It links to all kinds of archives and describes costs and geographic coverage. It also has a terrific new site for foreign newspapers as well. This is the key site to help you find out what archives are online and available.

Favorite Journalism Collection Sites

Some of the top reporters, editors and producers around the world have pulled together very thorough collections of links of great research sites geared to other journalists. My web site **DeadlineOnline** at www.deadlineonline.com has links to hundreds of valuable news resources and many of this book's key sites. Here are some other favorites:

NewsBot
www.newsbot.com

NewsBot is HotBot's and *Wired Magazine's* news search tool. It indexes hundreds of newspapers, magazines and television broadcasts, and it is searchable by subject for the preceding 30 days.

Newsindex.Com
www.newsindex.com

This is one of the few news-only search engines online, with a database of more than 250 newspapers and news sources from around the world. This site is very good when a quick and current global perspective is required.

Northern Light
www.northernlight.com/news.html

The combination of a robust search engine and an inexpensive but extensive clippings file makes this one-stop shopping for backgrounding a subject quickly. It also has one of the best current news collections available anywhere online with more than thirty different wire.

Poynter Institute's Hot News/Hot Research
http://www.poynter.org/research/reshotres.htm

This terrific site amasses valuable web resources on current and news topics. Compiled by Poynter researcher David Shedden, this should be your first place to check when trying to get up to speed on the big hot story gripping the country.

Reporters Desktop
www.seanet.com/~duff

A gem. This awe-inspiring site by *Seattle Times* Pulitzer prize-winning reporter Duff Wilson is an excellent starting point, with direct links to useful news tracking tools.

Sources & Experts
http://sunsite.unc.edu/slanews/internet/experts.html

An outstanding collection of experts lists compiled by *St. Petersburg Times* news researcher Kitty Bennett (see her sidebar, "How to Use This Resource Best") and posted on the SLA News Division web site.

SLA News Division
http://sunsite.unc.edu/slanews

The Special Libraries Association News Division is an international organization for news librarians and researchers. The site has a gold-mine of valuable tools for any researcher.

Time is money. If time is the overriding factor in your research, go with a fee-based service. Unless you know specifically where to look on the Web, you can search hundreds of publications simultaneously and restrict your search by date or subject.

Chapter 9

Business Tools

Business Resources in General

Information is the lifeblood of business. The Internet enables smaller firms to compete with larger ones and large ones to diversify. Business resources on the Web are plentiful. You can find company profiles, trade data, business news, corporate tax and legal advice, management strategies, small business information, executives' biographical data, financial reports and much more. The Web's free resources are a good starting point, but the most detailed information and sophisticated analyses are available through free-based companies. In this chapter, we'll describe both, including expensive and inexpensive options.

This chapter is divided into two parts: company and industry research, as well as personal finance research. The first section is further divided into company backgrounding, market studies, sales prospects, investment research and competitive intelligence.

Company & Industry Research

Backgrounding a Company

There are a number of reasons to background a company. Information about a company's hiring practices and material can help you prepare for a sales call, or provide the background material needed to evaluate potential vendors, suppliers or takeover targets. A basic overview, for example, might include:

- Company's formal name
- Address and telephone numbers of the company's main offices and major facilities
- Activities of the parent company, divisions and subsidiaries
- Executives' names, titles and salaries
- Board members' names, affiliations and backgrounds
- Number of employees
- Company history

- ◆ Assessments of the company by creditors, investors, analysts and competitors
- ◆ Company and industry analyses
- ◆ News reports

Where Do You Start?

First, pin down exactly the kind of information you really want. Narrow your focus and then, when you do go online, whether via the Web or proprietary services, select the *tool* most likely to hold the answer to your focused request.

A critical question is whether a company is privately-owned or publicly-held. It's the biggest factor in determining how much information is available to the public. Under US federal law, publicly-owned companies are required to disclose certain information about their operations – including many of the details mentioned above – to shareholders and also to the US Securities Exchange Commission (SEC) and other federal and state regulatory agencies.

The SEC web site is usually the best starting point for research on a publicly-held business. If the company is publicly-held, you can count on finding a great deal of information, including:

Profiles of the company

Company history

Market information

Facility locations

Names and positions of top executives

Financial statements

And, in some cases, ratings and credit information.

On the other hand, private companies are subject to much looser requirements; their public profiles tend to be less distinct, and therefore, your data-gathering strategy must be different. A company's web site isn't a bad place to start, but keep in mind that the information on their site is what the company wants you to know. That information is often an "exaggerated" perspective rather than an honest one.

For private companies, you may have to use less conventional means to get meaningful information – such as news clippings, state tax office and Secretary of State registrations, rival companies' web pages. You can consult business directories, industry analyst and broker reports, newspapers, magazines, newsletters and former employees and vendors. Some data can be found via commercial services or on the company's web site, some from a company's or an individual's credit report. Yet another source is companies that specialize in corporate research.

Also, just about every company in America strives to maintain a web presence; their web sites contain company-generated information.

Company Directories: How to Find Basic Information

Company directories are plentiful. A few resources stand out above the rest. Each offers information with varying degrees of reliability, and it pays to take the time to try several: you'll be surprised at the range of difference in the results.

CompaniesOnline
www.companiesonline.com

The information on this valuable site comes from **Dun & Bradstreet (D&B)** – which houses one of the largest business databases – and from its partner **Lycos**. The data here is reliable and includes company name, mailing address, phone number, CEO's name, annual sales, number of employees and other basic information. The free information is merely *a fraction* of the data that Dun & Bradstreet has.

Company Link
www.companylink.com

Company link provides contact information, ticker symbol (if public), location of operations and industry. This site is linked to press releases from the companies themselves, stock quotes, news articles and financial filings. If you register, you can also access information about competitors.

Corporate Information
www.corporateinformation.com

This site is a good starting point to find companies and corporate data from around the world. Organized by country, it offers links to corporate directories and other useful sites.

Hoover's Online
www.hoovers.com

Like its major competitor Dun & Bradstreet, Hoover's has a free site of information capsules that include company descriptions, information about key competitors, rankings, and subsidiaries as well as current news related to the company. Hoover's is also available on AOL using the keyword "Hoovers."

INTERNET.ORG!
www.internet.org

Internet.org offers a good, free look-up site for companies and domain names. Though primarily an Internet research company, it can also search within industries.

NetPartner's Company Site Locator
http://netpart.com/company/search.html

This is one of the easiest-to-use free tools and a good place to start. It doesn't list every business, but it searches a database of web addresses from **InterNIC/ICANN**, which provides Internet registration services. Its database consists primarily of US firms.

PRARS (Public Register's Annual Report Service)
www.prars.com

This service lets US-based investors order annual reports free via the Web.

In addition to their free services, Hoover's, Dun & Bradstreet, NewsPage and other companies also offer much more extensive company profile information – for a fee. For details, consult the Web Site Profiles at the back of this book.

SEC & Related Resources

Securities & Exchange Commission
www.sec.gov/edgarhp.htm

The single most important and most impressive business resource is the Securities and Exchange Commission's EDGAR web site. EDGAR — Electronic Data Gathering, Analysis and Retrieval — is a resource of unparalleled depth and breadth. Visit it first regardless of the size of your research budget.

Its holdings are vast but not totally comprehensive, and it's important to know what they comprise. Since May 1996, all public domestic companies have been required to file all their mandatory statements electronically. These documents are available on EDGAR. Electronic filing was optional during the 1994-1995 phase-in period, and online document availability for that period is inconsistent. You can search and/or request manually-filed documentation in person or by phone, however. Also, keep in mind that some SEC-related documents are not made public, and consequently these are unavailable on EDGAR.

Needless to say, the information found within EDGAR is likely to be more detailed and more reliable than a company's own web site because the company is reporting to its federal regulator.

It's well worth spending the time to familiarize yourself with the myriad of SEC forms that companies are required to file. From the SEC's Home Page, click on Quick Forms Lookup for descriptions of the many, many forms that public companies are required to file. For example, a 10-K form will give you an overview of a company's future plans. Knowing what's been filed can give you a good idea of the company itself. Form 13-F is a quarterly report of equity holdings by institutional managers holding equity assets of $100 million or more.

Notably unavailable are 13-G filings, which declare when a stockholder sells 5% or more of his or her shares. It's a required filing but for some reason isn't available on the web site. It is available from some fee-based services, however.

EDGAR contains other valuable information, such as the SEC Digest, which chronicles daily agency activities and enforcement actions. The main SEC site also describes enforcement activities. Currently, neither is searchable, but that may change soon.

Here are some of the many web sites that harvest and enhance SEC data:

Disclosure Inc SEC Site
http://edgar/disclosure.com/ea

Disclosure Inc offers an inexpensive way to track companies. For $5.00 per month, you can receive up to 25 company reports dating back to 1993. These reports can be full-text EDGAR filings or summaries. In addition, the EDGAR database is searchable from this site by ticker symbol, company name and SIC code. Also offered is an alert service that notifies you via e-mail when companies of interest have filed new SEC documents.

EDGAR Online People
http://people.edgar-online.com/people

This service allows users to search SEC filings using executives' names. Information is available from the last six months of proxy statements and includes company position, corporate board memberships, stock ownership, options, sales and executive compensation. You can register and run the index for free, but you must subscribe to the pay service for more detail.

NYU EDGAR Development Site
http://edgar.stern.nyu.edu

The SEC filings found on EDGAR are also found here, on the "Get Corporate SEC Filings" page. It allows you to search using some added features, such as Zacks

Industry Code, which isn't available on the SEC site. Also, it's very valuable when the SEC site is busy or down. There's a one-day delay on SEC information, however. This is a free site sponsored by New York University.

SEDAR (System for Electronic Document Analysis & Retrieval)
www.sedar.com

Canada's version of the EDGAR system and similar to EDGAR in structure. It is bilingual, free and includes most filings required of public companies

Many of the major business resource companies – such as Standard & Poors, Moody's, Dun & Bradstreet and others – also offer SEC data — for a fee.

Should You Pay for SEC Documents?

When does it make sense to pay for SEC documents? It generally comes down to time versus money. When saving time is more worthwhile than worrying about the money, fee-based tools are irreplaceable.

Jan Davis Tudor, who runs Portland, Oregon-based JT Research specializing in business research, often uses SEC documents to get information. She doesn't always get them from EDGAR: "If I need just one document, chances are I'll obtain it from one of the non-SEC web sites." But if she has a specific question, she prefers to visit Global Securities Information's LIVEDGAR at www.gsionline.com which is also available via dial-up connection and dedicated line. It provides enough value-added features, she says, to justify paying for the documents. What she really likes is its ability to search across the entire EDGAR database using keywords, SIC (standard industry code) or form type. Pricing is fair — pay as you go, on a per-minute basis — and documents are pre-formatted so they're predictable and easy to use.

Company Information from News Sources

News tools are great sources of corporate information. Four particularly valuable sites are mentioned in this section. The Business section of the Web Site Profiles at the back of this book lists many more.

Business Wire and **PR Newswire** are valuable sources of company-generated information, such as new product announcements, joint ventures, management changes, dividends distributions, mergers and acquisitions. As with company web sites, however, the information reflects the company's interests.

Access them through the Web:

Business Wire
www.businesswire.com

PR Newswire

`www.prnewswire.com`

or through vendors like CompuServe, America Online and others.

Another way to look at business news is by region. Here are two outstanding tools:

American City Business Journals

`www.amcity.com`

It's a free site where more than thirty-five local business publications have pooled their coverage. They provide in-depth reporting about companies headquartered in their regions. You can limit your search to a specific city or search across the entire web site. It's especially valuable because it gives you a community perspective.

Crain's Business Publications

`www.crainsny.com`

Additionally, there are the Crain's business publications online. Crain's has several publications but no centralized site, so to find the regional information for business news from Detroit, Chicago, Cleveland and New York, go to the Crain's New York site and navigate to the site you need.

Other Tools in Your Online Arsenal

You can also use the regular news wires – the Associated Press and Reuters and the valuable but pricey Bloomberg business news wire (`www.bloomberg.com`) — to ferret out business company profile information.

Vendors like Dow Jones, IAC Insite and DIALOG are excellent for tracking of historical business data, while other fee-based services like CDB Infotek, DBT Autotrack, IRSC and Information America profile companies and employees using government and public data, not news stories.

Don't forget to check general news outlets when searching for business information!

▬▬ Market Research

Market research is information that helps you decide if you have a viable product or service (whether new or existing) and how you can sell it. It includes any and all information about companies and their products – including product reviews, launch plans, campaign strategies, company rankings, market size and share – that can identify new opportunities and influence existing plans.

Usually, market analysis includes extensive chart comparisons, analyst recommendations, income estimates, equity return calculations, risk profiles and an overall assessment as well as continuous monitoring and appraisal of ongoing developments. Market research is critical to funding decisions made by venture capitalists and other potential investors. The Internet is an excellent platform for doing market research, and many companies use it to research and develop market reports.

Free Sources of Market Research Data

Market research is quite lucrative and most reputable research companies charge enormous prices for their work. You can assume that nothing in this field is even close to free. However . . . research companies often release their best, most interesting reports or portions thereof to the press to generate publicity. As a result, many of the most valuable market research reports are summarized in trade publications and general business publications online, and you can read these news articles in lieu of paying for the actual high-priced reports.

The federal government also has terrific free resources for marketing information. If you're looking for marketing statistics or demographic information about a city or community, the best starting point is the **US Census Bureau** web site at www.census.gov. It's searchable by city, state, ZIP Code or industry. Also valuable is the Labor Department's Bureau of Labor Statistics (BLS) at www.bls.gov.

The Commerce Department's Bureau of Economic Analysis (BEA) at www.bea.doc.gov handles most of the key economic indicators for the US Government. BLS focuses on labor, employment and those types of statistics, while BEA takes a more global, market-oriented perspective. Both are excellent sites with mountains of good information.

Another valuable repository of federal data is **STAT-USA** at www.stat-usa.gov. STAT-USA's statistics, based on the US Census, cover most economic sectors, all the way down to the regional and community level. This data is critical to market research because it gives you demographic profiles of specific communities.

Trade associations are also valuable resources for information on industries. The central clearinghouse for the thousands of trade associations is the American Society of Association Executives (www.asae.org) based in Washington, DC. This links to more than 1700 associations, all searchable by name.

Another good site for finding associations is the Internet Public Library's Associations on the 'Net list at www.ipl.org/ref/AON.

If you can't find what you are looking for from an association or by researching it yourself, another option is to choose from among the hundreds of firms that offer specialty market research.

In considering marketing information sources, ask yourself: who would care passionately about this information? Those with an interest or stake in the information you seek will be more likely to have the data.

Market Research Data Vendors

There are many market research data vendors, and they are costly. Research companies worth considering include:

Datamonitor
www.datamonitor.com

Datamonitor provides another extensive database, this one considerably more international than the others listed here.

FIND/SVP
www.findsvp.com

Like others, FIND/SVP offers a thorough database. It also provides considerable information for free, including responses to non-client questions from previously published materials.

First Call
www.firstcall.com

First Call is a high-end, high-cost service that provides same-day real time reports issued by the brokerage firms that own First Call. Access is limited to selected customers, such as money managers, mutual funds and other "buy-side" firms, but it is worth mentioning here because it's so high-powered — and because you might know someone who can run a report for you. First Call provides corporate and industry research to the desktop via the Internet. You'll need Adobe Acrobat freeware to read these reports.

Frost & Sullivan
www.frost.com

This marketing company has an extensive research database but it's accessible only to paying clients.

Investext Group
www.investext.com

Investext's reports, from more than sixty research firms that monitor thousands of companies, are among the Internet's most powerful and costliest. Some reports are also available a la carte through DIALOG and Dow Jones Interactive. All files are formatted in Adobe Acrobat. Like Investext, another Thomson company, MarkIntel, offers broad selections of research from many publishers – mostly compilations of magazines and letters – via the Investext web site.

Jupiter Communications

www.jup.com

This site contains reports of this industry leader, which are reserved and password-protected for its top-dollar-paying clients.

Zacks

www.zacks.com

Zacks specializes in market analysis with analyst recommendations of many industries and companies. Zacks offers lots of good free material and more extensive information if you're willing to pay for it.

The Giant Databases

If you decide to use pay services to gather information, one of the best and most thorough services in this field is DIALOG, which has extensive research capability – specifically its Trade and Industry Database and Business and Industry or Table Base. These three databases, recently purchased by Dialog Corporation, generate tables and charts about an extensive range of business-related information – micro, macro and international (www.rdsinc.com).

DIALOG features a terrific Market Research Reports full-text file, available on its DIALOGWeb.com site. You can also buy the reports on a page-by-page basis. LEXIS-NEXIS MKTRES, another valuable service, also packages market reports from some of the major market research firms.

The major supermarket-style database companies – DIALOG, Dow Jones, LEXIS-NEXIS, all specialize in gathering and using existing market research reports from generating companies. They add value to these reports by packaging them with other incoming data, such as business news stories.

Dow Jones Interactive, an irreplaceable resource for this kind of research, allows you to search publications by industry. You can access DJI by subscribing online to the *Wall Street Journal* Interactive version.

Other companies, like Dun & Bradstreet and Hoover's, also provide detailed market analysis and reports. These companies allow you to search high-quality market studies that focus on particular industries, products and specific companies.

Expertise counts! Since market research is very expensive, it's best to enlist the aid of someone familiar with the field and its resources. If you plan to go directly to a pay service, study the online help files carefully and thoroughly beforehand in order to familiarize yourself and avoid paying hundreds of unnecessary dollars.

Business Valuation: an Example

by Eva M. Lang

Eva M. Lang is an authority on electronic research for business and litigation support services. She is also technology columnist for *CPA Expert* Newsletter. Her e-mail address is: `lemay_lang@csi.com`

One of the fastest-growing areas in the accounting/financial consulting industry is the business valuation sector. Business appraisers, also referred to as private equity analysts, determine the value of privately-held companies for a variety of purposes including mergers, estate tax planning and marital dissolution.

The IRS requires appraisers to consider the economic and industry conditions in which the client operates and to compare the subject company to other similar companies. Performing the requisite industry, economic and market analyses requires significant research. Recently, I prepared to value a small chain of restaurants in the upper Midwest. I set out to obtain information on the restaurant industry, including publicly-traded restaurant companies, and on economic conditions of the regional market. Normally, I check the Internet first, and then move on to commercial data vendors such as DIALOG.

Business appraisers use a variety of sources to gather information for an industry analysis. I started my search at Hoover's Online at www.hoovers.com, which provides both an industry snapshot and a list of public companies in the industry. The Hoover's Industry Snapshot provides information on industry structure, trends and major players. For example, the Hoover's Restaurant Industry Snapshot is five pages long and includes a chart detailing industry sales by sector, links to major players in the industry, a glossary of industry terms, links to related sites, and current industry news stories.

My next stop was the American Society of Association Executives at www.asaenet.org/gateway/onlineassocslist.html. This site is a searchable directory of more than 1,000 trade associations currently operating on the Web. The ASAE site pointed me to the web site of the National Restaurant Association, a site rich with data on both the restaurant industry and market conditions in selected areas.

After gathering the Hoover's data and trade association data, I wanted to find out what Wall Street analysts think of the restaurant industry. For this, I turned to the Multex web site (www.multexnet.com), where I was able to purchase analyst reports on the restaurant industry. I find that the Multex site, with pricing based by report, is often cheaper than other similar databases, such as Investext, which charges on a per-page basis.

To round out the industry analysis, I moved on to the many sites that offer articles from trade and industry publications. Options include the Electric Library (www.elibrary.com), the Dow Jones Publications Library (accessible with a subscription to the Wall Street Journal Interactive at www.wsj.com or Dow Jones Interactive at www.dji.com) and databases accessible through the DIALOG or LEXIS/NEXIS information services. For my restaurant industry research, I was able to locate a number of useful articles from the Dow Jones Publications Library.

The industry research turned up names of some of the public companies in the industry. To get a comprehensive list of companies in a particular industry, I did a search by SIC code in several different databases because not all contain the same universe of public companies or classify them in the same way. Disclosure Company database, Moody's Corporate Records, and Media General Financial Services (www.mgfs.com) all allow searches by SIC code. For a quick and cheap list of companies by industry, I also looked at the FreeEdgar site (www.freeedgar.com). Choosing the Search Filings option on its home page will take you to a search screen that allows you to search by Company Name, Ticker or SIC code. If you enter a SIC code, you will get a list of the companies in that industry that file with the SEC.

Finally, I assembled the data for an economic analysis. For national economic data, I usually go first to the to the federal government sites, such as the US Census Bureau (www.census.gov), the Bureau of Economic Analysis (www.bea.doc.gov) or the Bureau of Labor Statistics (http://stats.bls.gov). For my restaurant client, I needed regional information. I found the Federal Reserve Bank system to be helpful in this regard. Federal Reserve District sites, including the Minneapolis bank, are accessible from www.bog.frb.fed.us/otherfrb.htm (Federal Reserve Bank map with links). I found the most helpful information in the Federal Reserve Bank Beige Book at www.bog.frb.fed.us/BeigeBook.

At this point, I had looked at the subject company in the context of its economic and industry environment and in comparison to other companies. The information provided a solid foundation from which to assess whether the company is more or less valuable than others operating in similar conditions.

Sales Prospecting

Sales research is the process of identifying potential consumers who possess characteristics of interest to you. Screening that pool of potential customers is known to professionals as "sales prospecting."

Dozens of companies gather and sell mailing lists on and off the Internet. They include companies like:

Centrus Online

www.centrusonline.com

Sells mailing lists

Acxiom Direct Media

www.directmedia.com

Another mailing list broker

Direct Channel

www.directchannel.com

Brokers and manages mailing lists

All charge for their services. Dun & Bradstreet is also in the direct mail business.

Hunting for potential customers online by contacting them indiscriminately is feasible but tacky, and invites irate responses called flames. Most mailing lists and newsgroups are very sensitive to unsolicited e-mail that is not relevant to their main focus. Just because 1500 avid viewers of the TV show *Melrose Place* belong to a newsgroup (`alt.tv.melrose-place`) doesn't mean they'll be happy to read your solicitation for, say, insurance premiums. But you may get a warmer reception if you target a specific group with information of interest – for example, if you send a message about your new screenwriting software to `misc.writing.screenplay` or `alt.writing`. The trick is to make your posting relevant to the common interest.

On the other hand, companies don't seem to mind if you send a blanket posting to them about the gizmo for which you're seeking distribution. In that case, one of your best stops should be the online business directories like **BigBook** (`www.bigbook.com`) and others, which are discussed in Chapter 4: Specialized Tools. BigBook is especially good because it allows you to determine competitors by location. It can be searched by area code, company name or by category. For example, if you're thinking of opening a car dealership, BigBook enables you to find the locations of all your potential competitors.

Backgrounding tools like Hoover's can also help you identify potential customers by industry and/or region. Some of the more sophisticated databases – including Dun & Bradstreet, Hoover's and DIALOG – recognize SIC (standard industrial classification) codes.

Competitive Intelligence

Competitive intelligence (CI) is about collecting and using public information about rival companies' activities and plans. The best CI work allows companies to predict and their competitors' activities and strategies. CI involves detailed analysis.

CI Example

Suppose you hear a rumor that a global insurance company is planning a major relocation and you want to know more. CI specialist Melissa Pankove, of the New Jersey-based research company InSearch, recommends the following:

♦ Search online databases for press releases about relocation plans.

♦ Visit web sites that specialize in insurance news and information, including rating agencies that provide qualitative analysis on insurance companies and those of local insurance companies.

♦ Check rival companies' web sites, which are likely to offer extensive corporate information.

- ◆ Then go to the SEC's EDGAR database to glean information that may not be on the company's site.

- ◆ Research news resources. In this case, it's possible that a local newspaper reporter may have gotten wind of a relocation.

Call local government officials to ask about a relocation. Chances are that if a relocation has been given the green light, someone at the local government will know about it.

Best Competitive Intelligence Sites

FIND/SVP
www.findsvp.com

This site provides business research reports, including market research, on many subjects, as well as customized research services. One of its best resources is Robert Berkman's excellent *Information Advisor* newsletter. FIND/SVP's book, *Finding Business Research on the Web*, is useful also.

Fuld & Company Inc.
www.fuld.com

This is an extensive site by a leading consultant, and it offers Intelligence Pyramid, a CI primer, and an extensive Internet index. Fuld & Company also publishes *The Competitive Intelligence Guide*.

Montague Institute
www.montague.com

Montague institute is a newsletter company that focuses on intellectual capital, knowledge-based publishing and business intelligence. It generates a free newsletter that contains good researching tips.

OneSource
www.OneSource.com

This is a high-cost integrated web-based information tool that supplements the SEC's business files with more than 200 newswire research reports. It is used by most of the Fortune 1000 companies. It leverages huge volumes of business and financial information and analyzes it according to your specifications.

Open Source Solutions
www.oss.net

Washington Researchers, a directory publisher, has compiled a list of tips for locating competitor facilities, researching emerging technologies and locating competitor information. It offers many CI-related books, including an essential $885.00 three-volume set called *How to Find Information About Any Company*.

Society of Competitive Intelligence Professionals
www.scip.org

The site for the trade association for CI professionals. It includes online forums and an online library of publications designed for CI professionals but useful for everyone. It has a searchable database of professionals with CI expertise.

Transium
www.transium.com

A low-cost information service focused on business. You can search on a company name and bring up extensive business information like market share and strategy analysis.

Trade Show Central
www.tscentral.com

This site is searchable by industry, type of gathering, keywords, geographic range and date – but not by company name. It covers more than 30,000 trade shows, conferences and seminars worldwide.

Trade Show Channel
www.tschannel.com

This trade show site offers resources and links to searchable trade show web sites.

Check for contracts awarded and researchers' presentations posted at conference web sites. Helene Kassler of Fuld & Company Inc. recommends visiting a search engine and submitting the company name followed by words like conference, speaker, contract, project, client, customer vendor, alliance or joint venture.

Don't forget, commercial data vendors — including the large supermarket databases as well as smaller providers of tools that offer company and personal information about company officials that can be helpful as competitive intelligence data.

Quick, Effective & Free Competitive Intelligence Using AltaVista's Link & Refine Features

by Jennifer Kaplan

Jennifer Kaplan is president of JKreative Solutions Inc., an international management consultancy. She has no personal stake in AltaVista. Her e-mail address is `Jennifer@JKreative.com`.

Let's say you're launching a web business targeting business travelers. It's common knowledge that **Biztravel.com** (`www.biztravel.com`) is a player in this market and therefore a major competitor. Typing in biztravel.com leads us nowhere, but submitting `www.biztravel.com` brings us to the site. Here's our first valuable piece of data: our rival is a web-based business, but someone there hasn't yet figured out how to get us to the site without the "www" and nobody else there has noticed. (Any commercial site, particularly one that has invested heavily to build brand recognition of own domain name, or URL – should be reachable with and without the "www." If we weren't persistent, Biztravel.com would have just lost a prospective customer.)

With URL in hand, we then go to AltaVista at `http://altavista.com` and click on `Advanced Search`. I prefer the Advanced Search function because it lets me narrow my searches by date. Many of the other Advanced Search features are available in the ordinary Search mode, however. A Link feature is available on some other major search engines, but as of this writing, only AltaVista offers both Link and this type of Refine features.

The Link Feature

The Link feature is a powerful way to investigate your category and your competitors. It can be a great tool for uncovering promotion, advertising and sales opportunities.

Using the Link feature, we can learn a lot about our competitors. In the advanced search's Boolean expression box, type the following: `link:www.biztravel.com`. About 2,494 matches are found. These are sites that link to the Biztravel.com site. By the time you read this, these numbers will have increased considerably because the Web – as well as AltaVista's index – is expanding so quickly.

This information is quite valuable. Most of the time, people get to web sites by linking from another site. So the number and quality of sites pointing to your site is very important. If you think of sites that point in as sales leads, you'll understand that while quantity matters, quality is really more important. A hundred promising leads are always better than thousands of unqualified leads.

The Importance of Linked Sites

Although the number of sites linked to the site may not seem important, it can tell us a lot in context. For instance, how does the number compare to that of a similar site? Let's take a look at another travel site. Microsoft Expedia Travel is very popular, and it's backed by the Microsoft name, marketing prowess and dollars. By using the link command for the Microsoft Expedia Travel site (www.expedia.com), we find about 1,818 sites linked.

Before we draw any quick conclusions, we must first understand that Expedia has multiple entry points. If, for example, we try: link:expedia.msn.com, we get about 10,470 sites pointing in, and if we try link:expedia.com, we'll get only about 4,468 matches. Let's keep in mind that Expedia appeals to a broader travel audience – not just business travelers – and it's been around longer than Biztravel.com, so we would expect it to have more sites pointing in. Still, this is the type of competitive intelligence of which Biztravel should be aware.

Another way to use the link command count is to watch it over time. Noting the results before and after an online promotion campaign is a quick, easy free way to measure the campaign's effectiveness.

While you're researching online, don't forget to keep your eyes open for other valuable nuggets of marketing information. For example, advertising can provide us with good data. AltaVista – like most of the big search engines – sells keywords to advertisers. That means any time a visitor searches a word, or set of words, that has been purchased, a banner advertisement pops up. Travel is a very popular category – one of the biggest on the Internet – so each time we try one of these searches, a travel-related banner comes onscreen. From this we can quickly see whose spending money to target particular audiences. You may even want to type some of your own keywords into the Search box just to see what words have already been purchased and how competitors' advertising messages are focused.

The Refine Feature

The Refine feature is meant to help you find things quicker and more easily, but it's also a treasure trove of marketing and competitor data. Let's say we search using the term "travel." It's common word, so we can expect a lot of hits. In fact, we get more than fourteen million hits. AltaVista offers many ways to narrow a search, but let's try submitting "business travel" in quotes. When we use quotes in AltaVista, we'll find pages containing the exact expression. For example, if we type in "Business travel," we'll find only pages containing the exact phrase, with the capitalized B.

This search brings back more manageable results, but who has time to sift through 65,000 web pages? Let's try that "Refine" option (shown as Refine your search when using AltaVista). A window pops up instructing the user to "Refine your search by requiring a few relevant topics, excluding irrelevant ones, and ignoring others." And down the page is a list of Topic Areas with keywords following. We have the opportunity to require, exclude or ignore each Topic Area to further refine our search. Indeed, we could do this, but let's instead focus on the marketing applications of this powerful feature.

Looking down the column, we see the Topic Areas that are related to our search on business travel: travel, hotels, reservation, airlines, worldwide, airport, trade and more. This helps us understand how other people – including prospective customers and competitors – think about the category. That understanding is absolutely critical for us as we develop and launch our site. But even better is the graphical view. Click on the "Graph" button on the upper right corner of the Search box. Be patient – it can take time, particularly if you're connecting at a modem speed of 28.8 kbps.

The graphical view (see the image below) shows us the relationship among key topics and features a drop-down menu of further associated keywords. The graphical view allows us to include or exclude specific words in the Topic Areas. Of course, this allows a more precise search, but it also offers valuable marketing information. The graph shows the relationships among Topic Areas and the keywords associated with each Topic Area. Keywords are essential for both search engine placement (we'll use them in our site's HTML meta-tags and in our content) and for advertising when we considering keyword purchases.

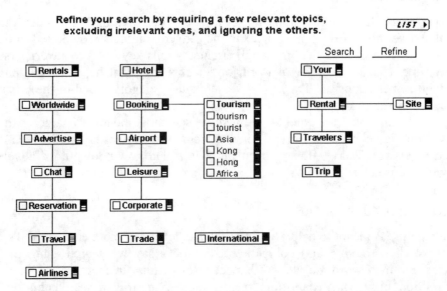

Whatever your field of business, try using the Link feature and the Refine feature on your site and on your competitors' sites. You'll be able to learn a lot. If you have an extra twenty minutes, make an excellent investment by reading through AltaVista's help section. AltaVista is a powerful search engine that's continuously improving and innovating. By learning its features and functions, you can add its power to your creativity and your business judgment for just a little time – no money needed. That's good business.

Patents & Trademarks

Patents are documents that give an inventor or employer the right to manufacture and market an invention. They are important because the holder of a patent or trademark *controls* the rights to it – rights that can be licensed or sold. To be patentable, the process, design, or device has to be useful, which means that it works and is unique or different from what others have done. Patent research is complex work and a true specialty.

In addition to looking up the actual patent, most researchers will consult scientific journals, popular magazines and conference papers and trade shows.

Here are some of the best patent research web sites:

US Patent & Trade Office

www.uspto.gov

The US Patent and Trade Office is the mother lode of patent data.

This government site is excellent for searching patent citations by company name, inventor, keyword and/or patent class. It's free, dates back to 1976 and is your best starting place. The search site is at http://patents.uspto.gov.

Derwent

www.derwent.co.uk

Derwent is a site that many professional patent searchers use. It is fee-based, searchable and can be tailored to your specific needs.

European Patent Office

www.european-patent-office.org

The European Patent office recently began offering free patent information for Europe.

IBM Patent Server

http://patent.womplex.ibm.com

This free IBM site takes the Patent Office's citation database back five years further to 1971 and makes it much easier to search. It has more than two million patents from all those years along with images. It also has some terrific links including one to Manning and Napier's MAPIT system, an analysis system that compares your patent to its competition.

Micropatent
www.micropat.com

Micropatent offers the US patent database in abstract form and in full-text for a fee. Also offers a subscription alert service for European, Japanese and other patent/intellectual property application filings, which is important because the US Patent Office doesn't publish patent information until patents are actually granted (up to two years later).

Patent research is best left to professionals. For a list of some of the best researchers in the business, contact the Association of Independent Information Professionals (www.aiip.org), which maintains a membership list searchable by subject specialty.

Personal Financial Information

Personal finance resources abound on the Internet. You can spend a lifetime exploring the swelling number of resources, checking leads and evaluating tips. Among the most valuable for getting up to speed on the art of investing are Quicken (www.quicken.com), Yahoo (http://quote.yahoo.com), Microsoft (http://investor.msn.com) and the terrific collection at the Mining Company (www.miningcompany.com — look under "Business"). In addition, some Internet gateways, such as America Online and CompuServe also offer extensive personal finance and business resources.

BANK Rate Monitor Infobank
www.bankrate.com

This site has very good how-to information for consumers and lenders. Includes the latest survey of the best deals in about seventy cities for mortgages, loans and home equity lines and money-market accounts.

CNNfn
www.cnnfn.com

Terrific for a quick review of the day's business and market news headlines. Its "Your Money" section regularly features stories about personal finance and guest experts who'll answer e-mail questions from the public.

Financenter
www.financenter.com

Got a financial situation you want to analyze? This is the site for you. It has more than 20 financial calculators that apply to household-related situations — refinancing a house, buying or leasing a car, etc.

INVESTools

www.investools.com

INVESTools is a "supermarket" of more than 30 financial newsletters and publications that you can buy piecemeal. There is a charge, but it's quite reasonable. Submit the company's name, symbol or other information and your hits will be displayed complete with hypertext links to the periodicals. Among the offerings: single copies of newsletters ($1.00 to $25.00), Morningstar Mutual Fund Reports ($5.00 each), Zacks Investment Research earnings estimates ($1.00 to $3.00 each), and Reuters Corporate News Service ($.25 per article, or $9.95 per month) as well as personalized e-mail updates of subjects you've selected.

Mutual Funds Interactive

www.brill.com

This free newsletter offers the inside scoop on mutual funds – lots of experts' commentaries, fund-manager profiles, basics of fund investing, etc. It also offers links to home pages of mutual funds and to fund-related web sites, such as the "Money Talks" site of investment columnists.

Quicken FN (formerly NETworth)

http://auth.quicken.com/login/http,3A,2F,2Fquotes,2Equicken,2Ecom,2Finvestments,2Fportfolio,2F

This is an all-in-one web site for investment research that searches the top twenty-five mutual funds by category or time period, then links directly to their Morningstar reports. Its database of 200 funds is searchable by total return, size, sales fees and other criteria. There's a great deal of useful information here. It's free, but you'll have to register for a password to access some sites. Also, skip the financial planning forum, where companies hawk their services.

PAWWS Financial Network

www.pawws.com

PAWWS is a fee-based connection to online brokerages and so forth. It also has non-subscription services that are worth checking – such as the ability to track the tax basis of your securities, which helps at tax time.

RAM Research Group

www.ramresearch.com

This unusual site hosts the "Payment Card Planet of Cyberspace," which has some lists of good no-fee and low-rate credit cards, rebate cards, secured cards, and even some credit union cards. You can apply for the cards online.

Investment Research

Investment research is well-represented on the Web. You can easily gather current and historical stock quotes, find investment advice, research companies and even buy, sell and manage your investments online. So much business information is available online that a number of Internet companies that specialize in personal finance matters are creating free gateway web sites as resource guides.

For more extensive information, please refer to The Company & Industry Research Section of this chapter – in particular the sub-sections on backgrounding companies, the SEC's EDGAR database, marketing information, and competitive intelligence. Also, note the extensive list of Business section of the Web Site Profiles Index at the back of this book.

Chapter 10

Managing & Filtering Information

Let's talk about overwhelming. Information comes at us from every direction – paper, paper and more paper! And then there's the endless Internet. Truly, it is a challenge to keep our colleagues, our clients and ourselves informed and updated. The problem is more complex if you are an information professional. You not only have to provide current information to your clients and colleagues, and stay updated on developments in your own field, but you have to do so quickly and accurately.

Yesterday we craved information. Now, we must learn to control its volume. A lot of today's information is useful and valuable, and there's also some garbage. That is why we need filtering — to let the important information in and shut out the rest.

While your computer may have contributed to the mess, it certainly can help get you out of it. Managed properly, technology can actually help you get organized. This chapter will show you how. You can be on top of e-mail, voice mail, faxes — the technology can even help remind you about things on your "to do" list.

There are lots of ways to organize your information and reduce overload. Much of this can be done before you ever get to the Web.

Managing Incoming Information

Managing E-Mail

E-mail is great – until you're suffocating under the weight of too much of it! Here are some ways to take control.

Be Selective	Read the subject heading first and make your decision whether to open it or kill it based on that. Deleting unopened mail is the only way to stay atop the mounting heap. It's ruthless but effective.

Note The Sender	Learn the difference between the person who sends you laughs and the person who controls your paycheck. Guess whose e-mail belongs on top of your priority list?
Delegate	Delegate or forward e-mail messages that shouldn't be yours in the first place – especially if you share e-mail duties with others.
Filter	Some people can ignore their e-mails. If you can't, then eliminate the volume by filtering them as they come in. Either route them to folders of your choosing – eliminating unnecessary ones in the process – or use a mail program that automatically routes your mail into folders. Pegasus Mail (a shareware program), Eudora Pro and Outlook '98 all do this. Nearly all e-mail programs allow you to sort mail by dates, by sender and, in some cases, by subject. Filtering will help eliminate *spam* (unsolicited e-mail). Filtering tools vary, but most allow you to select words and throw out messages that contain them. Or, you can choose words and prioritize messages that contain them. For example, filter e-mails containing the phrases "make money" and "$$$" and the program will send them to your delete file without you having to read them. Filtering software, such as Forté's Free Agent is effective. (For more filtering programs, see the Filtering section of the Web Site Profiles index.)

On your browser, locate the "Find" command when you are viewing your e-mail messages. All e-mail programs include a "Find" Command that will locate messages containing specified words. Use it to save time.

Managing Web Sites (Bookmark Folders)

Netscape calls them Bookmarks; Internet Explorer calls them Favorites. They're the web addresses that you want to save. Most people gather too many shortcuts and then can't find them when they're needed. Use the "Find" command in either of the major browsers. Better yet, Netscape 4.0 (and higher versions) lets you organize your bookmarks into folders and then lets you create new names for them – names that are easier to remember.

Managing Downloads

Some freeware/shareware programs help your browser schedule large file downloads while you're away. Programs such as Download Manager and Download Butler (for PCs) and the Midnight Download (for Macs) – can all be found at CNET's Download.com – www.download.com. They'll also automatically send you updates for the software.

Managing Your "Twinkie Time"

It is said that most Usenet content is as informative as Twinkies are nutritious. If you are going to subscribe to newsgroups, mailing lists and discussion groups, route them into folders where you can read them at your convenience. Learn to filter messages before you download them. When you do read them, apply the browsing tips described in the e-mail section above. Usenet filtering software, like Forté's Free Agent can also help you manage the avalanche.

Managing Your Offline Life

What's the point of having an organized online life if you're just going to dump it into the dumpster of your real life? Here are some options.

Handheld or palmtop computers, also known as personal information managers (PIMs) or personal digital assistants (PDAs). They function as calendars/schedulers, address books, phone books, to-do lists, project or task managers and note takers. Most of them transfer data seamlessly to and from your laptop and/or desktop computer.

Meetings can be coordinated electronically, insuring that everyone who needs to know is notified. Many companies use the Internet to post employee schedules.

Software programs like Microsoft Outlook and Eudora Pro can be programmed to send you e-mail reminders. Most palmtops have a reminder alarm function.

Alert services are offered by hundreds of companies and they've already become significant features of companies selling books, airline tickets and other forms of e-commerce. **Remind Me**, for example, notifies you a week or day before an event, or sends an alert for a specific time of a specific day, at your request. Need a nudge to make you remember it's time to take the cats to the vet for shots?

Ready for an off-beat but sure-to-save frustration reminder service? Try **Tow Zone**, from Phil Greenspun, who also offers Remind Me. Tow Zone warns drivers when the city is cleaning its streets. Tow Zone and Remind Me can be found at http://photo.net/philg/services.html.

If you want to be altered of bargain airfares, visit www.biztravel.com or www.travelocity.com or www.onetravel.com.

Be the first to find and buy the latest new book from your favorite author using Amazon's alert service (www.amazon.com), or when your favorite music group is coming to town (www.pollstar.com).

Business people use alert services to be notified when new documents on companies of interest are filed with the Securities and Exchange Commission (www.freeedgar.com or www.whowhere.com/Edgar/index.html).

Some Helpful Hard Drive Organizers

Enfish Tracker Pro

This new hard-drive organizing program coordinates everything that's on your hard drive, consolidating, collating and most important relating information from your e-mail, web searches, your PIM or PDA and it works like a desktop interface. This $80.00 program calls itself an automated assistant that can organize and file everything on your computer so you can find it when you need to.

Unifiers

Can't keep up with the voice mail, e-mail, pager and fax machines overwhelming you? What if they all came into a single mailbox? Several companies have new products coming out that will give you all of those in one unified manner.

Unified Messenger

Unified Messenger comes from Octel, a division of Lucent Technologies. It sells for about $200.00 per person, provides a single window into your e-mail and voice messages on your PC screen. This could be a real asset to download while you are on the road, though you don't need a laptop to check it. You can call the messaging system from a phone and a computer-generated voice actually reads messages to you. Faxes are also being linked to this process. It has a downside: this technology is based on Microsoft's Exchange software, so you will need to run that program in order to use the Unified Messenger. Centigram and other companies are developing similar technologies.

Filtering: Controlling the Deluge

Filtering is the process of culling, sorting and routing information into useful categories. Structuring your filtering right will save time and keep you on top of things. Filtering is a personalizing tool.

Currently, most general filtering tools and services claim to give you news you can use when you need it. To a large extent, these products promise more than they deliver. Often, you'll receive mail that you thought your filter would catch. Their overall weakness is that their filtering function is too general, and they don't make the connection between what you need and what they deliver. At least not yet.

Test filtering programs thoroughly. Most offer free trial periods. Remember, no one service is likely to meet every user's needs.

Filtering for Kids

Companies have developed filtering software to enable parents to set content and access preferences for children. Most filters today act simply as content filters. Through coding and dozens of other ways, these filters prohibit access to web pages containing specified words or pictures.

As software companies begin to add privacy preferences to their content filters, upcoming software should enable consumers to access only Internet sites that match their privacy preferences.

Content-screening software uses either a filtering or rating method. The filtering method allows access to the Internet, but blocks the sites (or materials) that the software-maker defines as objectionable. Typically, the software recognizes a database of banned sites and search words. This design is not foolproof. It does not prevent a user from clicking on a link to a site that is not in the database, and it cannot stop a clever search that avoids the search words listed in the database.

The rating method uses programs that identify a site's HTML code and permit access only to web sites with allowable ratings. Parents can, for example, restrict their children's access to sites that are rated as having no sexual material, foul language, or violence. The two currently operational rating systems are **Recreational Software Advisory Council on the Internet** (RSAC) at www.rsac.org/homepage.asp and **SafeSurf** at www.safesurf.com.

Phrases with dual meanings or contexts can also cause unintentional blocking. For example, filtering out the word "breast" removes not only pornographic sites, but also breast cancer sites.

The following are among the best filtering tools for children:

Cyber Patrol	www.cyberpatrol.com
CYBERsitter	www.cybersitter.com
Net Nanny	www.netnanny.com

Best Filtering Tools

Copernic 98
www.copernic.com

This is one of the best online search tools. However, you do need to download free software from the web site to use it. It searches through as many as thirty search engines, compiles the results, removes duplicates and then ranks them by relevancy. You can share the search results by sending them through e-mail. A more sophisticated version is available for about $30.00. Once you know how to use it, this one is a serious time saver.

NetMind
www.netmind.com/mindit

NetMind is a free alert service that informs you every time there is a change to a web page. It is great if you routinely monitor web sites – such as your competitors' sites. You can also use it to monitor web coverage by submitting the proper names of people, companies, and so forth.

NetMind also has a subscription service, Enterprise Minder for the Web or Intranets, that monitors designated web pages, intranets or extra-nets, and e-mails. The alerts monitor based on keywords, images and/or numbers.

JavElink
www.javelink.com

JavElink is a free monitoring service that watches up to twenty pages at a time. A more robust version that monitors up to fifty pages for $15.00 a month is available. It notes the changes, reports them to your secure account, highlights the location of each change and stores the history for you. It also lets you know what's new, what's notable and what's absent.

NewsBot
www.newsbot.com

As discussed in Chapter 8, NewsBot updates headlines in your areas of interest. NewsBot has one of the best collections of newspapers I've seen, rivaled only by News Index and Northern Light's current news collection. It is tailored specifically to search only news resources – general and international, business and other specialized news sites. Coverage goes back about a week, but it pulls from hundreds of daily newspapers, wire services, trade publications and broadcast news sites.

Daily Diffs
www.dailydiffs.com

Based on JavElink Secure Server technology, Daily Diffs monitors 3,500 of the most dynamic "changing" web pages each day – mostly news, companies, government and organizational web sites, including ones that may interest you. It shows the changes for each page every day. It is organized by topic, industry and company.

Electronic Library
www.elibrary.com

Electronic Library — or ELibrary — is a subscription service, though it's free for the first thirty days. It has vast news and information resources.

Inquisit!
www.inquisit.com

Inquisit! allows you to set up a filtering tool from about 600 sources including newswires, newspapers, newsletters. Subscriptions are $12.95 monthly or $129.95 yearly. To try it, they offer a fourteen-day free trial.

News Index
www.newsindex.com

An excellent compilation of searchable headlines from an enormous variety of sources, including an excellent collection of quality newspapers.

NewsHound
www.newshound.com

NewsHound is the Knight-Ridder chain news alert service. It is delivered by e-mail for $7.95 a month or $59.95 a year, allowing you access to an unlimited number of articles. Among its sources are the *Philadelphia Inquirer, Miami Herald, San Jose Mercury News* as well as the AP, Reuters and other news wires. NewsHound lets you construct your own search strategy using keywords. Once that is set up, you can set up your own relevance ranking.

Newspage
www.newspage.com

News Edge, a news delivery service, has developed Newspage, a subject-oriented alert service. Register at the site then personalized your edition by selecting from wide categories like energy, media and telecommunications.

Basic information is free. The premium service delivers personalized daily updates via e-mail for $6.95 per month. It offers news headlines and helps you track companies and business trends.

Wavephore's Newscast
`www.wavephore.com`

Newscast's subscription-based service delivers personalized business information from thousands of sources to more than 100,000 corporate employees and business-related subscribers using its own proprietary "pattern matching technology."

Commercial Filtering Tools Recommendations

Commercial filtering tools tend to be sophisticated and precise. And, of course, expensive. High-cost tools like Inquisit! deliver alerts via pagers, while e-mail services like NewsHound are less expensive but also push material to the user's desk at a moments notice. NewsHound uses e-mail to deliver its message, while another service – PointCast (`www.pointcast.com`) -- runs in the background of your computer at all times so it can always be viewed like a ticker scrolling across your screen.

Only the very high end tools, like WavePhore's Newscast or Desktop Data's News Edge meet professional competitive news filtering needs, and both are extremely costly – for instance, News Edge for 500 users costs about $85,000 a year. That kind of money buys real-time news – the kind that lets a stockbroker track the twenty worst performing stocks of the day and respond accordingly.

▬▬ Intelligence Agents

On the Internet, an intelligent agent (or simply an agent) is a program that gathers information or performs some other service on a regular schedule without your immediate presence. Typically, an agent program, using parameters you have provided, searches all or some part of the Internet, gathers information you're interested in, and presents it to you periodically.

These intelligence agents are sometimes called **bots**. For considerably more information go to **IBM's Intelligent Agent Center of Competence** at `http://www.raleigh.ibm.com/iag/iaghome.html`.

Other agents have been developed that personalize information on a web site based on registration information and usage analysis.

NetMind, referred to earlier under Best Filtering Tools, is an example of intelligent agent technology. You ask it to find when a site has been updated or to look for other events. This technology not only gathers the information but organizes and interprets the information for you.

Personalized "Opening Pages"

Another online trend is to have a web site custom-tailored to your needs, desires and interests. Most of the portal sites allow you to do this, and many of the nation's top news organizations have jumped into this as well, hoping to establish brand loyalty with their viewers.

Although not a comprehensive list, here are some of the better ones:

CNN Custom News

http://customnews.cnn.com

CNN allows you to customize your interests on all kinds of subjects, from news to sports, to business to features. This site has affiliations with over 100 newspapers and magazines as well as from CNN. It is very powerful and very strong.

Infoseek

www.infoseek.com

This is a narrowly focused personalization tool. It allows users to select keywords and only retrieves stories with those exact words and links them to your customized page. Also for stress relief, it has a quick link to corporate comic strip hero Dilbert.

Lycos Personal Guide

www.lycos.com

This personalized page, a relative newcomer to the field, has the same features as many of the others – headlines, weather, etc., but also provides a daily planner, a self-updating address book and home pages for users. It also has an "add a reminder" feature to alert you of things you don't want to forget.

Mercury Center Passport

http://www.sjmercury.com

Once at this site, click on Membership Passport. Not only do you get news headlines, great high tech coverage, but you also can customize your comics page so you don't miss any of your favorites. This site claims it has the largest collection of comics on the Web. It also has an e-mail key-subject notification system as well.

My Excite

www.excite.com

Like its Newstracker, Excite has developed an excellent personalized page for you. They recently added the first detailed daily horoscope on a personalized page.

MSNBC Personal News Alert

www.msnbc.com/tools/alert/alermain.asp

MSNBC will flash an alert icon on your desktop when news breaks. Click the icon to see the headline and a link to the article on MSNBC. Requires Windows '95 or Windows NT 4.0.

My Yahoo!

http://my.yahoo.com

This can also be personalized to the issues you care about. It also features news headlines, weather updates, airfare discounts from your home city and is constantly adding features.

Nando News Watcher

www.nando.net/nt/newswatcher

Nando News Watcher posts current headlines on your desktop from Nando's News Services.

News Edge's Newspage

www.newspage.com

News Edge's Newspage can be customized to highlight the companies you want profiled and to bring up coinciding news stories on the subjects you care about. A valuable tool.

New York Times Direct

http://www.nytimes.com/info/contents/services.html

From this site you can get the *Times* delivered to you electronically.

High-Tech Personalization Tools

There are many other personalization tools – especially for technology followers. For starters, check:

ZDNet's Personal View

http://members.zdnet.com/pview/login.cgi

and

CNET's News.com

www.news.com

Bots: Personal Search Tools

Chapter 3 discussed search tools and the concept of robots or spiders worming their way through the Internet to permit keyword searching of indexed documents. There are personal spiders — also called "bots" (short for "robots") — that share technology used by Excite's News Tracker, NewsBot and NewsHound to hunt through newspapers.

Bots are theoretically capable of three functions:

- Searching
- Monitoring
- Evaluating

You can get a bot to research the criteria and keywords you have outlined overnight while you sleep for, say, a capella music, and wake up to a collection of sites and sounds on your hard drive. Bots are particularly good at locating sound and picture files — a weakness of most search tools. Until recently, bots have been better at retrieving specific material than presenting overviews, and their ability to evaluate has been rudimentary.

But, that is changing rapidly. Now there are specialized bots that can be programmed to shop online for you, answer questions and retrieve music you may like based on your previous selections. Chat bots are adding dramatically to web site interactivity. Some bots host web site tours. Within the next few years, bots will become your servants on the Internet — carrying out orders that you've programmed from your computer, even when you're not actually online.

Best Bots

Alexa
www.alexa.com

Alexa's free software lets you track web traffic patterns by telling you the next destination of people who have visited the site you're currently visiting. Its ambitious Internet Archive has already archived huge portions of cyberspace equivalent to more than half of the Library of Congress.

BotSpot
http://botspot.com

BotSpot is a clearinghouse for all kinds of bot research. Stop in and try one.

CyBot
www.TheArtMachine.com/cybot.htm

CyBot is your personal web crawler, searching for what you need, bringing it back much faster than if you were to browse on your own. It uses artificial intelligence to adapt to your needs.

Databots with Imagination
www.imagination-engines.com

These bots use their own independent judgments in finding and understanding complex databases. Using artificial intelligence capabilities, Databots are being used by a Swiss banking company to do stock market analysis and make prediction models from market data.

Infogist
www.infogist.com

A timesaving researching tool that uses intelligent agent software technology, this fee-based tool offers a free trial.

Intelliseek
www.intelliseek.com

Intelliseek's Bullseye combines many customized intelligent agents to tap 300+ search engines and 600+ plus databases on the Internet, simultaneously, to find, analyze, filter, report, manage and track information. Definitely one to watch when you are trying to weed through oceans of information. It costs $50 (a one-time fee), and Intelliseek offers a thirty-day free trial.

Push Technology

In the past, search tools have been user-motivated, enabling a one-way communication to the Internet. Now, in addition to user-motivated information retrieval, sender-motivated material is sent to us via "push technology."

Push technology is a method of Internet data distribution in which information is "pushed" onto your computer screen, much like pre-selected television programs are broadcast onto your television set.

E-mail and instant messages are early forms of push technology. You can elect to block certain e-mail addresses, or allow instant messages only from pre-selected names and/or addresses.

Information is being gathered *about* you at the same time other information is being *delivered to you* at your request.

Push technology is only now coming of age, and the level and volume of interaction is increasing exponentially.

- Amazon.com and Barnes & Noble both use push technology quite successfully. They realized that ordinary book sales techniques wouldn't sustain their businesses. They needed to provide additional services. So, the Barnes & Noble web site at www.barnesandnoble.com lets you rank books you like. The site then identifies other users with similar tastes, then suggests their choices to you. You can also chat and exchange messages with readers with similar interests. Over time, the technology starts to recommend books based on your past preferences. It also takes into account your stated preferences. Amazon.com's site is similar.

- The site at www.cinemax.com uses push technology to identify people with tastes similar to your own and shows their recommendations.

- Another company, iVillage at www.ivillage.com recommends chat groups for consumers based on their personal profiles and online footprints.

- Infoseek, the search engine, lets advertisers track your online travels so that they can send targeted advertising to you based on your interests.

- Other companies can screen Internet content and push it to various groups of employees, sending industry news to one segment and a company announcements to another.

- Fidelity Management, a Boston-based mutual funds company, uses push technology to send volatile information, such as fund performance sales activities, to senior executives.

- Conference Plus of Illinois, which schedules and manages conference calls, pushes real-time customer statistics so managers know how long customers are waiting on the phone, and deploy backup operators so customers don't hang up.

Future intelligent marketing tools will ferret out new customers by tracking what groups of people are interested in and by aggregating the specific web sites people need quickly.

Push: The Downside

The downside of the new intelligent push agents is that they still rely on some form of interrupt to get the user's attention.

Interrupts in current push technologies include e-mail messages, system beeps, alerts, animated icons, scrolling tickers and screen savers. Interrupts can be turned off, but then push becomes much like e-mail.

Though interrupts can take a user's focus away from the task at hand, the real problem is that they're too frequent and generally unscheduled. Scheduled interrupts a couple of times a day, plus emergency information, makes sense, but this level of control isn't always available.

Chapter 11

Evaluating Accuracy, Credibility & Authority

The reality of the Internet is that anyone can be a publisher. Web page content can — and often does — goes straight from one person's fingertips into cyberspace. As a result, a credibility gap has developed as many people have found bogus information on the Internet, discount the medium altogether. It poses a problem for professionals who object to their life's work being lumped together with what's been called "gossip roadkill on the information superhighway." Is it credible? Is it authoritative or second-hand or third-rate? How can you tell? There are some fundamental questions you can ask that will lead you to credible information.

- Who wrote the material? Is the author identified — or anonymous?
- What authority and credentials do they have?
- What are their biases?
- Has anyone checked the work?
- Has anyone else reviewed the page you are seeing?
- Is the data from a traditionally reliable source?

It's helpful to think of the Internet as the messenger, not the message. As Barbara Quint, editor of *Searcher Magazine* says, "...don't put in your head what you wouldn't put in your mouth. Ask: . . . Where does this come from and why is this here?" She suggests, "It's like saying 'I got it from the Internet,' like 'I got it from the phone.' The quality of the information depends on who is on the line."

Consider the source. Professionals make mistakes, but, behind them stands a professional organization, with editors, fact-checkers and others who find and correct errors. At universities worldwide, original research is peer-reviewed before it's published, and often there is an internal review process, as well. At many companies, many people's eyes see a statement before it is posted.

After something has been put online, has there been a reaction to it? Can you find that reaction? In traditional newspapers, they print corrections if there were fact errors, but few newspapers even have correction policies when it comes to what is put material up on a web site.

When evaluating how accurate and reliable a web page is, there are several aspects to consider — credibility, authority and timeliness as well as coverage and objectivity.

Credibility

Good data can be verified; suspect data can't.

There are no sure-fire indicators of reliability, but the nature of the information sources can provide a good initial hint. If the data comes from a traditionally reliable outlet, such as a well-known publisher or research center, chances are better that the report is credible than if that same data is cited in a web site of unknown origin. Here are some questions to consider:

♦ What can you tell from the web site about its accuracy and credibility? Are there footnotes, cited references or just bold unattributed or unverifiable statements?

♦ Are there spelling errors and grammatical mistakes? An absence of proofreading can be a tip-off. At the very least, it indicates inattention to detail that might carry over to the information itself.

♦ Why is this information being provided? Is the reason clear? Is the reason likely to be correct? If not, the web site author's motivation bears further checking.

Verify web site authorship before using information from that site. A web site's main page — also called its home page — should identify its author/compiler. You can find a main page quickly by deleting parts of the URL, starting from the right and working your way toward the left. A tilde ~ sign embedded in an address usually signifies a personal home page. Try to verify the information elsewhere before assuming it's authoritative.

If you want to determine the credibility of something that's published, try *Ulrich's International Periodical Directory* available on DIALOG. *Gale's Directories*, similar to Ultrich's, are also online (www.gale.com). Both are gated web sites that charge for service. You can always call a nearby library and check the print versions of these books.

Authority

Know where a web site's content originates. It can be difficult to identify the author of a web page and the author's qualifications. If there is no contact person, no credit taken for the web site, don't trust it. If someone won't stand behind their work or at least provide their name, be wary.

Is the information itself *authoritative*? Trust is critical. For example, if you found these on the Internet, which would you trust more: a statement from John Smith, an employee of Cedar Hospital *or* a statement from Cedar Hospital itself?

Most people would agree that Cedar Hospital is far more trustworthy than John Smith, provided, of course, that the statement was in fact issued by the hospital.

If a company or organization is willing to put its reputation on the line, online, it should give the site's statements more credibility.

Another trick is to go with a known brand. If you regularly read *The New York Times* and count on its high standards of accuracy and credibility, its web site will likely hold to the same standard.

Use trustworthy organizations as guides to credible web sites. For example, government agencies, trade groups and professional associations and major universities all have web sites with credible links and references. So do reference tools like the Encyclopedia of Associations available on services such as **Silver Platter** (www.silverplatter.com) and the American Society of Association Executives (www.asae.org). Once you've identified the name of an authoritative source, use search tools to find their actual web sites.

Double-checking domain names via web and Internet sources is also a valuable verification tool. If a document is supposed to be from a university but the domain name doesn't end in .edu, it may not be legitimate.

Commercial online sources routinely compile source data and publications. Some fee-based companies compile several pieces of information – like phone numbers from phone companies, change of address forms and voter registration databases — into a single report. They may not identify the source of each item, but they will always tell you their sources, for instance, "state DMV records" as their source of driving records. But there are some databases that don't tell you directly where they get their information.

How much of an "authority" do you need? First figure out what you are going to use the information for. If you are taking something to court, you need a higher level of credibility than if you are just settling a bet. If it reads whitehouse.net and claims to be the official White House government site, be wary, because the official site's address should end in .gov.

Verify domain names! If a document is supposed to be from a university but its source web site's URL doesn't end in .edu, **then something just isn't right.**

Check the URL! Companies that are serious about establishing their presence on the Internet will buy a domain name that includes their company name in the address or a URL that includes a word that relates to their products or services. For example, www.XYZ.com **if the company's name is XYZ, or** www.translation.com **if XYZ specializes in foreign language translations.**

How to Use InterNIC/ICANN to Trace Web Authorship

Every time someone gets a web page, to secure their domain name or the first part of an Internet address, they must pay $150.00 to a federal government contractor InterNIC, which registers all sites. **InterNIC's whois** is a searchable list of anyone that has registered a domain name. While not foolproof, it often provides the real address, phone number, e-mail information and contact person for each web site. Submit a domain name in the search blank, and see what information comes up. The answers come directly from the registrants, so it may be outdated or incorrect.

Normally, there are two ways to find out who is responsible such a web page:

1. Contact the Source

Often there is an e-mail address, and you can write the person and ask for their credentials and information sources. Good content providers give you enough information to judge their authority.

2. Contact the Domain Registry

The domain registry can be checked to see who is paying for a site to be on the Internet. To do that, you go to Network Solution's **InterNIC**, http://rs.internic.net, which regulates the registration of domain names. As of January 2000, a new non-profit corporation (known as ICANN) takes over responsibility for managing domain names, and the web address will be www.icann.net. Also, another way to get at the same information is through **Inet's whois page** at www.inet.net/cgi-bin/whoisgw.

For example, when news of the Heaven's Gate mass suicide broke in 1997, Margot Williams, a researcher at *The Washington Post*, quickly went to InterNIC to find out who had registered the cults' Higher Source web site. Further checking revealed that the names probably were faked and the telephone numbers rang to pay phones. If you looked now, you may find an entry created after the event that lists David Koresh, Jim Jones and Jack Kevorkian as contacts.

Also on the InterNIC site is the **WebFinder Search Form** which allows you to locate web pages associated with organizations from a database of almost two million entries. Enter the word "university" and the clue "California" and you will get a list of university sites in that state with clickable links.

InterNIC also has a **DNS Lookup** on its site. This is how you translate a URL into its actual Internet Protocol address which is a series of numbers. The IP address of the web site www.deadlineonline.com, for example, is "38.8.94.2."

If your provider's DNS server isn't working, or if the URL isn't in there yet, you'll see an error message like "failed DNS lookup." If you type in the IP address instead, you will get into the site – unless some other problem caused the error.

You can use the DNS lookup to final URL's valid IP address and do the reverse to find the web address from a mysterious series of numbers.

InterNIC in Action

Not long ago, a wonderfully offbeat creative site showed up on the Internet. www.fractalcow.com/Bert. The site is now down but it has been mirrored, and you can connect to the mirrored versions from the original address.

Called Bert is Evil, it was a wickedly funny parody of Bert, the puppet character from *Sesame Street*. Its considerations of why Bert went bad included:

♦ E-mail relationship with mass murderer, Jeffrey Dahmer.

♦ Participation in a lost Pamela Anderson video excerpt.

♦ His involvement in the JFK assassination.

♦ An appearance on *The Jerry Springer Show*.

♦ His secret connection to O. J. Simpson.

The site included photos of Bert in many compromising situations. The page contained no mention whatsoever of who put it up or why.

To find its creator, we looked up the URL — fractalcow.com. It belonged to a Dino Ignacio who has an address, phone number and e-mail address in the Philippines. A 22-year-old graphic designer, he had built the web page for fun — and to promote his struggling graphics-design firm.

Finding Experts Online

by Kitty Bennett

Kitty Bennett is a news researcher for the *St. Petersburg Times*.

In my work as a news researcher for a daily newspaper, I'm requested to help unearth reputable, quotable experts for reporters in a very short amount of time. But journalists aren't the only ones with a need for experts — attorneys, writers, conference planners, medical researchers, engineers and businesspeople are also constantly on the prowl.

None of us has time to waste on "authorities" with questionable credentials, so what follows are some suggestions for finding experts and verifying their qualifications. While the ideal scenario would be to have Internet capability in addition to access to commercial online sources of information such as LEXIS-NEXIS and print resources such as *Who's Who*, in reality, the Internet may be the only tool available. Fortunately, much can be accomplished with a browser and a willingness to approach information sources with a fresh and innovative eye.

Here are some suggestions for getting started:

Check Directories of Experts Published Online by Universities, Think Tanks & Government Agencies

These are typically found in a section of an organization's web site that is produced by the public affairs office. Authorities are usually searchable by their subject expertise, and listings may include photos, e-mail addresses and home phone numbers. One of the best examples of this kind of directory is produced by the Wharton School of the University of Pennsylvania (www.wharton.upenn.edu/wharton/fac_resc.html). For other such sites, see my "Sources and Experts" page at http://sunsite.unc.edu/slanews/internet/experts.html.

Think Creatively: Repositories of experts come in many different forms

When you're looking for experts, **Amazon.com** (www.amazon.com) isn't just a place to buy books. It's a database of more than a million experts, otherwise known as authors. Using Amazon's very sophisticated "Power Search" option, accessed by clicking Book Search on the opening screen, I recently found a forensic psychologist and author of a book called *Kids Who Kill* for a reporter who needed an expert to interview about a rash of school shootings. *The New York Times* Book Review (www.nytimes.com/books) is not only a great place to check an author's credibility, but also a good place to search for experts. A periodicals directory such as **Mediafinder** (www.mediafinder.com), can also serve as a database of nearly 100,000 magazine editors, who are often authorities in their fields.

Search in Newsgroup & Listserv Postings — But Be Cautious

Newsgroups and listservs are usually unmoderated, and searching through them can swallow huge chunks of your valuable time. It's tedious to wade through irrelevant and trivial postings, and gauging credentials can be a dicey process. **Deja News** (www.dejanews.com) is by far the best place to search for newsgroup postings. Learn how to search its database by printing out its "Search Language Help" page (www.dejanews.com/help/help_lang.shtml) and placing it at your side so you can construct more advanced queries.

A good strategy is to search in particular hierarchies, or types, of newsgroups (see "A Newsgroup Primer" in Chapter 4). For example, if looking for experts on turtles, you might try searching like this: "expert ^10 turtles and ~g sci*," which means you're looking for the word "expert" within ten words of "turtle," and you only want to search in the "sci" hierarchy. The "~g" is Deja News shorthand for "newsgroup."

The caret (^) means "near." In this case, I used the number "10" because I wanted the two search words to be within ten words of each other. If I hadn't specified the number "10," the query would have defaulted to "5" – meaning that Deja News would search and deliver newsgroup postings in which the two keywords were within five words of each other.

There are far fewer options for searching Listservs. **Reference.Com** (www.reference.com) is currently the best alternative, but even it has fewer than 10% of the estimated total number of Listserv postings. Unless it's vital that you keep your search project a secret, you can also poll Newsgroup and Listserv members for their recommendations on experts.

Use Search Engines that Help You Focus on Particular Topics

Always use more than one search engine because each contains a unique database of records. **AltaVista** (www.altavista.com) supports proximity searching, truncation and all sorts of sophisticated options that make it ideal for finding experts. You can do seemingly complicated but effective searches, like this: "(expert or author* or research* or professor) near astron* and (url:mit or url:princeton or url:stanford)." This search statement means you're looking for any one of several words that are synonyms for expert, like "author" or "authority" or "researcher," "near" (within ten words of) variations of the word "astron," like "astronomy" or "astronomical." The term "url:mit" means you're looking for a URL address containing the acronym "MIT." I typed "mit" in lower case, following AltaVista's directions to use lower case when submitting search terms.

If you did this search, you would find, among others, the faculty members of the Department of Astrophysical Sciences at Princeton University and of the Stanford Solar Center. From there you would be able to read descriptions their research.

While it's an excellent search engine, HotBot can't handle truncation, which means you'd have to type in all the possible variations of words you're looking for. Still, you can't ignore HotBot because its database is huge. Some search engines that might help you focus on particular topics include **Beaucoup!** (www.beaucoup.com), **Search.com** (www.search.com) and **The Mining Company** (www.miningco.com). The Mining Co. offers 500 interest areas about everything from the aviation industry to 'zines, all moderated by guides who are themselves experts.

Check Your Expert's Credentials & Credibility

If you found him or her at a reputable institution, you're on pretty firm ground. Somebody else checked them out before the organization hired them. See if your expert has been quoted in respectable publications, but don't use that as the sole criterion. Many publications have free searchable online archives that can be accessed via their web sites or through a compilation web site (see the meta-tools section of Chapter 4 and News Resources Chapter 8). For example, the News Division of the Special Libraries Association maintains a good publications guide (sunsite.unc.edu/slanews/internet/archives.html). You can also run your expert's name through a couple of search engines. **Northern Light** (www.northernlight.com) is a particularly good search engine in general, and it offers a "special collection" of thousands of journals, books and magazines. All abstracts in this collection are free and may give you a good sense of your expert's renown or lack thereof. Don't forget to check your expert in **Deja News**.

Be aware that some Directories of "Experts" are run by Businesses that Charge a Fee for a Listing

These companies may do little or nothing to verify credentials. For example, recently I checked out the qualifications of an "expert" on aging issues listed on a site that specializes in providing guests for talk shows. The price for a listing here starts at $199. This alleged expert claimed many qualifications, few of which could be verified. Among other things, he claimed to be a "senior associate" of a particular think tank.

It was a simple matter to go to the organization's web site and determine that the sole criterion for becoming a senior associate there was an annual donation of between $250 and $5,000. According to the person's biographical information, he held a Ph.D. in Psychology, so I looked for his dissertation in **Dissertation Abstracts Online**, which is available through DIALOG and many other services. I found none. However, when I checked with the university listed on his resume, the school did confirm that he had indeed been awarded a Ph.D.

CompuServe's Knowledge Index is a great place to background someone who claims academic credentials. In this particular case, I checked for mentions of his name in Knowledge Index's Life Sciences Collection, Current Biotechnology Abstracts, ERIC, Academic Index, Medline (from 1966-present), PsycINFO, Mental Health Abstracts, Sociological Abstracts and Ageline. These are indexes to mostly scholarly journals, dating back as far as the late 1960s. In Knowledge Index, which costs $21.00 an hour, I was able to search these databases in about five minutes, so the total search amounted to less than $2.00 It's accessible only after 6 PM EST and on weekends, but it's far cheaper than, say, DIALOG even though it uses DIALOG's information. Although this expert had claimed to have "authored a number of scientific papers" in his web site biography, I found nothing that he had written and no references to him in anyone else's work.

By then, I had serious questions about this man's lack of substantial credentials. Still, since he made mention of a book he had written, I wanted to verify that it appeared in *Books in Print* (BIP), which is accessible through many online venues as well as through your local library. He was indeed the author of the book, but I discovered that he also owned the publishing company that had published it.

💻   💻   💻

▬▬▬ Timeliness

How can you tell when a web page was last updated? The date can be anywhere on the page.

If there is none, Netscape Navigator's View menu will list an option called "Document Information" or something similar. Look for a date in the Last Modified field. About half of the time, it will read "unknown," and in some cases, the Last Modified date will be more current than the date listed on the web page, because the author failed to update the date reference on the page itself. But when it works, it's a good way to check timeliness.

AltaVista's **Range of Dates** feature (available on its advanced search page) can check dates without your having to visit the actual site.

InterNIC's Whois will tell you when the page was posted and/or last updated.

The web archives of most reputable periodicals will carefully note the coverage dates of the articles within the archives. This goes for both free and commercial database holdings.

Coverage & Objectivity

Veteran journalist David Brinkley once said that objectivity is not the determining criteria for journalism, fairness is. Being as fair as you can be should hold for web pages as well.

> **EXAMPLE**: if you see an article titled "Should you buy or lease your car?" find out who is writing the piece, and think about what they have to gain by convincing you. If it is written by an auto-leasing firm, you should be skeptical, but if it is written by the non-profit consumer organization *Consumer Reports*, which doesn't accept corporate advertising, it would have a little more legitimacy. It's always a judgment call.

In the wild, wild West of the Internet, the masking of biased information as objective data is a more common phenomenon than you might think.

Eyeball the entire web site to assess the breadth and depth of its coverage. Look for what it's *not* telling you, especially when it takes a position or editorializes. For example, some political advocacy pages neglect to mention their organizational sponsor(s).

Ask yourself *why* the information is being published.

Watch for these telltale clues, which should raise doubts as to a site's objectivity:

♦ sweeping statements like "most important, unquestionably the best"

♦ over-claims like "millions are being killed every minute"

♦ harsh language like "the shrill cries of my extremist opponents"

Over time you'll develop an instinct for statements that make you question the credibility of the entire site. Don Ray calls them JDLRs — Just Doesn't Look Rights.

Because web sites change without warning, if you think you'll need proof that information existed on a certain date, download, print or save a copy of the source so that a record is preserved of your visit and your findings.

Stephen Miller of the *New York Times* developed a ranking scale for journalists to use when assessing the credibility of a site. He suggests that, in general, government sources should be trusted more than other sources, with federal government resources being rated a little higher than state and local governments.

Next on his trust meter are university studies, because nearly all of them are peer-reviewed and many have footnotes attached detailing bibliographic information. Special interest groups appear next on Miller's list. He notes that they publish lots of data, and even if they have a political agenda, it doesn't mean that their data is flawed.

Finally, Miller suggests that all others, including personal home pages, are a toss-up in terms of validity. The saving grace of personal home pages is that there is usually some information about the owner and a way of contacting them, which allows for further research.

Regardless, you can always report something you've found on the Web, and accompany it with a citation as to where you found the information.

Evaluating Web Site Information

Here are several good sites for helping you better evaluate web site information:

Evaluating Quality on the 'Net
www.tiac.net/users/hope/findqual.html

Babson College Library Director Hope Tillman has posted her thoughts on information assessment. This site offers a good overview.

Evaluating Web Information
http://thorplus.lib.purdue.edu/research/classes/gs175/3gs
175/evaluation.html

Purdue University has a solid step-by-step guide to evaluating the quality of information on the Web.

Evaluating Web Resources
www.science.widener.edu/~withers/webeval.htm

This is a practical tutorial from reference librarians at Widener University that indexes lists of questions and criteria to apply when evaluating sites.

Evaluating Information Found on the 'Net
http://milton.mse.jhu.edu:8001/research/education/net.html

A good resource from the Johns Hopkins University Eisenhower Library.

Thinking Critically about Web Information
www.ala.org/rusa/mars/ets98.html

This site represents the American Library Association Training session on web thinking skills.

The Quick Link Credibility Test

You can judge a site by the company it keeps. AltaVista's Link feature to do a quick and fairly reliable credibility test. In Chapter 9, Jennifer Kaplan describes a way to use the Link feature for free competitive intelligence research; the same principle applies to credibility research as well.

> **EXAMPLE 1:** Visit Catalaw (www.CataLaw.com), self-described as the "Internet's Grand Central Legal Station" and "the catalog of catalogs of law on the 'Net." Go to AltaVista at www.altavista.com and type the following: link:catalaw.com. A list will appear of more than two-hundred sites that link to Catalaw. That means that 200+ other sites think Catalaw is credible enough to link to their web sites. Browse the sites. Notice that most are law schools, universities, libraries and other institutions — a good indication of credibility.

Let's try it again:

> **EXAMPLE 2:** Say you're researching extra-terrestrial visits to earth, and you find the site www.saucers.com. On AltaVista, type the following: link:saucers.com. A list of links appears, including a web site called the "Fringe Page." Jump to that web site and you'll notice references to a Dr. Saucer, who is "not, technically speaking, a real medical doctor, psychologist or even a dentist. In fact, he lacks a college degree of any kind but he does have enormous insight into the study of saucers. .The site says that "Dr. Saucer is an experienced potter and designer of fine porcelain vases, pots, plates and, yes, saucers." The lesson? Be aware that the credibility of the site is questionable. Satire pages and parodies abound on the Web.

Useful Evaluative Tools

Many search tools – especially portals – have begun to review web sites, treating them as restaurants, destinations and the like.

Argus Clearinghouse

www.clearinghouse.net

This site, affiliated with the University of Michigan, rates sites on a scale of 1 to 5. An e-mail address is furnished for the evaluator. If contacted, the page's reviewer will usually respond.

Lycos Top 5% Reviews

www.lycos.com

Lycos says it has the largest and best collection of site reviews. It gives three evaluations: a content review, a design review and an overall review, all of which are rated 1 to 100. However, it gives no indication as to how or why sites reviewed are chosen.

Excite

www.excite.com

Excite offers its own series of review sites that are subjective but seem reliable. Select a subject, then look for the Our Top Picks link. You can find Excite's reviews on Magellan as well.

HotBot

www.hotbot.com

Direct Hit is a software company that ranks sites based on how often they are visited. HotBot has a "Ten Most Requested List" (generated by Direct Hit), which is helpful when trying to find similar sites.

Mining Company

www.miningcompany.com

This site has more than 500 different subject areas, maintained by a human. Essays are posted on key subjects. It also features bulletin boards, chat groups on many subjects, and you can even subscribe to newsletters. While the quality level of the subjects varies, when it is good, it is very good. The Mining Company is a solid starting point.

Yahoo!

www.yahoo.com

Yahoo! has a whole series of evaluation tools on its web site. Yahoo! is able to find large numbers of sites, but its recommendations are weak. Yahooligans for Children, which is a subject directory that has been screened for children, does a good job.

Accuracy: A Pop Quiz

See if you can figure out which one of the following addresses is the real page and which are parodies of America Online.

www.aol.com

http://www.bobsfridge.com/aologon.htm

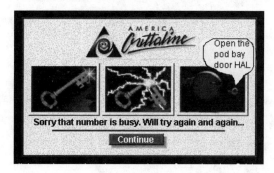

and

♦ http://members.aol.com/elmothecow/aoh/index.html

Be wary of fake web sites, or sites that appear to be legitimate. They may be a parody, or worse, a deliberate attempt to mislead you away from the information and message of the true site.

Chapter 12

Sample Searches

Okay, ready to rumble? It's time to see if you are ready for some creative searching. Here's where you can see how you would solve a few search dilemmas.

A lot of times, you look for information, but don't know for certain whether it exists. In many cases, you have only a minimal knowledge of the subject you need to research, so the terminology you use when searching may not match the jargon of experts on the subject.

If you've read the book most of the way through, you are now armed with knowledge about all the tools you can use to search with, a framework for how to research and thousands of valuable research sites. Now it's time to put all the component pieces together. But, realize you can do these searches many different ways. The key is getting the quality answer you are looking for.

The three sample types of searches discussed here are all types of searches you may need or want to do on your own. They are:

- Backgrounding a person
- Finding information about a business
- Learning about a medical condition.

While you may never have to conduct these particular searches, the tools and techniques used along the way will help you if you want to research people, a business or health-related issues, and it will help you become more familiar with tools themselves and the techniques that work best for you.

Put yourself into "researcher mode," plan a strategy and then discover what you would do in each of these cases. Remember, there are no right or wrong answers, and most importantly, you should enjoy the process.

Sample Search 1: People Finder

The Assignment

You are a researcher who gets a call from some rabid baseball fans that are going to host a 40th reunion for the 1959 Los Angeles Dodgers team. Your clients have already located team members and its coaching staff that are still alive, but they are missing the batboy from that year. You are asked to help find him.

So What Do You Do?

The solution involves two tasks. First, you must figure out his name, then you must locate him.

Given this situation, going online *immediately* would not be the best way to begin. If you do, it would be a swing, miss and strike one.

It would be a long shot to find anything online from that distant year. You could check for some kind of Los Angeles Dodgers history page, which might give you some leads to follow, but finding any "good" leads is a "long ball play" at best.

Rather, start by *calling* the Dodgers organization. Ask its employees if they would be willing to tell you his name by viewing the annual photo of the team for 1959. Remember, you don't always find everything online, and sometimes it's still easier to call someone or pick up a book to get you started.

After a little while, they tell you his name is Arnold Tesh, and that his nickname was "Red." Red could be his hair color, which might help if you find a driver's license or a picture provided that his hair hasn't turned gray by now. Later you may find out about a rumor that says he was called "Red" because he was a Communist. "Red" would certainly be consistent with the slang of that era.

Can I Go Online Now?

Your instinct might be to go to a search engine and input "Dodgers." However, the result would be a wide range of links to pages that probably aren't specific enough to satisfy your search needs.

Getting hits on a search engine for "Arnold Tesh" would be relatively easy. However, finding connections between the names found and the 1959 Dodgers – which would be a grand slam – may be a daunting task.

A search on Northern Light for `batboy,Dodgers` returns 144 hits, including a link to a fascinating web page about an article in the *Brooklyn Eagle* newspaper. The Dodgers moved from Brooklyn, NY in 1958. The article, located at `www.bayou.com/~brooklyn/batboy.html`, relates the illustrious batboy career of Charlie Digiovanna, who was affectionately known as "the Brow" and was the batboy for the 1955 Dodgers season. At the very least, you've found someone worth trying to locate who might have information about other batboys. Put that on your "Follow Up Later" list.

Next, on the Excite search engine, you search for `batboy, dodgers` and get 18,945 results. The first few are about the Dodgers. But, sometimes you don't always get close to what you want: several references are found about a Japanese man who calls himself the "batboy." Another example was "Batboy sightings" at `http://walden.mo.net/~waxler/wanted.htm`. Another site says "Batboy News Articles. BATBOY CAPTURED!/BAT BOY THREAT IS REAL – IF HE RUNS OUT OF BUGS, HUMANS WILL BE NEXT!" You'll find the *Weekly World News* headline with photo of the "Batboy wanted by the FBI" at `http://kulpatron.com/bboy.htm`; another batboy site makes reference to his love of frozen pizza. These are not quite the baseball references you're looking for, but they're highly entertaining.

Another idea might be to check online phone books for all the "Arnold Tesh's" in America. Such a search might result in a great deal of people across the country, and you wouldn't know which one is *the* one.

Essentially, although the above mentioned results might be helpful, they are the result of *unfocused* research. Before you search *online*, get "focused" by assessing what you know and what you *need* to know. This is the key to your ultimate success!

That leads to the next search question: what other clues do we have to eliminate people, like middle name, or age or something unique.

Before Going Online – Q & A

The first thing you need is a clear question to help you figure out *precisely* what you are looking for. Then you need to determine if what you are looking for can be found online.

Before you spend hours searching for any tenuous connection between the Dodgers and batboys, you should ask yourself the questions suggested by Nora Paul in Chapter 2, Framing Your Questions and Determining Your Sources.

What follows some of these questions and possible answers as they relate to this sample search:

Who

Who is the research about . . . ?

Our subject is Arnold Tesh, a Dodger batboy in 1959.

Who is key to the topic you are researching? Are there any recognized experts or spokespersons you should know about?

Experts and other people who might know of Tesh include baseball aficionados, memorabilia collectors and former sports reporters. It is also worth determining if there is a batboy association of some sort.

Books about "the end" of the Dodgers in Brooklyn or the Dodgers' move to Los Angeles might also be worthwhile sources.

Who has the data I need? Does the database I'm considering include information from the time period I want?

There probably isn't a database of batboy statistics. Imagine it – statistics like "best handshake at home plate" or "fastest bat retrieval."

However, news databases may contain a mention. Likewise public records databases are likely sources of information about Arnold, the man, rather than Arnold, the batboy.

What

What are you trying to do . . . ?

You are trying to find someone specific – Arnold Tesh.

What type of information will be useful: full-text articles or reports, specific facts, referrals to a person, public records?

Any of the above will suffice, provided that the materials can lead to Arnold Tesh. Essentially, you need as many good background leads as you can find.

What would be the best source of the information . . . ?

♦ Tesh's home page noting that he was once a batboy for the Dodgers.

♦ An article on "Where They Are Now," with leads.

♦ A batboy association.

♦ An article with a bio.

♦ California driver's license records 1959 to 1965 or so.

♦ Players from the 1959 Dodgers, or Dodgers 1959 employment records.

♦ A definitive history of the Dodgers with current contact names and addresses.

What information do you already have? What do you already know about the topic or person?

You know his name. Also, you can assume that Tesh was a teenager in 1959, and that if he's alive, he would be between fifty-five and sixty years-old.

Age is especially important because it is one of the few unique identifying features you have to distinguish him from anyone else named Arnold Tesh, aside from "Red," and you still aren't sure what that means.

Later, you should check the Social Security Death Index at www.ancestry.com to make sure Tesh is still alive.

What would the ideal answer look like?

Ideally, you would find "The Arnold Tesh Home Page," complete with a bio, photo, current address and phone number as well as a photo of him with the Dodgers.

When

When did the event being researched take place?

1959 is the last date associated with Tesh by your clients. Nothing was online in 1959 and, as such, very little may be online for that year now. With that in mind, the use of information-rich archives from fee-based services may be necessary.

When will you know you should stop searching?

When you find him, and you can be sure you have the right guy.

Where

Where is the biggest collection of the type of information you're looking for likely to be . . . ?

It's not exactly clear. A baseball historical group would be good. Someone at the Baseball Hall of Fame might have a Dodgers program from that year. However, a paper program would probably only reveal his name – a piece of information you already have courtesy of the phone call to the Dodgers.

Where did the person you're backgrounding come from?

Your clients informed you that Tesh lived in California back in 1959. Although it's unlikely, he could have moved to California along with the Brooklyn Dodgers when they relocated in the late 1950s. For all you know, he could be from New York originally.

Later, when you've narrowed down the list of "Arnold Tesh's," you could check "past addresses" using a fee-based tool. Using that information, you could try talking with neighbors. But remember, this is forty year old information; this could be a time-consuming task.

If time is not a critical factor, you could search Usenet newsgroups for baseball card collectors, Dodger fan discussion groups, etc. By doing so, you might find someone who knows something. From there, you could send out some e-mails and then see what happens.

Where might there have been previous coverage: newspapers, broadcasts, trade publications, court proceedings, discussions?

A good library might have old *Los Angeles Times* newspapers on microfilm, but you have to consider the effort involved when going in-person and viewing reel after reel of microfilm. Maybe the Dodgers organization has more information; they got you his name pretty easily — maybe they have a photo?

This is a case where you want to look where the light is best. If you lose your keys in the parking lot, and there is a light source nearby, you first check under the light source before you start groping around on the ground in the dark.

How

How much information do you need . . . ?

You just need the answer or information that will lead you to the target.

Information enough that lets you talk to Arnold Tesh.

How far back do you need to research . . . ?

Anything from 1959 to the present may be useful.

People Finder Search Plan

Okay, you get the idea about the importance of properly "framing" your query.

You have thought through what you want and how you might get it. You have considered many options, including whether to contact all the Arnold Tesh's in America, go to the Dodgers home page, contact baseball memorabilia collectors. You realize that the best way to go - after a quick few checks just to see what's there for free on the Internet - is to find all the Arnold Tesh's and see if you can find someone who might fit the right age range. Lucky for us, his name isn't as common as John Smith.

Realize that you are not limited to searching online. Contacting baseball experts and lifelong Dodger fans might be *the* most productive option. However, among your online resources are **Public Record Providers.**

In this case, there are several public record providers that would be useful. Merlin, a west-coast-based search company, is *regionally* focused and terrific for California. KnowX is a *national* public records vendor, and LEXIS-NEXIS has some public records, but more importantly, they have extensive news clippings files. You will definitely want to spend some time rummaging through news clips to distinguish one Arnold Tesh from another.

The other key factor is time versus money. First, let's see what you can do for free or inexpensively.

You need to consider the Andy Warhol principle as it applies to searching. Warhol once said that everyone will be world-famous for fifteen minutes. In other words, you need to figure out if the person you are looking for is a celebrity of some sort.

As a batboy, Tesh was on "the edge of celebrity" in the sense that he was surrounded by those who had achieved fame. In fact, his glory might not have been as a batboy. He could been famous for his other accomplishments. Essentially, it's worth checking him out on the Web using a few search engines.

One option is to submit his name in double quotes (" ")to a search engine and see if you obtain any hits. Another initial search to do is to see if there is a picture of the 1959 Dodgers team online.

When searching, keep a notepad next to your computer. Make a running list of the URLs you've visited, and what links you should check out later. Sometimes, at the end of a search, researchers realize that they were only a few keystrokes away from the information they needed. Keeping track of things to follow up on can prevent that crucial lead from getting lost.

So, you can begin by using a great search engine, Northern Light (www.northernlight.com)

A search for "Arnold Tesh" with his name in quotes gets seven hits.

Northern Light's **first hit** is www.cre.org/states/t_last.htm, which lists an Arnold Tesh as the new head of the Counselors of Real Estate. It also mentions that he is a partner in Tesh & Daly Advisors, LLC, based in Washington, DC and lists his phone number. It says that the company specializes in counseling for litigation, investments in commercial-industrial portfolios, health care facilities, railroad and public utility acquisitions. It says he also does litigation consulting/strategy and works as an expert witness.

Darn! Nothing about squeeze plays.

THE COUNSELORS OF REAL ESTATE

MEMBER SEARCH

SEARCH BY AREA

SEARCH BY NAME

SEARCH NEW
MEMBERS

RETURN TO INDEX

MEMBER SEARCH

Alphabetical Index of CRE Members T

Send email to change your information: cre@interaccess.com

TESH, ARNOLD, Tesh & Daly Advisors, LLC, Washington, DC

Telephone: (202) 785-0635

Specializes in counseling for litigation, investments in commercial-industrial portfolios, health care facilities, railroad and public utility acquisitions, studies for resort and mixed-use projects. Assignments are both international and domestic.

Litigation Consulting/Strategy, Eminent Domain, Expert Witness

Resorts, Railroads

TESSLER, MARTIN, Chase Manhattan Bank, New York, NY

If this is *the* Arnold Tesh for which you are searching, three possible leads are gained from this information.

- ◆ His company is a limited liability corporation, which means there are papers filed that might provide more detail on the company.

- ◆ As a counselor for litigation, chances are he is a lawyer.

- ◆ As an expert witness, his conference presentations may be posted online.

Northern Light's **second hit** is at www.flrrt.com/results/law9810.txt, which contains the results of the Lawyers Have Heart running race. It says that Arnold Tesh of Washington, DC finished 122nd overall. The site also says that he was second in the 55-59 age group, and he is 56 years old.

121	2	MARY CATH MALIN	39	F	ARLINGTON	VA	43:26	7:00
122	2	ARNOLD TESH	56	M	WASHINGTON	DC	43:30	7:01
123	4	LY PHAM	33	F	ALEXANDRIA	VA	43:32	7:01
124	3	JEFFREY ZAHLER	14	M	BETHESDA	MD	43:33	7:01
125	17	BENJAMIN LIEBER	29	M	WASHINGTON	DC	43:33	7:01
126	5	AMY JONES	31	F	HEATHSVILLE	VA	43:35	7:02
127	40	TOM GILES	33	M	CHEVY CHASE	MD	43:45	7:03
128	41	NICK PURINTON	34	M	WASHINGTON	DC	43:45	7:03
129	16	WILLIAM KISSINGER	37	M	WASHINGTON	DC	43:50	7:04
130	42	ROGER SHERMAN	32	M	WASHINGTON	DC	43:50	7:04
131	17	FRED WHITE	38	M	WALDORF	MD	43:52	7:05

This is an important finding because *this* Arnold Tesh fits the predicted age range. This could be your guy.

Also, having once been a batboy, the Arnold Tesh for which you are searching was, at least for a part of his life, interested in sports. The fact that this site mentions an athletic achievement could be a good sign. Maybe it is wishful thinking, but this Arnold Tesh's involvement in sports is certainly more encouraging than if the site mentioned that he was a chess champion.

The **third hit**, located on the same site as the previous one, is yet another road race. The site places him 759th at 1:11:53 for 10 miles, which is really very good for someone his age. It also says he is from Vienna, VA, a bedroom community of Washington. The fact that these two hits mention that this Tesh is from Washington, DC suggests that the Arnold Tesh in all three of these hits is indeed the same person. We also find a few more running race results with an Arnold Tesh. Whether *this* Arnold Tesh is the one for which you are searching still remains to be seen.

Northern Light's **sixth hit** is www.indigomagick.com, a web site for a company owned by Suzanne Snell Tesh, a writer who lives in Bethesda, MD, and Bradley Tesh. On the web site is a genealogy page that includes the following entry:

Bryon Arnold TESH	Rebecca MATLOCK
b. 17 Oct 1951	b. 2 Feb 1952
d.	d.
bur.	bur.
occ.	occ.
edu.	edu.
rel.	rel.
res.	res.

All of the remaining hits from Northern Light pertain to running. The Arnold Tesh of Washington, DC is definitely a serious runner.

Going for the "long ball" play, you decide to try another search engine. In this case, you choose AltaVista (www.altavista.com).

At this point you have two options. We can look for an image, using AltaVista's excellent Image Search capability http://image.altavista.com/cgi-bin/avncgi, which you can find on the main AltaVista site. If you go that way, make sure to check photos, color and black and white images and realize that if you search for Dodgers, you will get hundreds of photos. If you search for batboy, you may get nothing you can use. Try "1959 LA Dodgers" but don't expect it to be fruitful. Try the same thing on HotBot (www.hotbot.com), which is also great for finding photos. Make sure to check the Image box on the search engine.

The second option is to look for stories and references to the LA Dodgers from that year. Just on an instinct — and to avoid getting many references to the current LA Dodgers team — try looking for the LA Dodgers home page and/or sites that focus on the Brooklyn Dodgers, where you might find loyal followers and, possibly, references to batboys.

You discover an excellent memorabilia site — www.brooklyn-dodgers.com. On that site, there are some wonderful items, including a video of the 1959 season when the Dodgers won the World Series (www.dodgers.com/1950.html). However, you are unable to find a team photo. After looking at the dodgers.com site, and knowing that you really need to link Tesh to the Dodgers, one option would be to write to the Dodger's webmaster and see if somewhere in the files there is a photo of the team. Dodgers' webmaster Ben Platt sends you the following photo, but of course you won't get it until tomorrow – too late for your search.

Since, at the moment, you are unable to easily find the photo online, the next thing to try would be news clips. While at the Dodgers' site, you may have noticed a place to look up old newspaper clips, plus there's an option to subscribe to a regular newsletter. A subscription might result in the names of people who might have the information you need.

AltaVista's remaining hits for "Dodgers" are fruitless. Therefore, you decide to search for "Arnold Tesh."

You discover three more hits pertaining to the Arnold Tesh of Washington, DC. In addition, there is a reference to an Arnold Tesh in the *Pacific Business News* (www.amcity.com/pacific/stories/081897/calendar.html), which says that Tesh was the keynote speaker at a conference of the National Association of Industrial and Office Properties, Hawaii Chapter's breakfast meeting. According to the site, Tesh was speaking about real estate investment trusts, which seems to be another link to the Arnold Tesh of Washington, DC.

At this point, you could use fee-based services to determine how many Arnold Tesh's exist, but you decide to try additional search engines since they are free.

This time you choose HotBot (www.hotbot.com). You submit Arnold Tesh *without* using quotation marks because HotBot does that automatically.

The first HotBot hit is for a JM Zell Partners site (www.jmzell.com/apprais.htm) announcing that they have built an alliance with the DC-based Arnold S. Tesh Advisors.

Once again the site seems to refer to the Arnold Tesh of Washington, DC. However, this particular site gives you a very valuable tidbit – his middle initial. It also may have a bio on him or include links to several of Tesh's potential clients.

The links page for this site — www.jmzell.com/links.htm — also has several industry sources for the real estate world, including:

www.inman.com

www.amrex.com

and, International Real Estate Digest
www.ired.com

These links are sources of information on people who work in real estate. They might be worth checking to find more information about the Arnold S. Tesh of Washington, DC. It may be worth checking the Securities and Exchange Commission to do a search on owners' and officers' names, after you check to see if he is an attorney.

In addition, the Zell site has an extensive client list and names four key players in the company. These people may have information about Tesh, but if Arnold S Tesh never mentioned or never had a past in baseball, contacting these people might be a waste of time even if you have the right person. The client list consists of hundreds of big-name companies, and it is still unclear what this particular Arnold Tesh does for them. Investigating this information could take hours, so, for now, it must be put on a back burner.

The next hit from HotBot is www.mrhat.simplenet.com/celeb101.htm and it is certainly one of the most intriguing. It lists the "101 People we'd like to see on *South Park* by everyone who submitted to our survey." *South Park* is a racy, no-holes-barred, satirical TV show on cable's Comedy Central. The names on the list include:

- Wayne Gretsky

- Dilbert

- Bill Murray

- Sean Connery

- William Shatner

- Dan Akroyd

- ♦ Tim Allen

- ♦ Gumby

So why is Arnold Tesh on this list? It is not likely that the authors of this web site are roasting *everyone* and have worked their way to the batboys of forty years ago.

The site probably has the names John Tesh and Arnold Schwarzenegger together or "in proximity," leading the search engine to find Tesh and Arnold next to or near each other, which results in this HotBot hit.

After a brush with *South Park*, you decide to try a *meta*-search tool. You choose Inference Find at www.infind.com. get lots of hits concerning John Tesh, Arnold Schwarzenegger and Saint Arnold Brewing, a beer company, but nothing new on the Arnold Tesh of Washington, DC or any Arnold Tesh for that matter.

Now you decide to check him out using two lawyer look-up tools on the Web. Both of these tools offer biographies of every lawyer who practices. You go to the Martindale-Hubbell Lawyer Locator site at www.martindale.com/maps/../locator/home.html, which may let you search, or you try the other lawyer site, Westlaw's West Legal Directory, located at www.wld.com/ldsearch.htm. To your surprise, you don't find anything. You thought that if the DC Arnold Tesh is advising lawyers on litigation strategy then he too might be a lawyer. Guess not.

He is either not a lawyer, or does not practice law.

Just to be thorough, you check www.ancestry.com to make sure Arnold Tesh is still alive. No matches. That means he is most likely still living.

Now you try the phone books. You do a quick search on InfoSpace.com (www.infospace.com) and find three Arnold Tesh's. One is in North Carolina. The other two are Arnold S. Tesh. One is in Santa Monica, CA and the other in Vienna, VA. The latter is clearly the real estate/runner guy.

InfoSpace.com gives you phone numbers, addresses, maps, directions and can even send your "hits" a gift, if you want to. You're really curious who the California guy is because you haven't stumbled across him before, and the North Carolina person intrigues you.

So you check a couple of more phone books. You use Who Where (www.whowhere.lycos.com) and AnyWho (www.anywho.com), but come up with much of the same information.

Finally, you try yet one more phone book, just to see what you can find. You find seven people listed under Arnold Tesh, plus more detail:

- ♦ The Virginia Tesh's companion's name is Adriana.

- ♦ The Arnold in North Carolina is also listed under the name Solomon Tesh.

- ♦ There is an e-mail address for the North Carolina Tesh.

- ♦ Four more A. Tesh's from around the country are included in the findings.

At this point, re-evaluate the search and the plan. Assuming your man has a listed phone number, you've narrowed it down to three people pretty quickly and have not spent a dime to get there. What's your gut instinct?

Try the telephone — and for a few dollars you can contact all three and ask if they were ever a Dodger batboy.

Or, taking another approach, you proceed to some of the fee-based online services. Since you're curious about the Arnold Tesh in Santa Monica, you try Merlin, the West Coast-based company that specializes in public records. You also try KnowX, a national web-based public records company. Both have a web presence.

Among the things you find are:

Arnold S. Tesh Advisors, the DC-guy's company, has a Los Angeles office and that means the Santa Monica guy and the DC guy are probably the same, or father and son. Since the DC guy was 56, he looks like your best shot. It also looks like he has done well for himself and moved up in the world since his batboy days.

You find he owns a house in Vienna, Virginia, had one in Hawaii as well as one in Arizona. It also tells you the value, size and details of each property.

Then you go on to LEXIS-NEXIS, and use **reQUESTer**, the company's web-based clipping service. You run several Arnold Tesh searches to see if you can connect him to baseball and any news events.

You find eight stories. Among them are:

- A 1994 *Baltimore Sun* piece saying Tesh had become the president of the Counselors of Real Estate, the professional consulting affiliate of the National Association of Realtors.

- Another piece from the same time period in which he was listed as that group's new Vice President.

- A 1994 Greensboro NC *News and Record* clipping. showing that a Solomon Arnold Tesh sold a house. Now you know there is a second Arnold to seriously consider, and you need to check further. You don't know if this is the right one, but you can't rule him out.

- Another clipping shows the DC Tesh is the "financier" behind an ambitious $1 billion Costa Rican building project linking a warehouse, pier, port, two harbors and a rail link that is schedule to open in 1997.

However, you still haven't found *anything* that links any of these Tesh's to baseball.

Sometimes it is easier to use a dialup service than the web. In researching on LEXIS-NEXIS, experienced hands are much more comfortable using the dial-up version than the web version. You can also do considerably more advanced searching on the non-web version, including detailed Boolean searching, truncation, using wildcard and other precision searching techniques. So, you move to the dial-up version of LEXIS-NEXIS and start in the All News category of the News Library. Again, you are spending money, so be efficient with your time.

You input: **los angeles OR la OR l.a. OR l a OR dodgers W/15 1959 OR tesh OR arnold W/25 batboy OR bat boy**

Okay, it takes a while to get a sophisticated, narrow search like the one above. However, with the techniques in this book, you'll figure it out pretty quick.

In English, that means Los Angeles or la or la or Dodgers within fifteen words of 1959 or Tesh or Arnold and also within twenty-five words of batboy or bat boy.

Unfortunately, there are no sources that identify Arnold Tesh as the batboy for the Los Angeles Dodgers in 1959. However, several documents identify *Rene Lachmann* as a batboy for the Los Angeles Dodgers in 1959. You theorize that there were several batboys that year and, maybe if you find Rene, he will know where Arnold is. At least it's another lead.

In the process of researching using other fee-based tools, you also find out that

♦ The DC Arnold Tesh has two daughters.

♦ His Social Security Number was issued in California between 1955 and 1956.

♦ He has a Pennsylvania appraiser's license.

♦ He has no liens, judgments or bankruptcies outstanding.

♦ He and his wife have or had another house in Beaufort County, South Carolina.

♦ He has a Virginia driver's license.

♦ No links to baseball. Now, it's definitely time to make phone calls.

Other things you might do under normal circumstances include thoroughly checking back in the *Los Angeles Times* to see if you could make a link to his baseball career. That might include sending e-mail to people you find on the newsgroup `alt.sports.baseball.la-dodgers`.

You could also check online biographies to see if he shows up in places like Marquis Who's Who (in DIALOG's pay service), as well as looking for collectors' associations and baseball groups to contact.

Postscript to the Tesh Search

I called Arnold Tesh at his Washington, DC office and can now fill in some of the hole's in the research. After getting permission to use his name for the book, he says that he went to Loyola Law School in Los Angeles, but didn't graduate, leaving instead for a job in the assessor's office. That led him to a real estate career. He does still have red hair. He was never a Communist. He has fond memories of the 1959 World Series Champion Dodgers team.

Rene Lachmann, by the way, was the batboy for the *1960* team, and ended up becoming a major league baseball manager.

Tesh said when he was a batboy, his photo was regularly in the *Los Angeles Times* and the old (now-defunct) *Herald-Examiner* because it was a custom back then for the batboy to be the first person to congratulate players when they hit home runs. His grand Costa Rican project took two years out of his life, but never materialized.

Sample Search 2: Business Profile

The Assignment:

A foreign-owned distributor of pet products is interested in buying half a million dollars worth of pet products from a company called Veterinarian's Best. They call you to "find out what you can" about the kinds of products the Veterinarian's Best company offers, the quality of their products, the company's track record, its stability and some background on the owners. The products, they tell you, are supposed to be all natural and designed by an actual veterinarian. You have only hours to provide a response.

Again, as with any search, start by "framing" your research — figuring out what exactly you're trying to find. Less time is no reason to try shortcuts.

One of the first critical questions is whether or not this company is publicly-held. As discussed in Chapter 9, if it is a public company, then you have a whole group of online resources to pull from, including government resources like the Securities and Exchange Commission, and then business-oriented web sites such as Hoover's, and others.

If Veterinarian's Best is a private company, the best places to start are the Secretary of State's office for the state where the company is located, and other public records vendors who would have some details on the company's track record. You'll check clippings to find out what's been written about the company. As you work through your framing the research checklist, there are several important things to consider.

♦ It is definitely worth checking to see if the company has a web site.

♦ Animal supply industry people, pet stores, magazines that cover those industries and analysts who follow the trends in those industries will be important contact points. So will veterinarians, groomers, pet activists, and of course, the company's competitors.

Always ask yourself the most important of the Nora Paul "framing" questions: if you could envision the perfect answer, what would it look like?

In this case it would be a research paper or an article detailing everything you ever wanted to know about Veterinarian's Best — a company history, details about product lines, its place in the marketplace. It is most important that this be from a credible independent business publication, research company or analyst.

Business Finder Search Plan

So, where to begin? All you have to start with is a name, a kind of product and that's about it. Here's are some thoughts:

Start on the Web just to see what can be found quickly. Later, move to fee-based tools, which are probably inevitable in this case.

If you're a subscriber, you would start out on the fee-based DIALOG because you can search by company name. Dialog has great indexes. You could do the same kind of research on LEXIS-NEXIS or Dow Jones Interactive. Go with DIALOG on this because it is easier to maneuver around in.

I do the DIALOG search before moving back to a free search engine because I know exactly what I need from DIALOG, and I can find it quickly before I start ringing up big charges. If I wasn't familiar with DIALOG or other of the fee-based services, then I would stick to the free services of the Web instead. But knowing how to maneuver DIALOG can save time and won't cost a fortune.

Once you're comfortable with your findings about the basics about the company, then you can look for lawsuits and any kind of negative input just to make certain that you're giving your client everything they may ask for when you make your report to them later.

Turning your attention to the free search tools on the Internet, try company finders to locate Veterinarian's Best and, of course, look for their web site.

The best researchers online always search using the rule of concentric circles. They start out by:

1) Looking at the company

2) Then find the key people in the company

3) Profile the key people

4) Do a layered search until they you start coming back on where they started.

That will ensure they don't miss too much.

Next, you will check for press releases involving Veterinarian's Best. You'll definitely need to look at public records, too. If you can find them, industry marketing reports on the pet food and pet supplies industry will be a great help. Also check the wire services to see how often and in what capacity news was written involving the company.

Remember, there are two kinds of data on any company:

♦ information a company wants you to find about them.

♦ information they don't.

Not being honest with stockholders can get you arrested, so public companies are pretty thorough in their reporting to the regulating agencies. That's one of the reasons the US government's SEC site is so valuable. Few companies want to face off with their regulator over inaccurate information.

Private companies are held to a much lower standard of openness. That makes the finding of information about them a much harder research effort. In this sample, I chose a private company intentionally. The reasoning is, if you can find information on a private company, researching a public one will be much easier.

On a hunch, start with www.veterinariansbest.com.

No luck. If they have a web site, this is not its URL.

Next, search the Internet to see if the company has a web presence. Several search engines bring up hits, but nothing that points to a specific web site for Veterinarian's Best company.

The web sites do show lots of companies that carry the Veterinarian's Best product line, which, you'll find, includes Vita-Derm Shampoo Conditioner Spray and HotSpot Spray, two of the companies products.

Once you find the names of some of their products, string together a search like: Veterinarian's Best, Vita Derm Shampoo and Hot Spot Spray. Just starting, try Dogpile, a good meta-search tool. Another option would be to go to a Yahoo kind of index or subject directory site. There you may find lists of pet product vendors. That will give a list of potential competitors.

By searching on Excite first, just to see what comes up, you'll find thousands and thousands of pet-related sites. Among these sites are several places that carry the Veterinarian's Best line, and several more that post photos of the entire line. But, none of these sites link directly to a web site for the company. Even though you may not be zeroing in on the company's web site, the mere fact that you're finding so many of its products out there is, in itself, valuable information to your client.

Faced with so many pet sites out there, you can turn to Northern Light because it puts sites into categories and subject folders in your initial search. Northern Light also has a collection of newspaper clips, so you may be able to do two things at once: narrow the search down, and begin a search for news articles about the company.

When you search Northern Light for "veterinarian's best," you quickly come up with several hits for a www.Vetsbest.com.

The following image is the main screen for www.vetsbest.com:

This company's web site is nicely designed and loaded with material about the company. Let's check some of the other sites first and come back to this in a moment.

At another site, you find that Veterinarian's Best has a Hypo-allergenic Shampoo, which comes in several sizes, also three sizes of conditioner, three sizes of Hot Spot Shampoo at $47.50 a gallon, and Top Coat, a combination shampoo and conditioner.

Along the way, you're learning a lot about their products.

♦ These are all-natural products designed to avoid drugs, alcohol, steroids, pesticides and chemicals. They are gentle for dogs with sensitive skin, and help provide relief from itching and scratching.

♦ The Hot Spot Shampoo is a natural medicated shampoo with tea tree oil, whatever that is.

♦ The medicated stuff is supposed to provide relief from itching and relieves "hot spots" and red, raw, inflamed skin.

This all comes from sites that sell their products — sites that are found by simply doing a "veterinarian's best" search on Northern Light. You may also find a People for the Ethical Treatment of Animals-related site that notes "The Santa Barbara-based Veterinarian's Best doesn't test its products on animals and their products are all vegan." At www.allforanimals.com/cruelfree1.htm you find *Veterinarian's Best, P.O. Box 4459, Santa Barbara, CA 93103 800-866-PETS.

Another site, www.petgroomer.com, which is a directory of veterinarian products, lists the company address as Veterinarian's Best, Inc., 712 E. Mason Street, Santa Barbara, California 93193, Telephone: 805-963-5609, Fax: 805-963-

2921. The "notes" include that they make kennel supplies and equipment, dog and cat products, veterinary products.

Look at their web site. The first thing to catch your attention is the little gray terrier frolicking around the web site in Java script. Nice touch.

In fact, this site is loaded with information about the company, including a history and profile. Of course, it's what they want us to know about them, but it says the company was founded by veterinarian Dr. Dawn Curie Thomas. It is a family-owned company with a full line of pet products including foods, dog cookies, flea and tick products, leashes, etc.

Their web site says the company owners are veterinarian Dawn Curie Thomas, DVM, (make a note to check the state agency for confirmation of her vets license) and her husband, William S. Thomas. He is former newspaper editor and professor of journalism. If time permits, you can check the online archives for stories he once wrote, although with a name like Thomas, finding him quickly may be a long shot.

"Veterinarian's Best, Inc., was," the site tells you, "founded in 1989 when Dr. Thomas developed several very popular and effective all-natural skin care products for her dermatology patients at the Southern California Veterinary Hospital & Animal Skin Clinic in Los Angeles." So, there is another company to check out.

"There was such a demand for the products," the site continues, "that Veterinarian's Best, Inc., was formed to manufacture and distribute the products worldwide."

Now you have lots of leads to check out.

With this information, move to the company finders. A list of these is found in the Company Directories section of Chapter 9. Assuming that Veterinarian's Best is a private company may be incorrect, so, it's worth always doing a quick check of public companies on the government's SEC sites. And, much of this same information can be accessed via three free web-based public business finders that do capsule profiles of every company they list.

The SEC `www.sec.gov/edgarhp.htm`

Hoover's Online `www.hoovers.com`

Company Link `www.companylink.com`

CompaniesOnline `www.companiesonline.com`

Checking these, you find nothing about Veterinarian's Best, so you can begin to assume that it is a private company. Finding news clippings about the company is becoming even more important.

The Veterinarian's Best web site told you they're a California company, so, with a location, it's time to check fee-based tools, which are categorized by state locations. Start with DIALOG Select at `www.dialogselect.com`, which is the lite version of the powerful DIALOG database. DIALOG Select is geared for web users who are not skilled in DIALOG command language.

By starting with a search of Business News — Company News — you find three stories that talk about new Veterinarian's Best products:

- February '97 piece about "Nature's Creation," new dog cookies

- June '92 story about Hot Spot, the anti-itch shampoo

- A similar story in the same issue about Vita-Derm food supplement.

These three stories all come from an industry newsletter called *Marketing Intelligence Service*. Put that on the list of people to contact later. The newsletter may have a reporter who covers the pet products industry who is worth getting some analysis from.

Next, run what is called a Duns profile. What you want is a profile of the Veterinarian's Best company put together from company information in the Dun and Bradstreet database. A Duns report on a company, which you could have run through Dun and Bradstreet on the Web — or through LEXIS-NEXIS, DIALOG, Dow Jones or others — finds the company's address, phone number, employees, sales growth percentage, net worth, type of business, sales (current and historical), date of incorporation and state, president, size of property, and whether the property is owned or rented.

A more detailed Duns report on Veterinarian's Best includes information on sales, worth, payment history, type of business, president (Dawn Curie Thomas), payment rating, payments by industry, assets, liabilities, ratio, working capital, other financial data, lien information, UCC filing information, when the business was started, whether there was a change of address, education and biographical information on Dr. Thomas, and information on a related company called Curie, Inc. Among the more interesting details, are:

- The company was incorporated in 1989

- Annual sales were $1.9 million in 1997, similar in 1996, $675,000 in 1994

- The company has five employees

- The company has grown 185 percent over the past five years and also has a net worth statement

- They have a 2,000 square-foot rented workspace, based in a single location

- They have over one hundred accounts

- They *do* export products overseas

So far, you're getting general information and, the business newsletter re-writes of Veterinarian's Best PR releases. Now you need some objective information. Staying in DIALOG, look for news clippings to see what's been written about the company. Let the search go as far back to 1988. This search finds a handful of articles. These include:

- A June 1990 *San Francisco Examiner* story about how Dr. Dawn Curie Thomas of Veterinarian's Best has set up a fund to help to the animals caught in wildfires.

- A *Los Angeles Daily News* piece from 1990 that shows Dawn as the owner and director of the Southern California Veterinary Hospital in Los Angeles.

♦   Three other news clips.

News about her involvement in a veterinary hospital is worth going into other business files and checking. You'll also want to check property records.

Another news clip says she is the author of a book called "Ask The Vet," from BookWord Press. If there's time, the book company would be worth finding and talking to see if they have her bio, book sales figures, etc.

You may also find an August 13, 1995 *Arizona Republic* newspaper story that talks about Dr. Dawn as "Dawn Curie Thomas, a former Valley resident, in town for the grand opening of a PetSmart store at Pima and Shea. Thomas, a veterinarian who went to school at Camelback High and Arizona State, will talk about a line of natural skin-care products for pets and will push her book, *The 100 Most Common Questions That Pet Owners Ask the Vet.*"

Yet another story is a column she wrote where she claims to be the owner of the Southern California Veterinary Hospital and Animal Skin Clinic in Woodland Hills, a Los Angeles suburb.

Now you have two more businesses to check out. Your best bet is to return to the fee-based service, which, by now, you're becoming very familiar with: DIALOG. Go back and check out her other businesses to confirm them, and, if you still have time, you can turn to public records and the California Secretary of State's office. Among the public records of the California veterinary agency, you may want to find her veterinary license. You may be able to do this with a phone call, or you can move to Merlin at www.merlindata.com since it is a California search firm. Merlin can help you find all kinds of public records on the company. These include a Uniform Commercial Code filing showing that Dawn and her husband secured a loan with Wells Fargo Bank in San Jose, plus another from the Bank of Montecito. You may find considerably more detail on the company, including that Bill is the chief executive officer and Dawn is the president. You may find her veterinary medicine license dating back to 1981, and still current.

The Merlin filings, some of which come from the California Secretary of State's office, also include articles of incorporation for the Veterinarian's Best company as well as addresses for the company, its warehouse, and also information on another company they run called Curie Inc.

Looking deeper, you also find family trust documents for the Thomas' as well as a court record index showing two lawsuits in civil court. If you had more time, you could check details on these.

Now, focus on learning more about Bill and Dawn, the people. For this, quickly, you can move to another fee-based search tool, DBT Autotrack, and find:

♦   Dawn was born in Arizona in 1948

♦   her Social Security Number

♦   her last four addresses

♦ property records, including the value of their residency as well as the value of the warehouse that they rent. This suggests that they are the owners and that they rent the facility to themselves, a smart tax move.

A search reveals the same kinds of information on Bill, also the names, ages and addresses of their children.

A couple of other pieces of information are quite interesting. While two lawsuits are found, you also find that she has no liens or judgments against her. Through public records you may also find that she has a Drug Enforcement Administration license to dispense certain kinds of drugs. This would make sense for a vet.

Next, run market analyst reports on their products and on the company, on tools like Investext and Dun and Bradstreet, then add those findings into your market reports about the pet supplies industry.

Among the other tools to use, given more time or instead of using the web to find much of this, you could have looked at the Marketing and Advertising Reference Service on DIALOG or the Publisher's, Distributors and Wholesalers Database. This would certainly have found some information about them and Veterinarian's Best. Additionally you could do some research on trademarks for their products, and might use the Web to look up some of their competitors to find some people to talk to who have opinions and perhaps some information not found on databases.

Now you are ready to produce a detailed report on the corporation, Veterinarian's Best. Some conclusions are:

♦ The people behind the company are upstanding community citizens.

♦ Veterinarian's Best is a solid company.

♦ Since everything checks out, you can recommend that your client go ahead with the purchases.

♦ You may wish to check into some of their products for your own cat and dog.

Postscript to the Veterinarian's Best Business Profile

When I talked to Bill Thomas and got his final okay to use Veterinarian's Best as a sample search, I asked him if anything was missed. As it turns out, had we gone further we might have found his erstwhile career as a political adviser to the UN Ambassador of Papau, New Guinea. It seems that Bill and a friend were asking directions to a hotel after a week out in the New Guinea jungle, when the person they asked the directions from volunteered to let them stay at his house.

Dinner was served, politics discussed, and in particular the conversation turned into a discussion of limited democracy and its potential. The next thing he knew, Bill was on a national radio program debating the merits of limited democracy.

You would have needed a few more minutes online to find that story.

▬ Sample 3: Problem Solving

For our third scenario, I'll walk you through what I would do as I search on one topic, and leave it to you to pick a second topic, and you can do the actual searching on it. This lets you pick a medical or health topic of interest to you, rather than mine. The concepts involved in both my searches are the same, so your search should produce results, and, those results should be of some help to you.

My Assignment

Let's say my father is diagnosed with a prostate problem and is deathly scared of having surgery. He asks us to research alternative forms of treatment to the knife. He's going to see his doctor tomorrow morning. Time is the most critical factor.

Your Assignment

Your father, too, is diagnosed with a serious medical problem. He is concerned about the treatment he may receive, and would like to know more about *all* the alternatives.

So What Do You Do?

In the previous two searches I talked about using online tools to find specific information. But many times, you have something vague and general. Keep in mind, the Internet is about communication and using many of the human resources online like discussion groups, e-mail, listservs and newsgroups. Among these we should find people who have had genuine experience with the same kind of medical conditions we are looking into.

These many online sources can help you find support groups, better doctors, and subject directory lists of inter-related web-sites — in addition to medical information and treatment prospects.

Online sources are also incredibly valuable in helping us figure out how to ask the right questions.

In this Sample Search, there is a pitfall. With every medical condition, there are frustrated consumers — loved ones who are often unsatisfied with the information they have. Often, the prognosis is not good. Many are willing to devote long hours to remedying the unfortunate situation, perhaps grasping for any shred of hope. Frustrated, "hurt" people are vulnerable to quackery. You must always be careful to ask ourselves who is behind a web site and why is it up there, with medical conditions especially, or anytime the stakes are high. Don't be led into doing the wrong things by the wrong advisors who might prey on our vulnerability.

Now, before we go further, this tip. If, at any time, you don't know much about a subject and are just foraging, it's suggested that you look at Barbara Quint's superb sidebar on page 239 where she talks about protecting yourself by checking and double checking online information. She speaks of how to deal with swimming in data, and the critical nature of it.

Can I Go Online Now?

Before we go online, let's plan your search.

Remember, while I'm researching alternatives to prostate surgery, you could be doing a similar search on your topic, perhaps diabetes, heart surgery or any other health or medical condition.

Let's think through the situation first. In a medical situation, the first key is to find out where good information can be found and to determine if you want or need to spend money for information.

There should be plenty of information for free, but if you want absolute credibility in our sources – and if it is your parent's life in the balance, you certainly do — a combination of fee-based and free resources is recommended.

In addition to finding the right focus for the search, you also need to figure out what keywords will help locate trustworthy, reliable documents. In this case, since you know little or nothing about the subject to start with, you'll need to do some preliminary searches to get familiar with the terminology in use.

Always ask yourself where the most reliable data would be found. In this case, the federal government should have some good information, but medical experts would be the first place to turn.

To get the right phrases and starting points, I turn to my medical expert of choice, Susan Detwiler and her wonderful compilation at www.detwiler.com.

Though this is getting ahead of ourselves and our search, a trip to her web site would be a good short-cut. She wrote the medical sidebar in Chapter 4, and her excellent web site has links to most of the really good medical sites online.

If you don't know much about a subject, find someone who does. When you find an authority — someone you trust or someone you think really knows what they are talking about — check to see if they have a list of favorite sites (and their links) before you turn to more general search tools.

For this sample search, rather than compiling a long list of good sites, let's try finding one good medical site with the proper name for the medical condition you're researching. We'll use that web site to locate "alternatives to surgery."

You need a site that "speaks the right language" and contains what you're looking for -- to find health information, preferably from the government. Put that all together in one URL: "healthfinder.gov."

You're in luck: Healthfinder at www.healthfinder.gov/default.htm is a federal government list of previewed consumer health information sites. Here I can search for the scientific words for enlarged prostate, and you can search for whatever disease you are researching.

After finding some of the keywords, including

- Prostatitis
- BPH/ Benign Prostatic Hyperplasia
- PSA/ Prostate Specific Antigen
- TURP, TUNA and TUMT

...the next thing is to think of all the terms we would expect to find in an ultimate results page. Make a list of them.

My list might include all the medical terms above as well as prostate, radiation, risk factors, symptoms, enlarged prostate, urinary, and also words like "alternate choice" or "alternative" or choice, blockage, diagnosis, and treatment.

Put several words in a search string, separated by commas and without quote marks, in a Search Field of a search engine. What comes back? Now, enter a somewhat different variation (add or subtract words) to the search string in the Search Field. What comes back? The results are different, but not *all* that different. Create another search string and see what sites the engine brings up again. Expert searchers use the list concept because if several of the search strings result in the same hits over and over, the search engines will rank those sites higher This helps identify the top few sites.

Switching search engines lets you see what else there is to find on a particular topic.

One of the reasons to do this is to get the medical name or names for the condition you are trying to find out about. One warning about your medical list is necessary: you might want to specify "human being conditions" because an animal might have the same condition (in our sample, a cat certainly could) and you might find a ton of veterinary sites.

When searching, you have to get into the right language to find what you're specifically looking for. For example, the dictionary of searchable sports terms is different from the terms in medicine. Further, the dictionary of terms for the sport of bowling are different from that of football. If you are trying to find out the best bowling score and you keyed in the phrase "highest points," you'd probably end up with the Bowling Green football score. Bowlers count pins, not points, so, for bowling scores, include the term "pins."

Knowing the differences between domain names, like .com, .org, .gov. and .edu, can make all the difference in the world when judging a site's credibility. .com sites are commercial vendors whose only goal may be to sell us products. .org sites may also be dependent on you for financial support, or they may be advocating something. .gov sites may be accurate, but they may not offer information about "alternatives."

Knowing the terminology also makes all the difference in successful searching.

Look for bias. Ask yourself, is this site one-sided or is there balance? As you consider the value of a site, ask questions, ones like, are there contradictions and complications that someone with a differing viewpoint might point out?

Another way to pin down the disease and the technical lingo is to plow through medical journals. Here, you will find people who are familiar with your topics. Their work may be available for you to build on.

Since, at this point, you are searching by topic, using subject directories or indexes like Yahoo! or the Mining Company will help locate sites. Judging by the large number of hits your searches produce, it is clear you're not alone in looking for alternatives in medicine.

While searching the news features isn't likely to find many media stories unless someone famous has the same medical problem, celebrity news searches are a trick best-selling author Carole Lane uses. Think of a few famous people who may have had the illness in question. In the case of prostate problems, there are quite a few cases, including former Sen. Bob Dole, baseball player Darryl Strawberry, two-time Nobel Prize winner Dr. Linus Pauling, civil rights advocate Stokely Carmichael, actors Don Ameche and Bill Bixby, Jordan's King Hussein and Time-Warner Chairman Steven Ross. Each made news for having or fighting prostate problems, yet they would not have if they weren't well-known first. An article listing them could also include the rest of what we're looking for.

As you visit sites in search of "our medical condition," you may find many "alternative treatments." This gives a "field" of possibilities to consider. Included in the list of prostate treatments is one that involves heat, another that involves micro-waving, and several others. As you move forward, it would be wise to use our search engine tools to find more sites that contain these terms

Not surprisingly, you'll find web sites that claim their procedure is best. But in looking at the domain name, quickly realize that many are from doctors advocating their own procedures. Only when you turn to the government and media sites do we find reliable information and both the upside *and* downside of each procedure.

Since some of the information you are finding for free on the Web has us a bit worrisome or troubling, the next move is to fee-based databases like DIALOG or LEXIS-NEXIS, which are loaded with reliable science, medical and health information. The free sites on the Web gave us a lot of good terminology and background information, so, when you turn to the fee-based services, you won't be wasting time.

LEXIS-NEXIS has several medical resources that will help us find specific doctors, including:

♦ ABMS (The Official American Board of Medical Specialties Directory of Board Certified Medical Specialists)

- AMDIR (The American Medical Information's Physician & Surgeons Database

DIALOG offers MANTIS, an incredibly good medical database for alternative and natural therapies. DIALOG also has

- The Dictionary of Substances and their Effects

- Drugs of the Future (which talks about side effects among other things)

- Many powerful medical-related databases.

- Information Access Corp's Health and Wellness database (a terrific layman's guide to medical information)

Did You Find Enough "Right Information?"

Since the final Sample Search was about something you care about, by now you are more "informed" about something that, probably, affects your life and your future. How long did it take to collect that information? That's one of the true "beauties" of the Internet: it gives you same day access to information that, just a decade ago, would have taken you weeks to collect. And, the next time you're confronted with a medical emergency, you'll be able to take on tough search like this one and get results quickly.

Here's another "beauty" of the Internet: once you know what to look for, you have access to the "top experts" You can get to their published articles and news stories, ask them questions via e-mail, find and compare their businesses, learn about their backgrounds, who they "link with." No longer do you have to rely on just one family doctor, or one phone call to one expert, or whoever puts out the most advertisements.

A crucial part of Sample Search 3 is evaluating the information once you get it. Since it was a health question, you have realized the absolute importance of being sure of the source. And, when you find a good source, you learn a lot. For medical questions, especially, if you really want to feel safe, a fee-based service can be the most helpful. More about that in the next section.

Final Thoughts on Search Strategies

Susan Feldman, who wrote the searching strategies sidebar (on the next page) originally for *Searcher Magazine,* did a study comparing fee-based tools to free web-based resources. As part of *The Internet Search-Off.*[§], she compared DIALOG and Dow Jones Interactive (fee-services) results with those of free Web searching tools. Using experienced librarians, professional searchers and real life examples and case studies, Feldman drew the following conclusions:

DIALOG and Dow Jones retrieved more relevant documents than those found on the web.

[§] *Searcher Magazine,* Feb 1998 article by Susan Feldman

Total search time was more than double for finding information on the web. But, Feldman warns this may change as browsers get faster, smarter and bandwidth increases.

For finding relevant documents, the searchers found twice the number of useless documents (ranked number one) came out of the top thirty documents from web searches compared to the top thirty retrieved by the fee-based services.

Both the web and fee-based tools support different uses.

The Web was better for:

◆ Current information

◆ Finding pictures and illustrations

◆ Conference coverage and papers

◆ Product information directly from the company

◆ Small company information

◆ Current medical statistics

Fee-based services were better for finding

◆ Histories of companies and background information

◆ Scientific and engineering information

◆ Historical figures

◆ Market reports and industry reports

◆ Industry newsletter and journals

◆ Scholarly journal articles

◆ Quick searches when you know the information is likely to be there

◆ When time is a factor

Broken links proved a plague to searchers in many of the entries. They represented lost time as well as lost information, a unique problem for the web.

Perhaps more important, Feldman noted, the searchers themselves had different expectations from the different types of tools. In using the fee-based tools they *assumed* that information exists on the subject, it is high quality, the information is current and expensive, that it will take some training and know how to find what you are looking for. Often, they were surprised when they could not find something as long as they searched.

On the Web, the expectations of the skilled professional searchers were much lower. On the Web there might be information on a topic, but its quality and timeliness is unpredictable. The information is free, but there's no telling how effectively search engines work. Many test participants thought it would be a surprise if they found something.

In the search assignment, many searchers used *both online vendors and the Web* to supplement each other, especially for getting the facts on:

- Articles on topics of general interest

- Popular science

- Organizations

- Standards

- Directory information

- Reviews, evaluations and how to information

- Government regulations and other agency information

- Competitive Intelligence

- Obscure topics

- Clues for finding information online and offline

Feldman also pointed out that time is money: "Free information that takes too long to find and format is expensive information."

Her conclusion was that there is no longer a clear dividing line between the fee-based services and the Web. Time is the most relevant factor.

If you want to look through thousands of newspaper articles to find what you want, you can do it on the Web and you will also find the graphics, charts and tables missing from the fee-based services. But, it will likely take you longer *and* you probably will not be as thorough as if you used the fee-based tools.

Of course, as with everything online, this is an evolving world, so things could change again tomorrow.

One thing that is not going to change is your need to understand how to use these tools to keep some sense of your own privacy while online, which is the topic of the next chapter.

When you do specific research on a subject you don't ever expect to come back to (for instance, you need to go out on Usenet to track down leads), set up your own separate e-mail address just for this. Go to Hotmail or any service offering free e-mail. Get a free password. When your project is over — and you no longer care — just ignore replies to that e-mail service. That way, your regular e-mail won't be cluttered with unwanted e-mail replies.

Perhaps the most insightful conclusions, I've seen on the "dos" and "don'ts" of searching come from two of the best search gurus in the business — Dr. Susan Feldman and *Searcher* Editor, Barbara Quint.

Tips from The Internet Search-off

By Dr. Susan Feldman

> Dr. Susan Feldman was the coordinator of The Internet Search-Off for *Searcher Magazine*, February, 1998. She also runs Data Search in Ithaca, NY as well as teaching at Cornell University. Here she explains her conclusions of the Internet Search-Off contest, including the following "Tips and Recommendations."

Web search engines all attach weights to different words and rankings in order to put the most valuable finding at the top of your results query. To do this, nearly every Search Engine [detailed in Chapter 3] uses a different formula.

Here are some rules that can be gleaned from some of the expert searchers who participated in the Internet Search-off:

♦ Since Search Engines generally have little overlap in coverage, use more than one Search Engine for your extensive searches.

♦ Rare or unusual words are easier to find than common ones. Try searching for the rare term first.

♦ Know the default parameters of the site: AND or OR, etc.

♦ Find and use synonyms for your most important concept. If you use only one term for your most important concept, and then use many synonyms for less vital aspects, you can skew the weighting of the query away from the most important term.

♦ Use "More Like This" on **Excite** to refine a search.

♦ Use **AltaVista** for finding foreign sites and information in foreign languages. While their Translation feature may not be robust enough to try on Shakespeare, it does return a nice approximation of the original, unless you have idioms involved.

♦ Use **Northern Light** for subject searches. Northern Light seems to find useful information quickly on both the Web and in their special collection of journals, and you can't beat the price. Navigation using Custom Folders makes the service easy to use.

♦ Use **HotBot** if you need a specific format, date or field within a document such as the title or the URL.

♦ Use a meta-search engine to give you a quick overview of what might become a very broad search with many returns. Meta-search engines have one major drawback: they do not return enough information to make a considered decision of whether to view a page. Titles alone do not suffice usually.

♦ If too many pages come back, then add other concepts to the query.

- Ignore false drops. Don't waste time wondering why the German/English Running Dictionary showed up in a search on "the effect of jet lag on shining a light behind the knee." I never could figure that one out.

- Shorten a URL if you get a broken link, then use the features of the site to find the page you seek.

- Stick to a few search engines that work best for you. Knowing how to use them well will save searching time.

Don't let the numbers of results fool you. Each search service has its own idiosyncratic way of figuring out how many pages relate to a query. Some add all pages that have at least one of the query words. Others seem to limit that number or list only those which include all the concepts.

Product reviews, particularly for computer-related equipment are easy to find on the Web. **Ask Jeeves** often lists the best sites for reviews of various products.

"...Our Lives, Our Fortunes, & Our Sacred Honor" Protecting Yourself Online

by Barbara Quint

Barbara Quint is editor of *Searcher Magazine*. Her e-mail address is
bquint@netcom.com

The Signers of the *Declaration of Independence* defined the stakes they had riding on their actions very carefully. As Ben Franklin said, "If we don't all hang together, it's certain we'll all hang separately."

The warning applies as well to web work. If you have any of the above – life, fortune, or sacred honor – riding on the outcome of your web search, check and double check its quality. If you only plan to squander a pleasant hour or two in surfing the Web for amusement or entertainment, no problem, but if you plan to gather medical information or research your stock portfolio or hand someone your credit card data, *protect yourself.*

Rule One:

Don't put anything into your mind you wouldn't put into your mouth.

- Where did this information come from?

- Who stands behind it?

- What axes are they grinding?

Approval of a source can vary from situation to situation. For example, an ardent environmentalist and a timber industry lobbyist might have widely different opinions as to the value of information from a Sierra Club web site, but both should appreciate verification that the material came from the actual Sierra Club.

Tips:

Check the entire URL. Clicking through to a document with a foot long URL (usually ending in ".htm" or ".html") may expedite your trip to your target source, but it also skips the verification process. To check who or what brought you this far, just strip off the layers between the back slashes. Re-enter the URL up to the first back slash and see where you start.

Watch out for the domain name. If you're looking for a company site, it shouldn't end in ".org". If you're tracking government statistics, it shouldn't end in ".com". Sometimes there's a reasonable explanation. For example, one company selling laser printers might have a lovely collection of reference material, including poetry, quotations, statistics, etc., as a giveaway to lure users to its site. The data is probably reliable, but any smart searcher would have clicked around the site to see if anything "just doesn't seem right."

Look for contact information – the old-fashioned snail mail kind. Ignore this tip at your peril. In a desperate search for a cheap toner cartridge, I found a company that claimed to sell new ones $30.00 cheaper than my usual office supply house. But when I called the 800 number on a Saturday, the guy answered the phone, "Hello," and I could hear kids hollering in the background. When I rechecked the full web site, the contact section had no mailing address. I don't know about you, but I'm not handing over credit card data to businesses that don't tell me what state they're in. I need to deal with people who will stand behind the information they carry and the goods they sell.

Rule Two: Kick the tires!

♦ Stay cynical.

♦ Ask embarrassing questions.

♦ Play devil's advocate.

Assume next Monday you'll face a board of inquiry or an angry boss with a set of questions designed to de-bunk the data. What questions would be on that list? Can you answer them?

Tips:

The old adage, "You get what you pay for" doesn't hold true in web research. Commercial services that charge high fees for data may offer wonderful, reliable data and solid information, but they can also carry lightweight or biased information. The free web certainly has a sky load of cloudy data, but it can also carry rock-solid, reliable information – sometimes from the same sources as the commercial services. Look at each question and each answer, one at a time.

Verify bias. Judge web output with at least the same rigorous standards you would apply to any other source of data. A professional searcher colleague of mine tells the story of a client who wanted a list of the top ten mutual funds. When she had cleared enough earlier projects to work on his question, the client told her he had already found the list he needed on the Web. Actually, he had gotten the data from a promotional piece on a single mutual fund's company web site. Do you believe phone company representatives when they tell you about studies that show their company has cheaper long distance rates than any other? Just because it comes off the computer doesn't make it more reliable. On the other hand, if the data came from an established financial journal or a trade association or a government study, then you might place more faith in it. But check them out too.

Identify critical factors. Timeliness and currency often affect the value of information. The perfect study from the most authoritative source filled with relevant detail may have little or no value if written three years ago. Sometimes web versions of reports may contain more current information than print ones, but you must verify the date of the most recent revision. If not apparent on the document, e-mail the webmaster. Even if the study hasn't been updated recently, the webmaster may be able to suggest alternative sources. Remember built-in delay factors. For example, scholarly journals can have a two-year or three-year delay between the submission of a research study and its publication. Again, contacting authors, their research organizations and/or their web sites may provide more current information, and perhaps more detailed reports.

Make sure you can find the information again. Too much material on the Web is ephemeral: here today, gone tomorrow. Newspaper web sites, for example, usually only carry one day's worth of data. Some offer archives, but rarely is the archived material complete or in an identical format. If you think you might face future questions about the information a transaction, then archive it or document it yourself. Print it out straight from the browser and stick it in a file. Download it into your computer. Or find out whether and where archives appear. Many newspapers, trade press journals, company financial reports, etc. exist in commercial database archives. Libraries hold backruns of journals and magazines, government reports, etc.

Rule Three: When in doubt, hire it out.

If you lack confidence in your ability to do quality research on the Web, get a professional searcher to do the job for you. This rule applies to non-web research as well. Your company may have a corporate library with expert searchers on staff. Your community may have a public library with a cost-plus-fee search service. Information brokers do research for hire.

Tips:

Use the searchers with the best match of skills and price. Don't let geography determine the hire. The Internet has eliminated distance as a barrier. If you have an institutional library available to you, its staff will probably know your subject area well and have a vested interest in serving you. If you need a personal search done, they may still offer help – at least, help to find you the right searcher. Check trade and professional associations. The American Library Association at `http://www.ala.org` has a section called FISCAL that lists all the intermediated searching operations at public and academic libraries around the country. The Association of Independent Information Professionals `http://www.aiip.org` lists ethical information brokers from around the world.

Explain the full question to your searcher. Tell them how you plan to use the information. Online searching can offer a considerable range of choices.

Turn your search into a tutorial. Get double value from hiring a searcher by having them explain the logic and techniques they used to gather information. Next time, you can try doing it yourself. In fact, most searchers are happy to teach clients how to improve their research skills.

Rule Four: Just Do It!

A little knowledge is a dangerous thing, as the poet says, but the real enemy is ignorance. The most expensive and risky step you can take is just "going dumb." How many incurable diseases have cures that the patient or doctor just don't know exist? How many business losses result from not checking basic business data sources? How many mistakes can a person make in their life from sheer ignorance? The answers aren't pretty.

Tips:

Travel with the experts. Meta-sites are home pages that offer massive collections of links to related sites. Some come from libraries and academic institutions. Some come from individuals who have just said NO when they were advised to "Get a life!" Some come from commercial publishers working to retain their dominance in a print universe in the new digital world.

Check for update frequency. Whatever the source, webmasters behind major meta-sites have made a commitment to tracking the quality of their listings. Many of these sites will document when they last checked each and every listing.

Ask for help. The only bad question is an unasked question. If you find an expert, but don't find your answer or don't understand the answer you've found, contact them. Before the Internet had a web to hold all its research, it still held out open arms to connect all its people. Marvelous communities exist in the Internet. Use them. But watch out! Never let warm and fuzzy feelings about a friendly source deter you from cool-headed, critical examination of the information they give you.

Caveat searcher!!

Chapter 13

Privacy & Protection

Privacy discussions tend to be emotional ones. Who among you wants others to know what you paid for your house? But, we all want to know what our neighbors paid for theirs. You want to be able to check a potential caregiver's criminal history. It's an information age, and information is a two-edged sword.

Do you have any rights to privacy online? A few, and even those are narrowly defined. In most forums, you should assume no privacy whatever; it's wiser to presume the reverse – that any of your communications (except e-mail, with notable exceptions) can be copied and posted throughout cyberspace without your knowledge or consent.

Online Interactions: A Reality Check

Web Browsing

As mentioned in Chapter 1, when you journey on the Web, you leave imprints all over cyberspace that identify you, your ISP, the sites you've visited and your movements within each web site. Some web browsers are programmed to transmit your e-mail address to every web site you visit. Also, your browser's cache file is an ongoing record of everything you've viewed and read. Therefore, you should assume that everything you've sent or viewed can be accessed by someone somewhere out there.

The other half of the process occurs at the web site itself, which notes who you are and what you did at the site. Some sites make their logs available to anyone who wants access.

Internet Service Providers (ISPs)

Assume that all information you provide your ISP, other than your password, can and probably will be sold. That information includes online member profiles, directories and preferences.

There have been some troubling incidents regarding ISPs and their self-perceived roles as information carriers. For example, an America Online subscriber posted her opinion about a Caribbean resort — which happened to be an unfavorable opinion — to an AOL bulletin board.[**] The resort's lawyers demanded that AOL identify the woman to them. AOL complied. Needless to say, the resort is merely a private entity and posting an opinion isn't a crime – at least not yet. If online providers will release names to anyone who asks, how safe is your information that passes through an ISP?

In 1997, AOL announced it would sell its subscribers' information, including telephone numbers, to marketers – only to hastily retract the announcement under a firestorm of public outrage.

AOL is not alone. These kinds of problems happen with ISP's all over the world. All have different rules and policies on privacy.

Gated Communities

Safeguards such as passwords and registration processes are no guarantee of privacy in any forum. As a result, content from your postings may be copied, stolen, mangled, re-posted or sold – without your knowledge or consent. Unless a web site has an explicit privacy policy (read the fine print!), consider your name and e-mail address to be public property.

Discussion Groups

When you post to a discussion forum, millions can see that message. Chat groups in particular are notoriously permeable forums – for example, jokes are transmitted like lightning through the Internet.

Mailing Lists

As a subscriber, you may feel camaraderie with your fellow enthusiasts. Fellowship doesn't prevent contents from being lifted, changed and/or re-posted. Some lists prohibit their contents from being quoted or attributed to the list or its members – but that doesn't prevent information from reappearing elsewhere.

Bulletin Boards

Your postings can be traced back to you. For example, a male accountant harassed a woman through vindictive postings and foul language on a bulletin board for escorts/prostitutes and customers. Her ISP and the board's ISP warned him to cease. He didn't. So she posted his name, address, job title and company on the bulletin board and in accounting forums. Legal? You bet. Though the man assumed his communications were private (perhaps because of the nature of the bulletin board), not only was he wrong, but thousands of his professional colleagues now know how wrong he was. So do the zillions of other people who can access his postings – and hers – through Deja News and other archivers. Now you know one way law enforcement officials track predators and other Internet criminals.

[**] "Beware of E-mail Privacy Limits," CNET News.com, Nov., 27, 1997.
www.news.com/News/Item/0,4,91,00.html

Usenet Newsgroups

Your Usenet postings are readable by anyone. All Usenet postings are indexed automatically by Deja News, Reference.Com and other sites. Internet lore is rich with stories of people who posted casually only to find their words returning to haunt them. For example, an innocent posting to an AIDS newsgroup (perhaps you had a question or were doing research) posts your e-mail address where any one can read it – including life insurance companies, potential employers and others.

Privacy & E-mail

Normally, e-mail is considered private just as regular mail is considered private. The Federal Electronic Privacy Act makes it illegal for anyone to read or disclose the contents of an electronic communication unless one of the two people involved in the e-mail has complained to law enforcement authorities about harassment. There are three exceptions to e-mail privacy – and they are big exceptions.

1. In cases of suspected crime, law enforcement officials can obtain warrants that enable them to access your e-mail. Similarly, an online service can access your e-mail if it suspects attempted damage or harm, even if no crime has been committed (as in the case of stalkers and predators).

2. Your ISP can disclose private e-mails if it has the sender's consent. Most providers obtain that consent during the mandatory sign-up process. It's all in the fine print.

3. If your employer owns your computer and/or the e-mail system through which the e-mails are sent, then the e-mails belong to the employer, *not* to you. Repeat: in this case, your mail is not your mail. Several lawsuits are contesting the notion of full employer access to its employees' e-mail, but they're treading shaky ground because most companies don't have a "bill of privacy rights" for employees and there is no legal presumption of employee privacy. Even if there were, you probably signed away your rights away when you signed your employment contract. Generally speaking, whatever you do at work belongs to your employer, not you – and that goes for web site activity, too, because your time at work is assumed to belong to your employer. Feeling nervous? You may have a good reason.

Commercial providers like America Online, CompuServe and the Microsoft Network routinely record e-mail messages that pass through their networks. AOL, CompuServe and Microsoft say that when requested, they cooperate with law enforcement entities in criminal investigations involving stalkers, pedophiles, kidnapPers and others. And they say that when they are served with a warrant, they turn over information to law enforcement entities. The same applies to many of the large ISP companies.

The Ultimate Gold Mine: You

By now it should be clear that you are the answer to data-miners' dreams and fortunes. Data-miners, when in suits and ties, refer to the records of your online travels as "transaction-generated information." When they loosen their ties, they call them the "clickstream," and when they think you're not listening, they call them "mouse droppings." Whatever the name, the goal is to make an easy buck off your navigational habits online — actually, multiple bucks, since they can sell the information over and over again.

The Golden Trail of Cookie Crumbs

Here is how your data trail is generated:

When you visit a web site that is programmed to collect information about you, it creates a file about your browser called a "cookie." Cookies allow web sites to greet you personally ("Welcome back, Alan. It's been ten days since your last visit. If you're still interested in baseball, we have a special promotion just for you") and furnish local weather, sports and TV listings. Cookies enable companies to record your online activities every movement because they are placed on your computer's hard drive without your prior consent.

In reality, cookies are simply text files that are up to 255 characters long. They aren't software programs. They cannot scan your hard drive. Cookies from early versions of Netscape Navigator and JavaScript collected e-mail addresses; current versions don't; future versions may.

In short, cookies are a convenience. They allow a site to remember your previously registered information, preferences and passwords, for example. And they can facilitate interactivity.

If you set your browser to warn you each time a web site tries to slip you a cookie, you'll be quite surprised at how often it happens in the course of a single online session.

Cookie Taste Test at www.geocities.com/SoHo/4535/cookie.html **will introduce you to many sites and the multitude of ways they use cookies.**

Get to Know Your Cache

When a browser retrieves a page you want to see, it stores the page on your disk. Go to the same page again ten minutes later, the program doesn't have to retrieve the page again because it can reuse the copy it already has stored. It actually retrieves the page from your cache (pronounced "cash"), which is the space your browser uses to store pages. The more space you tell your browser to use for its cache, the faster pages appear the next time you look at them.

Be aware that for your privacy, you want to clear your Cache, or others who look at your computer can see where you have been.

You can find details about the cache in Netscape Navigator under Options, Network Preferences or Edit Preferences, depending which version you use. For Microsoft Internet Explorer, you can find it under View, Internet Options.

In Netscape, you can also use the Window/History option from the pull down menu to track which sites you've already visited. You also want to delete sites from your history file that may prove embarrassing. Double click on any you want to visit again. Also, the home button on the top of the browser will take you back to the opening page (the home page).

Under the Windows '98 operating system, you can manually locate your cache file (for Internet Explorer) in the Temporary Internet Files subdirectory of your Windows directory (C:\Windows\Temporary Internet Files). The files contained in Temporary Internet Files include cookies and downloaded items necessary to view the pages visited on your computer. Anything in this subdirectory may be deleted in order to protect your privacy.

Four Major Privacy Threats

1. Identity Fraud: A Devastating Epidemic

Identity fraud artists use their victims' personal information to assume the victims' personas and rack up bills in their names. While no firm statistics are available, police, regulators and privacy specialists say such crimes have become epidemic in recent years.

The impact on victims can be devastating. Take the case of Sandra Montgomery of St. Louis. In 1995, a woman using a similar name opened an account at the same credit union, where a customer service representative mistakenly divulged Montgomery's account information. First the woman milked Montgomery's accounts. Then she embarked on a year-long spending spree, using Montgomery's Social Security Number and mother's maiden name. The thief spent nearly $150,000 on a car, jewelry, and other goods before she was arrested and convicted of fraud. Montgomery's credit record is in tatters. Her attorneys had to sue credit bureaus, retailers and collection agencies to force them to clear her financial records. Montgomery told the Washington Post. "It has impacted every single part of my life. I can't get a credit card. I can't get a loan. I can't get a house."[tt]

Online information and credit companies have made it easier than ever to obtain once-private personal data. At the same time, Social Security Numbers, birth dates and other personal details are used increasingly often as identity verifiers in telephone and computer transactions. Also, identity thieves have long understood that most stores will absorb the loss of one person's fraudulent credit card usage

---

[tt] Robert O'Harrow and John Schwartz, "A Case of Taken Identity, Thieves With a Penchant for Spending Are Stealing Consumers' Good Names," *The Washington Post*, May 26, 1998

rather than lose a slew of customers by making security procedures more complex. They count on that.

Documented identity fraud cases are collected and archived by the San Diego-based Privacy Rights Clearinghouse at www.privacyrights.org.

2. Medical Records: A Privacy Meltdown Waiting to Happen

Nowhere are the stakes as high as when it comes to that most intimate of data: your medical records.

Nearly all US (and Canadian) medical records are compiled by the Medical Information Bureau (MIB) into a single database. The MIB is a consortium of insurance companies that maintains millions of records taken from insurance applications, doctors and hospitals. When you apply for a health insurance policy, insurers dive into MIB's computers for information about preexisting health conditions that might affect their decision to issue a policy to you.

Imagine that you have a non-communicable disease but find that, all of a sudden, your co-workers won't work with you any more. And they won't tell you why. Or that a rumor causes your health insurer to cancel your policy. Or that you're fired – or not hired for a job you deserve – because someone took an unauthorized peek at your medical history and then blabbed. You'll probably never know the real reason you were blacklisted.

Federal privacy law protects only three types of records: Your credit report can be released only to people you've authorized (as well as to banks, law enforcement people and some others). Also protected are your video rental records – as a result of background checks of certain Washington politicians and a Supreme Court nominee as to whether they'd ever rented adult movies. Thirdly, the law protects your cable TV viewing habits.

Your other personal records are unprotected and undefended. Think about that. It means that you have no legal recourse even if you are able to prove abuse or misuse of your private information.

3. Children: Prime Targets for Data-Miners

Kids under eighteen spend more than $80 billion a year and influence another $160 billion in parental purchases, according to 1998 Federal Trade Commission statistics. It's not surprising, then, that 89% of children's web sites in a 1998 FTC survey admitted to collecting personal information from child visitors.[‡‡] The same survey found that 46 percent of the sites didn't disclose their information collection practices; and less than 10 percent let parents control the data-mining. That last finding is echoed by the Center for Media Education (CME), a nonprofit children's

---

[‡‡] "CHILDREN AND PRIVACY," Federal Trade Commission, June 1998.

advocacy group, which discovered that more than 90 percent of child-oriented web sites didn't consult parents about the data taken from their children.

Children are favorite targets for marketing information about their families. Many web sites lure kids with "rewards" in order to have them fill out questionnaires for marketable personal data. After all, how many children can recognize and reject the temptation of a "prize" or "free membership?"

Collecting online information from a child is very different from the cereal box forms you may have filled out as a child because computerized data can be sold – or transferred – to other sites or marketers.

Soliciting online information from a child is unconscionable, according to *Privacy Journal* editor Robert Ellis Smith, because we don't allow strangers to ask children in a school playground for their names, addresses, phone numbers and family demographics. Many such sites solicit detailed information from children, such as home address, household size, birth date, favorite TV programs and toys. The FTC found the questions too invasive and has restricted data-mining of children without their parents' consent. In 1998, Congress passed legislation to curtail data solicitation from children.

4. Workplace Privacy

Employers love to keep tabs on their workers. Technology now makes it easy for companies to monitor employees every minute of the workday. Employers can read your e-mail, view your personal computer files and eavesdrop on your phone calls. There are no laws regulating electronic surveillance in the private sector workplace. There simply is nowhere to hide. Employers are deemed to have a legitimate interest in monitoring work to ensure efficiency and productivity – even though the surveillance often goes well beyond legitimate management concerns.

The number of people electronically observed at their workplace is skyrocketing.

Digital technology lets supervisors monitor employees' web use, keystrokes, phone call lengths and time spent away from the desk. Olivetti and Xerox have developed an "active badge" that tracks employee movements on company property. Software programs like Sequel's Net Access Manager by Sequel www.sequeltech.com and Webster's Network Strategies' Web Track www.webster.com enable employers to unobtrusively monitor employees' online activities in detail – and block certain online activities.

It's no accident that electronic surveillance is on the rise. It's not illegal, and it's facilitated by technology advances. Court rulings have deemed workplace time and output to be an employer's property. Since there's no strong legislation that specifically addresses electronic privacy concerns, it's not surprising that the courts have overwhelmingly supported employers in cases of workplace monitoring.

In one notable case, an Epson America Inc. employee named Alana Shoars discovered her supervisor reading and printing out other employees' e-mails. She questioned the practice and said she was told to mind her own business. A day later, she was fired for insubordination.

Shoars filed a class-action suit claiming invasion of privacy under California's constitution and a wiretapping statute – and lost. The state court ruled that state law didn't cover e-mail and that the state constitution didn't apply to business information. She also lost her wrongful termination lawsuit. Yet, California's privacy laws are considered the most progressive in the country.

Your Data & Industry Concerns

Who owns your personal data trail? Is that information public and usable for any purpose by anybody who can pick it up and read it – or does it belong to you? Sadly, nobody seems to be talking about this subject. Rather, the industry discussion starts from the premise that the information should be standardized, so that all industry participants have an equal chance to obtain it.

That standard would function as an identification card attached to your online presence as you journey through cyberspace. It would eliminate the need for you to sign in or register at various sites (also eliminating any inconsistencies in your identity). It would allow you to control site access to your profile, which would include your name, address, phone number, e-mail address, interests, hobbies and sites visited and activities at those sites. The entire profile would be stored and encrypted on your computer's hard drive, where you could view and modify it. Each time a web site requests your personal data, you can evaluate the request and offer some, all or none of your information. The standard was proposed and endorsed in mid-1997 by sixty-plus online companies (with the notable exception of Microsoft, which subsequently added its endorsement).

The next step will likely be a proposed implementation plan and then a formal request for approval.

So, how can you really protect yourself? What concrete steps and actions can you take to prevent privacy invasion? Carole Lane, who has testified on privacy issues before the Federal Trade Commission and the California State Legislature, offers some terrific tips.

Ten Tips for Protecting Your Privacy Online

by Carole A. Lane

> Carole A. Lane is the author of *Naked In Cyberspace: How To Find Personal Information Online*.

First of all, don't let online paranoia keep you up nights or stop you from enjoying the rich and remarkable resources of the Internet. Contrary to all of the horror stories circulated since the popular emergence of the Internet, most crime isn't perpetrated online, and your chances of becoming a crime victim are still greater offline. Although there's very little privacy left in life, these simple precautions will help to limit the risk factors that could put your in harm's way, as well as to defend what privacy you do have:

1. Protect your computer.

Anyone with access to your computer can obtain information about you, read your documents, find out what you do online (by reading your cookies or cache), and otherwise compromise your security. Don't store your best-kept secrets on your PC. Delete and erase sensitive documents, cookies and cache files. (Sending them to your PC's trash file is not enough.) Change the passwords in the BIOS setup program of your PC and in Windows for added security, or consider purchasing one of the many security software packages available on the market.

2. Keep your private life away from the workplace.

Your employer has the right to monitor all of your online transactions, to intercept your e-mail, read your files, and even to remove your PC altogether. If you don't want your boss to know that you're looking for a new job online, or checking out the latest porn sites during your coffee break, don't do it from work.

3. Carefully select and protect your passwords.

Anyone having access to your passwords could pretend to be you online (a practice called "spoofing"), order products or services in your name, or invite the unwanted attention of others. Change your passwords often, and don't leave them on or near your computer. Don't select passwords that could be guessed by someone who knows you, and don't use the same password on more than one site. Combinations of eight or more alphabetic and numeric characters are your best bet when selecting a password.

4. Don't tell secrets.

Much personal information gathered by companies is collected from warranty cards, "free" product offers, surveys, and other data that you may readily volunteer. Online, information about you is gathered when you sign up for services, select your preferences, sign guest books, register as a user of a site, or reveal your interests. If you don't want your personal information to be shared with the world, stop filling out surveys, stop giving your unlisted number to strangers, and stop filling in all of the blanks for marketers. Whether online or off, when sensitive information is requested (such as your Social Security Number, mother's maiden name, medical history, etc.) find out why it's needed and how it will be protected before you give it away. Assume that all of your personal information will be sold and resold by anyone who requests it, unless they tell you otherwise. Even then, there's no guarantee that it won't be sold later, so be cautious with whatever you consider private.

5. Find your own records.

Some information about you is probably already available online, even if you've never surfed the Internet. Search all the online phone books for your listing. Check the web sites of each organization that you belong to in order to find out if they list your name, address, telephone number, or anything else about you in their directories. Remember to include alumni, professional, and even hobbyist associations, company sites of your current and previous employers, and the directory of your Internet service provider in your search. Use several search engines to find out if you are mentioned elsewhere on the Internet. If having information about you displayed at these sites makes you uncomfortable, ask that it be removed. In most cases, web site owners will comply with your wishes. (This is not true of public records, DMV records, and some other types of records, however.)

6. Stop chatting or become anonymous.

When you express opinions or reveal anything about yourself online, there's no telling who's listening or sending your thoughts on to others. When you participate in online (Usenet) newsgroups, the information is routinely archived and searchable for years to come. If you're determined to participate in newsgroups, an anonymous re-mailer can be used to strip the identifying information from your messages and send them on to the newsgroup, or even to an individual. A List of Reliable anonymous re-mailers can be found at `www.cs.berkeley.edu/~raph/re-mailer-list.html`.

7. Stop the archiving.

You can request that one of the biggest archives, Deja News `www.dejanews.com`, not archive your messages by entering "x-no-archive: yes" in the first line of your message, followed by a blank line. That won't stop any other services or individuals from archiving or sharing your messages, so it's still best to post only what you're willing to share with the world. If you've already sent messages that you'd like to remove from Deja News' archive, use their Article Nuke Form at `www.dejanews.com/forms/nuke.shtml` to remove your messages one-by-one.

8. Surf under another identity.

If your Internet service provider allows you to set up more than one account, use one for correspondence with friends, family, business associates, and anyone else that you know and trust. NEVER surf the Internet with that account or register it at web sites. Use another account for all Internet surfing. NEVER give that e-mail address to anyone, or connect it with your information in any way. Also, change your surfing e-mail address often, if possible. These steps will help to distance you from the data being gathered about you as you surf, as well as keep your "real" e-mail account mailbox free from spam (junk e-mail).

9. Hide behind a firewall.

Even if you only have one e-mail address, you can still surf anonymously. A proxy server can be used to retrieve web pages and then pass them to you, serving as a firewall between you and the web site. If you access the Internet through a direct dial-up connection (rather than through a proxy server), Anonymizer at `www.anonymizer.com` can serve as your proxy server. Instructions for use are available at this site.

10. For added e-mail privacy, use encryption software.

There are many types of encryption software available for use when sending private e-mail, and some of these, such as PGP (Pretty Good Privacy) for Personal Privacy at www.pgp.com/products/pgpfreeware.cgi are available free-of-charge on the Internet, or may even be included with your current e-mail software. If the information that you're sending is sensitive in nature, encrypt it before sending it.

More Ways to Protect Your Privacy

Visit Informational Resources

Visit the privacy demonstration project web site run by The Center for Democracy and Technology (www.cdt.org) a privacy advocacy group that monitors federal government activities. This excellent resource shows you what information your computer is giving away when you travel the Internet.

Visit the extensive resources of Junkbusters at www.junkbusters.com/ht/en/cookies.html. Here you can have your browser checked, find form letters to end the flood of junk mail, read reports about the privacy wars, and so forth.

Visit the Privacy Rights Clearinghouse at www.privacyrights.org, another privacy advocacy group mentioned earlier, which offers excellent fact sheets on how to protect yourself.

Deep Clean Your Computer

Delete your e-mail messages after you've read them from your computer and from the central server. This isn't a foolproof method, but it makes it harder for others to read your mail for the time being.

Clean out your computer's hard drive. Password-protected files and deleted material can be recovered.

Clean your computer's cache through your browser's preferences. Purging your cache will delete the record of your online travels. It will also slim down and speed up your browser.

Disable Your Cookies.

If you're using a **Netscape Navigator 3.x** Browser, look in the Options menu for Network Preferences, then Protocols. Then click "Show an Alert before Accepting a Cookie." Then save your option settings.

In **Netscape Navigator 4.0 or higher,** go to Edit, then Preferences, then Advanced; click on "Never Accept Cookies" or "Warn Me Before Accepting a Cookie." Some versions offer the option of accepting only cookies that are stored in the original server.

If you're using a **Microsoft Internet Explorer (MS-IE) 3.0,** look under View, then Options, then Advanced, then check the box "Warn Before Accepting Cookies."

In **MS-IE 4.0,** go to Edit/Preferences/Cookies/Never Accept or View Internet Options/Advanced/Security/Cookies/Disable all cookie use. You can also right-click IE Shortcut/Properties/Advanced/Cookies and then Options.

With **Web TV,** there's is no way to block cookies.

If you use an early version of any of the above-mentioned browsers, upgrade. They are not secure.

Anonymizers & Encryption

Download **Pronto,** another shareware e-mail program that works in conjunction with encryption software, from www.shareware.com.

Erase unwanted files so they can't be recovered using **Mutilate,** another shareware program downloadable from www.cnet.com. The program offers three defined security levels and a customizable level and includes an uninstall utility.

Buy one of the many memory protection programs designed to prevent unauthorized access to your home computer. They encrypt each directory with a different password that requires log-in from the user. Some include "audit trails" that record all activity on your computer's drives.

Become anonymous. Lists of more anonymous re-mailer sites, in addition to the one mentioned by Carole Lane on the previous page, can also be found at www.replay.com/re-mailer/anon.html.

Padlock Your ISP

Request your ISP's policies about subscriber information. Inform it that you don't want your data sold, exchanged or given away. Request removal from your ISP's online directory, and check the fine print on its registration contract.

See Yourself as Others See You

Stalk yourself. Find out everything you can about yourself on the assumption that whatever you can discover, others can, too. Try every online tool you can. Then visit the courthouse and see what public records may eventually end up online.

Are you being fingered? A finger is an Internet command that prompts ISPs to release your e-mail address and other personal information. Many small ISPs aren't configured to reject fingering commands.

To learn more, visit the following:

- www.yahoo.com/computers_and_Internet/internet/ World_Wide_Web/Gateways/Finger_Gateways

- www.best.com/~ii/internet/faqs/launchers/ signature_finger_faq

- http://alabanza.com/kabacoff/Inter- Links/cgi/finger.cgi

Check online web sites of conferences, trade shows, exhibitions and other events in which you participate. Sometimes event organizers will post information about you derived from registration forms without your knowledge – including home addresses and phone numbers. If you are a speaker or presenter, the posted content of your presentation may include personal information, as well.

End Marketing/Telemarketing

Request removal from marketing and telemarketing lists. The Federal Trade Commission has a form letter available www.ftc.gov/privacy/cred- itr.htm. The Direct Marketing Association also lets consumers remove themselves from junk mail and telemarketers' lists. Contact DMA at www.the- dma.org.

Notify the three credit bureaus that you want no more pre-approved offers of credit. You can also request a copy of your credit report for $8.00 from any of the three. Their numbers:

- Equifax, 1-800-685-1111

- Experian, 1-800-682-7654

- Trans Union, 1-800-888-4213

Order a free copy of your Personal Earnings and Benefits Estimate Statement (PEBES) from the Social Security Administration once every three years or so. Make sure your earnings are accurately recorded and that no one else is using your Social Security Number. The SSA's toll-free number is 1-800-772-1213.

Stop Giving Out Personal Information

Give out your Social Security Number only when it's required (for banking/stock/real estate transactions). Don't carry the card itself in your wallet, don't list the number on business cards or checks, and don't give the number to merchandisers.

Government agencies that require your SSN must state in writing if the number is required or optional and how it will be used. Make private businesses do the same.

Don't participate in informal health screenings offered at pharmacies and shopping malls. They collect information that is sold to businesses that will solicit you to buy medications and related products.

Don't e-mail or post confidential and/or personal information

The State of the Law

At the start of 1999, there were no federal laws that protect the online release of your medical records, phone logs, phone numbers or bank account numbers.

Congress approved its first Internet privacy legislation, the Children's Online Protection Act (COPA), on Oct. 21, 1998. It applies only to children and imposes criminal penalties against any commercial web site that makes material that is "harmful to minors" available to anyone under 17 years of age. It requires commercial sites to seek parental approval before collecting or posting personal information from children under age 13. It also requires X-rated web sites to turn away minors. However, enforcement is still an open question.

Separately, Congress passed a 1998 roving wiretap proposition that allows law enforcement agencies to tap anyone in the vicinity of the person they've targeted. With telephone companies converting their systems from analog to digital, law enforcement agents can eavesdrop using wireless technology. In cases where a warrant isn't required (for example, in cases where national security is arguably at stake), federal eavesdropping is quick and easy.

And finally, a third new law called the "identity theft law," also passed in late 1998, bars the transfer and/or use of someone's personal information if it is used to commit a crime. Penalties have been ratcheted up to 20 years in prison and restitution to the victims. Previously, federal law criminalized the fraudulent possession, transfer and production of identity documents, but required culprit to be arrested in actual possession of the data.

There are legal limits on the collection and transfer of personal data by US government agencies (both on and offline) and citizens can sue agencies that violate those laws. For example, federal employees and agencies cannot perform a background check using someone's SSN, credit history or other information without a legitimate work-related reason. While existing federal law also limits access to credit information to only those with legitimate need, such as banks and insurance companies, the law has been extended to include online use of personal information, as well.

More than 30 states are considering privacy law changes. While the proposal vary widely, they are intended to protect individuals against privacy intrusions by government, corporations, and others.

Interestingly, the European Union (EU) views US privacy laws as inadequate. In the fall of 1998, the EU passed a Directive on Data Protection that bars the transfer of personal information from EU countries to the US and other countries whose privacy regulation is deemed insufficient. Consequently, US data companies may not be able to buy and/or sell personal data with the EU. Already, Privacy International, a watchdog group, is investigating 25 multinational data vendors for violations of European privacy laws. Companies under scrutiny include Electronic Data Systems, Ford, Hilton International, Microsoft and United Airlines.

Some Perspectives on the Larger Debate

Do you have any rights related to how any released information will be used and disseminated? The absence of documented privacy policies by web sites and online entities represent a noticeable void on the Internet. Despite efforts by a nonprofit, privacy rights organization called eTRUST, documented privacy policies continue to remain overwhelmingly absent on the Internet. Users beware. Your privacy concerns aren't a priority. There are no rules of thumb, no international information treaty, no United Nations commission on privacy. The technology and its capability to gather information has seriously outstripped any policies to protect you. Lawmakers around the world are only now starting to mull privacy policies to control the sale or barter of personal information online.

Meanwhile, the potential for abuse looms increasingly large. Nobody knows exactly who has access, or exactly what information can be accessed. Occasionally, bits of information do fall into public view, leaving everyone to wonder at the ramifications. For example, in the fall of 1996, Great Universal Stores, a UK company that owns Burberry Raincoats, bought Experian, the credit reporting agency formerly known as TRW and with it the credit reports of a 190 million Americans. Great Universal Stores now owns the financial profiles of 708 million people in 40 countries and is, presumably, selling and re-selling the data. But also, it is now a company that owns stores, does marketing and owns personal consumer data, including credit histories and other personal financial information. Surely the company must be tempted to use the confidential personal data to support its other operations. And even if not, surely the possibility exists for abuse of the confidential personal information.

The centralization of information continues as data-holding companies buy smaller companies and the industry consolidates. The trend can only mean that personal information will become easier than ever to search and obtain. Your privacy — and expectations of privacy — will continue to shrink. Being aware of what is happening to you and how to use the technology remains your best weapon.

Indexes

Government Public Records By State

Private Online Sources of Public Records

Web Site Profiles

Contributors

Glossary

Page Index

Government Public Records Online

There Is No Consistency

As previously mentioned, government-held records can be one of the best sources to use to find information about people or businesses. Generally, government public records are defined as records of incidents or actions filed or recorded with a government agency for the purpose of notifying others (the public) about the matter.

Government agencies maintain records in a variety of ways. While many agencies are computerized, others use microfiche, microfilm and paper storage of files and indexes. Agencies that have converted to computer will not necessarily place complete file records on their system; they are more apt to include only an index, pointer or summary data to the files.

It costs a lot of money for county and state agencies to maintain records, therefore fees are normally incurred when accessing the records. The reality is that if you think you are going to log on the Internet and find all kinds of public records for free, forget it. In fact, BRB Publications, a leading research and publishing company, estimates that only 15% of public records are online.

Nonetheless, there are a large number of county, state and federal level agencies that offer Internet or direct dial-up access to their records. The pages that follow describe over 500 of these agencies. Finding and profiling every agency that has public records online is like hitting a moving target, but the list is pretty inclusive and you will find a wealth of information.

A final caution — very little of what you may perceive as public record information is truly open to the general public. One government agency may make their records open to the public, the same type of records in another jurisdiction (even an adjoining county) may have severe restrictions to release. Or, in another jurisdiction, the record may not be released at all.

Online Access at the Federal Level

Certainly, if all the web sites for federal government agencies were listed, *Find It Online* would require more than one volume. However, there are many excellent web sources discussed in Chapters 6 and 7 that will lead you to thousands of federal government resources.

The Securities and Exchange Commission (SEC) and the US Court System are both excellent places to search online for information on people and businesses. For more information on the SEC, see pages 162-164.

Federal Court Records

There are over 500 bankruptcy and US District Court locations in the USA. These courts house all bankruptcy records and civil or criminal cases where violations of federal law have occurred. The Administrative Office of the US Courts has an excellent web site at www.uscourts.gov. For detailed information on individual courts and their record access procedures, the products from BRB Publications, Inc (1-800-929-3811) are recommended.

PACER & Online Access

PACER is an acronym for Public Access to Court Electronic Records. PACER allows any user with a personal computer to dial-in to a district or bankruptcy court computer and retrieve official electronic case information and court dockets. The user fee is $.60 per minute. Each court controls its own computer system and case information database; therefore, there are some variations among jurisdictions as to the information offered. Be aware that the district courts and bankruptcy courts provide PACER in different formats.

A recent development is PACER-Net, a pilot project to migrate PACER to the Web. Four courts are participating in the project.

All sign-up and technical support is handled at the PACER Service Center in San Antonio, Texas (1-800-676-6856). You cannot sign up for all or multiple districts at once. In many judicial districts, when you sign up for PACER access, you will receive a PACER Primer that has been customized for each district. The primer contains a summary of how to access PACER, how to select cases, how to read case numbers and docket sheets, some searching tips, who to call for problem resolution, and district specific program variations.

Before the ascendancy of PACER, some courts had developed their own electronic access systems. They have names like NIBS, JAMS and BANCAP. All but a few of these are now available for sign-up at the PACER Center in San Antonio.

Seven federal courts now offer free online access through the Internet.

Arizona Bankruptcy Court (limited data): http://ecf.azb.uscourts.gov

Southern District Court of California: www.casb.uscourts.gov/html/fileroom.htm

Northern District Court of Georgia: http://ecf.ganb.uscourts.gov

District & Bankruptcy Courts in Idaho: www.id.uscourts.gov/doc.htm

Southern Dist. of New York Bankruptcy: www.nysb.uscourts.gov

Northern District Court of Ohio: www.ohnd. uscourts.gov.

Eastern District Court of Virginia: http://ecf.vaeb.uscourts.gov

Alabama

State Agencies Online

Secretary of State Corporations Division PO Box 5616 Montgomery, AL 36103-5616 334-242-5324 334-240-3138 Fax www.alalinc.net/alsecst	Corporation Records Limited Partnership Records Limited Liability Company Records Limited Liability Partnerships The online access system is available for free from 7 AM to 12 PM for corporation and UCC records. Contact Robina Wilson at 334-242-7200 to sign up.
State Court Administrator Director of Courts 300 Dexter Ave Montgomery, AL 36104 334-242-0300 334-242-2099 Fax	Criminal Records The State Court Administration has an online system (SJIS) containing criminal records from all 75 county courthouses in the state. There is a $100 setup fee, $35 per month fee, and $.35 per minute charge. The system is open 24 hours a day, but interruptions in service can occur after 7 PM. All modem speeds work. Call 800-392-8077 for more information.
Department of Public Safety Driver Records-License Division PO Box 1471 Montgomery, AL 36102-1471 334-242-4400 334-242-4639 Fax	Driver Records Alabama offers real time batch processing access via the AAMVAnet 3270 Terminal Connection. There is a minimum order requirement of 500 requests per month. Requesters must provide their own connection device and terminal emulation software. Generally, requests are available 30 minutes after request transmission.
Alabama Legislature State House 11 S Union St Montgomery, AL 36130-4600 334-242-7826 Senate 334-242-7637 House 334-242-8819 Fax www.legislature.state.al.us	Legislation-Current/Pending/Passed The online access system is called "ALIS" and provides state code, bill text, bill status, voting history, statutory retrieval, and boards/commission information. The initial fee is $400 plus $100 per month. You must sign up for 12 months. The fees entitle you to 30 hours of usage per month. The system is open 24 hours a day, 7 days a week. For details, call Angela Sayers at 334-242-7482.

UCC Division	Uniform Commercial Code
Secretary of State PO Box 5616 Montgomery, AL 36103-5616 334-242-5231 www.alalinc.net/alsecst	Federal Tax Liens State Tax Liens There is no charge for their dial-up access system. The system is open from 7 AM to 12 PM. Corporation data is also available. Call Jim Brasher at 334-242-7000 for more information.

County Agencies Online

All County Circuit and District Courts	Civil Cases
	Criminal Cases A statewide system is available. See the State Court Administrator in the state agencies section for details.

Alaska

State Agencies Online

Department of Commerce	Corporation Records
Division of Banking, Securities & Corporations PO Box 110808 Juneau, AK 99811 907-465-2530 907-465-3257 Fax commerce.state.ak.us/dced/bsc/ search.htm	Fictitious Name Assumed Name Limited Partnership Records Limited Liability Company Records At the web site, one can access status information on corps, LLCs, LLP, LP (all both foreign and domestic) as well as registered and reserved names. There is no fee.
Division of Motor Vehicles	Driver Records
Driver's Records PO Box 20020 Juneau, AK 99802-0020 907-465-4335 Motor Vehicle Reports Desk 907-463-5860 Fax	Online access is $5.00 per record. .Inquiries may be made at any time, 24 hours a day. Batch inquires may call back within thirty minutes for responses. Search by the first four letters of driver's name, license number and date of birth. At present, there is only one phone line available for users; you may experience a busy signal.

Alaska State Legislature	Legislation-Current/Pending/Passed
State Capitol	
130 Seward St, Suite 313	All information is available on the Internet.
Juneau, AK 99801-1182	State statutes are on the Internet.
907-465-4648	
907-465-2864 Fax	
www.legis.state.ak.us	
Workers' Compensation	Workers' Compensation Records
PO Box 25512	
Juneau, AK 99802	Online access is available for pre-approved
907-465-2790	accounts. Request in writing to the Director.
907-465-2797 Fax	
www.state.ak.us	

Arizona

State Agencies Online

Corporation Commission	Corporation Records
1300 W Washington	Limited Liability Company Records
Phoenix, AZ 85007	
602-542-3026 Status	The online system is called STARPAS. It
602-542-3285 Annual Reports	functions 24 hours a day, 7 days a week. The
602-542-3414 Fax	initial set-up fee is $36 and access costs $.30
www.cc.state.az.us	per minute. Call Ann Shaw at 602-542-0685
	for a sign-up package.
Motor Vehicle Division	Driver Records
Record Services Section	
PO Box 2100, Mail Drop 539M	Arizona's online system is interactive and is
Phoenix, AZ 85001	primarily for those requesters who are
602-255-0072	exempt. For more information call "Third
	Party Programs" at 602-255-7235.
Arizona Legislature	Legislation-Current/Pending/Passed
State Senate - Room 203	
1700 W Washington	Most information, beginning with 1997, is
Phoenix, AZ 85007	available through the Internet (i.e. bill text,
602-542-3559 Senate Information	committee minutes, committee assignments,
602-542-4221 House Information	member bios, etc.). There is no fee.
602-542-3429 Senate Fax	
602-542-4099 House Fax	
www.azleg.state.az.us	

UCC Division Secretary of State State Capitol, West Wing, 7th Floor Phoenix, AZ 85007 602-542-6178 602-542-7386 Fax www.sosaz.com	Uniform Commercial Code Federal Tax Liens State Tax Liens UCC records can be searched over the web site. Searching can be done by debtor, secured party name, or file number. From this site you can also pull down a weekly microfiche file of filings (about 10 megabytes).
Motor Vehicle Division Record Services Section PO Box 2100, Mail Drop 504M Phoenix, AZ 85001 602-255-8359	Vehicle Ownership Vehicle Identification Online access is offered to permissible users. The system is open 24 hours a day, seven days a week. For more information, call 602-255-7235.

County Agencies Online

Maricopa County Superior Court 201 W Jefferson Phoenix, AZ 85003 602-506-3360 602-506-7619 Fax www.supcourt.maricopa.gov	Civil Cases Criminal Cases Online access is available via the Internet site at no charge. This system shows the entire case file, rather than merely an index. Searching is by name or case number.
Maricopa County County Recorder 111 S 3rd Avenue Phoenix, AZ 85003 602-506-3535 602-506-3069 Fax http://recorder.maricopa.gov	Liens Real Estate Access is available by direct dial-up or on the Internet. On the Internet, one may view document images. Official copies can be ordered for $1.00, certified copies are $3.00. Hours are 6AM-12AM M, 6AM-1AM T-F and 8AM-5PM S-S. For online access, there is a one time setup fee of $300, plus $.06 cents per minute. The system operates 8AM-10PM M-F and 8AM-5PM S-S. Records date back to 1983. There are no fees for using the Internet. Baud rates up to 28.8 are supported. One can search by name, Grantee/Grantor and recording number. For additional information, contact Linda Kinclhloe at 602-506-3637.

Pima County County Accessor's Office 115 N Church Tucson, AZ 85701 520-740-8630 520-792-9825 Fax www.asr.co.pima.az.us	Tax Assessor Records Records are available on the Internet for no fee. One may search by name, parcel and street name and number.

Arkansas

State Agencies Online

Secretary of State Corporation Department-Aegon Bldg 501 Woodlane, Rm 310 Little Rock, AR 72201-1094 501-682-3409 501-682-3437 Fax sosweb.state.ar.us/corps/ incorp	Corporation Records Fictitious Name Limited Liability Company Records Limited Partnerships The Internet site permits searches, at no fee, of corporation records. You can search by name, registered agent, or filing number.
Department of Driver Services Driving Records Division PO Box 1272, Room 127 Little Rock, AR 72203 501-682-7207 501-682-2075 Fax www.state.ar.us	Driver Records Access is available through the Information Network of Arkansas (INA). The system offers both batch and interactive service. The system is only available to INA subscribers who have statutory rights to the data. There is an annual $50 fee plus to the record fee of $8.00 ($11.00 if CDL). For more information, visit the web site or call 800-392-6069.
Arkansas Secretary of State State Capitol Room 256 Little Rock, AR 72201 501-682-1010 501-682-3408 Fax www.arkleg.state.ar.us	Legislation-Current/Pending/Passed The best way to search is through their Internet site.
Secretary of State Trademarks Section 501 Woodlane, #301 Little Rock, AR 72201 501-682-3405 501-682-3437 Fax www.sosweb.state.ar.us/corps/ trademk	Trademarks/Servicemarks Searching is available at no fee over the Internet site.

California

State Agencies Online

Secretary of State Information Retrieval Unit 1500 11th Street Sacramento, CA 95814 916-657-5448 916-653-3794 LLCs 916-653-3365 LPs	Corporation Records Limited Liability Company Records Limited Partnerships The state offers a corporate online system. There is a $300 set-up fee and usage charges of $1.00 for the first screen and $.25 thereafter. The system is available 24 hours a day. For more information, call 916-953-8905.
Department of Motor Vehicles Information Services PO Box 944247, Mail Station G199 Sacramento, CA 94244-2470 916-657-8098 916-657-5564 Alternate Telephone	Driver Records The department offers online access, but a $10,000 one-time setup fee is required. The system is open 24 hours, 7 days a week. For more information call the Analysis and Coordination Unit at 916-657-5582.
California State Legislature State Capitol Room B-32 (Legislative Bill Room) Sacramento, CA 95814 916-445-2323 Current/Pending Bills 916-653-7715 State Archives www.leginfo.ca.gov	Legislation-Current/Pending/Passed The Internet site has all legislative information back to 1993. The site also gives access to state laws.
UCC Division Secretary of State PO Box 942835 Sacramento, CA 94235-0001 916-653-3516 www.ca.gov	Uniform Commercial Code Federal Tax Liens State Tax Liens Direct Access provides dial-up searching via PC and modem. Fees range from $1-3 dollars, depending on type of search. Each page scroll is $.25. Requesters operate from a prepaid account.
Department of Motor Vehicle Public Contact Unit PO Box 944247, Sacramento, CA 94244-2470 916-657-8098 Walk-in/Mail-in Phone 916-657-7914 Commercial Accounts 916-657-6739 Vessel Registration 916-657-9041 Fax	Vehicle Ownership Vehicle Identification Boat & Vessel Ownership & Registration Online access is limited to certain Authorized Vendors. Hours are 6 AM to midnight. Requesters are may not use the data for direct marketing, solicitation, nor resell for those purposes. For information, call 916-657-5582.

County Agencies Online

Contra Costa County Superior Court 725 Court St Rm 103 Martinez, CA 94553 925-646-2951 www.co.contra-costra.ca.us	Civil Cases Access is available for free through the a remote dial-up system. This includes all municipal courts within the county. Accessible information includes: parties names, court dates, court calendars and a list of all documents filed.
Los Angeles County All consolidated courts throughout Los Angeles County www.latrialcourts.org/civil.htm	Civil Cases WEBCOURT online access is available for these courts in the county from the Internet Site. Traffic records are also available.
Riverside County Consolidated Courts-Criminal Division 4100 Main St Riverside, CA 92501 909-275-2300 Criminal 909-275-4007 Fax www.co.riverside.ca.us/depts/courts	Criminal Cases Online access is available by modem at $225.00 plus $16.00 per hour. Civil, family law, and traffic cases are also included on the system. Call Melinda Pierpoint at 909-275-5940 for more information.
Riverside County Consolidated Courts-Civil Division 4050 Main St Riverside, CA 92501 909-275-1960 909-275-1751 Fax www.co.riverside.ca.us/depts/courts	Civil Cases Probate Online access is provided at a subscription fee of $225.00 and an hourly online charge of $16.00. Criminal, probate, family law and traffic cases are also included in the system. Call Melinda Pierpoint at 909-275-5940 to subscribe.
Ventura County East County Superior & Municipal Court PO Box 1200 Simi Valley, CA 93062-1200 805-582-8080 www.ventura.org/courts/vencrts.htm	Criminal Cases Online access is open 24 hours daily and is the same system used by the Ventura Superior Court.
Ventura County Ventura County Superior & Municipal Courts 800 S Victoria Ave PO Box 6489 Ventura, CA 93006-6489 805-662-6620 805-650-4032 Fax	Civil Cases Criminal Cases Contact Gloria Moreno at 805-654-3745 for information about remote access. Cost is $100 for civil and $100 for criminal access plus $60 per user key. The system is open 24 hours

	daily.

Colorado

State Agencies Online

Secretary of State Corporation Division 1560 Broadway, Suite 200 Denver, CO 80202 303-894-2251 Corporations 900-555-1717 Status-Name 303-894-2242 Fax	Corporation Records Trademarks/Servicemarks Fictitious Name Limited Liability Company Records Assumed Name Online access is gatewayed through another agency -The Colorado Central Indexing System, 303-894-2175. The system can be accessed from their web site (www.cocis.com) or from a separate dial-up mode. There is an annual $29.50registration fee. Accounts can be set up to pay on a per search basis or for unlimited access. There are two plans, one including corporate officers and directors, and one not (corporate name searching only). The system holds UCC records from both the Secretary of State and the counties as well vehicle lien records.
Bureau of Investigation, State Repository Identification Unit 690 Kipling St, Suite 3000 Denver, CO 80215 303-239-4230 303-239-0865 Fax	Criminal Records There is a remote access system available called the Electronic Clearance System (ECS). This is an overnight batch system, open M-F from 7AM to 4PM. The fee is $7.00 per record. There is no set-up fee, but requesters must register. Billing is monthly. For more information, call 303-239-4230.
Colorado General Assembly State Capitol 200 E Colfax Ave Denver, CO 80203-1784 303-866-3055 Bill Data (during session) 303-866-2358 Archives www.state.co.us/gov_dir/ stateleg.html	Legislation-Current/Pending/Passed The web site gives access to bills, status, journals, 1997 and 1998 sessions, and much more.
UCC Division Secretary of State 1560 Broadway, Suite 200	Uniform Commercial Code Federal Tax Liens State Tax Liens

Denver, CO 80202 303-894-2200 303-894-2242 Fax	The online access is available through the Colorado Central Indexing System (CIS). It is accessed from the Internet at www.cocis.com or by direct dial-up. The fee is $15.00 to search by name or $2,500 per 6 months for unlimited access. There is no fee to search notice of farm product liens or for the sales tax by address locator. This system has filings from the state and the counties and lien records from the DMV. CIS can be reached at 303-894-2175. They do not permit mail, in person or phone searching.

Connecticut

State Agencies Online

Secretary of State Commercial Recording Division 30 Trinity St Hartford, CT 06106 860-509-6003 860-509-6068 Fax www.state.ct.us/sots	Corporation Records Limited Partnership Records Trademarks/Servicemarks Limited Liability Company Records There is no set-up fee, but a "bank" of $500.00 must be established. The communications network is AAMVAnet and charges are incurred. The cost to view a screen of data figures to less than $.01. The system supports baud rates to 28.8. Call David Pritchard at 860-509-6154 for more information.
Department of Motor Vehicles Copy Records Section 60 State St, Room 305 Wethersfield, CT 06109-1896 860-263-5154	Driver Records Online access is provided to approved businesses that enter into written contract. The system is open 24 hours a day, 7 days a week. The address is part of the record. For more information, call 860-566-3596.
Connecticut General Assembly State Library 231 Capitol Ave, Bill Room Hartford, CT 06106 860-566-5736 860-566-2133 Fax www.cga.state.ct.us	Legislation-Current/Pending/Passed From the web site you can track bills, find update or status, and print copies of bills.

Department of Motor Vehicles Copy Record Unit 60 State St, Branch Operations Wethersfield, CT 06109-1896 860-566-3720	Vehicle Ownership Vehicle Identification The Department has started a pilot program for online access that is not yet open to the general business public. This program, when available to all, will have the same restrictions and criteria as described in the Driving Records Section.

Delaware

State Agencies Online

Division of Motor Vehicles Driver Services PO Box 698 Dover, DE 19903 302-739-4343 302-739-2602 Fax	Driver Records Online searching is single inquiry only, no batch request mode is offered. Searching is done by driver's license number or name and DOB. A signed contract application and valid "business license" is required. Hours of operation are 8 AM to 4:30 PM. Access is provided through AT&T's 900 at a fee of $1.00 per minute. Records at $4.00 each. For more information, call 302-739-4435.
Division of Motor Vehicles Correspondence Section PO Box 698 Dover, DE 19903 302-739-3147 302-739-2042 Fax	Vehicle Ownership Vehicle Identification There is an additional $1.00 per minute fee to the $4.00 record fee for using the on-line "900 number" system. The system is single inquiry mode and is open from 8 AM to 4:30 PM. For more information, call 302-739-4435.

District of Columbia

State Agencies Online

Department of Motor Vehicles Driver Records Division 301 "C" St, NW Washington, DC 20001 202-727-6761	Driver Records Online requests are taken throughout the day and are available the next morning after 8:15 am. There is no minimum order requirement. Overnight tape-to-tape batches are not available. Billing is a "bank" system which

	draws from pre-paid account. Requesters are restricted to high volume, ongoing users. Each requester must be approved and sign a contract. For more information, call 202-727-5692.

Florida

State Agencies Online

Division of Corporations Department of State PO Box 6327 Tallahassee, FL 32314 850-488-9000 Telephone Inquires 850-487-6053 Copy Requests 850-487-6056 Annual Reports www.dos.state.fl.us	Corporation Records Limited Partnership Records Trademarks/Servicemarks Assumed Name Fictitious Names The state has an excellent Internet site which gives detailed information on all corporate, fictitious names, partnerships, and UCC records. They also offer electronic filing. The site is available from 7 AM to 7 PM, EST Monday-Friday. Recently, they have added a corporations document image delivery system which includes fictitious name filings and corporation annual reports since 01/96, all other corporation filings since 11/97, and all partnership filings.
Florida Department of Law Enforcement User Services Bureau PO Box 1489 Tallahassee, FL 32302 850-488-6236 850-488-1413 Fax	Criminal Records Access is available for pre-approved, pre-paid accounts. This is a batch inquiry system. All criminal history records are available. There is no sign-up fee, but requesters must establish an escrow account. The turnaround time is 48 hours. For more information, call Julie Boland at 850-488-6236.
Department of Highway Safety & Motor Vehicles Division of Drivers Licenses PO Box 5775 Tallahassee, FL 32314-5775 850-488-0250 850-487-7080 Fax www.hsmv.state.fl.us	Driver Records Online requests are $2.10 for a three year record and $3.10 for a seven year record. There is also a $.10 transaction fee per record. The system is open 24 hours a day, 7 days a week. The state differentiates between high and low volume users. Call Information Systems Administration at 850-488-6264 for details.

Joint Legislative Mgmt Committee Legislative Information Division 111 W Madison St, Pepper Bldg, Rm 704 Tallahassee, FL 32399-1400 850-488-4371 850-487-5285 Senate Bills 850-488-7475 House Bills 850-488-8427 Session Laws 850-921-5334 Fax www.leg.state.fl.us	Legislation-Current/Pending/Passed Their Internet site contains full text of bills and a bill history session outlining actions taken on bills. The site is updated every day at 11 PM. Records go back to 1995. There is a more extensive online information service available from the Legislative Data Center at 850-488-8326. This system also includes information on lobbyists. Fees are involved.
UCC Division Secretary of State PO Box 5588 Tallahassee, FL 32314 850-487-6055 850-487-6013 Fax www.dos.state.fl.us	Uniform Commercial Code Federal Tax Liens The state has a great Internet site that allows access for no charge. The site is open 7AM to 7PM M-F (EST). The collateral for the UCC filing is not mentioned in this database. The state also has a document image delivery system on the web site. This includes all UCC filings since 01/97 and all documents that were filed electronically since 03/95.
Division of Motor Vehicles Information Research Section Neil Kirkman Bldg, A-126 Tallahassee, FL 32399 850-488-5665 850-488-8983 Fax www.hsmv.state.fl.us	Vehicle Ownership Vehicle Identification Florida has contracted to release vehicle information through TML Information Services 800-743-7891, accounts must be approved by the state first. For each record accessed, the charge is $.50 plus the subscriber fee. Users must work from an estimated 2 1/2 month pre-paid bank. New subscribers to TML must contact the company prior to completing an application with the Department 850-488-6193.

County Agencies Online

Alachua County Circuit and County Courts PO Box 600 Gainesville, FL 32602 352-374-3611 352-338-3201 Fax	Civil Cases Criminal Cases For information about the remote access system and requesting searches by e-mail, call Jack Crosetti at 352-338-7323. The annual fee is $360 plus a one time setup fee of $50. The system is open 24 hours daily. Records can be searched by name or case number.

Brevard County Circuit Court 700 South Park Ave (PO Box H, 32781-0239) Titusville, FL 32780 407-264-5245 Civil 407-264-5350 Criminal 407-264-5395 Fax www.clerk.co.brevard.fl.us	Civil Cases Criminal Cases Liens Vital Records The annual fee for online access to the Indexing and ORM systems is $25.00, which includes unlimited use of the databases. The system is open 24 hours daily. Search by name or case number. Contact Lori Raulerson at 407-264-5245 to open an account.
Brevard County County Appraisers 400 South Street, 5th floor Titusville, FL 32780 407-264-6700 www.appraiser.co.brevard.fl.us	Real Estate Access is free through the Internet. One may search by owner name or address.
Broward County Circuit and County Courts 201 SE 6th St Ft Lauderdale, FL 33301 954-831-5729 954-765-4573 Criminal 954-831-7166 Fax	Civil Cases Criminal Cases The online system has a $40.00 setup fee plus security deposit. The monthly access fee is $49.00 which includes 2 free hours, afterward there is a $.34 per minute charge. Search by name or case number or case type. Call 954-357-7022 for more data.
Clay County Circuit Court PO Box 698 Green Cove Springs, FL 32043 904-284-6302 904-284-6390 Fax www.state.fl.us/clayclerk	Civil Cases Criminal Cases Probate Liens Real Estate The setup fee is $500 and there is a monthly usage fee of $50. Any VT 100 emulation software will work. The records date back to 1984. The system operates 24 hours daily and supports baud rates up to 33.6. One may search by name, case number, Grantee/Grantor and book and page. Lending agency information is available. Records include domestic and traffic. For further information, contact Carol Johnson at 904-284-6371.

Clay County County Court PO Box 698 Green Cove Springs, FL 32043 904-284-6316 904-284-6390 Fax `www.state.fl.us/clayclerk`	Civil Cases Criminal Cases This is the same system used by the Circuit Court in Clay County.
Collier County Circuit and County Courts PO Box 413044 Naples, FL 34101-3044 941-732-2646	Civil Cases Criminal Cases Probate The online access system has a $100.00 setup fee, a monthly $10.00 fee and a $.05 per minute access charge. The system is open 24 hours daily. Records include probate, traffic and domestic. Call 941-774-8339 for more information.
Collier County County Clerk of the Circuit Court 3001 E Tamiami Trail Administration Building, 4th Floor Naples, FL 34122 941-774-8261 941-774-8408 Fax	Liens Real Estate Birth Records Death Records Marriage Records Divorce Records The subscription fee is $100, plus a $50 deposit. The monthly fee is $10, plus $.05 per minute. The records date back to 1986. The system operates 24 hours daily and supports baud rates up to 9,600. One may search by name and Grantee/Grantor. Lending agency information is available. For additional information, contact Judy Stephenson at 941-774-8339.
Dade County Circuit and County Courts-Civil/Criminal 73 W Flagler St Miami, FL 33130 305-275-1155 305-375-5819 Fax	Civil Cases Online access includes a $125.00 setup fee, $52.00 monthly and $.25 per minute after the first 208 minutes each month. Open 24 hours daily, docket information can be searched by case number or name. Call 305-596-8148 for more information.
Dade County County Clerk 44 W Flager Street, 8th Floor Miami, FL 33130 305-275-1155 305-372-7775 Fax	Liens Real Estate Marriage Records Tax Assessor Records An initial setup fee of $125 is required, and

	there is a minimum monthly fee of $52, which includes 208 minutes of use. Additional minutes are $.25 each. The records date back to 1975. The system operates 24 hours daily, and supports a baud rate of 56k. 11 databases are available to search, including property appraisal, building permits, tax collection and permit public hearings, and others. One can search by name, Grantee/Grantor, folio number, address and by date. For additional information, contact Jerry Kiernan at 305-596-8148.
Duval County Circuit and County Courts- 330 E Bay St, Rm M106 Jacksonville, FL 32202 904-630-2039 Civil 904-630-2070 Criminal 904-630-7505 Fax www.ci.jax.fl.us/pub/clerk/ default.htm	Civil Cases Criminal Cases Contact Mike O'Brien at 904-630-1140 for information about remote access. Costs include $100 setup, $30 per month and $.25 per minute. System available 24 hours per day at minimum 9600 baud. Records go back to 1992.
Escambia County County Clerk of the Circuit Court 223 Palafox Place, Old Courthouse Pensacola, FL 32501 850-595-3930 850-595-3925 Fax	Liens Real Estate Divorce Records An initial subscription fee of $150 is required. The monthly fee of $42 is all inclusive. The records date back to 4/82. The system operates 24 hours daily. One may search by name, Grantee/Grantor or by document type. Lending agency information is available. No addresses can be viewed. For additional information, contact Joanne Duckworth at 850-595-3923.
Gadsden County Clerk of the Circuit Court 10 E Jefferson Street Quincy, FL 32351 904-875-8603 904-875-8612 Fax	Liens Real Estate Death Records Marriage Records Divorce Records A written request needs to be sent to the Clerk of the Court to sign up for online access. The subscription fee varies, as does the monthly fee. The records date back to 1985. The system operates 24 hours daily. A baud rate of 19.2 is supported. The database can be searched by name, Grantee/Grantor, file

	number, date and document type. Lending agency information is available. For additional information, contact Jim Cleek at 904-875-8629.
Hernando County Circuit and County Courts 20 N Main St Brooksville, FL 34601 352-754-4201 352-754-4239 Fax	Civil Cases Criminal Cases Liens Real Estate Marriage Records A refundable deposit is required. The monthly minimum fee is $5.00, with a per minute charge of $.10. The records date back to 1983. The system operates 24 hours daily and supports baud rates up to 28.8. The database can be searched by name, Grantee/Grantor, book and page, instrument number, and parcel and case. Lending agency information is available. A fax back service for specific pages is available for $1-$1.25 per page. Plans are underway to move the public record access to the Internet. For more information, contact Bob Piercy at 352-754
Hillsborough County Circuit and County Courts 419 Pierce St Tampa, FL 33602 813-276-8100 813-272-7707 Fax	Civil Cases Criminal Cases Probate Liens Real Estate Online access has a $50.00 setup fee which includes software. Access is $.25 per minute or $5.00 per month, whichever is greater. Traffic and domestic records included. Contact the help desk at 813-276-8100, Ext. 7000 for more information.
Indian River County County Clerk of the Circuit Court 2000 16th Avenue Vero Beach, FL 32960 561-770-5174 561-770-7008 Fax	Liens Real Estate Birth Records Death Records Marriage Records Divorce Records There is a $200 all inclusive monthly fee. The records date back to the mid 1980s. The system operates 24 hours daily. The system supports baud rates up to 33.6. All records recorded in this office are available online.

	One may search by name, Grantee/Grantor and case number. For further information, contact Gary Tummond at 561-567-8000.
Jacksonville (City) www.ci.jax.fl.us/pub/depot.htm#prop	Real Estate The Jacksonville Public Data Depot is a free access to property records for the city of Jacksonville, FL.
Lake County County Clerk of the Circuit Court 550 W Main Street Travares, FL 32778 352-742-4114 352-742-4166 Fax	Liens Real Estate Marriage Records There is a set up fee of $75, plus an annual renewal fee of $50. The system operates from 8:30AM-5PM M-F and supports a baud rate of 19.2. The records date back to 1974. One may search by name and book and page. Lending agency information is available. For further information, contact Sandra Squires at 352-742-4156
Lee County Circuit and County Courts PO Box 2469 Ft Myers, FL 33902 941-335-2283	Civil Cases Criminal Cases Online access entails a $150.00 setup, $15.00 per month fee and a per minute charge based on usage. The system is open 24 hours daily and includes probate records. Call Natalie at 941-335-2975 for more information
Leon County Circuit and County Courts PO Box 726 Tallahassee, FL 32302 850-488-7539 850-488-2131 Criminal 850-488-8863 Fax www.clerk.leon.fl.us	Civil Cases Criminal Cases There is both a free and access to online records. Search the Internet for free by name or instrument code (not all records up). The pay system, which is much more thorough, is $100 setup and $100 per month. The system is open 8am to 7pm daily. Records date back to 1984.
Leon County County Clerk of the Circuit Court 301 S Monroe Street, Room 123 Tallahassee, FL 32301 850-488-7538 850-921-1310 Fax www.clerk.leon.fl.us	Liens Real Estate Marriage Records Access is through their Internet site, there is no fee. One can search by name, Grantee/Grantor, type of document, recording date, document and instrument code. Information is available for no fee in their

	site. A search by lending agency gives a range of that agency's loans and dates. The earliest date documents are available is 01/01/84.
Manatee County Circuit and County Courts PO Box 1000 Bradenton, FL 34206 941-749-1800 941-741-4082 Fax	Civil Cases Criminal Cases Real Estate Probate Remote online access system, CHIPS, costs $50 for setup with an annual fee of $120. System includes civil and criminal indexes as well as property appraiser, tax assessor, probate and domestic data. Modem rates up to 9600. Call Terry Turner at 941-741-4003 for more information.
Manatee County County Clerk 1115 Manatee Avenue W Bradenton, FL 34206 941-741-4041 941-749-7194 Fax	Real Estate Death Records Marriage Records Divorce Records There are no fees to view, but you are limited to 2 hours access per day. The records date back to 1978. The system operates 24 hours daily. One can search by name, Grantee/Grantor, book and page, case number and instrument type. Lending agency information is available. They also offer a fax back service for a fee, which requires a $400 deposit. For further information, contact Martha Pope at 941-741-4051.
Martin County Circuit and County Courts PO Box 9016 Stuart, FL 34995 561-288-5576 561-288-5990; 288-5991 (civil) Fax	Civil Cases Criminal Cases Probate Online access entails a $100.00 setup fee (half of which is refundable), a monthly fee of $40.00, and access fee of $.10 per minute. The system is open during working hours only. ProComm Plus is required. Records available include traffic and domestic. The system offers a fax back option for actual page copies for $1-1.25 per page. For more information, call 561-288-5985.
Okaloosa County Circuit and County Courts 1250 Eglin Pkwy Shalimar, FL 32579	Civil Cases Criminal Cases Probate Liens

850-651-7200 850-651-7230 Fax	Real Estate Vital Records The system has a flat monthly usage fee of $100. The system operates 24 hours daily and supports baud rates up to 28.8. The records date back to 1982. One may search by name, Grantee/Grantor, book and page and by document type. Lending agency information is available. Records include traffic and domestic records. For further information contact, Don Howard at 850-689-5821.
Orange County Circuit and County Courts 37 N Orange Ave #550 Orlando, FL 32801 407-836-2060	Civil Cases Criminal Cases Probate The Teleclerk remote online system costs $100 one time fee and $30 per month, including 5 hours of online time. Additional time is charged at $.25 per minute. The system is open 24 hours daily and includes traffic and domestic records. For more information call 407-836-2064.
Orange County County Comptroller 401 S Rosalind Avenue Orlando, FL 32801 407-836-5115 407-836-5101 Fax www.comptroller.co.orange.fl.us	Liens Real Estate Marriage Records Access to public records is through the Internet, there is no fee. Records date back to 1955. Marriage records are available beginning 3/98. One can search by name or book and page. Lending agency information is available.
Palm Beach County Circuit and County Courts 205 North Dixie West Palm Beach, FL 33401 561-355-2986 Civil 561-355-2519 Criminal 561-355-3802 Fax	Civil Cases Criminal Cases Probate Contact Betty Jones at 561-355-6783 for information about remote access. Fees include $145 setup and $65 per month. Criminal and civil records are available back to 1988. Other records available include traffic and domestic The system is open 18 hours daily.
Pasco County Circuit and County Courts 38053 Live Oak Ave Dade City, FL 33523	Civil Cases Criminal Records Probate

352-521-4482	Online access requires a $100 deposit, $50 annual fee and minimum of $10.00 per month. There is a $.10 per screen charge. The system is open 24 hours daily. Search by name or case number. Call Barbara Alford at 352-521-4201 for more information.
Pasco County County Clerk of the Circuit Court 38053 Live Oak Avenue, Room 205 Dade City, FL 33523 352-521-4464	Liens Real Estate Marriage Records To sign up, there is a $25 annual fee plus a $50 deposit. One is billed at the rate of $.05 per minute from 7AM-6PM, and $.03 per minute at all other times. There is a $3.00 monthly minimum. The records date back to 1975. Baud rates up to 56k are supported. There is a fax back service and the cost per page is $1.25. One may search by name, Grantee/Grantor and by date. No addresses are listed. Lending agency information is available. For further information, contact Mike Stubs at 352-521-4529.
Pinellas County Circuit and County Courts-Civil Division 315 Court St Clearwater, FL 33756 813-464-3267 813-464-4070 Fax County Court-Criminal Division 14250 49th St N Clearwater, FL 34622-2831 813-464-6800 Criminal 813-464-6072 Fax	Civil Cases Criminal Cases Contact Sue Maskeny at 813-464-3779 for information about remote access. Setup fee is $60 plus per minute charges. The civil index goes back to 1973, the criminal index goes back to 1972. The system is open 24 hours daily and includes probate and traffic records.
Polk County Circuit and County Courts PO Box 9000 Bartow, FL 33830 941-534-4000 941-534-4089 Fax	Civil Cases Criminal Cases Real Estate Vital Records Online access requires a $150 setup fee and $.15 per minute with a $50 per quarter minimum. Call Ann Hoaks at 941-534-7575 for more information.
Putnam County Circuit and County Courts PO Box 758 Palatka, FL 32178	Civil Cases Criminal Cases Real Estate

904-329-0361 Civil 904-329-0249 Criminal 904-329-0888 Fax	Write Lonnie Thompson to register; include a check for $400 as a setup fee. The monthly charge is $40 plus $.05 per minute over 20 hours. Criminal records go back to 1972. Civil index goes back to 1984. The system operates 24 hours daily.
Putnam County County Clerk 518 St. Johns Avenue, Bldg. 1-E Palatka, FL 32177 904-329-0258 904-329-0889 Fax	Liens Real Estate Marriage Records Divorce Records Tax Assessor Records The initial online access fee is $400. There is a $40 per month fee, which includes 20 hours of use. Additional minutes are billed at $.05 per minute. Records date back to 10/83. The system operates 24 hours daily and supports baud rates up to 33.6. One can search by name, Grantee/Grantor, instrument number and 911 street address. For additional information, contact Lonnie Thompson at 904-329-0353.
Sarasota County Circuit and County Courts-Civil Division PO Box 3079 Sarasota, FL 34230 941-951-5206	Civil Cases Probate Contact Tom Kay for information about remote access. Cost is $15 per month minimum against $.15 per minute, with an initial deposit of $300. System operates 8-5 daily at 9600 baud. Index goes back to 1983. Domestic records included.
St. Johns County Circuit and County Courts PO Drawer 300 St Augustine, FL 32085-0300 904-823-2333 904-823-2294 Fax	Civil Cases Criminal Cases Online access requires dedicated phone line. Setup is $200 and there is a monthly fee of $50. The system is open 8-5 during the week. Searching is by name or case number. The index and dockets are available from 1984. Call Mark Dearing at 904-823-2333 X361 for more information.
Volusia County Circuit and County Courts PO Box 43 De Land, FL 32721-0043 904-736-5915 904-822-5711 Fax	Civil Cases Criminal Cases Online access is available from 8am to 4:30pm. Setup is $125 and the monthly fee is $25. Windows 95 or 98 is required. Search by

	name or case number back to 1988. Call Tom White for more information.
Volusia County County Clerk 235 W New York Avenue De Land, FL 32720 904-736-5912 904-740-5104 Fax	Liens Real Estate Death Records Marriage Records Divorce Records The initial set up fee is $125, with a flat monthly fee of $25. Once you sign up, you are given the commercial Internet site used for access. The records date back to 1988. You can search by name, Grantee/Grantor, case number, document type, and parcel number since 1995. Lending agency information is available. For further information, contact Virginia Threlkeld at 904-822-5710.
Walton County Circuit and County Courts PO Box 1260 De Funiak Springs, FL 32433 850-892-8115 850-892-7551 Fax	Civil Cases Criminal Cases Probate Liens Real Estate Death Records Divorce Records The initial set up fee ranges between $300-$450, with a flat monthly access fee of $100. The records date back to 1800. The system operates 24 hours daily and baud rates up to 28.8 are supported. One can search by name, Grantee/Grantor and recording date. Lending agency information is available. For further information, contact either David Langford or Alex Alford at 850-892-8115.

Georgia

State Agencies Online

| **Secretary of State**
Corporation Division
2 M L King Dr, Suite 315, W Tower
Atlanta, GA 30334-1530
404-656-2817
404-656-2817 Filing Questions
404-651-9059 Fax | Corporation Records
Limited Partnership Records
Limited Liability Company Records

Records are available from the Internet site. The corporate database can be searched by entity name or registered agent for no fee. |

www.sos.state.ga.us/corporations/	There is a $10.00 charge for a Certificate of Existence (Good Standing) or a certified copy of Corporate Charter. Other services include name reservation, filing procedures, downloading of forms and applications.
General Assembly of Georgia State Capitol Atlanta, GA 30334 404-656-5040 Senate 404-656-5015 House 404-656-2370 Archives 404-656-5043 Fax www.ganet.org/services/leg/	Legislation-Current/Pending/Passed The Internet site has bill information back to 1995. Statutes are not available online.
Superior Court Clerks' Cooperative Authority 1875 Century Blvd, #100 Atlanta, GA 30345 404-327-9058 404-327-7877 Fax gsccca.org	Uniform Commercial Code Online access is available for regular, ongoing requesters. There is a $50.00 set-up fee, a monthly charge of $25.00, and a $.32 per minute access fee. Billing is monthly. The system is open 24 hours a day, 7 days a week. Minimum baud rate is 9600; 28.8 is supported. Information from 01/01/95 forward is available. Call 800-304-5175 or 404-327-9058 for a subscription package.

Hawaii

State Agencies Online

Business Registration Division PO Box 40 Honolulu, HI 96810 808-586-2727 808-586-2733 Fax www.state.hi.us/dbedt/start.html	Corporation Records Fictitious Name Limited Partnership Records Assumed Name Trademarks/Servicemarks Online access is available through Hawaii FYI at 808-587-4800. There are no fees, the system is open 24 hours. For assistance during business hours, call 808-586-1919.
Hawaii Legislature 415 S Beretania St Honolulu, HI 96813 808-587-0700 Bill # and Location 808-586-6720 Clerk's Office-Senate 808-586-6400 Clerk's Office-House 808-586-0690 State Library	Legislation-Current/Pending/Pending To dial online for current year bill information line, call 808-296-4636. Or, access the information through the Internet site. There is no fee, the system is up 24 hours.

808-587-0720 Fax
www.hawaii.gov

Idaho

State Agencies Online

Secretary of State Corporation Division PO Box 83720 Boise, ID 83720-0080 208-334-2301 208-334-2847 Fax idsos.state.id.us	Corporation Records Limited Partnerships Trademarks/Servicemarks Limited Liability Company Records Fictitious Names, Trade Names The system is named PAIS. To subscribe, you must become a pre-paid customer. An initial deposit of $200 is requested. There is a monthly subscription of $10.00 and an online usage charge of $.10 per minute. Their current baud rate is 9600. The system is available from 8 AM to 5 PM, M-F. If PAIS is only used for corporation recaps and UCC, then initial deposit is only $25.
Idaho Transportation Department Driver's Services PO Box 34 Boise, ID 83731-0034 208-334-8736 208-334-8739 Fax www.state.id.us/itd/dmv.html	Driver Records Idaho offers online access (CICS) to the driver license files to approved vendors through the AAMVAnet/Advantis network. The system is interactive and open 24 hours per day. There is a minimum of 1,000 requests per month; however, this may change. The system not only permits access to driver records, but also to non-CDL title and registration records, and offers a dealer inquiry screen. Information: 208-334-8761.
Legislature Services Office Research and Legislation PO Box 83720 Boise, ID 83720-0054 208-334-2475 208-334-2125 Fax www.state.is.us/legislat/ legislat.html	Legislation-Current/Pending/Passed Statutes and bill information can be accessed from their web site.
UCC Division Secretary of State PO Box 83720 Boise, ID 83720-0080	Uniform Commercial Code Federal Tax Liens The deposit is $25-200 is required with a

| 208-334-3191
208-334-2847 Fax
`www.idsos.state.id.us` | monthly subscription fee of $10.00 and a usage fee of $.10 per minute. This is the same system described under Corporation Records. |
| **Idaho Transportation Department**
Vehicle Services
PO Box 34
Boise, ID 83731-0034
208-334-8773
208-334-8542 Fax
`www.state.id.us/itd/dmv.htm` | Vehicle Ownership
Vehicle Identification

Idaho offers online access (CICS) to the registration and title files to approved vendors through the same system used for driving record requests. At present, only non-commercial information is available. The system is open 24 hours daily. A dealer inquiry screen is also offered. For more information, call 208-334-8659. |

Illinois

State Agencies Online

| **Department of Business Services**
Corporate Department
Howlett Bldg, 3rd Floor, Copy Section
Springfield, IL 62756
217-782-7880
217-782-4528 Fax | Corporation Records
Limited Partnership Records
Trade Names
Assumed Name
Limited Liability Company Records

Potential users must submit in writing the purpose of the request. Submit to: Sharon Thomas, Dept. of Business Srvs, 330 Howlett Bldg, Springfield, IL 62756. Also, call 217-782-4104 for more information. |
| **Illinois State Police**
Bureau of Identification
260 N Chicago St
Joliet, IL 60432-4075
815-740-5164
815-740-5193 Fax
`www.state.il.us/isp/`
`isphpage.htm` | Criminal Records

Online access costs $7.00 per page. Upon signing an interagency agreement with ISP and establishing an escrow account, users can submit inquiries over modem. Replies are still sent via US mail. Turnaround time is approximately 4 business days for a "no record" response. Modem access is available from 7AM-4PM M-F, excluding holidays. Users must utilize LAPLINK for windows, version 6.0 or later. The system is called UCIA - Uniform Conviction Information Act. |

Illinois General Assembly State House House (or Senate) Bills Division Springfield, IL 62706 217-782-3944 Bill Status Only 217-782-7017 Index Div-Older Bills 217-782-5799 House Bills 217-782-9778 Senate Bills 217-524-6059 Fax	Legislation-Current/Pending/Passed The Legislative Information System is available for subscription through a standard modem. The sign-up fee is $500, which includes 100 free minutes of access. Thereafter, access time is billed at $1.00 per minute. The hours of availability are 8 AM - 10 PM when in session and 8 AM - 5 PM when not in session, M-F. Contact Craig Garret at 217-782-4083 to set-up an account. There is no Internet site available.

County Agencies Online

Champaign County Circuit Court 101 E Main Urbana, IL 61801 217-384-3725 217-384-3727 Criminal 217-384-3879 Fax	Civil Cases Criminal Cases Online available for cases back to 1992. The system is called PASS. There is a setup fee and an annual user fee. Contact Jo Kelly at 217-384-3767 for subscription information.
De Kalb County County Recorder 110 E Sycamore Street Sycamore, IL 60178 815-895-7156	Liens Real Estate A $350 subscription fee is required to sign up and there is a per minute charge of $.25, $.50 if printing. The records date back to 1980. The system operates from 8:30AM-4:30PM and supports a baud rate of 28.8. One may search by name, Grantee/Grantor, lot block subdivision, section, township and range, file number and parcel number. Lending agency information is available. For further information, contact Sheila Larson at 815-895-7152.
Du Page County County Recorder 421 N County Farm Road Wheaton, IL 60187 630-682-7200 630-682-7214 Fax	Liens Real Estate Tax Assessor Records One must lease a live interface telephone line from AT&T or a similar carrier to establish a connection. The only other fee is a $.05 per transaction charge. An IBM 3270 emulator is also required. The system operates from 12AM-6:30PM and supports a baud rate of 56K. Records date back to 1977. One may search by name, Grantee/Grantor or document

	number. For further information, contact Fred Kieltcka at 630-682-7030.
Macon County Circuit Court 253 E Wood St Decatur, IL 62523 217-424-1454 217-424-1350 Fax www.court.co.macon.il.us	Civil Cases Criminal Cases The online system is open 24 hours daily on the Internet. Docket information is viewable since 04/96. Search by name or case number. There is no fee.
McHenry County Circuit Court 2200 N Seminary Ave Woodstock, IL 60098 815-338-2098 815-338-8583 Fax www.co.mchenry.il.us	Civil Cases Criminal Cases Online is available 24 hours daily, there are no fees. Records date back to 1990. Civil, criminal, probate, traffic, and domestic records are available. For more information, call Bill Case at 815-334-4302.
McHenry County County Recorder 2200 N Seminary Avenue, Room A280 Woodstock, IL 60098 815-344-4110 815-338-9612 Fax	Liens Real Estate A subscription fee of $350 applies. In addition, there is a monthly fee of $25.00 and a per minute charge of $.25. Name search results can be printed for $1.00. Records date back to 1987. The hours of operation are 7AM-12PM and baud rates of up to 28.8 are supported. Searches can be made by name, Grantee/Grantor, tax ID number, legal description and recorded document number. Lending agency information is available. For further information, contact Phyllis Walters at 815-344-4110.
Rock Island County Circuit Court 210 15th St, PO Box 5230 Rock Island, IL 61204-5230 309-786-4451 309-786-3029 Fax	Civil Cases Criminal Cases Probate Online access is open 24 hours daily. There is a $200 setup fee and additional deposit required. The access fee is $1.00 per minute. Civil, criminal, probate, traffic, and domestic records can be accessed by name or case number.

Indiana

State Agencies Online

Corporation Division Secretary of State 302 W Washington St, Room E018 Indianapolis, IN 46204 317-232-6576 317-233-3387 Fax www.state.in.us/sos	Corporation Records Limited Partnerships Fictitious Name Assumed Name Limited Liability Company Records Limited Liability Partnerships This subscription service is available from the Access Indiana Information Network gateway over the Internet. In general, search fees are $1.00 per search. For more information, visit the web site.
UCC Division Secretary of State 302 W Washington St, Room E018 Indianapolis, IN 46204 317-233-3984 317-233-3387 Fax www.state.in.us/sos	Uniform Commercial Code This subscription service is available from the Access Indiana Information Network gateway over the Internet. The search fee is $3.00 with an additional $.50 to view an image of the lien. For more information, visit the web site.
BMV-Driving Records 100 N Senate Ave Indiana Government Center North, Room N405 Indianapolis, IN 46204 317-232-6000 2	Driver Records Online access costs $5.00 per page. Access Indiana Information Network (AIIN) is the state owned interactive information and communication system which provides batch and interactive access to driving records. There is an additional $.10 fee if accessing through AIIN's 800 number. However, there is no access fee if you come in through the Internet (www.ai.org). The system is open 24 hours per day, 7 days a week. Generally, batch transmissions are available 6 hours after request is made. For more information, call AIIN at 317-233-2010.
Legislative Services Agency State House 200 W Washington, Room 302 Indianapolis, IN 46204-2789 317-232-9856 www.state.in.us	Legislation-Current/Pending/Passed All legislative information is available over the Internet. The Indiana Code is also available.

Bureau of Motor Vehicles Records 100 N Senate Ave, Room N404 Indianapolis, IN 46204 317-233-6000	Vehicle Ownership Vehicle Identification Boat & Vessel Ownership Boat & Vessel Registration The Access Indiana Information network (AIIN) at 317-233-2010 is the state appointed vendor. The fee is $5.00 per record plus an access fee of $.10 per minute if through an 800 number or no access fee if via the Internet (record fee still applies). The system is open 24 hours 7 days a week. Both interactive and batch (6 hour turnaround time) are available. The web address is www.ai.org.

County Agencies Online

Adams County Circuit & Superior Court 2nd St Courthouse Decatur, IN 46733 219-724-2600 X206 219-724-3848 Fax	Civil Cases Criminal Cases Online access is available through www.civicnet.net. Fees vary by search, the system is open 24 hours. Civil records date back to 1991, criminal to 1988.
Elkhart County County Recorder 117 N 2nd Street, Room 205 Goshen, IN 46526	Liens Real Estate Tax Assessor Records The annual fee is $50, plus a minimum of $20 per month if you use the system. The minimum fee gives 2 hours of access. Additional usage is billed at $10 per hour. The system operates 24 hours daily and supports baud rates up to 9,600. One can search by name, Grantee/Grantor and instrument type. Lending agency information is available. For further information, contact Nick Cenova at 219-535-6777.
Marion County Circuit & Superior Court 200 E Washington St Indianapolis, IN 46204 317-327-4724 317-327-4733 Criminal	Civil Cases Criminal Cases Remote access available through www.civicnet.net (Internet). The setup fee is $50, other fees vary by Criminal records go back to 1988.

Marion County County Recorder 200 E Washington, Suite 721 Indianapolis, IN 46204 317-327-4020 317-327-4733 Fax www.indygov.org	Liens Real Estate The set up fee is $200, plus one is required to maintain an escrow balance of at least $100. Additional charges are $.50 per minute, $.25 display charge for the 1st page and $.10 for each additional page. The system operates 24 hours daily and supports baud rates up to 19.2. Records date back to 1987 and images from 2/24/93. One may search by name, Grantee/Grantor and document type. Federal tax liens and UCC information are available. The fax back service is $2.00 per page. For further information, contact Mike Kerner at 317-327-4587.

Iowa

State Agencies Online

Secretary of State Corporation Division 2nd Floor, Hoover Bldg Des Moines, IA 50319 515-281-5204 515-242-6556 Other Fax Line 515-242-5953 Fax sos.state.ia.us	Corporation Records Limited Liability Company Records Fictitious Name Limited Partnership Records Assumed Name Trademarks/Servicemarks The state offers the DataShare Online System. Fees are $175.00 per year plus $.30 per minute. The system is open 5 AM to 8 PM daily. All records are available, including UCCs. Call 515-281-5204 and ask for Cheryl Allen for more information.
Iowa General Assembly Legislative Information Office State Capitol Des Moines, IA 50319 515-281-5129 www.legis.state.ia.us	Legislation-Current/Pending/Passed Access is available through the Legislative Computer Support Bureau or through their web site. Note that the agency is going to discontinue the Bureau access and make all information available through the Internet site.

UCC Division Secretary of State Hoover Bldg, East 14th & Walnut Des Moines, IA 50319 515-281-5204 515-242-5953 Other Fax Line 515-242-6556 Fax sos.state.ia.us	Uniform Commercial Code Federal Tax Liens Online access is available at $.30 per minute with a $175.00 annual fee. The system is up daily from 5 AM to 8 PM and is the same system used to obtain corporation records online.

Kansas

State Agencies Online

Secretary of State Corporation Division 300 SW 10th St, 2nd Floor Topeka, KS 66612-1594 785-296-4564 785-296-4570 Fax www.ink.org/public/sos	Corporation Records Limited Partnerships Limited Liability Company Records Corporate data can be ordered from the Information Network of Kansas (INK), a state sponsored interface. Both independent online and Internet (www.ink.org) access modes are offered. The system is open 24 hours a day, 7 days a week. Corporation records are $.25 per search. There is a $.10 a minute access charge, unless you connect through the Internet where there is no connect charge. Minimum baud rate is 14.4. For more information, call INK at 800-452-6727.
Department of Revenue Driver Control Bureau PO Box 12021 Topeka, KS 66612-2021 785-296-3671 785-296-6851 Fax	Driver Records Kansas has contracted with the Information Network of Kansas (INK), 800-452-6727, to service all electronic media requests of driver license histories. INK offers connection through an "800 number" or can be reached via the Internet (www.ink.org). Cost is $4.00 for batch records or $4.50 for interactive records with a $.10 charge per minute if using the 800 number, and a $50 annual subscription fee. There is a $15 minimum requirement per month, unless you pay by credit card. The system is open 24 hours a day, 7 days a week. Batch requests are available at 7:30 am (if ordered by 10 PM the previous day).

Kansas State Library Capitol Bldg 300 SW 10th Ave Topeka, KS 66612 785-296-2149 785-296-6650 Fax www.ink.org	Legislation-Current/Pending/Passed The web site has bill information for the current session. The site also contains access to the state statutes.
UCC Division Secretary of State State Capitol, 300 W Tenth, 2nd Floor Topeka, KS 66612-1594 785-296-3650 785-296-3659 Fax www.ink.org/public/sos	Uniform Commercial Code Federal Tax Liens Online service is provided the Information Network of Kansas (INK). The system is open 24 hours daily. There is an annual fee. Network charges are $.10 a minute unless access is through their Internet site (www.ink.org) which has no network fee. UCC records are $8.00 per record. This is the same online system used for corporation records. For more information, call INK at 800-452-6727.
Division of Vehicles Title and Registration Bureau 915 Harrison Topeka, KS 66612 285-296-3621 285-296-3852 Fax	Vehicle Ownership Vehicle Identification Online batch inquires are $3.00 per record; online interactive requests are $4.00 per record. See the Driving Records Section for a complete description of the Information Network of Kansas (800-452-6727), the state authorized vendor.

County Agencies Online

Johnson County District Court 100 N Kansas Olathe, KS 66061 913-764-8484 X5015 913-791-5826 Fax	Civil Cases Index online through the Information Network of Kansas. See www.ink.org for subscription information.
Sedgwick County District Court 525 N Main Wichita, KS 67203 316-383-7311 316-383-7253 Criminal 316-383-8070 (Civil) 383-8071 (Criminal) Fax 316 383 8066 (Recorder) Fax	Civil Cases Criminal Cases Probate Liens Real Estate Tax Assessor Records The setup fee is $225. There is a monthly fee of $49 and a per transaction charge of $.03-

	$.04. Records date back to 1980. The system operates 24 hours daily and supports baud rates up to 28.8. System connections can be made using Windows 95/98. The database can be searched by name, Grantee/Grantor, address, key number and book and page. Lending agency information is available. For further information, contact John Zukovich at 316-383-7384.
Wyandotte County District Court 710 N 7th St Kansas City, KS 66101 913-573-2901 913-573-2905 Criminal 913-573-4134 Fax	Civil Cases Criminal Cases Online access requires specific software and a $20 setup fee. Transactions are $.05 each. The system is open 8am to 10pm M-F, and 8-4 on Sat. For more information call 913-573-2885.
Wyandotte County Register of Deeds Courthouse 710 N 7th Street Kansas City, KS 66101 913-573-2841 913-573-3075 Fax	Liens Real Estate Death Records Marriage Records Divorce Records A setup fee of $20 applies. The monthly fee is $5 and $.05 after the first 100 transactions. VT 100 emulation software is required. Records date back to 1/97. The system operates 8AM-10PM M-F and 8AM-4PM S and supports a baud rate of 9,600. Searches can be made by name, Grantee/Grantor, plat or subdivision name. Lending agency information is available. For information, contact Louise Sachen at 913-573-2885.

Kentucky

State Agencies Online

Secretary of State Corporate Records PO Box 718 Frankfort, KY 40602-0718 502-564-7330 502-564-4075 Fax www.sos.state.ky.us	Corporation Records Limited Partnerships Assumed Name Limited Liability Company Records The Internet site, open 24 hours, has a searchable database with over 340,000 KY businesses. The site also offers downloading of filing forms.

Department for Public Health Vital Records 275 E Main St - IE-A Frankfort, KY 40621-0001 502-564-4212 502-227-0032 Fax	Death Records In cooperation with the University of Kentucky, there is a searchable death index at http://ukcc.uky.edu:80/ ~vitalrec. This is for non-commercial use only. Records are from 1911 through 1992.
Department for Public Health Vital Records 275 E Main St - IE-A Frankfort, KY 40621-0001 502-564-4212 502-227-0032 Fax	Divorce Records In cooperation with the University of Kentucky, there is a searchable index on the Internet at http://ukcc.uky.edu:80/ ~vitalrec. This is for non-commercial use only. The index is for 1973-1993.
Division of Driver Licensing State Office Bldg, MVRS 501 High Street, 2nd Floor Frankfort, KY 40622 502-564-6800 2250 502-564-5787 Fax	Driver Records This is a batch method for higher volume users. There is a minimum order of 150 requests per batch. Input received by 3 PM will be available the next morning. Either the DL# or SSN is needed for ordering. The state will bill monthly. For more information, call 502-564-6800, ext. 2111.
Kentucky General Assembly Legislative Research Commission 700 Capitol Ave, Room 300 Frankfort, KY 40601 502-372-7181 Bill Status Only 502-564-8100 Bill Room 502-564-8100 LRC Library 502-223-5094 Fax www.lrc.state.ky.us	Legislation-Current/Pending/Passed The web site has an extensive searching mechanism for bills, actions, summaries, and statutes.
Department for Public Health Vital Records 275 E Main St - IE-A Frankfort, KY 40621-0001 502-564-4212 502-227-0032 Fax	Marriage Certificates In cooperation with the University of Kentucky, a searchable index is available on the Internet at http://ukcc.uky.edu:80/ ~vitalrec. The index runs from 1973 through 1993. This is for non-commercial use only.
UCC Division Secretary of State, PO Box 718 Frankfort, KY 40602-0718 502-564-2848 401 502-564-4075 Fax www.sos.state.ky.us	Uniform Commercial Code Only information on out-of-state debtors can be obtained from their web site for no charge.

Department of Motor Vehicles Division of Motor Vehicle Licensing State Office Bldg, 3rd Floor Frankfort, KY 40622 502-564-4076 Title History 502-564-3298 Other Requests 502-564-1686 Fax	Vehicle Ownership Vehicle Identification Online access costs $2.00 per record. The online mode is interactive. Title, lien and registration searches are available. Records include those for mobile homes. For more information, contact Gale Warfield at the number listed above.
Boyd County County Clerk 2800 Louisa Street, Courthouse Catlettsburg, KY 41129 606-739-5116 606-739-6357 Fax	Liens Real Estate The usage fee is $10 monthly. The system operates 24 hours daily and supports baud rates up to 56K. Records date back to 1/79. One may search by name, Grantee/Grantor and book and page. Lending agency information is available. for further information, contact Maxine Selbee or Kathy Fisher at 606-739-5166
Oldham County County Clerk 100 W Jefferson Street, Courthouse LaGrange, KY 40031 502-222-9311 502-222-3208 Fax oldhamcounty.state.ky.us	Liens Real Estate Marriage Records Tax Assessor Records The set up fee is $200, plus a monthly fee of $65. The system operates 24 hours daily. Records date back to 1980 and viewable images date back to 1/95. One may search by name, Grantee/Grantor, book and page, instrument number, subdivision and date. Lending agency information is available. For further information, contact Donna Schroeder at 502-222-9311.

Louisiana

State Agencies Online

Commercial Division Corporation Department PO Box 94125 Baton Rouge, LA 70804-9125 225-925-4704 225-925-4726 Fax sec.state.la.us	Corporation Records Limited Partnership Records Limited Liability Company Records Trademarks/Servicemarks The system is $360 per year for unlimited access. Almost any communications software

	will work with up to a 14,400 baud rate. The system is open from 6:30 am to 11pm. For more information, call Brenda Wright at 225-922-1475.
Dept of Public Safety and Corrections Office of Motor Vehicles PO Box 64886 Baton Rouge, LA 70896 225-922-1175 225-925-6009 Alternate Telephone 225-925-6915 Fax	Driver Records An online, interactive mode is available from 7 AM to 9:30 PM daily. Records are $6.00 each. There is a minimum order requirement of 2,000 requests per month. A bond or large deposit is required. For more information, call 225-925-6032.
Louisiana House (Senate) Representative State Capitol, 2nd Floor PO Box 44486 Baton Rouge, LA 70804 225-342-2456 Information Help Desk 225-342-2365 Senate Documents (Room 205) 225-342-6458 House Documents (Room 207) 800-256-3793 General Information, In-state www.legis.state.la.us	Legislation-Current/Pending/Passed The Internet site has a wealth of information about sessions and bills.
Secretary of State UCC Records PO Box 94125 Baton Rouge, LA 70804-9125 800-256-3758 225-342-5542 Fax	Uniform Commercial Code An annual $400 fee gives unlimited access to UCC filing information. The dial-up service is open from 6:30 AM to 11 PM daily. Minimum baud rate is 9600. Most any software communications program can be configured to work. For further information, call Brenda Wright at 504-922-1475.
Department of Public Safety & Corrections Office of Motor Vehicles PO Box 64884 Baton Rouge, LA 70896 225-922-6146 225-925-3979 Fax www.dps.state.la.us/laomv.html	Vehicle Ownership Vehicle Identification Online access costs $6.00 per record. Minimum usage is 2,000 requests per month. The online system operates similar to the system for driving records. For more information: Dept. of Public Safety and Corrections, PO Box 66614, Baton Rouge, LA 70896, 225-925-6032, Attn: Jimmy Thibodeaux.

County Agencies Online

Caddo Parish Parish Clerk of the Court 501 Texas Street, Room 103 Shreveport, LA 71101 318-226-6783 318-227-9080 Fax	Liens Real Estate Marriage Records The set up fee is $50, plus a monthly fee of $30.The system operates 24 hours daily and supports baud rates up to 19.2. Record dates vary. Mortgages and indirect conveyances date back to 1981, Direct conveyances date back to 1914. One may search by name, Grantee/Grantor and registry number. Lending agency information is available. UCC information is available through the Secretary of State. For further information, contact Susan Twohig at 318-226-6523.
East Baton Rouge Parish 19th District Court PO Box 1991 Baton Rouge, LA 70821 504-389-3950 504-389-3392 Fax	Civil Cases Criminal Cases The online system is open 24 hours daily. The setup fee is $100, the monthly minimum is $15 at $.33 per minute. Civil, criminal, probate (1988 forward), traffic and domestic index information is available by name or case number. Call Wendy Gibbs at 504-389-5295 for more information.
East Baton Rouge Parish Clerk of Court 222 St. Louis Street Baton Rouge, LA 70821 504-389-3958 504-389-3392 Fax	Liens Real Estate The setup fee is $100. There is a monthly fee of $15 and a per minute fee of $.33. Four years worth of data is kept active on the system. The system operates 24 hours daily and supports a baud rate of 9,600. Searches are done by name. UCC information is located at the Secretary of State. Lending agency information is available. For further information, contact Wendy Gibbs at 504-398-5295.
Iberia Parish 16th District Court PO Drawer 12010 New Iberia, LA 70562-2010 318-365-7282 318-365-0737 Fax	Civil Cases Probate Liens Real Estate Marriage Records Divorce Records

	A monthly usage fee of $50 applies. Records date back to 1959. The system operates 24 hours daily and supports baud rates up to 56k. Searches can be made by name, Grantee/Grantor and Book and Page. UCC lien information is available through the office of the Secretary of State. Lending agency information is available. For further information, contact Mike Thibodeaux at 318-365-7282.
Lafayette Parish 15th District Court PO Box 2009 Lafayette, LA 70502 318-233-0150 318-269-6392 Fax www.lafayetteparishclerk.com	Civil Cases Criminal Cases Remote access available for $100 setup fee plus $15 per month and $.50 per minute. Civil index back to 1986. Modem speeds up to 9600 supported 24 hours per day. For more information, call Mike Prejean at 318-291-6232.
Lafayette Parish Parish Clerk of Court 800 S Buchanan Street Lafayette, LA 70501 318-233-0150 318-269-6392 Fax www.layfayettecourthouse.com	Liens Real Estate Marriage Records The set up fee is $100. A monthly fee of $15 applies, plus $.50 per minute. The system operates 24 hours daily and supports baud rates up to 9,600. Conveyances date back to 1936, mortgages back to 1948 and all other records back to 1986. One may search by name, file number and date range. Tax and UCC lien information is for this parish only. Lending agency information is available. For further information, contact Derek Comeaux at 318-291-6433.
Orleans Parish Civil District Court 421 Loyola Ave, Rm 402 New Orleans, LA 70112 504-592-9100 X122 504-592-9128 Fax	Civil Cases CDC Remote provides access to civil cases from 1985 and First City Court cases from 1988, as well as mortgage and conveyance indexes for the county. The setup fee is $100, and usage is charged at $.25 per minute. Call 504-592-9264 for more information.

Orleans Parish Recorder of Mortgages 421 Loyola Avenue, B-1 Civil Court Building New Orleans, LA 70112 504-592-9176 504-592-9192 Fax	Liens Real Estate The setup fee is $100 and a $300 deposit for 1,200 minutes of usage is required. One is billed $.25 per minute. Records date back to 9/87. The system operates 24 hours daily and supports baud rates of 9,600-19.2. Searches can be made by name, lot number and district number. No lending agency information is available. For further information, contact John Rabb at 504-592-9264.
St. Tammany Parish Parish Clerk of Court 510 E Boston Street Covington, LA 70433 504-898-2430 `stp.pa.st-tammany.la.us`	Liens Real Estate The set up fee is $100, plus a $.30 per minute fee. The system operates 24 hours daily and supports baud rates up to 33.6. Records date back to 1961. Viewable images are available for conveyances back to 1985 and Mortgages back to 8/93. One may search by name, Grantee/Grantor and instrument number. UCC lien information is with the Secretary of State. For further information, contact Mark Cohn at 504-898-2890 or Christy Howell at 504-898-2491.
Tangipahoa Parish 21st District Court PO Box 667 Amite, LA 70422 504-748-4146 504-748-6503 Fax	Civil Cases Probate Online access is $125 per month and is available 24 hours daily. Civil and probate information can be searched by name. For more information, call 504-748-4146.
Tangipahoa Parish Parish Clerk of Court 110 N Bay Street Amite, LA 70422 504-549-1611 504-748-6503 Fax	Liens Real Estate Marriage Records A monthly fee of $125 applies. The system operates 24 hours daily and supports baud rates up to 28.8. Record dates vary. One may search by name, Grantee/Grantor, book and page, document type, instrument type and number and date. Lending agency information is available. For further information, contact Alison Carona at 504-549-1611.

Maine

State Agencies Online

Secretary of State Reports & Information Division 101 State House Station Augusta, ME 04333-0101 207-287-4190 207-287-4195 Main Number 207-287-5874 Fax www.state.me.us/sos/ corpinfo.htm	Corporation Records Limited Partnerships Trademarks/Servicemarks Assumed Name Limited Liability Company Records The Internet site gives basic information about the entity including address, corp ID, agent, and status.
Bureau of Motor Vehicles Driver License & Control 29 State House Station Augusta, ME 04333-0029 207-287-9005 207-287-2592 Fax www.state.me.us/sos/bmv/mbv.htm	Driver Records This is considered a non-certified record, thus the fee is $5.00 per request. The system is a PC modem access mode and is fairly new. Call 207-287-8590 for further details.
Maine Legislature 2 State House Station Legislative Document Room, 3rd Floor Augusta, ME 04333-0002 207-287-1692 Bill Status or LD # 207-287-1408 Document Room 207-287-1456 Fax www.state.me.us/legis	Legislation-Current/Pending/Passed There is a Link Service that requesters can subscribe to. Call Information Systems at 207 287-1692. Also, the web site offers bills, status, and access to text of state laws.
Department of Motor Vehicles Registration Section 29 State House Station Augusta, ME 04333-0029 207-287-3556 207-287-5219 Fax www.state.me.us/sos/bmv/bmv.htm	Vehicle Ownership Vehicle Identification Maine offers online access to title records via PC and modem. The system is open 24 hours daily. To set up an account, call 207-287-8590.

Maryland

State Agencies Online

Department of Assessments and Taxation Corporations Division 301 W Preston St, Room 809 Baltimore, MD 21201 410-767-1340 410-767-1330 Charter Information 410-333-7097 Fax www.dat.state.md.us/ datanote.html	Corporation Records Limited Partnerships Trade Names Limited Liability Company Records Fictitious Name At press time, this site was under construction, but the indication is it will be up and running sometime in mid 1999. The site currently provides a statewide search of real estate records and UCC records; however, a name search cannot be performed. Note there is a secondary web site in the state with corporate information - www.dat.state.md.us/ datanote.html.
Administrative Office of the Courts Court of Appeals Bldg, 361 Rowe Blvd Annapolis, MD 21401 410-260-1400 410-974-2169 Fax www.courts.state.md.us	Criminal Records Civil Case Records Land Records The State Court Administrator's office has online access to criminal records from all state district courts, 2 circuit courts, and 1 city court. The system, called JIS, is available 24 hours daily. There is a one-time $50 fee to register and a $.50 per minute fee. Call 410-260-1031 for a registration package.
MVA Driver Records Unit 6601 Ritchie Hwy, NE Glen Burnie, MD 21062 410-787-7758 mva.state.md.us	Driver Records The network is available 6 days a week, twenty-four hours a day to qualified and bonded individuals and businesses. Access is through PC and modem at up to 9600 baud. The communication network is the Public Data Network (BellAtlantic). The driver's license number, name, and DOB are needed when ordering. The fee is $5.00 per record. For signup, call 410-768-7234.

Maryland General Assembly Dept of Legislative Services 90 State Circle Annapolis, MD 21401-1991 410-841-3810 Bill Status Only 410-841-3000 Alternate Telephone 800-492-7122 In-state 410-841-3850 Fax http://mlis.state.md.us	Legislation-Current/Pending/Passed The Internet site has complete information regarding bills and status.
UCC Division Department of Assessments & Taxation 301 West Preston St Baltimore, MD 21201 410-767-1340 410-333-7097 Fax www.dat.state.md.us/bsfd	Uniform Commercial Code Real Property Records The Internet site offers free access to UCC index information. There is also a related site offering access to real property data for the whole state at www.dat.state.md.us/realprop.
Department of Motor Vehicles Vehicle Registration Division Room 206, 6601 Ritchie Hwy, NE Glen Burnie, MD 21062 410-768-7520 410-768-7653 Fax mva.state.us	Vehicle Ownership Vehicle Identification The state offers vehicle and ownership data over the same online network utilized for driving record searches. Line charges will be incurred. For more information, call 410-768-7234.
Workers Compensation Commission Six N Liberty St Baltimore, MD 21201 410-767-0900 410-333-8122 Fax	Workers' Compensation Records Request for online hook-up must be in writing on letterhead. There is no search fee, but there is a $7 set-up fee, $5 monthly fee and a $.01-03 per minute connect fee. The system is open 24 hours a day. Write to the Commission at address above, care of Information Support Division, or call Lili Joseph at 410-767-0713.

County Agencies Online

All County District Courts **Anne Arundel and Carroll County Circuit Courts** **Baltimore City Court**	Civil Cases Criminal Cases A statewide system is available. See the State Court Administrator in the state agencies section for details.

Massachusetts

State Agencies Online

Secretary of the Commonwealth Corporation Division One Ashburton Pl, 17th Floor Boston, MA 02108 617-727-9640 Corporations 617-727-2850 Records 617-727-8329 Trademarks 617-727-9440 Forms request line 617-742-4538 Fax `state.ma.us/sec/cor/coridx.htm`	Corporation Records Trademarks/Servicemarks Limited Liability Partnerships Limited Partnership Records The agency offers "Direct Access." The annual subscription fee is $149.00 and there is a $.40 a minute access fee. System is available from 8 AM to 9:50 PM. This system also provides UCC record data. Call 617-727-2853 for a sign-up packet.
Massachusetts General Court State House Beacon St, Room 428 (Document Room) Boston, MA 02133 617-722-2860 Document Room `www.state.ma.us/legis.legis.htm`	Legislation-Current/Pending/Passed The web site has bill information for the current session and the previous session.
UCC Division Secretary of the Commonwealth One Ashburton Pl, Room 1711 Boston, MA 02108 617-727-2860	Uniform Commercial Code Federal Tax Liens State Tax Liens "Direct Access" is available for $149 per year plus a $.40 per minute network fee. The system is open from 8 AM to 9:50 PM. Call 617-727-2853 to obtain information packet.
Registry of Motor Vehicles Customer Assistance-Mail List Dept. PO Box 199100 Boston, MA 02119-9100 617-351-9384 617-351-9524 Fax	Vehicle Ownership Vehicle Identification Permissible users are limited to Massachusetts based insurance companies and agents for the purpose of issuing or renewing insurance. This system is not open to the public. There is no fee, but line charges will be incurred.

County Agencies Online

Barnstable County County Register of Deeds 3195 Route 6A Barnstable, MA 02630 508-362-7733 508-362-5065 Fax `www.bcrd.co.barnstable.ma.us`	Liens Real Estate A $50 annual fee applies along with a $.50 per minute charge. The system operates 24 hours daily and supports a baud rate of 56K. The records date back to 1976. One may

	search by name, Grantee/Grantor, street address and document number. Lending information is available. For information, contact Janet Hoben at 508-362-7733.
Berkshire County County Register of Deeds (Southern District) 334 Main Street Great Barrington, MA 01230 413-528-0146 413-528-6878 Fax County Register of Deeds (Middle District) 44 Bank Row Pittsfield, MA 01201 413-433-7438 413-448-6025 Fax County Register of Deeds (Northern District) 65 Park Street Adams, MA 01220 413-743-0035 413-743-1003 Fax	Liens Real Estate A one time signup fee of $100 is required and there is a $.50 per minute charge. This system provides access to all three District Recorders' records in the county. The records date back to 1985. The system operates 24 hours daily and supports baud rates up to 9,600. Searchable indexes are recorded land, plans and registered land. You can search by name and Grantee/Grantor. Lending agency information is available. For further information, contact Sharon Henault at 413-443-7438.
Bristol County County Register of Deeds (Southern District) 25 N 6th Street New Bedford, MA 02740 508-993-2605 508-997-4250 Fax County Register of Deeds (Northern District) 11 Court Street Taunton, MA 02780 508-822-0502 508-880-4975 Fax County Register of Deeds (Fall River District) 441 N Main Street Fall River, MA 02720 508-673-1651 508-673-7633 Fax	Liens Real Estate There is a set up fee of $100, and at $.50 per minute access fee. All three districts are on this system. The record dates vary by district. The system operates 24 hours daily and supports baud rates up to 9,600. At this time one can only search by name and Grantee/Grantor. There are plans to expand search capabilities sometime in 1999. Lending agency information is available. For further information, contact Rosemary at 508-993-2605
Essex County County Register of Deeds (Northern District) 381 Common Street Lawrence, MA 01840 978-683-2745 978-688-4679 Fax	Liens Real Estate Online access requires a $25 deposit, with a per minute charge of $.25 per minute. The records date back to 1981. The system

	operates 24 hours daily and supports baud rates up to 9,600. You can search by name and Grantee/Grantor. Lending agency information is available. For further information, contact David Burke at 978-683-2745.
Essex County County Register of Deeds (Southern District) 36 Federal Street Salem, MA 01970 978-741-0201 978-744-5865 Fax	Liens Real Estate Public record information available on the Internet for no fee. Images are available from 01/92 to present. Index includes records from 01/84 to present. Search by name, Grantee/Grantor, street address, book and page, town and date. Lending agency info is available.
Hampden County County Register of Deeds 50 State Street, Hall of Justice Springfield, MA 01103 413-748-8662 413-731-8190 Fax	Liens Real Estate A $50 annual fee applies along with a per minute charge of $.50. The records date back to 1965. The system operates 24 hours daily and supports a baud rate of 28.8. Searchable indexes are bankruptcy (downloaded from PACER), unregistered land site and registered land site. One may search by name, Grantee/Grantor and address. Lending agency information is available. For information, contact Donna Brown at 413-748-7945.
Hampshire County County Register of Deeds, Hall of Records 33 King Street Northampton, MA 01060 413-584-3637 413-584-4136 Fax	Liens Real Estate A $100 annual fee applies and per minute charges are $.50 for in-state and $.60 for out-of-state. The records date back to 9/2/86. The system operates 24 hours daily and supports baud rates up to 9,600. One may search by name, Grantee/Grantor, town location and book and page. Lending agency information is available. For further information, contact MaryAnn Foster at 413-584-3637.
Middlesex County County Register of Deeds (Northern District) 360 Gorham Street Lowell, MA 01852 978-458-8474 978-458-7765 Fax www.tiac.net/users/nmrd	Liens Real Estate The system is called "Telesearch." The set up fee is $100, plus a $50 deposit and access is billed at $.20 per minute. To connect, one must be able to emulate the Wang screen.

	Wang emulation software is $95. The system operates from 5AM-10:30PM. One can search the Grantee/Grantor index, recorded land plans, registered land documents and recording information. Records date back to 1976. A fax back service is available. For further information, contact customer service at 978-458-8474.
Middlesex County County Register of Deeds (Southern District) 208 Cambridge Street East Cambridge, MA 02141 617-494-4550 `www.tiac.net/users/nmrd`	Liens Real Estate The system is called "LandTrack." The Annual fee is $100, plus $.50 per minute. One also needs Wang 2110/2110A terminal emulation software. The system operates 24 hours daily. A minimum baud rate of 9,600 is recommended. One may search by name, Grantee/Grantor, address, document detail, book and page, date and instrument number, plans, and registered owner files. Lending agency information is available. They have a fax back service for documents since 1987. For further information, contact Grace Abruzzio at 617-494-4510.
Norfolk County County Register of Deeds 649 High Street Dedham, MA 02026 781-461-6122 781-326-4742 Fax	Liens Real Estate There is a set up fee of $25.00, $1.00 fee for the first minute and $.50 per minute thereafter per session. The system operates from 2AM-10:30PM M-F and 24 hours on weekends and holidays. The system is only accessible from within Massachusetts. The system supports a baud rate of 9,600. One may search by Grantee/Grantor, plan index by proprietor, town and street, tax index and by land court index. Lending agency information is available. For further information, contact Pam at 781-461-6116.
Plymouth County County Register of Deeds 7 Russell Street Plymouth, MA 02360 508-830-9200 508-830-9280 Fax	Liens Real Estate To access "Online Titleview" there is a usage charge of $.60 per minute. The records date back to 1971. The system operates 24 hours daily and supports baud rates up to 14.4. One may search by name, Grantee/Grantor, tax

	lien and land courts. Lending agency information is available. They have a fax back service. There is a service charge of $3.00 plus $1.00 per page (in county). If out of county, the service charge is $4.00, plus $1.00 per page. For further information contact, Sandy, Cynthia or Graham at 508-830-9287.
Suffolk County County Register of Deeds 1 Pemberton Square The Old Courthouse Boston, MA 02108 617-725-8575 617-720-4163 Fax	Liens Real Estate To gain access to the online access system, you must sent a written request to Paul R. Tierney, Register of Deeds. Online charges are $.50 per minute. The records date back to 1/1/79. The system operates 24 hours daily and supports a baud rate of 19.2. One may search by name, Grantee/Grantor, address, type of document, date, district and town. They have a fax back service. For area codes 617, 781 and 508, the fee is $3.00 for the first page and $1.00 for the remainder. For all other area codes, the first page is $5.00 and $1.00 for the remainder.
Worcester County County Register of Deeds (Worcester North) Courthouse 84 Elm Street Fitchburg, MA 01420 978-342-2634 978-345-2865 Fax	Liens Real Estate Death Records Marriage Records The annual fee for "Northfield" is $50, plus $.25 per minute. The records date back to 1983. The system operates 24 hours daily and supports baud rates from 1,200-9,600. Viewable images are available from 1995. One may search by name, Grantee/Grantor, book and page, document number and date. Lending agency information is available. A fax back service is available. For information, contact Ruth Piermarini at 978-342-2637.
Worcester County County Register of Deeds (Worcester District) 2 Main Street Courthouse Worcester, MA 01608 508-798-7713 508-798-7746 Fax	Liens Real Estate The "Landtrack System" annual fee is $50, plus $.25 per minute. The index records date back to 1966. The system operates 24 hours daily and supports baud rates up to 19.2. One may search by name and book and page. Lending agency information is available. Fax

	back service is available at $.50 per page. Images are viewable from 1974. For further information, contact Joe Ursoleo at 508-798-7713 X233.

Michigan

State Agencies Online

Department of State Police Record Look-up Unit 7064 Crowner Dr Lansing, MI 48918 517-322-1624 517-322-1181 Fax www.sos.state.mi.us/dv	Driver Records Online ordering is available on an interactive basis. The system is open 7 days a week. Ordering is by DL or name and DOB. An account must be established and billing is monthly. Access is also available from the Internet. Call Carol Lycos at 517-322-1591 for more information.
Michigan Legislature Document Room State Capitol PO Box 30036 Lansing, MI 48909 517-373-0169 www.michiganlegislature.org	Legislation-Current/Pending/Passed Access is available from their Internet site. Adobe Acrobat Reader is required. Information available includes status of bills, bill text, joint resolution text, journals, and calendars.
Department of State Police Record Look-up Unit 7064 Crowner Dr Lansing, MI 48918 517-322-1624 517-322-1181 Fax www.sos.state.mi.us/dv	Vehicle Ownership Vehicle Identification Boat & Vessel Ownership & Registration Online searching is single inquiry and requires a VIN or plate number. A $25,000 surety bond is required. Direct dial-up or Internet access is offered. For information, call Carol Lycos at 517-322-1591.

County Agencies Online

Jackson County County Register of Deeds 120 W Michigan Avenue, 11th Floor Jackson, MI 49201 517-788-4350 517-788-4686 Fax	Liens Real Estate The per minute fee is $1.00. The system is being upgraded in 1999 and fees may change. The system operates 24 hours daily and supports a baud rate of 28.8. The records date back to 1985. The indexes that are available are Grantee/Grantor, deeds and mortgages.

	One may search by name, Grantee/Grantor, book and page, legal description, document type, date and address. Lending agency information is available. Vital records will be added to the system when it is upgraded. For information, contact Mindy at 517-768-6682.
Livingston County County Register of Deeds Courthouse Howell, MI 48843 517-546-0270 517-546-5966 Fax	Liens Real Estate Tax Assessor Records For the occasional user, the annual fee is $400, plus $.000043 per second. A dedicated line is available for $1,200. Records date back to 10/84. The system operates from 5:30AM-11PM daily. The system supports a baud rate of 28.8. One may search by name, Grantee/Grantor, legal description, instrument type, tax code and address. Lending agency information is available. For further information, contact Judy Eplee at 517-546-2530
Montcalm County County Register of Deeds 211 W Main Street, Courthouse Stanton, MI 48888 517-831-7337 517-831-7320 Fax	Liens Real Estate Death Records They have two public record access systems available. To view only the index, the monthly fee is $250. To view both the index and the document image, the monthly fee is $650. These fees are all inclusive. The records date back to 1/1/88. The system operates 24 hours daily and supports baud rates up to 28.8. One may search by name, Grantee/Grantor, legal description and book and page. Lending agency information is available. For further information, contact Laurie Wilson at 517-831-7321.

Minnesota

State Agencies Online

Business Records Services Secretary of State 180 State Office Bldg, 100 Constitution Ave St Paul, MN 55155-1299 651-296-2803 Information 651-297-9102 Copies 651-215-0683 Fax www.sos.state.mn.us	Corporation Records Limited Liability Company Records Assumed Name Trademarks/Servicemarks Limited Partnerships The program is called Direct Access and is available 24 hours daily. There is an annual subscription fee of $50. Records are $1-4, depending on item needed. Please call 651-297-9100 or 651-297-9097 for more information.
Driver & Vehicle Services Records Section 445 Minnesota St, #180 St Paul, MN 55101 651-296-6911 www.dps.state.mn.us/dvs	Driver Records Online access costs $2.50 per record. Inquiries can be processed either as interactive or as batch files (overnight) 24 hours a day, seven days a week. Requesters operate off of a "bank." Records are accessed by either DL number or full name and DOB. For more information, call 651-297-1714.
Minnesota Legislature State Capitol House-Room 211, Senate-Room 231 St Paul, MN 55155 651-296-2887 Senate Bills 651-296-6646 House Bill Status 651-296-2314 House Bill Copies 651-296-1563 Fax www.leg.state.mn.us	Legislation-Current/Pending/Passed Information available through the Internet site includes full text of bills, status, previous 4 years of bills, and bill tracking.
UCC Division Secretary of State 180 State Office Bldg St Paul, MN 55155-1299 651-296-2803 651-297-5844 Fax www.sos.state.mn.us	Uniform Commercial Code Federal Tax Liens State Tax Liens The program is called Direct Access and is available 24 hours. There is a subscription fee is $50.00 per year, plus $4.00 per search. Call 651-297-9100 or 651-297-9097 for more information.

Driver & Vehicle Services Records Section 445 Minnesota St St Paul, MN 55101 651-296-6911 General Information	Vehicle Ownership Vehicle Identification Online access costs $2.50 per record. There is an additional monthly charge for dial-up access. The system is the same as described for driving record requests. It is open 24 hours a day, 7 days a week. Lien information is included.

County Agencies Online

Anoka County County Recorder 2100 3rd Avenue Anoka, MN 55303 612-323-5400 612-323-5421 Fax	Real Estate Tax Assessor Records The set up fee is $250. The monthly fee is $20, plus $.25 per transaction. The system operates from 8AM-4:30PM M-F, and supports baud rates up to 33.6. The records date back to 1995. One may search by name, Grantee/Grantor and document number. Lending agency information is available. For further information, contact Pam LeBlanc at 612-323-5424.
Hennepin County County Recorder 300 S 6th Street 8-A Government Center Minneapolis, MN 55487 612-348-3066 www.co.hennepin.mn.us	Liens Real Estate The annual fee is $35. One is charged $5.00 per hour between 7AM-7PM and $4.15 the balance of the time. The system operates 24 hours daily and supports baud rates up to 28.8. Records date back to 1988. One may search by name, Grantee/Grantor, legal description, document number and address. Property tax information is at the treasurer's office. Only state UCC information is available. Lending agency information is available. For further information, contact Jerry Erickson at 612-348-3856.
Washington County County Recorder 14949 62nd Street N Stillwater, MN 55082 651-430-6755 651-430-6753 Fax	Liens Real Estate Tax Assessor Records The set up fee is $250. No fees apply to recorders office information. Fees may apply to other indexes on the system. The system operates 24 hours daily and supports baud rates up to 28.8. Records date back 3 years.

	One may search by name, Grantee/Grantor, geo code and legal description. UCC information is on a separate system. Lending agency information is available. For further information: Larry Haseman 651-430-6423.

Mississippi

State Agencies Online

Corporation Commission Secretary of State PO Box 136 Jackson, MS 39205-0136 601-359-1633 800-256-3494 Alternate Telephone 601-359-1607 Fax www.sos.state.ms.us	Corporation Records Limited Partnership Records Limited Liability Company Records Trademarks/Servicemarks The system is called "Success" and is open 24 hours daily. There is a $250 set-up fee and usage fee of $.10 per screen. Users are billed quarterly. Once registered, users can access through the Internet and avoid toll charges. Call 601-359-1548 for more information (ask for Tobie Curry).
Department of Public Safety Driver Records PO Box 958 Jackson, MS 39205 601-987-1274	Driver Records Both interactive and batch delivery is offer for high volume users only. Billing is monthly. Hook-up is through the Advantis System, fee apply. Lookup is by name only-not by driver license number. For more information, contact Donna Smith at 601-987-1337.
Mississippi Legislature Documents PO Box 1018 Jackson, MS 39215 601-359-3229 Senate 601-359-3358 House www.als.state.ms.us	Legislation-Current/Pending/Passed The Internet site has an excellent bill status and measure information program. Data included is for both the current and previous session.
UCC Division Secretary of State PO Box 136 Jackson, MS 39205-0136 601-359-1350 800-256-3494 Alternate Telephone 601-359-1607 Fax www.sos.state.ms.us	Uniform Commercial Code Federal Tax Liens The PC system is called "Success" and is open 24 hours daily. There is a $250 set-up fee and usage fee of $.10 per screen. Users can access via the Internet to avoid any toll charges. Customers are billed quarterly. For information, call Tobie Curry, 601-359-1548.

Missouri

State Agencies Online

Secretary of State Corporation Services PO Box 778 Jefferson City, MO 65102 573-751-4153 573-751-5841 Fax mosl.sos.state.mo.us	Corporation Records Fictitious Name Limited Partnership Records Assumed Name Trademarks/Servicemarks Limited Liability Company Records Searching can be done from the Internet site. The corporate name, the agent name or the charter number is required to search. The site will indicate the currency of the data.
Department of Revenue Driver License Bureau PO Box 200 Jefferson City, MO 65105-0200 573-751-4300 573-526-4769 Fax http://dor.state.mo.us	Driver Records Online access costs $1.25 per page. Online inquiries can be put in Missouri's "mailbox" any time of the day. These inquiries are then picked up at 2 AM the following morning, and the resulting MVRs are sent back to each customer's "mailbox" approximately two hours later. The system is designed to be accessed by both PCs and main frames. All network access charges are billed directly by Advantis. For further information, call 573-751-4391.
Legislative Library 117A State Capitol Jefferson City, MO 65101 573-751-4633 Bill Status Only www.moga.state.mo.us	Legislation-Current/Pending/Passed The web site offers access to bills and statutes. One can search or track bills by key words, bill number, or sponsors.

County Agencies Online

Cass County County Recorder of Deeds 102 E Wall Street County Court House Harrisonville, MO 64701 816-380-1510 816-380-5136 Fax	Liens Real Estate The monthly fee is $250, plus $.10 per minute after 50 minutes usage. The system operates 24 hours daily. The records date back to 1990. One may search by name, Grantee/Grantor and book and page. Images are viewable and one may print the image for $1.00. A fax back service is also available at $1.00 per page. For further information, contact John Kohler at 816-380-1510.
Jackson County Circuit Court 415 E 12th Kansas City, MO 64106 816-881-3926; 881-3522 www.state.mo.us'sca/circuit16 Independence Circuit Court 308 W Kansas Independence, MO 64050 816-881-4497 816-881-4410 Fax	Civil Cases Criminal Cases Probate Contact Becki Fortune at 816-881-3411 for information about remote access. No fee for service, but request to sign up must be on company letterhead and include indication of the business you are in. Fax requests to 816-851-3148. The county has indicated it may place the records on the Internet sometime in 1999.
St. Louis City Circuit & Associate Circuit Courts 10 N Tucker, Civil Courts Bldg St Louis, MO 63101 314-622-4367/622-4405 314-622-4537 Fax	Civil Cases Remote access is through MoBar Net and is open only to attorneys. Call 314-535-1950 for more information.

Montana

State Agencies Online

State Legislature of Montana State Capitol Room 138 Helena, MT 59620-1706 406-444-3064 406-444-3036 Fax www.mt.gov/leg/branch/branch.htm	Legislation-Current/Pending Legislation-Passed Information is available on the Internet. There is also a BBS which contains additional information such as actions taken on a bill. Special software is needed. Call 406-444-1626 for more information. Committee minutes and exhibits will be available on CD-

	ROM in the future; price has yet to be determined.
Business Services Bureau Secretary of State PO Box 202801 Helena, MT 59620-2801 406-444-3665 406-444-3976 Fax www.mt.gov/sos/	Uniform Commercial Code Federal Tax Liens The online system costs $25 per month plus $.50 per page if copies of filed documents are requested. A prepaid account is required. The system is open 24 hours daily.

Nebraska

State Agencies Online

Secretary of State Corporation Commission 1301 State Capitol Bldg Lincoln, NE 68509 402-471-4079 402-471-3666 Fax www.nol.org.home/SOS/	Corporation Records Limited Liability Company Records Limited Partnerships Trade Names Trademarks/Servicemarks The state has designated Nebrask@ Online (800-747-8177) to facilitate online retrieval of records. Access is through both a dial-up system and the Internet; however an account and payment is required. The state Internet site has general information only.
Department of Motor Vehicles Driver Records Division PO Box 94789 Lincoln, NE 68509-4789 402-471-4343 www.nol.org/home/dmv/driverec.htm	Driver Records Nebraska out sources all online and tape record requests through Nebrask@ Online (800-747-8177). The online system is interactive and open 24 hours a day, 7 days a week. There is an annual fee of $50.00 and a $.40 per minute connect fee or $.12 if through the Internet.
Clerk of Legislature Office PO Box 94604 Lincoln, NE 68509-4604 402-471-2271 402-471-2126 Fax www.unicam.state.ne.us	Legislation-Current/Pending/Passed The web site features the state statutes, legislative bills for the present and past sessions, and a legislative journal.
UCC Division Secretary of State PO Box 95104 Lincoln, NE 68509 402-471-4080	Uniform Commercial Code Federal Tax Liens Access is outsourced to Nebrask@ Online. The system is available 24 hours daily. There

402-471-4429 Fax	is an annual $50 fee and a $.12 per minute access charge. The access charge can be avoided by using their Internet site at www.nol.org. Call 800-747-8177 for more information.
Department of Motor Vehicles Titles and Registration Section PO Box 94789 Lincoln, NE 68509-4789 402-471-3918	Vehicle Ownership Vehicle Identification Boat & Vessel Ownership Electronic access is through Nebrask@ Online. There is a start-up fee and line charges are incurred in addition to the $1.00 per record fee. The system is open 24 hours a day, 7 days a week. Call 800-747-8177 for more information.
Workers' Compensation Court PO Box 98908 Lincoln, NE 68509-8908 402-471-6468 800-599-5155 In-state 402-471-2700 Fax	Workers' Compensation Records Access to data is available from Nebrask@ Online. There is a $50 set-up fee and $.12 per minute charge, unless you access through their Internet site at www.nol.org. This web site provides court information, name and address lists, and forms.

County Agencies Online

Douglas County Douglas County Court 1819 Farnam, 2nd Fl Omaha, NE 68183 402-444-5425	Civil Cases Online access is $25 per month for the first 250 transactions and $.10 per transaction thereafter. The system is open 24 hours daily and can be searched by name or case number. Call Jo Williams at 402-444-7705 for more information.

Nevada

State Agencies Online

Secretary of State Status Division 101 N Carson, #3 Carson City, NV 89701-4786 775-687-5203 900-535-3355 Status Line 775-687-3471 Fax	Corporation Records Limited Partnerships Limited Liability Company Records Limited Partnership Records Online access is offered on the Internet site for no charge. You can search by corporate

http://sos.state.nv.us	name, resident agent, corporate officers, or by file number.
Nevada Legislature 401 S Carson St Carson City, NV 89710 775-687-6825 Bill Status Only 775-687-6800 Main Number 775-687-6835 Publications 775-687-6827 Research Library 702-687-3048 Fax www.leg.state.nv.us	Legislation-Current/Pending/Passed Bills and bill status information is available via this agency's web site.
UCC Department Secretary of State Capitol Complex Carson City, NV 89710 702-687-5203 702-687-3471 Fax	Uniform Commercial Code Federal Tax Liens State Tax Liens This is a PC dial-up system. The fee is $24.50 per hour or $10.75 per hour on an 800 number for unlimited access. There is a $50.00 minimum deposit. The system is up from 7 AM to 5 PM. Call 702-687-4357 for a packet.

County Agencies Online

| **Clark County**
County Recorder
500 S Grand Central, 2nd Floor
Las Vegas, NV 89106
702-455-4336
www.co.clark.nv.us/RECORDER/or_srch.htm | Liens, Tax Assessor Records
Real Estate
Birth Records
Death Records
Marriage Records
Divorce Records

Access to public records is through the Internet. There is no fee. The records date back to 1988. You can search by name, Grantee/Grantor, book and instrument type, document type, UCC, and address. Lending agency information is available. |

New Hampshire

State Agencies Online

| **Department of Motor Vehicles**
Driving Records
10 Hazen Dr
Concord, NH 03305
603-271-2322 | Driver Records

Online access is offered for commercial accounts. The system is open 22 hours a day. Searches are by license number or by name |

	and DOBand are $7.00 per record. For more information, call Chuck DeGrace at 603-271-2314.
New Hampshire State Library 20 Part St Concord, NH 03301 603-271-2239 603-271-2205 Fax www.state.nh.us/gencourt/ gencourt.htm	Legislation-Current/Pending/Passed Online search: Information can be viewed from the web site. A dial-up system is also available. There is a $100 set-up fee, software is $75, and a $.75 charge per minute after the first month. This system offers more than web site. Call 603-271-2180 and ask Stan Kelly for more information.

County Agencies Online

Grafton County County Register of Deeds Route 10 North Haverhill, NH 03774 603-787-6921 603-787-2363 Fax	Liens Real Estate The set up fee is $100, plus a monthly fee of $40. Two years of data are kept on the system. Prior years are stored on CD-ROM. The system operates 24 hours daily and supports a baud rate of 9,600. One can search by name and Grantee/Grantor. Lending agency information is available. There is a fax back service for in-state only. The first page is $4.00, the second $3.00 and $2.00 for any additional pages. For further information contact Carol Elliott at 603-787-6921.

New Jersey

State Agencies Online

Department of Treasury Division of Commercial Recording PO 450 Trenton, NJ 08625 609-530-6400 609-530-6432 Copies 609-530-8290 Fax accessnet.state.nj.us/index.asp	Corporation Records Limited Liability Company Records Fictitious Name Limited Partnerships The New Jersey Business Gateway Service (NJBGS) provides Internet online searching for business entities records. Fees are involved. The system is open 24 hours daily. NGBGS is planning to offer UCC records online in the future. For more information, call 609-530-6419.
Motor Vehicle Services Driver's Abstract Section CN142 Trenton, NJ 08666 609-292-6500 888-486-3339 In-state only 609-292-6500 Suspensions www.state.nj.us/mvs	Driver Records The fee is $4.00 per record. Access is limited to insurance, bus and trucking companies, parking authorities, and approved vendors. There is a minimum of 400 requests per quarter.
New Jersey State Legislature State House Annex CN-068, Room B06 Trenton, NJ 08625-0068 609-292-4840 Bill Status Only 609-292-6395 Copy Room 800-792-8630 In State Only 609-777-2440 Fax www.njleg.state.nj.us	Legislation-Current/Pending/Passed The web site is a good source of information about bills. All statutes are online, also.
Motor Vehicle Services Certified Information Unit CN 146 Trenton, NJ 08666 609-292-6500 888-486-3339 In-state www.state.nj.us/mvs	Vehicle Ownership Vehicle Identification Boat & Vessel Ownership/Registration Limited online access is available for insurance companies, bus and trucking companies, highway/parking authorities, and approved vendors for these businesses. Participation requires a minimum of 100 requests per calendar quarter at $4.00 per request.

County Agencies Online

All County Superior Courts - Special Civil Part Superior Court Clerk's Office Electronic Access Program 25 Market St, CN971 Trenton, NJ 08625 609-292-4987 Main Number 609-292-6564 Fax	Civil Cases Online access is available through 3 systems (ACMS, AMIS, and FACTS). ACMS contains data on all active civil cases from the 21 counties. AMIS contains closed case information. FACTS contains information on dissolutions from all counties. The fee is $1.00 per minute. For more information and an enrollment form, call 609-292-4987.

New Mexico

State Agencies Online

State Corporation Commission Corporate Department PO Box 1269 Santa Fe, NM 87504-1269 505-827-4502 Main Number 800-947-4722 In-state Only 505-827-4510 Good Standing 505-827-4513 Copy Request 505-827-4387 Fax www.state.nm.us/scc/sccfind.htm	Corporation Records Limited Liability Company Records There is no charge to view records at the Internet site.
Motor Vehicle Division Driver Services Bureau PO Box 1028 Santa Fe, NM 87504-1028 505-827-2234 505-827-2267 Fax	Driver Records New Mexico Technet is the state authorized vendor for access. The costs are $2.50 per record for interactive, $1.50 per record for batch, plus a $.25 per minute network fee. The system is open 24 hours a day, batch requesters must wait 24 hours. There is a $35.00 set-up fee, also. Technet bills users on a monthly basis. All users must first be approved and sign a contract with the Director of the Motor Vehicle Division. Technet can be reached at 505-345-6555.
Legislative Council Service State Capitol Bldg, Room 311 Santa Fe, NM 87501 505-986-4600 505-986-4350 Bill Room (in Session Only) 505-986-4610 Fax legis.state.nm.us	Legislation-Current/Pending/Passed The Internet site is a complete source of information about bills and legislators. There is also a link to some state statute sites.

UCC Division Secretary of State State Capitol Bldg, Rm 420 Santa Fe, NM 87503 505-827-3610 505-827-3611 Fax www.sos.state.nm.us/ucc/ucchome.htm	Uniform Commercial Code The web site permits searches. A more extensive online access is available through the state appointed vendor New Mexico Technet. There is a $50 set-up fee and 3 levels of service with various access charges. Call 505-345-6555 for information.
Motor Vehicle Division Vehicle Services Bureau PO Box 1028 Santa Fe, NM 87504-1028 505-827-4636 505-827-1004 Alternate Telephone 505-827-0395 Fax	Vehicle Ownership Vehicle Identification Boat & Vessel Ownership/Registration Records are available, for authorized users, from the state's designated vendor New Mexico Technet. Cost is $2.50 per record plus a $.25 per minute network charge. There is a $35 set-up fee, also. Call 505-345-6555 for more information.

County Agencies Online

Bernalillo County 2nd Judicial District Court PO Box 488 Albuquerque, NM 87103 505-841-7437 505-841-7459 Criminal 505-841-7446 Fax	Civil Cases Criminal Cases Online access available through New Mexico Technet. There is a setup fee and an access fee. Civil records go back 7 years. Search by name, case number, SSN or arrest number. Call 505-345-6555 for information.
Bernalillo County Metropolitan Court 401 Roma NW Albuquerque, NM 87102 505-841-8110/841-8142 505-841-8192 Fax www.metrocourt.nmcjnet.org	Civil Cases Criminal Cases Online access available through New Mexico. A setup fee and access fees apply. Technet. Call 505-345-6555 for information.
Dona Ana County 3rd Judicial District Court 201 W Puecho, Suite A Las Cruces, NM 88005 505-523-8200 505-523-8290 Fax	Civil Cases Criminal Cases Remote access available through New Mexico Technet. Call 505-345-6555 for information. A setup fee and access fees apply.

Dona Ana County Assessor's Office 251 W Amador, Room 103 Las Cruces, NM 87504 505-647-7421 505-647-7464 Fax www.co.dona-ana.nm.us/newpages/assr/txparcel.html	Liens Real Estate Access is free on the Internet. Records date back to 1990. Records can be searched by name or street address or parcel number. For further information, contact Dan at 505-647-7449 or Cindy at 505-647-7426.
San Juan County 11th Judicial District Court 103 S. Oliver Aztec, NM 87410 505-334-6151 505-334-1940 Fax	Civil Cases Criminal Cases Civil: Remote access through New Mexico Technet. Call 505-345-6555 for information. There is a setup fee and access fees apply.
Santa Fe County County Clerk 102 Grant Avenue Santa Fe, NM 87504 505-986-6280 505-995-2767 Fax	Liens Real Estate The monthly fee is $20, plus $5.00 per hour. The system operates 24 hours daily and supports baud rates up to 9,600. The records date back to 1990. One may search by name, Grantee/Grantor, book and page and document number. Lending agency information is available. For further information, contact, Mary Quintana at 505-995-2782.

New York

State Agencies Online

Department of Motor Vehicles MV-15 Processing 6 Empire State Plaza, Room 430 Albany, NY 12228 518-474-0642 518-473-5595 Alternate Telephone www.nydmv.state.ny.us	Driver Records Online access costs $4.00 per record. NY has implemented a "Dial-In Inquiry" system enabling customers to obtain data online 24 hours a day. The DL# or name, DOB and sex are required to retrieve. If the DOB and sex are not entered, the system defaults to a limited group of 5 records. These may be expanded for an additional fee. Billing is pre-paid. The agency also offers a batch inquiry method for higher volume requesters with about a 6 hour turnaround time. For more information, call 518-474-4293.

NY Senate Document Room	Legislation-Current/Pending/Passed
State Capitol Room 317, State and Washington Sts Albany, NY 12247 518-455-7545 Bill Status Only 518-455-2312 Senate Document Room 518-455-3216 Calls Without Bill Numbers 518-455-5164 Assembly Document Room www.senate.state.ny.us	Both the Senate (senate.state.ny.us) and the Assembly (assembly.state.ny.us) have web sites to search for a bill or specific bill text. A much more complete system is the LRS online system. This offers complete state statutes, agency rules and regulations, bill text, bill status, summaries and more. For more information, call Barbara Lett at 800-356-6566.
Department of Motor Vehicles MV-15 Processing 6 Empire State Plaza, Room 430 Albany, NY 12228 518-474-0710 518-474-8510 Alternate Telephone www.nydmv.state.ny.us/index.htm	Vehicle Ownership Vehicle Identification Boat & Vessel Ownership & Registration New York offers plate, VIN and ownership data through the same online network for driving records. The system is interactive and open 24 hours a day, with the exception of 10 hours on Sunday. Call 518-474-4293 for more information.

County Agencies Online

Bronx County	Liens
City Register 1932 Arthur Avenue Bronx, NY 10457 718-579-6828 718-579-6832 Fax	Real Estate Tax Assessor Records This service supports the Boroughs of Brooklyn, Queens, Staten Island, Bronx and Manhatten. There is a $250 monthly fee and a fee of $5.00 per transaction. Records are kept for 2-5 years. The system operates from 9AM-5PM M-F. One may search by name, Grantee/Grantor and address. For information, contact Richard Reskin at 718-935-6523.
Kings County City Register 210 Joralemon Street Municipal Building Brooklyn, NY 11201 718-802-3590 718-802-3745 Fax	Liens Real Estate Tax Assessor Records This service supports the Boroughs of Brooklyn, Queens, Staten Island, Bronx and Manhatten. There is a $250 monthly fee and a fee of $5.00 per transaction. Records are kept for 2-5 years. The system operates from 9AM-5PM M-F. One may search by name, Grantee/Grantor and address. For information, contact Richard Reskin at 718-935-6523.

Monroe County Supreme and County Court 39 W Main St Rochester, NY 14614 716-428-5151 716-428-5447 Fax	Civil Cases Criminal Cases The online system is open 7am to 7pm daily. No special software is need. Access is $50 per hour. Fax back is available for $.50 per page. Plans are underway to place viewable images on the Internet sometime in late 1999. Call Tom Fiorilli for information.
New York County City Register 31 Chambers Street, Room 202 New York, NY 10007 212-788-8529 212-788-8521 Fax	Liens Real Estate Tax Assessor Records This service supports the Boroughs of Brooklyn, Queens, Staten Island, Bronx and Manhattan. There is a $250 monthly fee and a fee of $5.00 per transaction. Records are kept for 2-5 years. The system operates from 9AM-5PM M-F. One may search by name, Grantee/Grantor and address. For information, contact Richard Reskin at 718-935-6523.
Queens County City Register 90-27 Sutphin Boulevard Jamaica, NY 11435 718-298-7000	Liens Real Estate Tax Assessor Records This service supports the Boroughs of Brooklyn, Queens, Staten Island, Bronx and Manhattan. There is a $250 monthly fee and a fee of $5.00 per transaction. Records are kept for 2-5 years. The system operates from 9AM-5PM M-F. One may search by name, Grantee/Grantor and address. For further information, contact Richard Reskin at 718-935-6523.
Rockland County Supreme and County Court 27 New Hempstead Rd New City, NY 10956 914-638-5070 914-638-5647 Fax	Civil Cases Criminal Cases Liens Real Estate Online access is available 24 hours daily. Setup is $250, which includes software, and there is a minimum of $150 per month for access. Case file pages can be ordered and faxed back. The system includes criminal index since 1982 plus civil judgments, real estate records and tax warrants. . One may search by name, Grantee/Grantor, book and

	page and transaction number. Images are viewable from 6/96 and more are being added. Call Paul Pipearto at 914-638-5221 for more information.
Ulster County County Clerk 240-244 Fair Street County Office Building Kingston, NY 12401 914-340-3000 914-331-0754 Fax	Liens Real Estate Divorce Records The monthly fee is $25 and you must commit to 1 year of service to sign up. The per minute usage fee is $.05. All software is included. Records date back to 1984. The system operates 24 hours daily and supports baud rates of 9,600-28.8. One may search by name and Grantee/Grantor. Lending agency information is available. For information, contact Valerie Harris at 914-340-5300
Ulster County Supreme and County Court PO Box 1800 Kingston, NY 12401 914-340-3288 914-340-3299 Fax	Civil Cases Criminal Cases The online system is open 24 hours daily. There is a minimum fee of $25 per month, 12 months required to signup. Search by name or case number. Call Valerie Harris for more information.

North Carolina

State Agencies Online

Secretary of State Corporations Section 300 N Salisbury St Raleigh, NC 27603-5909 919-733-4201 Corporations 919-733-4129 Trademarks 919-733-1837 Fax www.secstate.state.nc.us/ business	Corporation Records Limited Partnerships Limited Liability Company Records Trademarks/Servicemarks Access is available through a dial-up system. There is an initial registration fee of $185 and a charge of $.02 each time the "enter key" is pushed. To register, call Bonnie Elek at 919-733-0418. Also, the web site offers a free search of status and registered agent by corporation name.
Division of Motor Vehicles Driver's License Section 1100 New Bern Ave Raleigh, NC 27697	Driver Records To qualify for online availability, a client must be an insurance agent or insurance company support organization. The mode is

919-715-7000 www.dmv.dot.state.nc.us	interactive and is open from 7 AM to 10 PM. The DL# and name are needed when ordering. A minimum $500 security deposit is required.
North Carolina General Assembly State Legislative Bldg 16 W. Jones Street, 1st Fl Raleigh, NC 27603 919-733-7779 Bill Numbers 919-733-3270 Archives 919-733-5648 Order Desk www.ncga.state.nc.us	Legislation-Current/Pending/Passed The Internet site has copies of bills, status, and state statutes.
UCC Division Secretary of State 300 North Salisbury St, #302 Raleigh, NC 27603-5909 919-733-4205 919-733-9700 Fax www.secstate.state.nc.us/ secstate/ucc.htm	Uniform Commercial Code Federal Tax Liens Dial-up access is offered. There is a one-time registration fee of $185 and a $.02 charge each time the "enter key" is pushed. The minimum baud rate is 9600. Call Bonnie at 919-733-0418 for more information.

North Dakota

State Agencies Online

Department of Transportation Driver License & Traffic Safety Division /08 E Boulevard Ave Bismarck, ND 58505-0700 701-328-2603 701-328-2435 Fax	Driver Records The system is interactive and is open 24 hours daily. Records are $3.00 each. For more information, call 701-328-4790.
North Dakota Legislative Council State Capitol 600 E Boulevard Ave Bismarck, ND 58505 701-328-2916 701-328-2900 Secretary of State 701-328-2992 Sec of State fax www.state.nd.us/lr	Legislation-Current/Pending/Passed Their Internet site offers an extensive array of legislative information at no charge.
UCC Division Secretary of State 600 E Boulevard Ave, 1st Fl Bismarck, ND 58505-0500 701-328-3662 701-328-4214 Fax www.state.nd.us/sec	Uniform Commercial Code Federal Tax Liens State Tax Liens Sign-up for access to the Central Indexing System includes an annual $125 fee and a one-time $50 subscription fee. The same $7.00 search fee applies.

Ohio

State Agencies Online

Department of Public Safety Bureau of Motor Vehicles 1970 W Broad St Columbus, OH 43223-1102 614-752-7600 www.ohio.gov/odps	Driver Records The system is called "Defender System" and is suggested for requesters who order 100 or more motor vehicle reports per day in batch mode. Turnaround is in 4-8 hours. The DL or SSN and name are needed when ordering. For more information, call 614-752-7692.
Ohio House of Representatives 77 S High Street Columbus, OH 43266 614-466-8842 In-State Only 614-466-9745 Out-of-State www.legislature.state.oh.us	Legislation-Current/Pending/Passed The Internet site offers access to bill text, status, and enactment.
Bureau of Motor Vehicles Motor Vehicle Title Records 1970 W Broad St Columbus, OH 43223-1102 614-752-7671 614-752-8929 Fax www.state.oh.us/odps/division/ bmv/bmv/html	Vehicle Ownership Vehicle Identification Ohio offers online access through AAMVAnet. All requesters must comply with a contractual agreement prior to release of data. Call 614-752-7692 for information.

County Agencies Online

Butler County Common Pleas Court 130 High St Hamilton, OH 45011 513-887-3996 513-887-3089 Fax	Civil Cases Criminal Cases Online access is free 24 hours daily using VT100 emulation software. Contact Vickie Robertson for more information.
Hamilton County Common Pleas Court 1000 Main St, Room 315 Cincinnati, OH 45202 513-632-8247 Civil 513-632-8245 Criminal 513-763-4860 Fax www.courtclerk.org	Civil Cases Criminal Cases Access is free from the Internet site. Civil index goes back to 1991. Criminal index goes back to 1986. Municipal civil case information is also included.
Hamilton County County Recorder 138 E Court Street, Room 205 Cincinnati, OH 45202	Liens Real Estate An escrow account of $100 is required. It

513-946-4600 513-946-4577 Fax www.hcro.org	costs $1.00 to connect to the system and $.30 per minute. The system operates 6:30AM-10:30PM daily and supports baud rates up to 9,600. Records date back to 6/88. One may search by name, document number and book and page. Lending agency information is available. The fax back service fee is $2.00 per page. For further information, contact Vicky Jones at 513-946-4571.
Lawrence County County Recorder S 4th Street, Courthouse Ironton, OH 45638 740-533-4314 740-533-4411 Fax	Liens Real Estate The set up fee is $600-700, plus a monthly fee of $150. The system operates 24 hours daily and supports baud rates up to 28.8. Mortgage records date back to 1988 and deeds back to 1986. One may search by name and Grantee/Grantor. Only Federal tax liens are online; state liens are kept with the Clerk of the Court. UCC liens date back to 1989. Lending agency information is available. For further information, contact Kim Estep or Sue Deeds at 740-533-4314.
Lorain County County Recorder 226 Middle Avenue Elyria, OH 44035 440-329-5148 440-329-5199 Fax	Liens Real Estate There is no set up fee and you are given 2 free months. Monthly charges are $10 for 2 hours, then one is billed $.10 per minute. The system operates 24 hours daily and supports baud rates up to 14.4. Records date back to 5/92. One may search by name, Grantee/Grantor and document number. Lending agency information is available. For further information, contact Rich Barrett at 440-329-5413.
Medina County Medina Municipal Court 135 N Elmwood Medina, OH 44256 330-723-3287 330-225-1108 Fax	Civil Cases Criminal Cases Online access requires Procomm Plus. The system is open 24 hours daily. There are no fees. Search by either name or case number. The computer access number is 330-723-4337. For more information, call Judy Schwartz at ext. 227.

Wood County	Civil Cases
Perrysburg Municipal Court	Criminal Cases
300 Walnut	
Perrysburg, OH 43551	Contact Judy Daquano at 419-872-7906 for
419-872-7900	information about remote access. Access is
419-872-7905 Fax	free using up to 14.4 modem speed. Civil and
	criminal indexes go back to 1988. The system
	is open 24 hours daily.

Oregon

State Agencies Online

Corporation Division	Corporation Records
Public Service Building	Limited Partnership Records
255 Capital St NE, #151	Trademarks/Servicemarks
Salem, OR 97310-1327	Fictitious Name
503-986-2200	Assumed Name
503-378-4381 Fax	Limited Liability Company Records
www.sos.state.or.us/corporation	
/corphp.htm	A dial-up system is available at $400 per year.
	Call 503-986-2343 for more information.
Oregon State Police	Criminal Records
Identification Services Section	
PO Box 430034	This service is a bulletin board used for
Salem, OR 97208	requesting and receiving criminal history
503-378-3070	reports. The hours are 10 AM to 1 PM and 5
503-378-2121 Fax	PM to 7 AM. Results are posted as "No
	Record" or "In Process" which means a
	record will be mailed in 14 days. Users must
	complete an application and will be billed.
	Call 503-373-1808, ext 230 to receive the
	application.
Oregon Legislative Assembly	Legislation-Current/Pending/Passed
State Capitol-Information Services	
State Capitol, Rm 49	Text and histories of measures can be found at
Salem, OR 97310	the Internet site for no charge.
503-986-1180 Current Bill Information	
503-373-0701 Archives	
503-373-1527 Fax	
www.leg.state.or.us	

UCC Division	Uniform Commercial Code
Secretary of State	Federal Tax Liens
255 Capitol St NE, Suite 151	
Salem, OR 97310-1327	UCC index information can be obtained for
503-986-2200	free from the web site. You can search by
503-373-1166 Fax	debtor name or by lien number. You can also
www.sos.state.or.us/corporation/ucc/ucc.htm	download forms from here.

County Agencies Online

All Circuit Courts	Civil Cases
	Criminal Cases
	Probate
	Online access to an index is available through the Oregon Judicial Information Network (OJIN). The OJIN databases contains civil, criminal, small claims, probate, and some, but not all, juvenile records from the Circuit Courts, but not from the Municipal or County Courts. There is a one-time setup fee of $295, plus a minimum monthly usage fee of $10. Usage fees vary by type of record, but are in the $10-13 per hour range. For a registration packet, call 800-858-9658.
Benton County	Liens
County Recorder	Real Estate
120 NW 4th Street	Tax Assessor Records
Corvallis, OR 97330	
541-757-6831	Access is through their Information Resources
541-757-6757 Fax	system. There are no fees. An Internet site will be available in March 1999, possibly sooner. The web site is www.co.benton.or.us. Records date back to 1988. The system operates 24 hours daily and supports baud rates up to 9,600. One can search by name, date of recording, map number, tax lot number, serial number and document type. For further information, contact Dan Miller at 541-757-6877.

Pennsylvania
State Agencies Online

Department of Transportation Driver Record Services PO Box 68695 Harrisburg, PA 17106-8695 717-391-6190 800-932-4600 In-state only	Driver Records The state is in the process of testing their online access system. This new interface will be available to high volume requesters only.

County Agencies Online

Berks County Court of Common Pleas 2nd Floor, 633 Court St Reading, PA 19601 610-478-6970 610-478-6969 Fax	Vital Records Probate The Registry of Wills has a free searchable web site at www.berksregofwills.com which includes records both for the county and the City of Reading. The birth and marriage records are extremely current.
Bucks County Court of Common Pleas 55 E Court St Doylestown, PA 18901 215-348-6191 Civil 215-348-6389 Criminal 215-348-6209 Recorder 215-348-6379 Fax	Civil Cases Criminal Cases Liens Real Estate Marriage Records Tax Assessor Records Probate To access their public records, one must have a Sprint ID number. The annual Sprint fee is $24. The user is charged .60 per minute (2 minute minimum). The records date back to 1980. The system operates from 8AM-9PM M-F and 8AM-5PM S-S and supports baud rates up to 9,600. One may search by name, Grantee/Grantor, address and book and page. Lending agency information is available, as well as the register of wills data. For further information contact Jack Morris at 215-348-6579.
Butler County Court of Common Pleas Butler County Courthouse, PO Box 1208 Butler, PA 16003-1208 724-284-5233 Criminal 724-284-5244 Fax	Criminal Cases Call Infocon Corp. at 814-472-6066 for more information about the remote online system.

Chester County County Recorder of Deeds 235 W Market Street, Suite 100 West Chester, PA 19382 610-344-6330 610-344-6408 Fax	Liens Real Estate Marriage Records Tax Assessor Records Probate The sign up fee is $50, plus a $.30 per minute charge. The records date back to 1992. The system operates 24 hours daily and supports baud rates up to 9,600. One may search by name, Grantee/Grantor and parcel number. Lending agency information is available, as is register of wills data. For further information, contact Lisa or Gail at 610-344-6884.
Chester County Court of Common Pleas 2 North High St, Ste 130 West Chester, PA 19380 610-344-6300	Civil Cases Criminal Cases Contact Gail Galliger at 610-344-6884 for information about remote access. Fee is $50 for subscription and $.30 per minute. Index goes back to 1990. Available 24 hours per day.
Delaware County County Recorder of Deeds 201 W Front Street, Room 107 Government Center Building Media, PA 19063 610-891-4148	Real Estate Tax Assessor Records Access is free by dialing 610-566-1507. The system operates 24 hours daily. Records date back to 1990. For further information, contact Data Processing at 610-891-4675.
Delaware County Court of Common Pleas-Criminal/Civil 201 W Front St Media, PA 19063 610-891-5399	Civil Cases There are no fees for online access. VT100 emulation is required. The system is open 24 hours daily. For more information, call 610-891-4675. The access number is 610-566-1507.
Lancaster County County Recorder of Deeds 50 N Duke Street Lancaster, PA 17608 717-299-8238	Liens Real Estate Marriage Records Tax Assessor Records Probate A monthly fee of $25 applies, plus a per minute charge of $.18. Their system holds 5 years of data. Use of Windows is required. The system operates 8AM-6PM M-S and supports baud rates up to 56K. One may

	search by name, Grantee/Grantor and by index number. Lending agency information is available, as is the register of wills data. For further information, contact Nancy Malloy at 717-299-8252.
Lancaster County Court of Common Pleas 50 N Duke St, PO Box 83480 Lancaster, PA 17608-3480 717-299-8282 717-293-7210 Fax www.co.lancaster.pa.us	Civil Cases Online access is available 8am to 6pm M-Sat. There is a monthly fee of $25 and a per minute fee of $.18. by name or case number. Call Nancy Malloy at 717-299-8252 for more information.
Lehigh County County Recorder of Deeds 455 Hamilton Street Allentown, PA 18101 610-782-3162 610-820-2039 Fax	Liens Real Estate Marriage Records Tax Assessor Records The set up fee is $10 and the annual fee is $288. Online minutes are billed at $.05. The system operates 24 hours daily and supports baud rates up to 56K. Records date back to 1984. One may search by name, Grantee/Grantor and book and page. Lending agency information is available. For further information, contact Al Johnson at 610-782-3189.
Lehigh County Court of Common Pleas 455 W Hamilton St Allentown, PA 18101-1614 610-782-3148 Civil 610-782-3077 Criminal 610-770-3840 Fax	Civil Cases Criminal Cases All types of county records, including criminal cases and real estate records are available online. The system is open 24 hours daily, fees are involved. Call Al Johnson at 610-782-3189 for more information.
Montgomery County County Recorder of Deeds One Montgomery Plaza, Suite 303 Swede & Airy Streets Norristown, PA 19404 610-278-3289 610-278-3869 Fax	Liens Real Estate Tax Assessor Records The initial sign up fee is $10, plus a $.15 per minute usage charge. Their records date back to 1900. The system operates 24 hours daily and supports baud rates up to 14.4. Lending agency and prothonotary information are both available. One must contact the outside agency, Berkheimer Associates at 800-360-8989 to sign up for access to the system.

Montgomery County Court of Common Pleas PO Box 311 Airy & Swede St Norristown, PA 19404-0311 610-278-3360 Civil 610-278-3346 Criminal 610-278-5188 Fax www.montcopa.org	Civil Cases Criminal Cases For information about remote access, call 800-360-8989, extension 5. There is a $10 registration fee plus $.15 per minute of usage. Index goes back 10 years.
Washington County County Recorder of Deeds Washington County Courthouse 1 S Main Street, Room 1006 Washington, PA 15301 724-228-6806 724-228-6737 Fax	Liens Real Estate Tax Assessor Records The system operates 24 hours daily and supports baud rates up to 56K. Records date back to 1952. One may search by name, Grantee/Grantor and book and page. Tax lien information in kept in the Prothonotarys office. The Register of Wills data is available, as is lending agency information. For further information, contact Jack Welty at 724-228-6766.
Washington County Court of Common Pleas 1 S Main St Suite 1001 Washington, PA 15301 724-228-6770 Civil 724-228-6787 Criminal 724-228-6890 Fax	Civil Cases Criminal Cases Probate Divorce Online access is open 24 hours daily, there are no fees. Criminal records date back to 1986. Call Sally Michalski at 724-228-6797 for more information.
Westmoreland County County Recorder of Deeds Main Street Courthouse Square, Room 503 Greensburg, PA 15601 724-830-3526 724-832-8757 Fax	Liens Real Estate A setup fee of $100 applies, which includes software. In addition, there is a monthly fee of $20 and a per minute charge of $.50 after 40 minutes. Records date back to 1957. The system operates 24 hours daily and supports baud rates up to 19.2. Searches can be made by name, Grantee/Grantor, book and page and by street. No tax lien information is available, only UCC liens. For further information, contact Phil Svesnik at 724-830-3874.

Westmoreland County Court of Common Pleas Courthouse Sq PO Box 1630 Greensburg, PA 15601-1168 724-830-3500 724-830-3734 Criminal 724-830-3517 Fax	Civil Cases Criminal Cases Online access is open 24 hours daily. The $100 setup fee includes software, the minimum monthly fee is $20. Records are available from 1992 forward. For more information, call Phil Svesnik at 724-830-3874.
York County Court of Common Pleas-Civil York County Courthouse, 28E Market St York, PA 17401 717-771-9611	Civil Cases Criminal Cases The online system is available from 4AM-PM, M-F. The setup fee is $200.00 and the access fee is $.75 per minute. Criminal records from mid-1988 forward are available. For further information, call (717) 771-9321.

Rhode Island

State Agencies Online

Secretary of State Corporations Division 100 N Main St Providence, RI 02903 401-222-3040 401-222-1309 Fax	Corporation Records Fictitious Name Limited Partnerships Limited Liability Company Records Limited Liability Partnerships The direct access system is free; however, special Wang software is needed. The system is open 24 hours daily. Call 401-222-3040 for more information.
Rhode Island General Assembly State House Room 38, Public Information Center Providence, RI 02903 401-222-3983 Bill Status Only 401-222-2473 State Library 401-222-1308 Fax Back Request Line 401-222-1356 Fax www.state.ri.us	Legislation-Current/Pending/Passed The Internet systems provides a means to search enactments and measures by key words.

South Carolina

State Agencies Online

Corporation Division Capitol Complex PO Box 11350 Columbia, SC 29211 803-734-2158 803-734-2164 Fax	Corporation Records Trademarks/Servicemarks Limited Partnerships Limited Liability Company Records Their program is called Direct Access. Information available includes corporate names, registered agents & addresses, date of original filings, and dates of amendments or merger filings. The system is open 24 hours daily and there are no fees. The system permits the retrieval of documents by fax return. For more information, call 803-734-2345.
Division of Motor Vehicles Driver Records Section PO Box 100178 Columbia, SC 29202-3178 803-737-2940 803-737-1077 Fax	Driver License Information Driver Records The online system offers basic driver data, as well as a 3 year and 10 year record. This is a single inquiry process. Network charges will be incurred as well as initial set-up and a security deposit. The system is up between 8 AM and 7 PM. Access is through the AAMVAnet (IBMIN), which requesters much "join."
South Carolina Legislature 937 Assembly Street, Rm 220 Columbia, SC 29201 803-734-2060 803-734-2145 Older Bills www.leginfo.state.sc.us	Legislation-Current/Pending/Passed Bill text and status data can be found at the web site.
UCC Division Secretary of State PO Box 11350 Columbia, SC 29211 803-734-2175 803-734-2164 Fax	Uniform Commercial Code "Direct Access" is open 24 hours daily, there are no fees. Inquiry is by debtor name. The system provides for copies to be faxed automatically. Call 803-734-2345 for registration information.

County Agencies Online

Charleston County Circuit Court PO Box 70219 Charleston, SC 29415 843-740-5700 843-740-5887 Fax www3.charlestoncounty.org	Civil Cases Criminal Cases The Internet offers access to records from 04/92 forward. Search by name or case number. There is no fee.

South Dakota

State Agencies Online

Dept of Commerce & Regulation Office of Driver Licensing 118 W Capitol Pierre, SD 57501 605-773-6883 605-773-3018 Fax www.state.sd.us/dcr/dl/sddriver.htm	Driver Records The system is open for batch requests 24 hours a day. It generally takes 10 minutes to process a batch. The current fee is $4.00 per record and there are some start-up costs. For more information, call 605-773-6883.
South Dakota Legislature Capitol Bldg - Legislative Documents 500 E Capitol Ave Pierre, SD 57501 605-773-3835 605-773-4576 Fax www.state.sd.us/state/legis/lrc.htm	Legislation-Current/Pending/Passed Information is available at their web site at no charge. The site is very thorough and has enrolled version of bills.
UCC Division Secretary of State 500 East Capitol Pierre, SD 57501-5077 605-773-4422 605-773-4550 Fax	Uniform Commercial Code Federal Tax Liens Online access costs $240.00 per year plus a transaction charge over 200 keystrokes per month. Prepayment is required. The system is open 24 hours per day. Place request in writing to set up an account. The agency is considering an Internet site in the future.

Tennessee

State Agencies Online

Tennessee General Assembly Office of Legislative Information Services Rachel Jackson Bldg, 1st Floor Nashville, TN 37243 615-741-3511 Status 615-741-0927 Bill Room www.legislature.state.tn.us	Legislation-Current/Pending/Passed Bill information can be viewed at the Internet site. The Tennessee Code is also available from the site.

Texas

State Agencies Online

Secretary of State Corporation Section PO Box 13697 Austin, TX 78711-3697 512-463-5555 Information 512-463-5578 Copies 512-463-5576 Trademarks 512-463-5709 Fax www.sos.state.tx.us	Corporation Records Fictitious Name, Assumed Name Limited Partnership Records Limited Liability Company Records Trademarks/Servicemarks Dial-up access is available M-TH from 7 AM to 8 PM (6PM on Fridays). There is a $3.00 fee for each record searched (secured party searches are ($10.00) Filing procedures and forms are available from the web site or from 900-263-0060 ($1.00 per minute). To sign up for online access, call Tina Passell at 512-475-2755. A second way to access information, although somewhat limited, is through the Office of the Comptroller for certification of franchise tax account status. You can determine status of a corporation or an LLC and obtain list of officers or directors. Go to www.window.texas.gov/ taxinfo/coasintr.html.
Crime Records Service Correspondence Section PO Box 15999 Austin, TX 78761-5999 512-424-2079 txdps.state.tx.us	Criminal Records Records can be pulled from the web site. Requesters must establish an account and have a pre-paid bank to work from. The fee established by the Department (Sec. 411.135(b)) is $3.09 per request plus an additional handling fee of $.57 to buy credits.

Legislative Reference Library PO Box 12488 Austin, TX 78711-2488 512-463-1252 Bill Status 512-463-0252 Senate Bill Copies 512-463-1144 House Bill Copies 512-475-4626 Fax www.capitol.state.tx.us	Legislation-Current/Pending/Passed The web is a thorough searching site of bills and status.
UCC Section Secretary of State PO Box 13193 Austin, TX 78711-3193 512-475-2705 512-475-2812 Fax www.sos.state.tx.us	Uniform Commercial Code Federal Tax Liens Direct dial-up is open from 7 AM to 6 PM. The fee is $3.00 per search, $10.00 for a secured party search. General information and forms can be found at the web site.
Department of Transportation Vehicle Titles and Registration 40th St and Jackson Austin, TX 78779-0001 512-465-7611 512-465-7736 Fax	Vehicle Ownership Vehicle Identification Online access is available for pre-approved accounts. A $200 deposit is required, there is a $23 charge per month and $.12 fee per inquiry. Searching by name is not permitted. For more information, call the number listed above.

County Agencies Online

Bexar County County Court-Criminal 300 Dolorosa, Suite 4101 San Antonio, TX 78205 210-220-2220 Criminal District Court 100 Dolorosa, County Courthouse San Antonio, TX 78205 210-220-2083	Civil Cases Criminal Cases Online access is open 24 hours daily. The setup fee is $100, the monthly fee is $25 plus inquiry fees. Call Jennifer Mann at 210-335-0212 for more information.
Cameron County District Court 974 E Harrison St Brownsville, TX 78520 956-544-0839	Civil Cases Online access is available 24 hours daily. The $125 setup fee includes software, there is a $30 monthly access fee also. For more information, call Eric at 956-544-0838 X475.

Collin County District Clerk PO Box 578 McKinney, TX 75069 972-548-4365 County Court 210 S McDonald St Rm 542 McKinney, TX 75069 972-548-4529 972-548-4698 Fax	Civil Cases Criminal Cases Online is available 7am to 7pm M-Sat, 6 to 6 on Sun. The access fee is $.12 a minute, there is a monthly minimum of $31.13. Procomm Plus is suggested. Call Patty Ostrom for subscription information
Dallas County County Court-Civil 509 W Main 3rd Floor Dallas, TX 75202 214-653-7131	Civil Cases Public Access System allows remote access at $1.00 per minute invoiced to your telephone bill. Access number is 900-263-INFO. ProComm Plus is recommended. Call the Administrator at 214-653-7807 for more information.
Dallas County District Court-Civil 600 Commerce Dallas, TX 75202-4606 214-653-7421	Civil Cases Public Access System allows remote access at $1.00 per minute to these and other court and public records. Access number is 900-263-INFO. ProComm Plus is recommended. The system is open 8am to 4:30pm. Searching is by name or case number.
Dallas County District Court-Criminal 133 N Industrial Blvd Dallas, TX 75207-4313 214-653-5950 Criminal 214-653-5986 Fax Criminal District Courts 1-5 133 N Industrial Blvd Dallas, TX 75207 214-653-7421 Criminal 214-653-5986 Fax	Criminal Cases The Public Access System makes felony and other records available remotely at a cost of $1.00 per minute, billed on your telephone bill. Access number is 900-263-INFO. The system is open from 8am to 4:30 PM. Search by name or case number. For more information, call 214-653-6807
Denton County District Court PO Box 2146 Denton, TX 76202 940-565-8528 940-565-8607 Fax http://justice.co.denton.tx.us	Civil Cases Criminal Cases Criminal searches are available on the web site at no charge. Records are available from 1998 forward. Access also includes sheriff bond and jail records. Search by name or cause number.

Fort Bend County County Clerk 301 Jackson Richmond, TX 77469 281-341-8650 281-341-8669 Fax	Liens Real Estate Birth Records Death Records A $100 escrow account is required. Monthly fee is $15, plus $.25 per minute. The system operates 24 hours daily and supports a baud rate of 14.4. Reach Out software is required to interface with their system. Records date back to the 1930's, viewable images back to 10/94. Images are printable for $.50, $.75 if long distance. One may search by name, Grantee/Grantor, book and page and instrument number. Lending agency information is available. For information, contact Linda Jordan at 281-341-8652.
Fort Bend County District and County Court 301 Jackson Richmond, TX 77469 281-341-4562 281-341-4542 Criminal 281-341-4519 Fax	Civil Cases Criminal Cases Online searching available through a 900 number service. The access fee is $.55 per minute plus a deposit. Call 281-341-4522 for information.
Galveston County County Clerk 722 Moody Avenue Galveston, TX 77550 409-766-2292 County Clerk (Leek City Annex) 174 Calder Drive, suite 149 Leek City, TX 77573 281-316-8732 281-316-8739 Fax	Liens Real Estate Marriage Records A $200 escrow account deposit is required. The monthly fee is $25, plus $.25 per minute. The system operates 8AM-12AM and supports baud rates up to 14.4. Index records date back to 1965. Viewable image documents date back to 1/95. One may search by name, Grantee/Grantor, date filed, instrument number and document type. A fax back service is available, $.75 per page for local, $1.00 long distance. Lending agency information is available. Reach out Software is required to interface with their system. For further information, contact Robert Dickinson at 409-770-5115.
Galveston County County Court PO Box 2450 Galveston, TX 77553-2450 409-766-2203 409-766-2206 Criminal	Civil Cases Criminal Cases A $200 escrow account is required to open online access. The fee is $.25 per minute. The system is available 24 hours daily and gives

	fax back capability. For more information about GCNET call Mary Ann Daigle at 409-766-2200.
Harris County County Court PO Box 1525 Houston, TX 77251-1525 713-755-6421	Civil Cases Probate Real Estate Vital Records Liens The online system is open 24 hours daily. There is a $300 deposit and access in $40.00 per hour. The online system also includes real property, assumed names, UCC, probate court dockets and marriages. For more information, call Ken Peabody at 713-755-7151.
Harris County District Court PO Box 4651 Houston, TX 77210 713-755-5711 713-755-5734 Criminal 713-755-5480 (civil) Fax	Civil Cases Criminal Cases Online access requires a separate deposit of $150 for both civil and criminal access plus access fees. Civil and criminal are in separate systems, however. The system is open 24 hours daily. Attendance at a training class is required. For more information, call Eric Engelking at 713-755-7815.
Tarrant County County Court 100 W Weatherford Rm 250 Fort Worth, TX 76196 817-884-1076	Civil Cases Probate Online access is by subscription only. There is a setup fee, deposit and monthly minimum fees of $25 (based on $.05 per minute). The system is open 24 hours daily and also includes probate, misdemeanor and traffic. For further information, call Laura Yanes at 817-884-3202.
Tarrant County District Court 401 W Belknap Fort Worth, TX 76196-0402 817-884-1240 817-884-1342 Criminal 817-884-1484 Fax	Civil Cases Criminal Cases The online system is open 7:30 am to 7pm daily. The $50 setup includes software. The per minute fee is $.05 with a $25 minimum per month. Call Ms. Ziton at 817-884-1782 for more information.

Utah

State Agencies Online

Commerce Department Corporate Division PO Box 146705 Salt Lake City, UT 84114-6705 801-530-4849 Administration 801-530-6205 Certified Records 801-530-6034 Non-Certified 801-530-6363 Good Standing 801-530-6111 Fax	Corporation Records Limited Liability Company Records Fictitious Name Limited Partnership Records Assumed Name Trademarks/Servicemarks The system is called "Datashare." User fee is $10.00 per month plus some records require search fees. The system is open 24 hours daily. A large variety of information is available including notary public commissions and state contractors licenses. Call 801-530-6443 for more information.
Utah Legislature Research and General Counsel 436 State Capitol Salt Lake City, UT 84114 801-538-1032 801-538-1588 Bill Room 801-538-1032 Older Passed Bills 801-538-1712 Fax www.le.state.ut.us	Legislation-Current/Pending/Passed Web site contains bill information and also the Utah Codes.
Department of Commerce UCC Division Box 146705 Salt Lake City, UT 84114-6705 801-530-6025 801-530-6438 Fax www.commerce.state.ut.us	Uniform Commercial Code User fee is $10.00 per month. There is no additional fee at this time; however, the state is considering a certification fee. The system is open 24 hours daily and is the same system used for corporation records. Call 801-530-6643 for details.

County Agencies Online

All District Courts	Civil Cases Criminal Cases Case index information from approximately 98% of all Utah Court records is available from XChange. Fees include a $55.00 registration fee and a $35.00 monthly usage fee. For more information, contact the Court Administrator's Office at 801-578-3843 or visit

http://courtlink.utcourts.gov.

Virginia

State Agencies Online

State Corporation Commission Clerks Office PO Box 1197 Richmond, VA 23218-1197 804-371-9733 804-371-9133 Other fax 804-371-9744 Fax dit1.state.va.us/scc/division/ clm/index.htm	Corporation Records Limited Liability Company Records Fictitious Name Limited Partnership Records Assumed Name There is a dial-up system, called Direct Access, for registered accounts. There are no fees. A wealth of information is available on this system. For more data, call 804-371-9654.
Virginia State Police CCRE PO Box C-85076 Richmond, VA 23261-5076 804-674-2084 804-674-2277 Fax	Criminal Records Certain entities, including screening companies, are entitled to online access. The system is ONLY available to IN-STATE accounts. Fees are same as manual submission with exception of required software package purchase. The system is windows oriented, but will not handle networks. The PC user must be a stand alone system. There is a minimum usage requirement of 25 requests per month. Turnaround time is 24-72 hours.
Department of Motor Vehicles Motorist Records Services PO Box 27412 Richmond, VA 23269 804-367-0538	Driver Records Online service is provided by the Virginia Information Providers Network (VIPNet). Online reports are provided on an interactive basis 24 hours daily. There is a $50 annual administrative fee and records are $5.00 each. All accounts must be approved in advance by the DMV and VIPNet. Call Rodney Willett at 804-786-4718 to request an information use agreement application.
House of Delegates Legislative Information PO Box 406 Richmond, VA 23218 804-698-1500 804-786-3215 Fax	Legislation-Current/Pending/Passed Information can be found on the web site. There is no fee.

`http://legis.state.va.us/` `vaonline/v.htm`	

UCC Division
State Corporation Commission
PO Box 1197
Richmond, VA 23218-1197
804-371-9189
804-371-9744 Fax
`dit1.state.va.us/ecc/division/`
`clk/index.htm`
	Uniform Commercial Code
	Federal Tax Liens
	
	This is a free, non-Internet service. Accounts must be registered. This is the same system used for corporation records. Call 804-371-9661 and ask Angela for a registration packet.

Motorist Records Services Customer Records Request Section PO Box 27412 Richmond, VA 23269 804-367-0538	Vehicle Ownership Vehicle Identification Online access costs $4.00 per page. The online system, managed by the Virginia Information Providers Network (VIPNet), is an interactive system open 24 hours daily. There is an annual $50 administration fee and records are $5.00 each. All accounts must be approved by both the DMV and VIPNet. Contact Rodney Willett at 804-786-4718 to request an information use agreement application.

County Agencies Online

All Circuit and District Courts **Court of Appeals** **Supreme Court**	Civil Cases Criminal Cases An online, statewide system called LOPAS allows remote access to the court case indexes and abstracts from most of state's courts. Although there are no fees involved, registration for an ID and password is required. Keep in mind that searching is by specific court; there is no combined index. Plus, a summary list of all included courts is not available. Anyone wishing to register should contact the Director of MIS, Supreme Court of VA, at 804-786-6455.
Danville City City Clerk of the Circuit Court 212 Lynn Street Danville, VA 24541 804-799-5168 804-799-6502 Fax	Liens Real Estate Marriage Records There are no fees. The records date back to 1993. The system operates 24 hours daily. Search by name, Grantee/Grantor, instrument type, finance and statements (UCC) and wills.

	Lending agency information is a available. Contact Leigh Ann Thomas at 804-799-5168.
Wise County Clerk of the Circuit Court 125 Main Street Courthouse Wise, VA 24293 540-328-6111 540-328-0039 Fax www.courtbar.org	Real Estate There are no fees for access to this system. Record dates vary. The system operates 24 hours daily and supports baud rates up to 56K. One may search by name and Grantee/Grantor. Lending agency information is available. For further information, contact Vickie Ratliff at 540-328-6111. Note: this system also includes real estate information for the City of Norton.

Vermont

State Agencies Online

Secretary of State Corporation Division 109 State St Montpelier, VT 05609-1101 802-828-2386 802-828-2853 Fax sec.state.vt.us/soshome.htm	Corporation Records Trademarks/Servicemarks Corporate and trademark records can be accessed from the Internet for no fee. All records are available except for LPs, LLCs, and Farm Product Liens (however, all of these records will eventually be up).
Department of Motor Vehicles DI - Records Unit 120 State St Montpelier, VT 05603 802-828-2050 802-828-2098 Fax www.aot.state.vt.us/dmv/ dmvhp.htm	Driver Records Driver License Information Online access costs $4.00 per 3 year record. Two methods are offered-single inquiry and batch mode. The system is open 24 hours a day, 7 days a week (except for file maintenance periods). Only the license number is needed when ordering, but it is suggested to submit the name and DOB also. The system is oriented towards PC and modem users. For more information, call 802-828-2053.
Vermont General Assembly State House-Legislative Council 115 State Street, Drawer 33 Montpelier, VT 05633 802-828-2231 802-828-2424 Fax www.leg.state.vt.us	Legislation-Current/Pending/Passed The web site offers access to bill information.

UCC Division Secretary of State 109 State St Montpelier, VT 05609-1101 802-828-2386 802-828-2853 Fax sec.state.vt.us/seek/ ucc_seek.htm	Uniform Commercial Code Searches are available from the Internet site. You can search by debtor name, there is no fee.

Washington

State Agencies Online

Secretary of State Corporations Division PO Box 40234 Olympia, WA 98504-0234 360-753-7115 900-463-6000 Records 360-664-8781 Fax www.wa.gov/sec/corps.htm	Corporation Records Trademarks/Servicemarks Limited Partnerships Limited Liability Company Records The Secretary of State has plans to make corporation information available via their Internet site sometime in 1999. However, information is available elsewhere. From the Dept of Licensing. Subscription is $18 per month, access is $60 per hour plus line charges of $.09-37 per minute. A $200 deposit is required to start. Hours are from 5 AM to 9 PM. Call Darla at 360-753-2523 in Licensing for more information. Also, there is a non-commercial use database available on the Internet from the Department of Revenue. This database contains state business records for tax license and registration. Go to- www.wa.gov/dor/prd/cgi_bin/prd2gif1.cgi.
Court Administrator Temple of Justice PO Box 41174 Olympia, WA 98504-1174 360-357-2121 360-357-2127 Fax	Criminal Records The State Court Administrator's office maintains a database of criminal records in their JIS-Link. Records do not include arrests unless case is filed. There is a $125.00 set-up fee and a $25.00 per hour access charge. Call 360-705-5277 for packet. This agency offers access through a system called WATCH, which can be accessed from their web site. The fee is $10.00. The correct DOB and exact spelling of the name is required. Credit cards

	are accepted for payment. To set up a WATCH account, call 360-705-5100 or e-mail to criminhis@wsp.gov.
Washington Legislature State Capitol Room 120, 1st Floor Olympia, WA 98504-0600 360-753-5000 Information 800-562-6000 Local Only 360-786-7573 Bill Room 360-786-1293 Fax http://leginfo.leg.wa.gov	Legislation-Current/Pending Legislation-Passed The web site offers bill text and status look-up.
Revenue Department Taxpayer Account Administration PO Box 47476 Olympia, WA 98504-7476 360-902-7180 800-647-7706 Alternate Telephone 360-586-5543 Fax www.wa.gov/dor/wador.htm	Sales Tax Registrations The agency provides a state business records database with free access on the Internet at www.wa.gov/dor/prd/. Lookups are by owner names, DBAs, and tax reporting numbers. Results show a myriad of data.
Department of Licensing Business & Professional Div PO Box 9034 Olympia, WA 98507-9034 360-664-1400 900-463-6000 Tradename Search 360-753-9668 Fax www.gov.gov/dol/bpd/limsnet.htm	Trade Names This is the same system for corporation and UCC records. A deposit is required (depends on usage), access is $60 per hour plus a $.09-.37 phone charge. Hours are 5 AM to 9 PM daily. Call Fran at 360-664-1400 to set up an account.
UCC Division Department of Licensing PO Box 9660 Olympia, WA 98507-9660 360-753-2523 360-586-1404 Fax www.wa.gov/dol/bpd/uccfront.htm	Uniform Commercial Code Federal Tax Liens Subscription fee is $18.00 per month. Online access costs $60.00 per hour. There is a deposit of $200 required which is replenished at end of the month. Line charges will vary from $.09 to .37 per minute. Hours are from 5 AM to 9 PM. Call Darla at 360-753-2523 for more information.

County Agencies Online

All Superior and District Courts	Civil Cases Criminal Cases Three separate statewide systems are available. See the State Court Administrator in the state agencies section for details.

King County County Records 500 4th Avenue Administration Building, Room 311 Seattle, WA 206-296-1570 206-296-1535 Fax	Liens Real Estate Marriage Records The set up fee is $200. Online charges are $.03 per minute for browsing and $.20 per minute for viewing images. Records date back to 1853. No new customers are being accepted at this time. The system operates from 6PM-4:30PM and supports baud rates up to 19.2. Lending agency information is available. For further information, contact Diane Mickunas at 206-296-1588.

West Virginia

State Agencies Online

Division of Motor Vehicles Driver Improvement Unit Building 3, Rm 124, State Capitol Complex Charleston, WV 25317 304-558-0238 304-558-0037 Fax www.state.wv.us/dmv	Driver License Information Driver Records Online access is available in either interactive or batch mode. The system is open 24 hours a day. Batch requesters receive return transmission about 3 AM. Users must access through AAMVAnet. A contract is required and accounts must pre-pay. For more information, call Lacy Morgan at 304-558-3915.
West Virginia State Legislature State Capitol Documents Charleston, WV 25305 304-347-4830 800-642-8650 Local wvlc.wvnet.edu/legisinfo/ legisht.html	Legislation-Current/Pending/Passed The Internet site allows one to search for status of bills. To receive full text, there is a fee of $80.00 per month. There is also a BBS system for non-web users. Call Carla Dyer at 304-347-4820 for more information.

Wisconsin

State Agencies Online

Division of Motor Vehicles Records & Licensing Section PO Box 7995 Madison, WI 53707-7995 608-266-2353 608-267-3636 Fax	Driver Records Online access is available for high volume users only. Call 608-266-2353 for more information.
Wisconsin Legislative Legislative Reference Bureau PO Box 2037 Madison, WI 53701-2037 608-266-0341 800-362-9472 Bill Status 608-266-5648 Fax www.legis.state.wi.us	Legislation-Current/Pending/Passed Information on current bills is available over the Internet. There is a Folio program to search text of previous session bills.
Department of Financial Institutions CCS/UCC PO Box 7847 Madison, WI 53707-7847 608-261-9555 608-264-7965 Fax	Uniform Commercial Code Federal Tax Liens State Tax Liens The system requires purchase of software to access a Wang system. There is an upfront fee of $144 (prorated annually) and a $.50 charge per minute, billing monthly. All current, open records are available. The system is open from 12 PM to 5 PM. Call Linda Schmidt at 608-267-3741 for details.

County Agencies Online

Kenosha County County Register of Deeds 1010 56th street Kenosha, WI 53140 414-653-2414 414-653-2564 Fax	Liens Real Estate Birth Records Death Records Marriage Records The set up fee is $500 and you are billed $6.00 per hour. The system operates 24 hours daily and supports baud rates from 14.4-56K. Records date back to 5/86. One can search by name, Grantee/Grantor, book and page, document number, legal description and track. Federal tax liens are listed. Lending agency information is available. For further

	information, contact Joellyn Storz at 414-653-2511.

Milwaukee (City)
Assessor's Office
200 E Wells
Milwaukee, WI 53202-3515
414-286-3651
414-286-8447 Fax
`www.ci.mil.wi.us/citygov/assess`
`or/assessments.htm`
	Real Estate
	
	The City of Milwaukee Assessor's Office provides an excellent Internet site for free property and assessment data.

Wyoming

State Agencies Online

Corporations Division Secretary of State State Capitol Cheyenne, WY 82002 307-777-7311 307-777-5339 Fax `soswy.state.wy.us`	Corporation Records Limited Liability Company Records Limited Partnership Records Fictitious Name Trademarks/Servicemarks Information is available through the Internet site listed above. You can search by corporate name or even download the whole file. Also, they have an excellent 2 page tip document.
Wyoming Legislature State Capitol Room 213 Cheyenne, WY 82002 307-777-7881 `legisweb.state.wy.us`	Legislation-Current/Pending/Passed The Internet site contains a wealth of information regarding the legislature and bills.
UCC Division Secretary of State The Capitol Cheyenne, WY 82002-0020 307-777-5372 307-777-5338 Alternate Telephone 307-777-5988 Fax	Uniform Commercial Code Federal Tax Liens Online search: All accounts must be approved by the Director and by Vendor Security. Fees include a $50 annual registration, $20 monthly, and long distant access fees of between $3 and $6 per hour. A word of caution, if user fails to log off the "clock" still keeps ticking and user is billed! The system is open 24 hours daily except 1:30AM to 5AM Monday through Sunday, and 4PM to 6PM on Sunday.

Private Online Sources of Public Records

If you go to a search engine and surf for "public records," you will find a myriad of sites offering access to public records. Many tout access to 10,000 databases and offer "national" searches. Most of these sites are legitimate, reputable vendors. Some sites even collect, purchase and store the data themselves, such as KnowX, a subsidiary of Information America and one of the largest private companies in the information industry. However, the majority of sites you will find are usually intermediaries — companies that access records upon demand from either government agencies or from private enterprise and then resell the data to the end user.

So, who are these private enterprise companies that have developed their own databases and how have they done this? Actually, there are not that many (if you don't count all the direct marketing companies). These private enterprise companies create their databases in one of two ways: they buy records in bulk from government agencies; or they send people to the government agencies and compile information using laptop computers or copy machines. This information can be sliced, diced and merged to create a powerful proprietary database for internal use or for resale purposes.

The pages that follow are profiles of these commercial database vendors, preceded by an index of typical application or use by their clientele. The profiles include product descriptions, methods of distribution, and general statements regarding their capabilities. This list is not limited to only companies proving online access. You will find many media outlets, including CD-ROM, disk, tapes and microfiche, and even good old-fashioned telephone service. Every vendor may not be here, but what you will find is quite extensive.

Keep in mind many of these companies are sources and do not necessarily sell their products to casual or infrequent users. However, people who use public records extensively will find these pages invaluable.

The first part of this section is a series of indices based on the "applications" or practical uses of the each company's services. Following these eighteen indexes, there are full profiles of each company. The indexes are:

Asset/Lien Searching/Verification
Background Info – Business
Background Info – Individuals
Collections
Competitive Intelligence
Direct Marketing
Employment Screening
Filing/Recording Documents
Fraud Prevention/Detection
Genealogical Research
General Business Information
Government Document Retrieval
Insurance Underwriting
Legal Compliance
Lending/Leasing
Locating People/Businesses
Litigation
Real Estate Transactions
Tenant Screening

If you find a company that may possibly fit you public record searching needs, call them or visit their web site.

For a more inclusive and updated list of online searchable of source, gateways and distributors of public records, visit `www.publicrecordsources.com`.

Application Indexes

Searching/Verification Asset/Lien

Access Indiana Information Network
Access Louisiana
AccuSearch Inc
Amerestate Inc
Attorneys' Title Insurance Fund
Banko Inc
Cal Info
CDB Infotek
ChoicePoint Inc
Commercial Information Systems Inc
Confi-Chek
Court PC of Connecticut
Cyberspace Information Services
Datalink
DataQuick
DCS Information Systems
Diversified Information Services Corp
Dun & Bradstreet
Electronic Property Information Corp (EPIC)
Experian Business Information Solutions
Finder Group, The
First American Real Estate Solutions
IDM Corporation
Information America Inc
Intranet Inc
IQ Data Systems
IRSC
KnowX
Law Bulletin Information Network
LIDA Credit Agency Inc
Lloyds Maritime Information Services Inc
Logan Information Services
Logan Registration Service Inc
Maine Public Record Services
Merlin Information Services
Motznik Computer Services Inc
National Service Information
Nebrask@ Online
Northwest Location Services
Pallorium Inc
Paragon Document Research

Professional Services Bureau
Property Data Center Inc
PROTEC
Public Data Corporation
Richland County Abstract Co
Search Company of North Dakota LLC
Search Network Ltd
Security Search & Abstract Co
SKLD Information Services LLC
Southwest InfoNet
Specialty Services
Superior Information Services LLC
The Search Company Inc
Todd Wiegele Research Co Inc
Tyler-McLennon Inc
UCC Retrievals Inc
Unisearch Inc
US Corporate Services
US Document Services Inc
Western Regional Data Inc

Background Info - Business

AcuSearch Investigations & Services LLC
American Business Information Inc
ARISTOTLE
Avantext Inc
Burrelle's Information Services
Cal Info
Capitol Lien Records & Research Inc
CCH Washington Service Bureau
CDB Infotek
ChoicePoint Inc
CompuServe
Corporate Screening Services Inc
Court PC of Connecticut
CourtLink
Cyberspace Information Services
Daily Report, The
Datalink
DCS Information Systems
Derwent Information
Dialog Corporation, The
Disclosure Incorporated

Dun & Bradstreet
Electronic Property Information Corp (EPIC)
Experian Business Information Solutions
Fidelifacts
Finder Group, The
First American Real Estate Solutions
Gale Group Inc, The
Hollingsworth Court Reporting Inc
Hoovers Inc
Information America Inc
Information Network of Arkansas
IQ Data Systems
IRSC
KnowX
LIDA Credit Agency Inc
Lloyds Maritime Information Services Inc
Logan Registration Service Inc
Martindale-Hubbell
Merlin Information Services
Motznik Computer Services Inc
National Service Information
Offshore Business News & Research
OPEN (Online Professional Electronic
     Network)
OSHA DATA
Owens Online Inc
Paragon Document Research
PROTEC
RC Information brokers
San Diego Daily Transcript/San Diego Source
SEAFAX Inc
Search Company of North Dakota LLC
Specialty Services
Tax Analysts
The Search Company Inc
Thomson & Thomson
UMI Company
US Document Services Inc
WinStar Telebase Inc

Background Info –
Individuals

AcuSearch Investigations & Services LLC
Agency Records
Agency Records Inc
Ameridex Information Systems
Avert Inc

BiblioData
Cal Info
CCH Washington Service Bureau
ChoicePoint Inc
Cleo
CompuServe
Confi-Chek
Corporate Screening Services Inc
Court PC of Connecticut
CourtLink
CQ Staff Directories Ltd
CrimeLine Information Systems
Cyberspace Information Services
Daily Report, The
Electronic Property Information Corp (EPIC)
Equifax Credit Services Division
Fidelifacts
Finder Group, The
First American Real Estate Solutions
Hogan Information Services
Infocon Corporation
Information Inc
Informus Corporation
IQ Data Systems
Logan Registration Service Inc
Maine Public Record Services
MDR/Minnesota Driving Records
Military Information Enterprises Inc
National Credit Information Network NCI
National Information Bureau Ltd
Offshore Business News & Research
OPEN (Online Professional Electronic
     Network)
Owens Online Inc
PROTEC
RC Information brokers
Specialty Services
The Search Company Inc
Thomson & Thomson
Todd Wiegele Research Co Inc
VitalChek Network

Collections

Banko Inc
Case Record Info Services
Commercial Information Systems Inc
Equifax Credit Services Division
Haines & Company Inc

Information Inc
Informus Corporation
Merlin Information Services
Northwest Location Services
RC Information brokers
Record Information Services Inc
Trans Union
WinStar Telebase Inc

Competitive Intelligence

American Business Information Inc
Aurigin Systems Inc
BiblioData
Burrelle's Information Services
Capitol Lien Records & Research Inc
CCH Washington Service Bureau
CompuServe
Confi-Chek
Cyberspace Information Services
Daily Report, The
DataTech Research
Derwent Information
Dialog Corporation, The
Disclosure Incorporated
FOIA Group Inc
Hoovers Inc
IRSC
KnowX
LEXIS-NEXIS
Maine Public Record Services
MicroPatent USA
Paragon Document Research
Progenitor
Public Record Research Library
Thomson & Thomson
UMI Company
US Corporate Services
West Publishing
WinStar Telebase Inc

Direct Marketing

Accutrend Corporation
Amerestate Inc
American Business Information Inc
ARISTOTLE
Avantext Inc
Banko Inc

Case Record Info Services
CQ Staff Directories Ltd
Daily Report, The
DataQuick
Dialog Corporation, The
Experian Target Marketing Services
Haines & Company Inc
IDM Corporation
Intranet Inc
Lloyds Maritime Information Services Inc
Logan Information Services
MDR/Minnesota Driving Records
Metromail Corporation
Nebrask@ Online
OSHA DATA
Progenitor
Property Data Center Inc
Record Information Services Inc
SKLD Information Services LLC
Thomson & Thomson
Western Regional Data Inc
WinStar Telebase Inc

Employment Screening

AcuSearch Investigations & Services LLC
Agency Records Inc
American Driving Records Inc
Avantext Inc
Avert Inc
Business Information Service
Capitol Lien Records & Research Inc
ChoicePoint Inc
Cleo
Commercial Information Systems Inc
Corporate Screening Services Inc
CourtLink
DAC Services
Database Technologies Inc
Datalink
DCS Information Systems
Equifax Credit Services Division
Experian Consumer Credit
Felonies R Us
Fidelifacts
Hogan Information Services
Information Inc
Information Network of Arkansas
Information Network of Kansas

Informus Corporation
Law Bulletin Information Network
LIDA Credit Agency Inc
Logan Information Services
National Credit Information Network NCI
OPEN (Online Professional Electronic
  Network)
Pallorium Inc
Paragon Document Research
PROTEC
Search Company of North Dakota LLC
Specialty Services
TML Information Services Inc
Todd Wiegele Research Co Inc
Tyler-McLennon Inc
Virginia Information Providers Network

Filing/Recording Documents

Access Indiana Information Network
AccuSearch Inc
AcuSearch Investigations & Services LLC
Amerestate Inc
Banko Inc
Capitol Lien Records & Research Inc
CCH Washington Service Bureau
Chattel Mortgage Reporter Inc
Daily Report, The
Diversified Information Services Corp
Hollingsworth Court Reporting Inc
IQ Data Systems
Maine Public Record Services
National Service Information
Professional Services Bureau
Richland County Abstract Co
San Diego Daily Transcript/San Diego Source
Search Company of North Dakota LLC
Search Network Ltd
Security Search & Abstract Co
SKLD Information Services LLC
Southwest InfoNet
Tyler-McLennon Inc
UCC Retrievals Inc
US Corporate Services
US Document Services Inc

Fraud Prevention/Detection

Cambridge Statistical Research Associates
Carfax
CDB Infotek
Cleo
Commercial Information Systems Inc
DAC Services
Database Technologies Inc
Datalink
DCS Information Systems
Felonies R Us
IDM Corporation
IRSC
Merlin Information Services
Metromail Corporation
National Fraud Center
Offshore Business News & Research
PROTEC

Genealogical Research

Ameridex Information Systems
CQ Staff Directories Ltd
Everton Publishers
Gale Group Inc, The
Infocon Corporation
Military Information Enterprises Inc
Progenitor
RC Information brokers
VitalChek Network

General Business Information

Accutrend Corporation
Agency Records
American Business Information Inc
Banko Inc
BRC Inc
Business Information Service
CompuServe
CrimeLine Information Systems
Cyberspace Information Services
Database Technologies Inc
DataTech Research
Dialog Corporation, The

Disclosure Incorporated
Dun & Bradstreet
Federal Filings Inc
Felonies R Us
Finder Group, The
Hollingsworth Court Reporting Inc
Hoovers Inc
Information Network of Arkansas
Information Network of Kansas
Intranet Inc
LEXIS-NEXIS
Lloyds Maritime Information Services Inc
National Information Bureau Ltd
Offshore Business News & Research
Owens Online Inc
Progenitor
Public Data Corporation
Public Record Research Library
SEAFAX Inc
Tax Analysts
Trans Union
UMI Company
WinStar Telebase Inc

Government Document Retrieval

AccuSearch Inc
ARISTOTLE
CCH Washington Service Bureau
Congressional Information Service Inc
Conrad Grundlehner Inc
CQ Staff Directories Ltd
Database Technologies Inc
DataTech Research
Dialog Corporation, The
FOIA Group Inc
Hogan Information Services
Hollingsworth Court Reporting Inc
KnowX
LEXIS-NEXIS
OSHA DATA
Public Record Research Library
Southwest InfoNet
The Search Company Inc
US Document Services Inc
West Publishing

Insurance Underwriting

Agency Records
Agency Records Inc
AM Best Company
American Driving Records Inc
DAC Services
Datalink
Diversified Information Services Corp
Electronic Property Information Corp (EPIC)
Explore Information Services
Haines & Company Inc
Information Network of Arkansas
Information Network of Kansas
Insurance Information Exchange (iiX)
MDR/Minnesota Driving Records
Nebrask@ Online
Property Data Center Inc
Silver Plume
TML Information Services Inc
Trans Union
Tyler-McLennon Inc
Virginia Information Providers Network
VISTA Information Solutions

Legal Compliance

Access Indiana Information Network
Access Louisiana
AccuSearch Inc
Agency Records
ARISTOTLE
Aurigin Systems Inc
Avantext Inc
Communications Systems Technology Inc
Congressional Information Service Inc
Conrad Grundlehner Inc
Corporate Screening Services Inc
CrimeLine Information Systems
Derwent Information
Disclosure Incorporated
Federal Filings Inc
Information Network of Kansas
Investigators Anywhere Resource Line
Legi-Slate Inc
LEXIS-NEXIS
MicroPatent USA
National Service Information
Nebrask@ Online

OSHA DATA
Public Data Corporation
Security Search & Abstract Co
Superior Information Services LLC
Tax Analysts
Thomson & Thomson
UCC Guide Inc, The
UCC Retrievals Inc
Unisearch Inc
VISTA Information Solutions
West Publishing
Western Regional Data Inc

Lending/Leasing

AccuSearch Inc
Amerestate Inc
Business Information Service
CDB Infotek
Chattel Mortgage Reporter Inc
Cleo
Communications Systems Technology Inc
DataQuick
Derwent Information
Equifax Credit Services Division
Experian Business Information Solutions
Experian Consumer Credit
First American Real Estate Solutions
Haines & Company Inc
Hogan Information Services
IDM Corporation
Information America Inc
Information Network of Kansas
National Information Bureau Ltd
National Service Information
Nebrask@ Online
Professional Services Bureau
Property Data Center Inc
Real Estate Guide Inc, The
SEAFAX Inc
Search Network Ltd
Southwest InfoNet
Superior Information Services LLC
Trans Union
Tyler-McLennon Inc
UCC Guide Inc, The
Unisearch Inc
US Corporate Services
VISTA Information Solutions

Litigation

Access Louisiana
Agency Records
Business Information Service
Chattel Mortgage Reporter Inc
ChoicePoint Inc
Confi-Chek
Conrad Grundlehner Inc
Court PC of Connecticut
CourtLink
CrimeLine Information Systems
Database Technologies Inc
Disclosure Incorporated
Federal Filings Inc
Felonies R Us
Fidelifacts
FOIA Group Inc
Hylind Courthouse Retrieval Co
Infocon Corporation
Information America Inc
Information Inc
Intranet Inc
Investigators Anywhere Resource Line
LIDA Credit Agency Inc
Motznik Computer Services Inc
Northwest Location Services
Offshore Business News & Research
OPEN
OSHA DATA
Pallorium Inc
Paragon Document Research
RC Information brokers
Southwest InfoNet
Specialty Services
Superior Information Services LLC
Tax Analysts
The Search Company Inc
Todd Wiegele Research Co Inc
UCC Retrievals Inc
Virginia Information Providers Network

Locating People/Businesses

AcuSearch Investigations & Services LLC
American Business Information Inc
Ameridex Information Systems

ARISTOTLE
Cambridge Statistical Research Associates
CDB Infotek
Cleo
Commercial Information Systems Inc
Confi-Chek
Court PC of Connecticut
CQ Staff Directories Ltd
CrimeLine Information Systems
DataQuick
DCS Information Systems
Finder Group, The
Folks Finders Ltd
Haines & Company Inc
Hoovers Inc
Information America Inc
Informus Corporation
IQ Data Systems
IRSC
KnowX
Law Bulletin Information Network
Merlin Information Services
Metromail Corporation
Military Information Enterprises Inc
Motznik Computer Services Inc
National Credit Information Network NCI
Northwest Location Services
OPEN
Owens Online Inc
Pallorium Inc
Progenitor
Public Data Corporation
Public Record Research Library
Western Regional Data Inc

Real Estate Transactions

Amerestate Inc
Attorneys' Title Insurance Fund

BRC Inc
Business Information Service
Capitol Lien Records & Research Inc
Chattel Mortgage Reporter Inc
DataQuick
Diversified Information Services Corp
Electronic Property Information Corp (EPIC)
Environmental Data Resources Inc
First American Real Estate Solutions
IDM Corporation
Infocon Corporation
LIDA Credit Agency Inc
Logan Information Services
Maine Public Record Services
Motznik Computer Services Inc
Professional Services Bureau
Property Data Center Inc
Real Estate Guide Inc, The
Record Information Services Inc
Richland County Abstract Co
San Diego Daily Transcript/San Diego Source
Security Search & Abstract Co
SKLD Information Services LLC
Todd Wiegele Research Co Inc
Trans Union
Unisearch Inc
US Corporate Services
Western Regional Data Inc

Tenant Screening

American Driving Records Inc
AmRent
Experian Consumer Credit
Felonies R Us
Information Inc
Logan Information Services
National Credit Information Network NCI

Vendor Profiles

Access Indiana Information Network

150 W Market #530
Indianapolis, IN 46204-2806
Telephone: **Fax:**
317-233-2106   317-233-2011
www.ai.org

Applications: Legal Compliance,
Filing/Recording Documents, Asset/Lien
Searching/Verification, Current Events

Proprietary Products:

Name/Desc: Premium Services
Info Provided: Driver and/or Vehicle
Media: Internet
Coverage: IN

Name/Desc: Free Services
Info Provided:
Licenses/Registrations/Permits
Media: Internet
Coverage: IN

Statement of Capabilities:
AIIN is a comprehensive, one-stop source for
electronic access to State of Indiana
government information. This company is
owned by the state itself. Access to the public
record information listed here requires a
subscription fee. They also specialize in
physician and nurse license verification. See
the Internet site for more information.

Access Louisiana

400 Travis St #1308
Shreveport, LA 71101
Telephone: **Fax:**
800-489-5620   800-705-8953
318-227-9730

Applications: Asset/Lien
Searching/Verification, Legal Compliance,
Litigation

Proprietary Products:

Name/Desc: LA UCC
Info Provided: Uniform Commercial Code,
Addresses/Telephone Numbers and Social
Security Numbers
Media: Printed Report
Coverage: LA

Name/Desc: LA Corporate Data
Info Provided: Corporate/Trade Name Data,
Trademarks/Patents and Addresses/Telephone
Numbers
Media: Printed Report
Coverage: LA

Statement of Capabilities:
Access Louisiana is a statewide legal research
company with a physical presence in every
Louisiana parish. Services include: public
records (UCC, accounts, receivable,
state/federal tax liens, suits, chattel mortgages,
bankruptcy records), corporate filing/retrieval,
court records and registered agent services.
They have extensive knowledge of where
information is recorded and how to effectively
retrieve Louisiana public records.

AccuSearch Inc

PO Box 3248
Houston, TX 77253-3248
Telephone: **Fax:**
800-833-5778   713-831-9891
713-864-7639

www.accusearchinc.com
sales@accusearchinc.com

Applications: Asset/Lien
Searching/Verification, Filing/Recording
Documents, Legal Compliance, Government
Document Retrieval, Lending/Leasing

Proprietary Products:

Name/Desc: AccuSearch
Info Provided: Corporate/Trade Name,
Uniform Commercial Code
Media: Direct Online
Coverage: TX,CA,PA,IL,WA,OH,OR,MO

Name/Desc: AccuSearch
Info Provided: Bankruptcy
Coverage: CA,IL,TX

Statement of Capabilities:
AccuSearch provides immediate access to
UCC, corporate, charter, real property and
bankruptcy search services via IBM-
compatible PCs or over the telephone.

Instantaneous access is available for each online database listed. Each online or over-the-phone search is followed by same-day mailing or faxing of the search report and any copies requested. AccuSearch also performs any of the above searches for any county or state nationwide. AccuSearch's Direct Access system allows multi-page, formatted reports which eliminates print screens, and selective ordering of UCC copies.

Accutrend Corporation

6021 S Syracuse Wy #111
Denver, CO 80111

Telephone: **Fax:**
800-488-0011   303-488-0133
303-488-0011

www.accutrend.com

Applications: Direct Marketing, General Business Information

Proprietary Products:

Name/Desc: New Business Database
Info Provided:
Licenses/Registrations/Permits and Corporate/Trade Name Data
Media: CD-ROM, Internet, Magnetic Tape and Lists or labels
Coverage: US

Statement of Capabilities:

Accutrend Corporation compiles a new business database monthly that contains 175 to 200 million new business registrations, licenses and incorporations. Data is collected from all levels of government and is enhanced with demographic overlays.

AcuSearch Investigations & Services LLC

PO Box 100613
Denver, CO 80250

Telephone: **Fax:**
303-756-9687   303-756-9687
AcuSearch9@aol.com

Applications: Background Info - Business, Background Info - Individuals, Employment Screening, Filing/Recording Documents, Locating People/Businesses

Proprietary Products:

Name/Desc: CO Criminal Information
Info Provided: Criminal Information
Media: Call-back Only
Coverage: CO

Statement of Capabilities:

AcuSearch specializes in locating and obtaining pertinent information for financial institutions, businesses and individuals. Instant access to nationwide people, credit, and vehicle information. 24 hour turnaround time on all Colorado and Washington criminal/civil, driving/plate records, and process service. They provide in depth investigation in trademark matters. Owner Layla Flora is a University of Colorado graduate and has extensive case investigation experience in civil and criminal matters. Guarantees quality and professional service.

Agency Records

PO Box 310175
Newington, CT 06131

Telephone: **Fax:**
800-777-6655   860-666-4247
860-667-1490

www.agencyrecords.com

Applications: Background Info - Individuals, Litigation, General Business Information, Insurance Underwriting, Legal Compliance

Proprietary Products:

Name/Desc: CT Court Convictions (1989)
Info Provided: Criminal Information
Media: Direct Online to Your Computer, Gateway via Another Online Svc, Automated Telephone Look-Up, 624, and Auto-Activated Fax-on-Demand
Coverage: CT

Name/Desc: MN Court Convictions (15 years)
Info Provided: Criminal Information
Media: Direct Online to Your Computer, Gateway via Another Online Svc, Automated Telephone Look-Up, 624, and Auto-Activated Fax-on-Demand
Coverage: MN

Name/Desc: FL Workers' Compensation Claims (20 years)
Info Provided: Workers' Compensation

Media: Direct Online to Your Computer, Gateway via Another Online Svc, Automated Telephone Look-Up, 624, and Auto-Activated Fax-on-Demand
Coverage: FL

Statement of Capabilities:

Agency Records provides instant access to MVRs for FL, AL, SC, NC, WV, NJ, NY, CT, VT, NH, and ME. They also provide instant access to court convictions for Connecticut and Minnesota. They offer computer, fax and phone ordering as well as volume discounts. Public companies may be invoiced.

Agency Records Inc

PO Box 310175
Newington, CT 06131
Telephone: **Fax:**
800-777-6655 860-666-4247
860-667-1617

www.agencyrecords.com

Applications: Employment Screening, Insurance Underwriting, Background Info - Individuals

Proprietary Products:

Name/Desc: ARI
Info Provided: Driver and/or Vehicle
Media: Online, Fax, Printed Report
Coverage: US

Statement of Capabilities:

Agency Records Inc, and its sister company Rapid Information Services, is a business to business provider of public record information. Agency records is committed to quality service and rapid turnaround of orders. They accept orders via their PC software, mainframe transmission, fax or telephone. The ARI product allows instant diring record access in many states.

AM Best Company

Ambest Rd
Oldwick, NJ 08858-9988
Telephone: **Fax:**
908-439-2200 908-439-3296
www.ambest.com

Applications: Insurance Underwriting, Insurance Ratings

Proprietary Products:

Name/Desc: Best Database Services
Info Provided: SEC/Other Financial
Media: Online Database, CD-ROM, Disk, Magnetic Tape, Call-back
Coverage: US

Statement of Capabilities:

AM Best, known worldwide as The Insurance Information Source, became the first rating agency to report on the solvency of insurers, and is considered the leading provider of insurance information. Their exclusive Best's Ratings are the original and most recognized financial strength insurance ratings in the world. AM Best offers comprehensive insurance information through more than 50 reference publications and services. AM Best is dedicated to providing the precise, objective insurance information. AM Best also has a branch office in London, England; their phone number is 011-44-171-264-2260.

Amerestate Inc

8160 Corporate Park Dr #200
Cincinnati, OH 45242
Telephone: **Fax:**
800-582-7300 513-489-4409
513-489-7300

www.amerestate.com

sales@amerestate.com

Applications: Asset/Lien Searching/Verification, Direct Marketing, Filing/Recording Documents, Lending/Leasing, Real Estate Transactions

Proprietary Products:

Name/Desc: PaceNet for Windows
Info Provided: Real Estate/Assessor, Mortgage Data and Addresses/Telephone Numbers
Media: CD-ROM and Direct Online to Your Computer
Coverage: KY, MI, OH

Name/Desc: PaceNet Online
Info Provided: Real Estate/Assessor, Mortgage Data and Addresses/Telephone Numbers
Media: Direct Online to Your Computer
Coverage: KY, MI, OH

Name/Desc: Pace Books
Info Provided: Real Estate/Assessor, Mortgage Data and Addresses/Telephone Numbers
Media: Printed Report
Coverage: KY, MI, OH

Name/Desc: PaceNet Mortgage Heads
Info Provided: Real Estate/Assessor, Mortgage Data and Addresses/Telephone Numbers
Media: Direct Online to Your Computer
Coverage: KY, MI, OH

Name/Desc: Prospect Services
Info Provided: Real Estate/Assessor, Mortgage Data and Addresses/Telephone Numbers
Media: Disk, Lists or labels, Magnetic Tape and Printed Report
Coverage: KY, MI , OH

Statement of Capabilities:
Amerestate maintains databases of existing real estate ownership and gathers and verifies data from courthouse public records and other sources on all real estate sales. They collect most information manually, assuring accuracy, completeness and timely information. Property addresses are standardized and updated quarterly to current CASS standards required by the USPS. Amerestate has recently introduced PaceNet Mortgage Leads, a product specifically designed for those in the lending industry who want to target prospects for refinance, lines of credit or seconds.

American Business Information Inc

PO Box 27347
Omaha, NE 68127
Telephone: **Fax:**
800-808-4636   402-331-5990
402-593-4500

www.infousa.com

Applications: Background Info - Business, Competitive Intelligence, Direct Marketing, General Business Information, Locating People/Businesses

Proprietary Products:
Name/Desc: Business Sales Leads
Info Provided: Addresses/Telephone Numbers, Credit Information, Foreign Country Information, News/Current Events and SEC/Other Financial
Media: CD-ROM, Direct Online to Your Computer, Disk, Gateway Via Another Online Service, Internet, Lists or labels, Magnetic Tape, Printed Report, Publication/Directory and Software
Coverage: US

Name/Desc: Consumer Sales Leads
Info Provided: Addresses/Telephone Numbers, Credit Information, Driver and/or Vehicle, Genealogical Information and Real Estate/Assessor
Media: CD-ROM, Direct Online to Your Computer, Disk, Gateway Via Another Online Service, Internet, Lists or labels, Magnetic Tape, Printed Report, Publication/Directory and Software
Coverage: US

Statement of Capabilities:
American Business Information compiles business information from telephone directories and other public sources. Over the past 20+ years, they have provided services to over two million customers. They telephone verify every name in their database before they offer it for sale. They phone-verify address changes from the USPS NCOA program. Their info is available in a variety of ways including online (SalesLeadsUSA.com), CD-ROM, and by telephone (Directory Assistance Plus). A division produces the Pro-CD Disk and another operates Digital Directory Assistance. For business leads call 800-555-5335. For SalesLeads USA call 402-593-4593.

American Driving Records Inc

PO Box 160147
Sacramento, CA 95816-9998
Telephone: **Fax:**
800-766-6877   800-800-0817
916-456-3200   916-456-3332

www.mvrs.com

sales@mvrs.com

Applications: Insurance Underwriting, Employment Screening, Tenant Screening

Proprietary Products:

Info Provided: Driver and/or Vehicle
Media: Online, Fax, Printed Report
Coverage: US

Statement of Capabilities:

Amercian Driving Record (ADR) services include driving records, registration information, and special processing for the insurance industry such as automatic checking (ACH), calculating underwriting points, and ZapApp™ - an automated insurance application from the agency to the carrier. Driving records can be instant, same day or overnight, depending on the state.

Ameridex Information Systems

PO Box 51314
Irvine, CA 92619-1314
Fax:
714-731-2116
http://kadima.com

Applications: Background Info - Individuals, Locating People/Businesses, Genealogical Research

Proprietary Products:

Name/Desc: SSDI
Info Provided: Addresses
Media: CD-ROM, Online, Lists
Coverage: US

Name/Desc: Military
Info Provided: Military Service
Media: CD-ROM, Online, List
Coverage: US

Name/Desc: Live Index
Info Provided: Addresses
Media: CD-ROM, Online, Lists
Coverage: US

Statement of Capabilities:

Ameridex presents several unique databases for people tracing on the Internet. Over 220 million names and 180 million with a data of birth are compiled from multiple public record sources. Speciality databases include a nationwide death index with supplements and an active military personnel database.

AmRent

9990 Richmond #100
Houston, TX 77042
Telephone: **Fax:**
800-324-3681   800-324-4595
713-266-1870   713-266-9146

Applications: Tenant Screening

Proprietary Products:

Name/Desc: AmRent
Info Provided: Tenant History
Media: Available on Trans Registry and Call-in
Coverage: IL, TX

Statement of Capabilities:

AmRent furnishes background checks in relation to their tenant screening services, utilizing proprietary in-house database information and public records. AmRent is an affiliate of Trans Registry, a database of tenant history and eviction information accumulated from affiliates nationwide.

ARISTOTLE

205 Pennsylvania Ave SW
Washington, DC 20003
Telephone: **Fax:**
800-296-2747   202-543-6407
202-543-8345

www.products.aristotle.org

Applications: Background Info - Business, Legal Compliance, Direct Marketing, Government Document Retrieval, Locating People/Businesses

Proprietary Products:

Name/Desc: ARISTOTLE
Info Provided: Voter Registration and Addresses/Telephone Numbers
Media: CD-ROM, Magnetic Tape and Online Database
Coverage: US

Statement of Capabilities:

ARISTOTLE maintains a nationwide file of registered voters. Information obtained from 3,400 counties and municipalities is standardized and enhanced with listed phone number, postal correction and national change of address, census geography, and age and vote history. Twenty-six states have no significant restrictions on the commercial use of their voter registration information.

Attorneys' Title Insurance Fund

PO Box 628600
Orlando, FL 32862

Telephone: **Fax:**
800-336-3863 407-240-1106
407-240-3863

www.thefund.com

Applications: Real Estate Transactions, Asset/Lien Searching/Verification

Proprietary Products:

Name/Desc: The Fund
Info Provided: Real Estate, Litigation/Judgments/Tax Liens,
Media: Online, Disk, Printed Report, Magnetic Tape
Coverage: FL-31 counties

Statement of Capabilities:

Although the primary business of The Fund (as they are called) is to issue title insurance, they offer access to over 100 million real estate records from 31 major counites in FL. The Fund has 14 branch offices and is expanding to SC and IL. Online users can access public records including mortgages, deeds, liens, assessments, right-of-way data, and even judgment and divorce proceedings.

Aurigin Systems Inc

1975 Landings Drive
Mountain View, CA 94043

Telephone: **Fax:**
650-237-0900 650-237-0910

http://aurigin.com

info@aurgin.com

Applications: Legal Compliance, Competitive Intelligence

Proprietary Products:

Name/Desc: SmartPatent
Info Provided: Trademarks, Patents
Media: Online, Software
Coverage: US, International

Statement of Capabilities:

Aurigin, formally known as SmartPatents Inc, offers the Aurigin IPAM System to manage a company's intellectual asset management needs. Other important products are SmartPatent Electronic Patents, indexed patents from the US Patent and Trademark Office, and the SmartPatent Workbench, a desktop software application.

Avantext Inc

Green Hills Corporate Center
2675 Morgantown Rd #3300Reading, PA 19607

Telephone: **Fax:**
800-998-8857 800-544-9252
610-796-2385 610-796-2392

www.avantext.com

sales@avantex.com

Applications: Background Info - Business, Direct Marketing, Employment Screening, Legal Compliance

Proprietary Products:

Name/Desc: FAA Data
Info Provided: Aviation/Vessels, Addresses, Legislation/Regulations
Media: CD-ROM
Coverage: US

Statement of Capabilities:

Avantext product line includes six powerful CDs for the aviation industry. The FAA Data CD includes a full listing of pilots and aircraft owners, schools, technicians, dealers and much more.

Avert Inc

301 Remington St
Fort Collins, CO 80524

Telephone: **Fax:**
800-367-5933 800-237-4011

www.avert.com

welsh@avert.com

Applications: Background Info - Individuals, Employment Screening

Proprietary Products:

Name/Desc: Workers' Compensation History
Info Provided: Workers Compensation
Media: Direct Online, Printed Report
Coverage:
AK,AL,AR,AZ,CA,CO,DC,DE,FL,HI,IA,ID, IL,IN,KS,KY,MA,MD,MI,MN,MO,MS,MT,

ND,NE,NH,NM,NV,OH,OK,OR,PA,RI,SC,S
D,TN,TX,VA,VT,WV,WY

Statement of Capabilities:
Avert helps employers minimize risk and hire safe, honest and competent employees. Use Avert's on-line ordering system, OrderXpert, and retrieve reports to your desktop. Avert offers services such as KnowledgeLink Help Desk for building a compliant pre-employment screening program to fit the need. Legal and fair to all parties, Avert is a good outsource for pre-employment screening as well as providing a proactive approach to reducing fraud, theft, turnover, and violence in the workplace.

Banko Inc
607 Marquette Ave #500
Minneapolis, MN 55402
Telephone: **Fax:**
800-533-8897   612-321-0325
612-332-2427
www.BANKO.com
SALES@BANKO.com

Applications: Asset/Lien Searching/Verification, Collections, Direct Marketing, Filing/Recording Documents, General Business Information

Proprietary Products:

Statement of Capabilities:
Banko Inc. provides up to the minute information about bankruptcy suppression and notification in a variety of electronic formats.

BiblioData
PO Box 61
Needham Heights, MA 02494
Telephone: **Fax:**
781-444-1154   781-449-4584
www.bibliodata.com
ina@bibliodata.com

Applications: Current Events, Competitive Intelligence, Background Info - Individuals, Risk Management

Proprietary Products:

Name/Desc: BiblioData
Info Provided: News/Current Events, Addresses/Telephone Numbers
Media: Internet

Coverage: US

Statement of Capabilities:
Bibliodata publishes directories and newsletters directly related to the online industry. Their products are targeted for researchers and librairies who must struggle daily with online pricing decisions.

BRC Inc
PO Box 4889
Syracuse, NY 13221
Telephone:
315-437-1283
Applications: General Business Information, Real Estate Transactions

Proprietary Products:

Info Provided: Real Estate
Media: Online
Coverage: ME-17 county registries

Statement of Capabilities:
BRC specilizes in online access to Maine Registries. Fees are involved. They are expanding into Illinois, also.

Burrelle's Information Services
75 East Northfiled Rd
Livingston, NJ 07039
Telephone:
800-631-1160
973-992-6600
http://burrelles.com
info@burrelles.com

Applications: Current Events, Background Info - Business, Competitive Intelligence

Proprietary Products:

Name/Desc: BIO
Info Provided: News/Current Events
Media: Online, CD-ROM, Publication
Coverage: US, International

Statement of Capabilities:
For over 100 years Burrelle's has been monitoring, organizing, and delivering media data to clients. Products include Press Clipping, NewsExpress, NewsAlert, Media Directories, Broadcast Transcripts, and Web Clips. The BIO - Burrelle's Information Office

- is software to receive and use information from Burrelle's.

Business Information Service

531 S Holland
Bellville, TX 77418
Telephone: **Fax:**
409-865-2547 409-865-8918
Applications: General Business Information, Lending/Leasing, Real Estate Transactions, Litigation, Employment Screening

Proprietary Products:

Name/Desc: Local Public Record
Info Provided: Real Estate/Assessor, Litigation/Judgments/Tax Liens, Uniform Commercial Code and Criminal Information
Media: Publication
Coverage: TX -Austin, Colorado, Waller, Washington Counties

Name/Desc: Bankruptcies
Info Provided: Bankruptcy
Media: Publication
Coverage: TX-Austin, Colorado, Waller, Washington

Statement of Capabilities:

Business Information Service (BIS) provides its information in the form of monthly subscription publications.

Cal Info

316 W 2nd St #102
Los Angeles, CA 90012
Telephone: **Fax:**
213-687-8710 213-687-8778
http://members.aol.com/
calinfola
calinfola@aol.com

Applications: Background Info - Business, Background Info - Individuals, Asset/Lien Searching/Verification

Proprietary Products:

Name/Desc: Guide to State Statutes
Info Provided: State Statutes
Media: Directory
Coverage: US

Name/Desc: Administrative Guide to State Regulations
Info Provided: State Regulations

Media: Publication

Statement of Capabilities:
Cal Info offers an information research and retrieval service that finds answers to questions that affect law firms and businesses everyday. Their personnel are trained to search computerized databases as well as the more traditional information sources, including libraries, publishers, government agencies, courts, trade unions and associations. They provide company reports, financial data, product information, people information, journals and news stories, real estate information, legal research, public records research, government information and document retrieval.

Cambridge Statistical Research Associates

53 Wellesley
Irvine, CA 92612
Telephone: **Fax:**
800-327-2772 800-327-2720
714-509-9900 714-509-9119

Applications: Locating People/Businesses, Fraud Prevention/Detection

Proprietary Products:

Name/Desc: Death Master File
Info Provided: Social Security Numbers
Media: CD-ROM, Online Database and Printed Report
Coverage: US

Statement of Capabilities:
CSRA traces its origin to an actuarial and programming service established in 1979. In recent years, its efforts moved toward bringing large mainframe databases to the desktop computing platform, including CD-ROM. CSRA specializes in nationwide death index by name and Social Security Number, death auditing service, database consulting, genealogical and probate research, and address trace service.

Capitol Lien Records & Research Inc

PO Box 65727
St Paul, MN 55165

Telephone: **Fax:**
800-845-4077   800-845-4080
612-222-2500   612-222-2110

Applications: Competitive Intelligence,
Background Info - Business, Employment
Screening, Real Estate Transactions,
Filing/Recording Documents

Proprietary Products:

Name/Desc: UCC
Info Provided: Uniform Commercial Code
Media: Disk
Coverage: MN

Statement of Capabilities:
Capitol Lien Records & Research provides
UCC, federal and state tax lien searches,
environmental lien searches, Minnesota
Watercraft, motor vehicle searches,
bankruptcy, suit and judgment searches,
corporate documents and a weekly tax lien
report. They provide an online ordering system
to clients.

Carfax

3975 Fair Ridge Dr #200N
Fairfax, VA 22033

Telephone: **Fax:**
703-934-2664   703-218-2465
www.carfax.com

Applications: Fraud Prevention/Detection, Risk
Management

Proprietary Products:

Name/Desc: Vehicle History Service
Info Provided: Driver and/or Vehicle
Media: Internet and Direct Online to Your
Computer
Coverage: US

Name/Desc: Motor Vehicle Title Information
Info Provided: Driver and/or Vehicle
Media: Online Database, Available on
CompuServe and Call-in
Coverage: US

Name/Desc: VINde (VIN Validity Check
Program)
Info Provided: Software/Training

Media: Disk
Coverage: US

Statement of Capabilities:
With perhaps the largest online vehicle history
database (728 million vehicle records), Carfax
can generate a Vehicle History Report based on
a VIN in less than one second. They collect
data from a variety of sources including state
DMVs and salvage pools. Reports include
details from previous titles, city and state,
odometer rollbacks, junk and flood damage,
etc, reducing the risk of handling used vehicles
with hidden problems that affect their value.

Case Record Info Services

2648 E Workman Ave #512
West Covina, CA 91791

Telephone: **Fax:**
626-967-6682   626-967-3782
caserecord@yahooo.com

Applications: Collections, Direct Marketing

Proprietary Products:

Name/Desc: Judgment Lists
Info Provided: Litigation/Judgments/Tax
Liens
Media: Disk, Lists or labels and Printed
Report
Coverage: CA

Statement of Capabilities:
Case Record Info Services provides judgment
lists in California. Their data is used by bulk
data providers, collection, and mediation
companies. They are also members of the
American Arbitration Association.

CCH Washington Service Bureau

655 15th Street NW
Washington, DC 20005

Telephone: **Fax:**
800-955-5219   202-508-0694
202-508-0600

www.wsb.com

custserve@wsb.com

Applications: Background Info - Business,
Background Info - Individuals, Competitive
Intelligence, Filing/Recording Documents,
Government Document Retrieval

Proprietary Products:

Name/Desc: SECnet
Info Provided: SEC Filings
Media: Direct Online to Your Computer and Internet
Coverage: US

Statement of Capabilities:
With an average of over seven years of SEC document experience, their research specialists can tackle tough assignments and meet the most pressing deadlines. Whether clients require examples of precedent language or detailed intelligence on a specific firm or industry, CCH Washington Service Bureau will quickly provide the precise information. Using state-of-the-art proprietary databases their research specialists quickly deliver a wide range of corporate and transactional information.

CDB Infotek

6 Hutton Centre Dr #600
Santa Ana, CA 92707
Telephone: **Fax:**
800-427-3747   714-708-1000
714-708-2000
www.cdb.com

Applications: Locating People/Businesses, Asset/Lien Searching/Verification, Background Info - Business, Fraud Prevention/Detection, Lending/Leasing

Proprietary Products:

Name/Desc: Real Property Ownership & Transfers
Info Provided: Real Estate/Assessor
Media: Online Database
Coverage: US

Name/Desc: Corporate & Limited Partnerships
Info Provided: Corporate Information
Media: Online Database
Coverage: US

Name/Desc: Uniform Commerical Code
Info Provided: Uniform Commerical Code
Media: Online Database
Coverage: US

Name/Desc: Bankruptcies, Tax Liens, Judgments, Notices of Default
Info Provided: Bankruptcy and Litigation/Judgments/Tax Liens
Media: Online Databases

Coverage: US

Statement of Capabilities:
CDB Infotek offers nationwide public records information, including instant access to more than 3.5 billion records and 1,600 targeted databases to efficiently locate people or businesses, conduct background research, identify assets, control fraud, conduct due diligence, etc. Subscribers learn search strategies at free, year-round seminars and have toll-free access to customer service representatives for help. CDB Infotek also offers direct marketing lists, monitoring services, hard copy document retrieval and high-volume processing services.

Chattel Mortgage Reporter Inc

300 W Washington #808
Chicago, IL 60606
Telephone: **Fax:**
312-214-1048   312-214-1054
www.chattelmtg.com
searches@chattelmtg.com

Applications: Lending/Leasing, Filing/Recording Documents, Real Estate Transactions, Litigation

Proprietary Products:

Name/Desc: Chattel Mortgage Reporter
Info Provided: Uniform Commercial Code
Media: Call-in, Fax, Online and E-mail
Coverage: IL-Cook County

Statement of Capabilities:
CMR is a national public record service organization specializing in Illinois. They have more than 95 years of experience, with emphasis on public record research in Cook County, IL and the counties surrounding the Chicago area. For fast copy retrieval, their UCC database for Cook County is backed up by microfilm dating back to 1973.

ChoicePoint Inc

1000 Alderman Dr
Alphretta, GA 30005
Telephone: **Fax:**
770-752-6000   770-752-6005
www.choicepointinc.com

Applications: Background Info - Business, Employment Screening, Asset/Lien Searching/Verification, Background Info - Individuals, Litigation

Proprietary Products:

Name/Desc: Corp Data
Info Provided: Corporation Information
Media: Online Database
Coverage: US

Name/Desc: Bankruptcy
Info Provided: Bankruptcy Data
Media: Online
Coverage: US

Name/Desc: UCC
Info Provided: UCC Fillings and Tax Liens
Media: Online Database
Coverage: US

Name/Desc: Real Property
Info Provided: Real Estate
Media: Online
Coverage: US

Name/Desc: Litigation
Info Provided: Litigation, Liens, Suits
Media: Online
Coverage: US

Name/Desc: Licenses
Info Provided: Licenses, Physicians
Media: Online
Coverage: US

Name/Desc: Fict. Bus Names
Info Provided: Fictious Business Names
Media: Online
Coverage: US

Statement of Capabilities:

ChoicePoint is a leading provider of intelligence information to help businesses, governments, and individuals to better understand with whom they do business. ChoicePoint services the risk management information needs of the property and casualty insurance market, the life and health insurance market, and business and government, including asset-based lenders and professional service providers. The company, with many branch offices nationwide, was spun off/out from Equifax in 1997. They offer a variety of useful online products.

Cleo

106 West 6th Ave
Rome, GA 30161
Telephone: **Fax:**
706-295-5777   706-295-9081
Applications: Background Info - Individuals, Employment Screening, Fraud Prevention/Detection, Lending/Leasing, Locating People/Businesses

Proprietary Products:

Name/Desc: Cleo
Info Provided: Addresses and Phone Numbers
Media: Direct Online to Your Computer and Fax
Coverage: US

Statement of Capabilities:

Cleo has no long distance charges for online access and offers 30 seconds or less turnaround time. No monthly minimum is required, but the client agreement must identify the legal "need to know." They offer a fraud detection program.

Commercial Information Systems Inc

4747 SW Kelly #110
Portland, OR 97201-4221
Telephone: **Fax:**
800-454-6575   503-222-7405
503-222-7422

www.cis-usa.com
cis@world1.worldstar.com

Applications: Asset/Lien Searching/Verification, Collections, Employment Screening, Fraud Prevention/Detection, Locating People/Businesses

Proprietary Products:

Name/Desc: Aircraft Registrations
Info Provided: Aviation/Vessels
Media: Direct Online to Your Computer
Coverage: US

Name/Desc: UCCs
Info Provided: Uniform Commercial Code
Media: Direct Online to Your Computer
Coverage: CA, ID, OR, WA

Name/Desc: Corporations & Limited Partnerships
Info Provided: Corporate/Trade Name Data
Media: Direct Online to Your Computer
Coverage: CA, ID, OR, WA

Name/Desc: Professional Licenses
Info Provided: Licenses/Registrations/Permits
Media: Direct Online to Your Computer
Coverage: ID, OR, WA

Name/Desc: Real Estate Records
Info Provided: Real Estate/Assessor
Media: Direct Online to Your Computer
Coverage: ID, NV, OR, WA

Name/Desc: Criminal Records
Info Provided: Criminal Information
Media: Direct Online to Your Computer
Coverage: ID, OR, WA

Name/Desc: Fish & Wildlife Records
Info Provided: Licenses/Registrations/Permits
Media: Direct Online to Your Computer
Coverage: ID, OR

Name/Desc: Driver's License & Registration
Info Provided: Hazardous Materials
Media: Direct Online to Your Computer
Coverage: ID, OR

Name/Desc: Hazardous Materials
Info Provided: Environmental
Media: Direct Online to Your Computer
Coverage: ID, OR

Statement of Capabilities:
Commercial Information Systems (CIS) is an online/on-site database of public records serving business and government entities, and they provide direct access to selected public and private database records on a national level through special gateway relationships. The CIS integrated regional database aggregates, co-mingles and cross-matches records at the state level by name, address, city, state, ZIP Code, birth date, driver's license, vehicle plates and other identifiers with a search engine that allows a subscriber to return all related records on a common identifier. The CIS system is always available through a PC and modem.

CIS provides the communication software. CIS also provides information on a manual retrieval basis, including credit bureau products and services as well as special data mining capabilities tailored to a clients' specific research or volume searching needs.

Communications Systems Technology Inc
5564 S Lee St
Littleton, CO 80127-1845
Telephone: **Fax:**
303-973-8111 303-973-1110
www.sni.net/~arte

Applications: Lending/Leasing, Legal Compliance

Statement of Capabilities:
Communications Systems Technology (CST) provides access to Colorado public records through a BBS system. Available records include: corporate, trade names and trademarks.

CompuServe
PO Box 20212
Columbus, OH 43220
Telephone: **Fax:**
800-848-8199 614-457-0348
614-457-8600

www.compuserve.com

Applications: General Business Information, Background Info - Business, Background Info - Individuals, Competitive Intelligence

Proprietary Products:

Name/Desc: Quest Research Center
Info Provided: Business Information and Patents & Trademarks
Media: Internet
Coverage: US

Name/Desc: Phonefile
Info Provided: Addresses and Telephone Numbers
Coverage: US

Statement of Capabilities:
Now a subsidiary of AOL, CompuServe is available in 185 countries and provides comprehensive services for serious Internet online users at home, in the workplace, and

globally. Business and professional resources, latest news and information are but a few of CompuServe's powerful communications capabilities.

Confi-Chek
1816 19th ST
Sacramento, CA 95814

Telephone: **Fax:**
800-821-7404   800-758-5859
916-443-4822   916-443-7420

www.Confi-check.com

Applications: Asset/Lien Searching/Verification, Background Info - Individuals, Competitive Intelligence, Litigation, Locating People/Businesses

Proprietary Products:

Name/Desc: Confi-Chek Online
Info Provided: Criminal History
Media: Online Database
Coverage: CA

Statement of Capabilities:
Confi-Check provides instant access to national and local records throughout the US. They also offer asset services. Their web site has almost all state records. Dial-up and fax call-in services are also available.

Congressional Information Service Inc
4520 East-West Highway
Bethesda, MD 20814-3389

Telephone: **Fax:**
800-638-8380   301-654-4033
301-654-1550

www.cispubs.com

Applications: Legal Compliance, Government Document Retrieval, Current Events

Proprietary Products:

Name/Desc: Current Issues Sourcefile
Info Provided: Legislation/Regulations
Media: CD-ROM, Disk, Publication
Coverage: US

Statement of Capabilities:
Congressional Information Service is an international publisher of reference, research, and current awareness information products

and services. Many of their products deal with economic and demographic issues. Their multiple databases are offered in electronic format and through partners such as LEXIS-NEXIS.

Conrad Grundlehner Inc
8605 Brook Rd
McLean, VA 22102-1504

Telephone:
703-506-9580

Applications: Litigation, Government Document Retrieval, Legal Compliance

Proprietary Products:

Name/Desc: Conrad Grundlehner
Info Provided: Bankruptcy, Litigation/Judgments/Tax Liens
Media: Disk, Magnetic Tape
Coverage: DC, MD, NC, VA, WV

Statement of Capabilities:
Conrad Grundlehner Inc (CGI) was among the first companies to use portable computers to collect legal data at courts and recording offices. The use of notebook computers combined with electronic data transmission data to the customer reduces the time between data collection and its availability to the customer. CGI's information processing expertise also allows it to provide a high degree of customized service to customers. Data can be delivered in a wide variety of ways on a broad spectrum of media.

Corporate Screening Services Inc
PO Box 36129
Cleveland, OH 44136

Telephone: **Fax:**
800-229-8606   888-815-4567
440-816-0500   440-243-4204

www.corporate-screening.com

Applications: Background Info - Individuals, Background Info - Business, Employment Screening, Legal Compliance

Proprietary Products:

Name/Desc: CSS EASE
Info Provided: Credit Information, Credit Information3, Driver and/or Vehicle, Education/Employment, Licenses/Registrations/Permits, Litigation/Judgments/Tax Liens, Social Security Numbers and Workers' Compensation
Media: Internet
Coverage: US

Statement of Capabilities:

Corporate Screening utilizes a national network of resources for public record search and retrieval services. They offer complete pre-employment and business background investigative packages, and can customize to fit needs. Their applicant Screening Engine (CSS EASE) allows registered users to access complete investigative results and updates over the Internet. This has recently expanded to include online public record search ordering, free and easy to use.

Court PC of Connecticut

PO Box 11081
Greenwich, CT 06831-1081
Telephone: 203-531-7866   **Fax:** 203-531-6899
Applications: Litigation, Background Info - Business, Asset/Lien Searching/Verification, Locating People/Businesses, Background Info - Individuals

Proprietary Products:

Name/Desc: Superior Index
Info Provided: Litigation/Judgments/Tax Liens, Criminal Information
Media: Fax-on-Demand and Printed Report
Coverage: CT

Statement of Capabilities:

Court PC is Connecticut's comprehensive source of docket search information from Superior Court and US District Court cases. Their database contains records of civil filings from 1984, family/divorce from 1988, and criminal conviction data from 1991. Indexes are used to supplement PACER data from 1970 to present. They also provide current corporation, UCC and tax lien data from the Conneticut Secretary of State database, and statewide real estate information from computerized assessor lists.

CourtLink

400 112th Ave NE #250
Bellevue, WA 98004
Telephone: 800-774-7317   **Fax:** 425-450-0394
425-450-0390
www.courtlink.com
panderson@courtlink.com
Applications: Background Info - Business, Background Info - Individuals, Litigation, Risk Management, Employment Screening

Proprietary Products:

Name/Desc: CourtLink
Info Provided: Case/Name Index
Media: Online Database, Printed Reports and Lists or Labels
Coverage: US

Statement of Capabilities:

CourtLink has created an online gateway through which the user gains interactive access to all federal district and bankruptcy courts on PACER, also to OJIN (Oregon) and to SCOMIS (Washington State) using one Windows-based interface program. The user can search one court at a time or any combination of courts simultaneously. Federal and state court searches can be combined into one step.

CQ Staff Directories Ltd

815 Slaters Ln
Alexandria, VA 22314
Telephone: 800-252-1722   **Fax:** 703-739-0234
703-739-0900
www.staffdirectories.com
Applications: Locating People/Businesses, Background Info - Individuals, Direct Marketing, Genealogical Research, Government Document Retrieval

Proprietary Products:

Name/Desc: Congressional Staff Directory
Info Provided: Addresses/Telephone

Media: Publication, CD-ROM, Disk, and available on Lexis, LegiSlate and America Online
Coverage: US

Name/Desc: Federal Staff Directory
Info Provided: Addresses/Telephone
Media: Publication, CD-ROM and available on Lexis.
Coverage: US

Name/Desc: Judicial Staff Directory (Federal)
Info Provided: Addresses/Telephone
Media: Publication, CD-ROM and avaiable on Lexis
Coverage: US

Name/Desc: Military Personnel (Active-US)
Info Provided: Addresses/Telephone
Media: CD-ROM
Coverage: US

Statement of Capabilities:
Staff Directories is a leading publisher of directory information about federal employees, including Congress, the federal judiciary, and the US military.

CrimeLine Information Systems
113 Latigo Lane
Canon City, CO 81212
Telephone: **Fax:**
800-332-7999   800-462-5823
www.CDROMINVESTIGATIONS.com
custserv@InterstateDataCorp.com

Applications: Background Info - Individuals, General Business Information, Legal Compliance, Litigation, Locating People/Businesses

Proprietary Products:

Name/Desc: CA Criminal
Info Provided: Criminal Information
Media: CD-ROM, Direct Online to Your Computer and Call back
Coverage: AZ, CA, CO

Name/Desc: CA Professional Licenses
Info Provided: Licenses/Registration/Permits
Media: CD-ROM, Direct Online to Your Computer and Call back
Coverage: CA

Name/Desc: CA Corporate Records

Info Provided: Corporate/Trade Name
Media: CD-ROM, Direct Online to Your Computer and Call back
Coverage: CA

Statement of Capabilities:
Crimeline provides a criminal background checking database as well as research on corporate requirements, professional licenses, Board of Equalization, fictitious business names, and others. Features online and CD-ROM technology at competitive prices.

Cyberspace Information Services
306 N West El Norte Pkwy #307
Escondido, CA 92026
Telephone: **Fax:**
888-809-3913   888-860-3994
760-809-3993   888-860-3994
http://members.home.net/stanjo/cyberinforserv.htm
stajo@home.com

Applications: Asset/Lien Searching/Verification, Background Info - Business, Background Info - Individuals, Competitive Intelligence, General Business Information

Proprietary Products:

Name/Desc: Newsfeeds on a Disk
Info Provided: News/Current Events
Media: CD-ROM, Disk and Internet
Coverage: US

Name/Desc: Public Records on a Disk
Info Provided: Aviation/Vessels, Credit Information, Driver and/or Vehicle, Genealogical Information, Licenses/Registrations/Permits, Legislation/Regulation, Military Service, Real Estate/Assessor, SEC/Other Financial, Trademarks/Patents and Workers' Compensation
Media: CD-ROM, Disk and Internet
Coverage: US

Name/Desc: Portable White Pages
Info Provided: Addresses/Telephone Numbers
Media: CD-ROM, Disk and Internet
Coverage: US

Name/Desc: Portable Yellow Pages
Info Provided: Addresses/Telephone Numbers
Media: CD-ROM, Disk and Internet
Coverage: US

Name/Desc: The Early Edition
Info Provided: News/Current Events
Media: CD-ROM, Disk and Internet
Coverage: US

Statement of Capabilities:
Cyberspace Information Services sells a myriad of useful information products on various mediums for end users of public information. The value-added information is very easy to understand. They specialize in public information and real estate documents

DAC Services
4110 S 100th East Ave
Tulsa, OK 74146-3639
Telephone: **Fax:**
800-331-9175   918-664-4366
918-664-9991
www.dacservices.com

Applications: Insurance Underwriting, Employment Screening, Risk Management, Fraud Prevention/Detection

Proprietary Products:

Name/Desc: Transportation Employment History; Drug/Alcohol Test Results, Security Guard Employment History
Info Provided: Education/Employment
Media: Online Database
Coverage: US

Name/Desc: Driving Records
Info Provided: Driver/Vehicle
Media: Online Database
Coverage: US

Name/Desc: 20/20 Insight
Info Provided: Criminal Information
Media: Online Database
Name/Desc: Claims and Injury Reports
Info Provided: Workers' Compensation
Media: Online Database
Coverage: AR, FL, IA, IL, KS, MA, MD, ME, MI, MS, ND, NE, OH, OK, OR, TX

Statement of Capabilities:
DAC has serviced employers and insurance businesses for more than 15 years, providing employment screening and underwriting/risk assessment tools. CDLIST contains summary information on more than 6,000,000 drivers. Customers request information by PC and modem via toll-free lines. Computer access is available through networks and mainframe-to-mainframe connections. Customers may opt to call or fax requests to their service representative toll-free.

Daily Report, The
310 H Street
Bakersfield, CA 93304-2914
Telephone: **Fax:**
800-803-6127   805-322-9084
805-322-3226
www.thedailyreport.com
inquires@thedailyreport.com

Applications: Background Info - Business, Background Info - Individuals, Direct Marketing, Filing/Recording Documents, Competitive Intelligence

Proprietary Products:

Info Provided: Address, Licenses/Registrations/Permits, Criminal Information, Litigation/Judgments/Tax Liens
Media: Internet
Coverage: CA

Database Technologies Inc
4530 Blue Lake Dr
Boca Raton, FL 33431
Telephone: **Fax:**
800-279-7710   561-982-5872
561-982-5000

Applications: Employment Screening, Fraud Prevention/Detection, General Business Information, Government Document Retrieval, Litigation

Proprietary Products:

Name/Desc: Auto Track Plus
Info Provided: Driver and/or Vehicle, Addresses, Real Estate, Corporate/Trade Name
Media: direct Online

Coverage: US

Name/Desc: Autotrack XP
Info Provided: Driver and/or Vehicle
Media: Direct Online
Coverage: US

Statement of Capabilities:
From a personal computer, Database Technologies' subscribers gain instant access to billions of publicly available records on individuals and companies. Information from both national and state sources includes: current/past addresses, telephone numbers, relatives, neighbors, assets, corporations and much more. Database Technologies offers these records in a uniquely integrated and cross-referenced system that is instantly accessible seven days a week, 24 hours a day. The system is available to qualified professionals in law enforcement, private investigation, insurance fraud investigation, legal professionals, news media and security investigations. Database Technologies offers two products. AutroTrack Plus is a DOS-based system with a low per-minute rate. AutoTrackXP is a Windows-based system with a flat-rate for searches and reports.

Datalink

PO Box 188416
Sacramento, CA 95818
Telephone: **Fax:**
800-742-2375 916-452-5096
916-456-7454
www.datalinkservices.com
sales@datalinkservices.com

Applications: Asset/Lien Searching/Verification, Background Info - Business, Employment Screening, Fraud Prevention/Detection, Insurance Underwriting

Proprietary Products:

Name/Desc: Driving, Vehicle & Dealer Records
Info Provided: Driver, Vehicle and Dealer Records
Media: Direct Online to Your Computer, Fax-on-Demand, Printed Report and Software
Coverage: US

Statement of Capabilities:
Datalink is a public record research firm that accesses records nationwide. Located just two blocks from the California DMV, they provide fast, accurate information to clients. They provide electronic record retrieval for California driving and vehicle records and dealer searches through a proprietary software program. They use a nationwide database to access most state DMV records. A commitment to customer service is their top priority. Their staff has over 15 years in the record research industry, providing reliable technical support on searches.

DataQuick

9171 Towne Centre Dr #600
San Diego, CA 92122
Telephone:
619-455-6900
www.dataquick.com

Applications: Real Estate Transactions, Lending/Leasing, Asset/Lien Searching/Verification, Direct Marketing, Locating People/Businesses

Proprietary Products:

Name/Desc: DataQuick
Info Provided: Real Estate
Media: Online, Tape, Disk, Print
Coverage: US

Statement of Capabilities:
A leading name in real property information products, Axiom/DataCheck services the title, mortgage, real estate and insurance industries. They provide property details such as ownership and address information, sale and loan details, characteristics such as sq footage, etc, and historical sales and data such as previous transactions for marketing and research purposes. They cover household development demographics and market trend data.

DataTech Research

726 Wilson Ave.
Green Bay, WI 54303
Telephone: **Fax:**
920-592-9617 920-592-9645
REILAND@NETNET.NET

Applications: Competitive Intelligence, General Business Information, Government Document Retrieval

Statement of Capabilities:
DataTech Research specializes in Federal and State procurement consulting and research, and provides daily observance of State and Federal acquisitions requests, and timely research of government agency forecasts and acquisitions in any market. Navy veteran Mark Reiland has worked with large and small companies in purchasing and defense contract administration. DataTech helps companies do business with the government, providing timely, accurate information on various government agencies.

DCS Information Systems

500 N Central Expressway #280
Plano, TX 75074

Telephone: **Fax:**
800-394-3274   800-299-3647
972-422-3600   972-422-3621

www.dnis.com

Applications: Locating People/Businesses, Background Info - Business, Fraud Prevention/Detection, Employment Screening, Asset/Lien Searching/Verification

Proprietary Products:

Name/Desc: DNIS
Info Provided: Addresses/Telephone, Credit Header, Real Estate/Assessor and Driver/Vehicle
Media: Online Database
Coverage: US

Name/Desc: Texas Systems
Info Provided: Driver/Vehicle, Criminal Convictions, Credit Header and Real Estate/Assessor
Media: Online Database
Coverage: TX

Statement of Capabilities:
DCS's premiere product, DNIS (DCS National Inquiry System) is a comprehensive skip tracing and locating tool. Both of their online systems utilize search technology that allows users access to information in ways not available from other providers. DCS offers customized information solutions for large volume users.

Derwent Information

1725 Duke Street #250
Alexandria, VA 22314

Telephone: **Fax:**
800-337-9368   703-838-0450
703-706-4220

www.derwent.com
info@derwent.com

Applications: Background Info - Business, Competitive Intelligence, Legal Compliance, Lending/Leasing, Current Events

Proprietary Products:

Name/Desc: Derwent World Patents Index Derwent World Patent Index
Info Provided: Trademarks/Patents, Corporate/Trade Name Data
Media: Direct Online to Your Computer, Internet, Publication/Directory, Printed Report,
Coverage: US,International

Name/Desc: Patent Explorer
Info Provided: Trademarks/Patents, Corporate/Trade Name Data
Media: US, International
Coverage: US, International

Statement of Capabilities:
With offices in London, Tokyo, and Alexandria, Derwent provides international patent information and recruitment data oriented to chemicals, engineering, and pharm. They are parent company to The Thomson Corporation. Online hosts include The Dialog Corp, Questel.Orbit, DIMDI, and STN as well as their own various media and networks, some customized to client's needs. Additional offices in Japan and London.

Dialog Corporation, The

2440 W El Camino Real
Mountain View, CA 94040

Telephone: **Fax:**
800-334-2564   650-254-7070
650-254-7000

www.dialog.com

Applications: General Business Information, Competitive Intelligence, Direct Marketing,

Government Document Retrieval, Background Info - Business

Proprietary Products:

Name/Desc: Profound; DIALOG Web
Info Provided: Foreign Country Information, Corporate/Trade Name Data, Trademarks/Patents, Legislation/Regulation, SEC/Other Financial
Media: Direct Online to Your Computer, Internet, CD-ROM, Software
Coverage: US,International

Name/Desc: Profound LiveWire
Info Provided: News/Current Events
Media: Direct Online to Your Computer, Internet, CD-ROM, Software

Statement of Capabilities:
The Dialog Corporation provides comprehensive, authoritative sources of information to professionals worldwide. The company was created by the merger of MAID plc and Knight-Rider Information Inc. The Dialog Corporation's complete line of Internet, intranet, CD-ROM and Windows-based products and services have been designed to specifically address individual as well as enterprise-wide information solutions. They include DIALOGWeb, DataStar Web, DIALOG Select, Profound, DIALOG@Site, and Profound LiveWire.

Disclosure Incorporated

5161 River Rd
Bethesda, MD 20816
Telephone: **Fax:**
800-945-3647 301-657-1962
301-951-1300

www.disclosure.com

Applications: Background Info - Business, Competitive Intelligence, General Business Information, Legal Compliance, Litigation

Proprietary Products:

Name/Desc: Compact D/SEC
Info Provided: SEC/Other Financial
Media: CD-ROM, Magnetic Tape, Online Database, Microfiche and Publication
Coverage: US

Name/Desc: Compact D/Canada
Info Provided: SEC/Other Financial
Media: CD-ROM and Publication

Coverage: CD

Name/Desc: Compact D/'33
Info Provided: SEC/Other Financial
Media: CD-ROM
Coverage: US

Name/Desc: Laser D SEC
Info Provided: SEC/Other Financial
Media: CD-ROM
Coverage: US

Name/Desc: Laser D International
Info Provided: SEC/Other Financial
Media: CD-ROM
Coverage: US, International

Name/Desc: Worldscope Global
Info Provided: SEC/Other Financial
Media: CD-ROM, Magnetic Tape, Online Database and Publication
Coverage: US, International

Statement of Capabilities:
Disclosure has specialized in public company information over the past 20 years. Their newest product, Global Access, provides online access to all EDGAR files. Disclosure's information products have grown from SEC documents filed by US public companies to include virtually every document available to the public. A subsidiary, FDR Information Centers, provides search and retrieval services. Disclosure was the first company to offer SEC documents via CD-ROM. Disclosure later teamed with Wright Investors' Service to provide Worldscope, an extensive database of international companies.

Diversified Information Services Corp

111 W Monroe St #720
Phoenix, AZ 85003-1720
Telephone: **Fax:**
602-256-0961 602-256-2074
discplats@aol.com

Applications: Asset/Lien Searching/Verification, Filing/Recording Documents, Insurance Underwriting, Real Estate Transactions

Proprietary Products:

Name/Desc: Real Property Records
Info Provided: Real Estate

Media: Online, Disk, CD-ROM, Printed Report, Fax
Coverage: AZ-Maricopa

Statement of Capabilities:
Diversified Information Services is owned by North American Title Agency, Old Republic Title Insurance Agency, Transnation Title, Lawyers Title of Arizona, Fidelity National Title Agency, Stewart Title & Trust of Phoenix, and Nations Title Agency.

Dun & Bradstreet

1 Diamond Hill Rd
Murray Hill, NJ 07974
Telephone:
800-234-3867
908-665-5000

www.dnb.com

Applications: Risk Management, General Business Information, Asset/Lien Searching/Verification, Background Info - Business

Proprietary Products:

Name/Desc: D & B Public Record Search
Info Provided: Addresses/Telephone Numbers, Bankruptcy, Corporate/Trade Name Data, Credit Information, Litigation/Judgments/Tax Liens and Uniform Commercial Code
Media: Call-in Only, Direct Online to Your Computer, Internet, Printed Report, Software and Disk
Coverage: US

Name/Desc: Business Credit Information
Info Provided: Credit Information
Media: Online Database and Call-Back
Coverage: US

Statement of Capabilities:
Dun & Bradstreet's Public Records Search database is the one of most extensive commercial public record information sites available. It is a powerful online database of corporate, UCC, litigation and tax lien information about businesses that covers all 50 states, the Virgin Islands, Puerto Rico and the District of Columbia. The 800 number listed above is for business credit information.

Electronic Property Information Corp (EPIC)

227 Alexander St #206
Rochester, NY 14607
Telephone: **Fax:**
716-454-7390   716-454-7409
Applications: Real Estate Transactions, Insurance Underwriting, Asset/Lien Searching/Verification, Background Info - Business, Background Info - Individuals

Proprietary Products:

Name/Desc: OPRA
Info Provided: Real Estate/Assessor, Uniform Commerical Code, Litigation/Judgments/Tax Liens and Wills/Probate
Media: Online Database
Coverage: NY-Erie, Monroe Counties

Name/Desc: OPRA
Info Provided: Bankruptcy
Media: Online Database
Coverage: NY-Northern & Western Districts

Statement of Capabilities:
EPIC provides online access to their proprietary database of all public records affecting real property in Erie and Monroe Counties, NY and bankruptcy records for New York's Western and Northern Districts. In addition to helping create abstracts and write title insurance, the database has been used for collections, asset search, and individual and business screening applications.

Environmental Data Resources Inc

3530 Post Rd
Southport, CT 06490
Telephone: **Fax:**
800-352-0050   800-231-6802
203-255-6606   203-255-1976

www.edrnet.com

Applications: Real Estate Transactions, Risk Management

Proprietary Products:

Name/Desc: NEDIS, WasteMonitor, Sanborn Maps
Info Provided: Environmental, Licenses/Registratoins/Permits, and Real Estate/Assessor
Media: Online Database, Call-in

Coverage: US

Statement of Capabilities:
Environmental Data Resources (EDR) is an information company specializing in providing data on environmental liabilities associated with companies and properties. EDR provides this data to environmental consulting firms, banks, insurance companies, law firms, corporations and accounting firms. EDR has compiled and organized more than 600 separate government databases, obtained at the federal, state and local levels, into an environmental database referred to as NEDIS, the National Environmental Data Information System. The WasteMonitor database contains detailed information about more than 5000 non-hazardous waste disposal facilities and more than 500 hazardous treatment, storage and disposal facilities. EDR Sanborn owns the largest and most complete collection of fire insurance maps, with more than 12,000 communities surveyed, dating back to the 1800s.

Equifax Credit Services Division
1600 Peachtree St NW
Atlanta, GA 30309
Telephone:
888-202-4025
404-885-8000
www.equifax.com

Applications: Background Info - Individuals, Employment Screening, Lending/Leasing, Collections

Proprietary Products:

Name/Desc: Acrofile
Info Provided: Credit Information
Media: Direct Online to Your Computer, Internet
Coverage: US

Name/Desc: Persona
Persona
Info Provided: Addresses/Telephone Numbers, Education/Employment, Social Security Numbers, Credit Information
Media: Direct Online to Your Computer, Internet
Coverage: US

Statement of Capabilities:
Equifax, like its two major competitors Experion and Trans Union, provides a full range of consumer credit and related information. Equifax credit services include consumer credit, locate services, fraud detection, and accounts receivable management. They operate globally - in 18 countries with sales in 40. North American Information Services is an Equifax company. Media Relations telephone is 404-888-5452. Consumers may order a credit report: 800-685-1111 or discuss its content at 888-909-7304. Government entities fax Equifax at 404-885-8215, or e-mail govetrelequifax.com.

Everton Publishers
PO Box 368
Logan, UT 84323
Telephone:
800-443-6325
801-752-6022
www.everton.com

Applications: Genealogical Research

Proprietary Products:

Name/Desc: Everton's Online Search
Info Provided: Addresses/Telephone, Social Security Numbers
Media: Online Database
Coverage: US

Statement of Capabilities:
Everton publishes "The Genealogical Helper."

Experian Business Information Solutions
600 City Parkway West
8th FlOrange, CA 92868
Telephone:
800-831-5614
www.experian.com

Applications: Lending/Leasing, Asset/Lien Searching/Verification, Background Info - Business

Proprietary Products:

Name/Desc: Business Credit Information
Info Provided: Uniform Commercial Code, Bankruptcy, Litigation/Judgments/Tax Liens, Corporate/Trade Name Data

Media: Direct Online to Your Computer, Printed Report
Coverage: US

Statement of Capabilities:
Experian Business Information Solutions is the business credit arm of Experian. Although this division is located in Orange, CA, they prefer inquiries to go through the main Experian switchboard (800-831-5614 in Allen, TX) first, then allow access to the California site at 714-385-7000.

Experian Consumer Credit
425 Martingale Rd #600
Schaumburg, IL 60173
Telephone:
800-831-5614
www.experian.com

Applications: Lending/Leasing, Employment Screening, Tenant Screening

Proprietary Products:

Name/Desc: Consumer File
Consumer File
Info Provided: Credit Information, Addresses/Telephone Numbers
Media: Direct Online to Your Computer, Printed Report
Coverage: US

Statement of Capabilities:
As the consumer credit arm of Experian, formerly TRW, data from here may be used for a variety of purposes related to individuals, subject to permissible purposes. Individuals who need assistance with reports should call 888-397-3742.

Experian Target Marketing Services
701 Experian Parkway
Allen, TX 70013
Telephone: **Fax:**
800-527-3933   972-390-5001
972-390-5000
www.experian.com

Applications: Direct Marketing

Proprietary Products:

Name/Desc: Various Experian Databases
Various Experian Databases

Info Provided: Addresses/Telephone Numbers, Driver and/or Vehicle
Media: Disk, Magnetic Tape, Printed Report
Coverage: US

Statement of Capabilities:
Experian Target Marketing Services is a list compiler that utilizes Experian's overall information - collected from such sources as the NCOA file - to provide support to direct marketers to businesses and individuals. Their MV database includes 42+ million vehicle owners and vehicle characteristics in 32 states. Combining vehicle selections with their demographic, lifestyle, and other selections allows for higher focused targeting. Other Experian divisions are profiled separately.

Explore Information Services
4920 Moundview Dr
Red Wing, MN 55066
Telephone: **Fax:**
800-531-9125   612-385-2281
612-385-2284
www.exploredata.com

Applications: Insurance Underwriting

Proprietary Products:

Name/Desc: EARS
Info Provided: Driver/Vehicle
Media: Online, Magnetic Tape and Disk
Coverage: CO, FL, IA, KY, ME, MN, MO, NE, NH, OH, TN, UT, WI

Statement of Capabilities:
Their Electronically Accessed Reunderwriting Service (EARS), is a database of driver information, including violation history, that can be customized for use by insurance industry clients. RiskAlert is a service that identifies all licensed drivers in a household.

Federal Filings Inc
601 Pennsylvania Ave NW
South Bldg #700 Washington, DC 20004-2601
Telephone: **Fax:**
800-487-6162   202-393-0974
202-393-7400
www.fedfil.com

Applications: General Business Information, Litigation, Legal Compliance

Proprietary Products:

Name/Desc: EDGAR
Info Provided: SEC/Other Financial
Media: Online Database
Coverage: US

Name/Desc: Federal Filings Business News
Info Provided: News/Current Events
Media: Online Database, Newsletters
Coverage: US

Statement of Capabilities:

Federal Filings provides a number of different services based on access to federal records, including SEC filings, bankruptcy and civil court cases, and research at other federal agencies in Washington, DC such as the FCC. SEC services include monitoring specific public company filings. Court services include monitoring companies for new cases and new pleadings in existing cases. Copies of 10Ks and 10Qs may be ordered through their online system. Federal Filings also has a library of bankruptcy documents dating back to 1988.

Felonies R Us

1423 W 3rd #21
Little Rock, AR 72201
Telephone: Fax:
501-376-4719   510-376-4619
Applications: Employment Screening, Fraud Prevention/Detection, General Business Information, Litigation, Tenant Screening

Proprietary Products:

Name/Desc: AR Felonies
Info Provided: Criminal Information
Media: Fax-on-Demand and Printed Report
Coverage: AR

Statement of Capabilities:

Felonies 'R' Us maintains an updated criminal database obtained form the Arkansas Administrative Office of the Courts. Able to run statewide searches, they retrieve documents desired by the client.

Fidelifacts

50 Broadway
New York, NY 10004
Telephone: Fax:
800-678-0007   212-248-5619
212-425-1520

norton@fidelifacts.com

Applications: Background Info - Business, Background Info - Individuals, Employment Screening, Litigation

Proprietary Products:

Name/Desc: Fidelifacts Data Bank
Info Provided: Criminal History
Media: Call-in
Coverage: US

Statement of Capabilities:

Among the oldest companies engaged in the business of providing background reports on individuals for employment purposes and on companies, Fidelifacts has a network of investigators in offices around the country, and local personnel who examine public records in less populated areas. Fidelifacts specialty is conducting background investigations, reference checks, screening checks of job applicants and due diligence investigations. They also provide asset location services, skip tracing and other services on legal matters. Their in-house database lists 1,500,000 names of persons arrested, indicted, convicted, and otherwise had problems with the law. Data is primarily for metro New York area, but also includes SEC/NASD filings where unlawful activity may be a question. Note: office is located 1/2 block from the NY State Office of Court Administration and they have personnel there on a daily basis.

Finder Group, The

PO Box 11740
Kansas City, KS 64138
Telephone: Fax:
800-501-8455   816-737-5225
816-737-5005

finder@solve.net

Applications: Asset/Lien Searching/Verification, Background Info - Business, Background Info - Individuals,

General Business Information, Locating People/Businesses

Statement of Capabilities:
The Finder Group is a p[rofessional search firm designed to bridge the gap between end users and repositories. Economical access to public records includes criminal, civil, MVR, asset, background and address information. Web site offers links to sites for public record searching.

First American Real Estate Solutions

5601 E. La Palma Ave
Anaheim, CA 92807

Telephone: **Fax:**
800-345-7334   800-406-2907
714-701-2150   714-701-9231

www.firstAm.com

Applications: Real Estate Transactions, Lending/Leasing, Asset/Lien Searching/Verification, Background Info - Business, Background Info - Individuals

Proprietary Products:

Name/Desc: Real Property Database
Info Provided: Real Estate/Assessor
Media: Online Database, CD-ROM and Microfiche
Coverage: AL, AZ, CA, CO, DC, DE, FL, GA, HI, IL, IN, LA, MA, MD, MI, MN, MS, NC, NJ, NM, NY, NV, OH, OK, OR, PA, SC, TN, TX, UT, VA, VI, WA, WI

Statement of Capabilities:
Now independent of Experian Inc (formerly TRW), First American Real Estate Solutions is now part of the First American Financial Corporation. They are a leading provider of real estate information from major counties in most US states. Call for specific coverage and access via online database, CD-ROM and microfiche information.

FOIA Group Inc

1090 Vermont Ave NW # 800
Washington, DC 20005

Telephone: **Fax:**
202-408-7028   202-347-8419
www.FOIA.com
FOIA@FOIA.com

Applications: Competitive Intelligence, Government Document Retrieval, Litigation

Proprietary Products:

Name/Desc: FOIA-Ware
Info Provided: Internet, Software and Disk
Coverage: US

Statement of Capabilities:
FOIA specializes in the Freedom of Information Act protocols. They help prepare and file FOIA requests, monitor and review documents, and service the legal profession and others seeking information through the Act. They also offer whistleblower assistance.

Folks Finders Ltd

PO Box 880, RR1
Neoga, IL 62447

Telephone: **Fax:**
800-277-3318   800-476-0782
217-895-2524   217-895-2418

www.pimall.com/folksfinders/folkfind.htm

Applications: Locating People/Businesses

Proprietary Products:

Name/Desc: NYC Birth Index
Info Provided: Vital Records, Voter Registration, Workers' Compensation, Tenant History and Genealogical Information
Media: Printed Report
Coverage: NY-New York City

Name/Desc: IL Birth Index
Info Provided: Vital Records, Voter Registration, Workers' Compensation, Tenant History and Genealogical Information
Media: Printed Report
Coverage: IL

Name/Desc: CA Birth Index
Info Provided: Vital Records, Voter Registration, Workers' Compensation, Tenant History and Genealogical Information
Media: Printed Report
Coverage: CA

Name/Desc: Cemetery Internment
Info Provided: Vital Records, Voter Registration, Workers' Compensation, Tenant History and Genealogical Information
Media: Printed Report
Coverage: US

Statement of Capabilities:
Folks Finders specializes in finding folks, missing persons, that may not object to being located. Most service charges are based on a "no find, no fee" philosophy. Categories of searches include no-name pension beneficiaries, health-related searches, and adoption searches. As part of their expertise, they obtain and provide vital records worldwide. They have begun "alternate identity" locating.

Gale Group Inc, The

27500 Drake Rd
Framington Hills, MI 48331-3535
Telephone:
800-877-4253
248-699-4253

www.gale.com

Applications: Background Info - Business, Current Events, Genealogical Research

Proprietary Products:

Name/Desc: GaleNet
Info Provided: Associations/Trade Groups, Addresses & Telphone Numbers and Business Information
Media: Online Database
Coverage: US, International

Statement of Capabilities:
As a major publisher of academic, educational, and business research companies serving libraries, educational institutions, and businesses in all major international markets, The Gale Group provides much of its material online through products such as Associations Unlimited, Biography and Genealogy Master Index, Brands and Their Companies, Gale Business Resources, and Peterson's Publications. It was formed Sept. '98 with the merger of Gale Research, Information Access Co., and Primary Source Material.

Haines & Company Inc

8050 Freedom Ave
North canton, OH 44720
Telephone: **Fax:**
800-843-8452   330-494-0226
330-494-9111
www.haines.com

criscros@haines.com

Applications: Collections, Direct Marketing, Insurance Underwriting, Lending/Leasing, Locating People/Businesses

Proprietary Products:

Name/Desc: Criss+Cross Directory
Info Provided: Address/Telephone Numbers
Media: Publication/Directory
Coverage: US

Name/Desc: Criss+Cross Plus CD-ROM
Info Provided: Address/Telephone Numbers
Media: CD-ROM
Coverage: US

Name/Desc: Criss+Cross Plus Real Estate
Info Provided: Real Estate/Assessor
Media: CD-ROM
Coverage: US

Name/Desc: Crrss+Cross Plus Online
Media: Direct Online to Your Computer
Coverage: US

Name/Desc: Criss+Cross Natl Look-Up Library
Info Provided: Address/Telephone Numbers
Media: Call-in Only
Coverage: US

Name/Desc: Americalist
Media: Disk, Lists or labels and Magnetic Tape
Coverage: US

Statement of Capabilities:
Varied products and full-service capabilities allow Haines & Company to satisfy the marketing and research needs of most industries. County Real Estate on CD-ROM has been noted for its ease of use, speed and marketing power. They also offer cross-reference directories in book form or on CD-ROM in 71 major markets, also business and residential lists on labels, manuscripts, CD-ROM, the Internet or bulletin boards (24-hour turnaround time available). Using their target list or a customer-provided list, they can provide complete direct marketing services, graphic design, printing and database maintenance -- all in-house.

Hogan Information Services

14000 Quail Springs Parkway #4000
Oklahoma, OK 73134

Telephone:
405-278-6954
www.hoganinfo.com
hogan.data@firstdatacorp.com

Applications: Lending/Leasing, Risk Management, Employment Screening, Government Document Retrieval, Background Info - Individuals

Proprietary Products:

Name/Desc: Hogan Online
Info Provided: Bankruptcy
Media: Online, Disk, Lists, Labels, Magnetic Tape
Coverage: US

Statement of Capabilities:

Hogan Information Services provides high-quality national public record information to credit bureaus, bankcard issuers, collection agencies, retail institutions, and other businesses through various First Data business units. Founded in 1990, in 1996 Hogan Information Services became a business unit of First Data Corp. Hogan gathers public record information on laptop computers in over 8,000 courthouses nationwide for business to business applications. They specialize in helping businesses make smarter decisions and manage risk by using public record information.

Hollingsworth Court Reporting Inc

10761 Perkins Rd #A
Baton Rouge, LA 70810
Telephone: **Fax:**
504-769-3386   504-769-1814
www.hcrinc.com

Applications: General Business Information, Background Info - Business, Government Document Retrieval, Filing/Recording Documents

Proprietary Products:

Name/Desc: Public Record Report
Info Provided: Litigation/Judgments/Tax Liens
Media: Online Database, Disk, and Magnetic Tape
Coverage: AL, AR, FL, GA, IL, LA, MS, TN

Statement of Capabilities:

HCR collects and compiles public record information in eight states and makes it available in a variety of formats, including call-in service. HCR processes criminal record searches nationwide with a 48-hour turnaround time. Orders may be placed through an online system. Their proprietary database is an excellent source of eviction information for apartment owners and managers. The principals of HCR have a combined 40 years experience in the public record field.

Hoovers Inc

1033 La Posada Drive #250
Austin, TX 78752
Telephone: **Fax:**
800-486-8666   512-374-4505
512-374-4500
www.hoovers.com
info@hoovers.com

Applications: General Business Information, Background Info - Business, Competitive Intelligence, Locating People/Businesses

Proprietary Products:

Name/Desc: Hoover's Company Profiles
Info Provided: Addresses/Telephone Numbers, Corporate/Trade Name Data, News/Current Events
Media: Direct Online to Your Computer, Printed Report, Internet
Coverage: US, International

Name/Desc: Real-Time SEC Documents
Info Provided: SEC/Other Financial
Media: Direct Online to Your Computer, Printed Report, Internet
Coverage: US

Statement of Capabilities:

Hoovers offers a wide range of company information, much for investing purposes. Their published materials are distributed electronically and in print, and they claim their databases are among the least expensive sources of information on operations, strategies, etc. of major US and global and private companies.

IDM Corporation

3550 W Temple St

Los Angeles, CA 90004
Telephone: **Fax:**
877-436-3282   213-389-9569
213-389-2793

Applications: Asset/Lien
Searching/Verification, Direct Marketing,
Fraud Prevention/Detection, Lending/Leasing,
Real Estate Transactions

Proprietary Products:

Name/Desc: Tax, Assessor and Recorders
Info Provided: Real Estate Information
Media: Disk and Direct Online to Your
Computer
Coverage: US

Statement of Capabilities:
IDM Corporation is one of the largest source
providers of real estate public records. They
convert 900 tax/assessor counties and 500
recorder's counties to a uniform format. Their
assessment files are updated once per year, and
recorder's are updated weekly.

Infocon Corporation

PO Box 568
Ebensburg, PA 15931-0568
Telephone: **Fax:**
814-472-6066   814-472-5019
Applications: Background Info - Individuals,
Real Estate Transactions, Litigation, Risk
Management, Genealogical Research

Proprietary Products:

Name/Desc: INFOCON County Access
System
Info Provided: Criminal Information, Vital
Records, Voter Registration,
Litigation/Judgments/Tax Liens, Real Estate
Media: Direct Online to Your Computer
Coverage: PA-12 Western Counties

Statement of Capabilities:
Infocon offers the Infocon County Access
System that offers online access to civil,
criminal, real estate, and vital record
information in Pennsylvania Counties of
Armstrong, Bedford, Blair, Butler, Clarion,
Clinton, Erie, Huntingdon, Lawrence, Mifflin,
Potter, and Pike. Fees are involved, access is
through a remote 800 number.

Information America Inc

Marquis One Tower #1400
245 Peachtree Center AveAtlanta, GA 30303
Telephone: **Fax:**
800-235-4008   800-845-6319
404-479-6500

www.infoam.com

Applications: Lending/Leasing, Background
Info - Business, Asset/Lien
Searching/Verification, Litigation, Locating
People/Businesses

Proprietary Products:

Name/Desc: Bankruptcy Records
Info Provided: Bankruptcy
Media: Online Database and Call back
Coverage: US

Name/Desc: Corporations and Partnerships
Info Provided: Corporate/Trade Name
Media: Online Database and Call back
Coverage: US

Name/Desc: Lawsuits, Judgments, Liens
Info Provided: Case Index
Media: Online Database and Call back
Coverage: US

Name/Desc: Professional Licenses
Info Provided:
Licenses/Registrations/Permits
Media: Online Database and Call back
Coverage: AZ, CA, CO, CT, FL, GA, IL, IN,
LA, MA, MD, MI, NJ, OH, PA, SC, TN, TX,
VA, WI

Name/Desc: Real Estate, Liens and Judgments
Info Provided: Real Estate/Assessor,
Litigation/Judgments/Tax Liens
Media: Online Database and Call back
Coverage: US

Name/Desc: UCCs
Info Provided: Uniform Commerical Code
Media: Online Database and Call back
Coverage: US

Name/Desc: Watercraft Locator/Aircraft
Locator
Info Provided: Aviation/Vessels
Media: Online Database and Call back
Coverage: US

Name/Desc: Business Finder/People Finder
Info Provided: Motor Vehicle Records
Media: Online Database, Internet and Call
back

Coverage: US

Name/Desc: Motor Vehicle Records
Info Provided: Driver and/or Vehicle
Media: Direct Online to Your Computer

Statement of Capabilities:
Information America combines and links public records and courthouse documents with information from private sources to address the relationships between corporations, people and their assets. Banks, financial service companies, corporations, law firms and government agencies across the nation use their online and document retrieval services to obtain background data on businesses, locate assets and people, retrieve official public records and solve business problems. Information America was founded by a practicing attorney and a computer systems expert acquainted with the needs of government, legal and corporate customers. A related company, Document Resources, is a national search firm.

Information Inc

PO Box 382
Hermitage, TN 37076
Telephone: **Fax:**
615-884-8000   615-889-6492
www.members.aol.com/
infomantn/info.html
infomantn@aol.com

Applications: Background Info - Individuals, Collections, Employment Screening, Litigation, Tenant Screening

Proprietary Products:

Name/Desc: Arrest Database
Info Provided: Criminal Information
Media: Direct Online to Your Computer
Coverage: TN-Nashville

Statement of Capabilities:
Information Inc provides a real time criminal arrest database for Davidson County, TN. This includes all agencies in the 20th Judicial District of Tennessee.

Information Network of Arkansas

425 West Capitol Ave #3565
Little Rock, AR 72201
Telephone:

800-392-6069
501-324-8900
www.ark.org/ina/
about_ina.html
info@ark.org

Applications: Background Info - Business, General Business Information, Employment Screening, Insurance Underwriting

Proprietary Products:

Name/Desc: INA
Info Provided: Driver and/or Vehicle
Media: Internet
Coverage: AR

Statement of Capabilities:
Information Network of Arkansas was created by the Arkansas Legislature with the responsibility of assisting the state in permtting citizens to access public records. More categories of records will soon be available. There is a fee for driving record access; there may not be fees for other record categories.

Information Network of Kansas

534 S Kansas Ave #1210
Topeka, KS 66603
Telephone: **Fax:**
800-452-6727   785-296-5563
785-296-5059
www.ink.org

Applications: General Business Information, Employment Screening, Insurance Underwriting, Lending/Leasing, Legal Compliance

Proprietary Products:

Name/Desc: Premium Services
Info Provided: Driver and/or Vehicle, Uniform Commercial Code, Corporate/Trade Name, Legislation/Regulations, Real Estate
Media: Internet, Online
Coverage: KS

Name/Desc: Premium Services
Info Provided: Litigation/Judgements/Tax Liens
Media: Internet, Online
Coverage: KS-Johnson, Sedgwick, Shawnee, Wyandotte

Name/Desc: Premium Services
Info Provided: Criminal Information

Media: Online, Internet
Coverage: KS- Sedgwick,Shawnee,Wyandotte

Statement of Capabilities:
INK is the official source for electronic access to the State of Kansas government information. Access to public record information listed here requires a subscription.

Informus Corporation

2001 Airport Rd #201
Jackson, MS 39208
Telephone:
800-364-8380
601-664-1900

www.informus.com

Applications: Employment Screening, Locating People/Businesses, Background Info - Individuals, Collections

Proprietary Products:

Name/Desc: Informus
Info Provided: Workers Compensation
Media: Online, Printed Report
Coverage: MS, US

Name/Desc: IntroScan
Info Provided: Addresses, Social Security
Media: US

Statement of Capabilities:
Informus provides an online pre-employment screening and public record retrieval service. Online access is available through the Internet. Some searches provide instant information, depending on state and category.

Insurance Information Exchange (iiX)

POBox 30001
College Station, TX 77842-3001
Telephone: **Fax:**
800-683-8553   409-696-5584
www.ixx.com

Applications: Insurance Underwriting

Proprietary Products:

Name/Desc: Motor Vehicle Reports
Info Provided: Driver and/or Vehicle
Media: Direct Online to Your Computer, Fax-on-Demand, Internet and Printed Report
Coverage: US

Name/Desc: UDI
Info Provided: Driver and/or Vehicle
Media: Direct Online to Your Computer, Fax-on-Demand, Internet and Printed Report
Coverage: US

Name/Desc: CLUE
Info Provided: Driver and/or Vehicle
Media: Direct Online to Your Computer
Coverage: US

Name/Desc: UNCLE
Info Provided: Driver and/or Vehicle
Media: Direct Online to Your Computer
Coverage: US

Name/Desc: A+
Info Provided: Driver and/or Vehicle
Media: Direct Online to Your Computer
Coverage: US

Name/Desc: MVP
Info Provided: Driver and/or Vehicle
Media: Direct Online to Your Computer
Coverage: US

Statement of Capabilities:
iiX is an established provider of information systems to the insurance industry. Their services and products include MVR, claims, undisclosed driver, and other underwriting services. Users still call this system AMS or AMSI.

Intranet Inc

107 E Erwin
Tyler, TX 75702
Telephone: **Fax:**
903-593-9817   903-593-8183
Applications: Asset/Lien Searching/Verification, Litigation, General Business Information, Direct Marketing

Proprietary Products:

Name/Desc: Bankscan
Info Provided: Bankruptcy
Media: Disk
Coverage: TX

Statement of Capabilities:
Intranet specializes in bankruptcy research and retrieval services for the state of Texas.

Investigators Anywhere Resource Line

PO Box 40970
Mesa, AZ 85274-0970

Telephone: **Fax:**
800-338-3463   602-730-8103
602-730-8088

www.IONINC.com
ION@IONINC.com

Applications: Risk Management, Litigation, Legal Compliance

Proprietary Products:

Name/Desc: Resource Line
Info Provided: Addresses/Telephone Numbers,
Media: Online Database
Coverage: US

Statement of Capabilities:

Investigators Anywhere Resources' Resource Line service provides access to over 30,000 investigators, prescreened for excellence of service levels. Callers are matched to appropriate investigators. No fee to the callers except for international and non-commercial projects.

IQ Data Systems

1401 El Camino Ave #220
Sacramento, CA 95815

Telephone: **Fax:**
800-264-6517   800-528-2813
916-576-1000   916-576-1005

www.IQDATA.com

Applications: Asset/Lien Searching/Verification, Background Info - Business, Background Info - Individuals, Filing/Recording Documents, Locating People/Businesses

Proprietary Products:

Name/Desc: UCC Data
Info Provided: Uniform Commerical Code
Media: Online
Coverage: US

Info Provided: Real Estate
Media: Online
Coverage: CA

Statement of Capabilities:

As a gateway and a compiler of some of their own data, IQ Data Systems offers over three billion public records, retrievable instantaneously via the Internet in an easy to use, point-&-click, full-color graphic interface. They offer UCC, tax lien, judgment searches in all states and can also hand-search criminal and civil county records from every US county. Driver records are available from all 50 states.

IRSC

3777 N Harbor Blvd
Fullerton, CA 92835

Telephone: **Fax:**
800-640-4772   714-526-5836
714-526-8485

www.irsc.com

Applications: Asset/Lien Searching/Verification, Background Info - Business, Competitive Intelligence, Fraud Prevention/Detection, Locating People/Businesses

Proprietary Products:

Name/Desc: IRSC
Info Provided: Social Security Numbers, Education/Employment, Aviation/Vessels, Credit Information, Addresses/Telephone Numbers, Environmental, Uniform Commercial Code and Litigation/Judgments/Tax Liens
Media: Online Database
Coverage: US

Name/Desc: IRSC
Info Provided: Corporate/Trade Name
Media: Online Database
Coverage: US

Name/Desc: IRSC
Info Provided: Bankruptcy
Media: Online Database
Coverage: US

Name/Desc: IRSC (Criminal Court Index)
Info Provided: Criminal History
Media: Online Database
Coverage: US

Name/Desc: IRSC
Info Provided: Workers' Compensation
Media: Online Database

Coverage: Ak, AL, AR, AZ, CA, CO, DC, DE, FL, IA, ID, IL, IN, KS, KY, MA, MD, ME, MI, MO, MT, NE, NH, NM, NV, OH, OK, OR, RI, SC, SD, TX, UT, VA, VT, WY

Name/Desc: IRSC
Info Provided: Real Estate/Assessor
Media: Online Database
Coverage: AK, AL, AR, AZ, CA, CO, CT, DC, DE, FL, GA, HI, IL, KY, LA, MA, MD, MI, MN, MO, MS, NC, NJ, NV, NY, OH, OK, PA, SC, TN, TX, UT, VA, WI

Name/Desc: IRSC
Info Provided: Driver and/or Vehicle
Coverage: US

Statement of Capabilities:
Information Resource Service Company (IRSC) has an investigative database that accesses more than one billion records about individuals and businesses. Their database is available online 24 hours a day. They do not charge for connect time. A Windows-based front end program is available.

KnowX
245 Peachtree Center Ave #1400
Atlanta, GA 30303
www.knowx.com
support@knowx.com

Applications: Asset/Lien Searching/Verification, Background Info - Business, Competitive Intelligence, Locating People/Businesses, Government Document Retrieval

Proprietary Products:
Name/Desc: KnowX
Info Provided: Addresses/Telephone Numbers, Credit Information, Bankruptcy, Licenses/Registrations/Permits, Corporate/Trade Name Data, Aviation/Vessels, Litigation/Judgments/Tax Liens, Uniform Commercial Code
Media: Direct Online to Your Computer, Internet
Coverage: US

Statement of Capabilities:
KnowX, a division of Information America (owned by West Group and Thomson Corp.) is one of the most comprehensive sources of public records available on the Internet.

Included is aircraft ownership, bankruptcies, business directory, partnerships, DBAs, DEAs, death records, Duns, judgments, liens, lawsuits, licensing, residencies, real property foreclosures & refinancings, tax records, property transfers, sales permits, stock ownership, UCC and watercraft records.

Law Bulletin Information Network
415 N State
Chicago, IL 60610-4674
Telephone: 312-644-7800 **Fax:** 312-527-2890
www.lawbulletin.com

Applications: Asset/Lien Searching/Verification, Locating People/Businesses, Employment Screening

Proprietary Products:
Name/Desc: Access Plus
Info Provided: Real Estate/Assessor
Media: Online Database
Coverage: IL-Cook County

Name/Desc: Access Plus
Info Provided: Litigation/Judgments/Tax Liens
Media: Online Database
Coverage: IL-Central, North Counties

Name/Desc: Access Plus
Info Provided: Addresses/telphone
Media: Online Database
Coverage: IL

Statement of Capabilities:
The Law Bulletin Publishing Company's Information Network, called access Plus, provides both online and access to Illinois Courts, vital public record information, corporate documents, realty sales, etc. They offer other useful DocuCheck services online, and also licensed investigative services.

Legi-Slate Inc
10 G Street NE #500
Washington, DC 20002
Telephone: 800-733-1131 **Fax:** 202-898-3030
202-898-2300
www.legislate.com
legislate@legislate.com

Applications: Current Events, Legal Compliance

Proprietary Products:

Name/Desc: Legi-Slate
Info Provided: Legislation/Regulations
Media: Online Database
Coverage: US

Statement of Capabilities:
Legi-Slate provides expert guidance on federal and state government issues. Includes federal regulations, analysis, news, and current events, with timely delivery and responsive custom support.

LEXIS-NEXIS

PO Box 933
Dayton, OH 45401-0933
Telephone:
800-227-9597
937-865-6800

www.lexis-nexis.com

Applications: Legal Compliance, Current Events, General Business Information, Competitive Intelligence, Government Documents

Proprietary Products:

Name/Desc: LEXIS Law Publishing
Info Provided: Litigation/Judgments/Tax Liens
Media: Direct Online to Your Computer, Internet
Coverage: US

Name/Desc: Shepard's
Info Provided: Litigation/Judgments/Tax Liens
Media: Direct Online to Your Computer, Internet
Coverage: US

Name/Desc: Congressional Information Service
Info Provided: Legislation/Regulation
Media: Direct Online to Your Computer, CD-ROM
Coverage: US

Statement of Capabilities:
For more than 10 years, LEXIS-NEXIS has been building the largest collection of public records in the US, and today leads the industry in providing information to a variety of professionals in law, law enforcement, business, research, and academia. Four main business units are LEXIS, NEXIS, Reed Technologies & Information Systems, and Martindale-Hubbell. Their Quick-Check provides clients with company news and credit rating changes, brokerage reports, SEC filings, trends and views/analysis of companies, their debts, equities, and earnings estimates, etc.

LIDA Credit Agency Inc

450 Sunrise Hwy
Rockville Centre, NY 11570
Telephone: **Fax:**
516-678-4600   516-678-4611
Applications: Litigation, Real Estate Transactions, Background Info - Business, Asset/Lien Searching/Verification, Employment Screening

Proprietary Products:

Name/Desc: LIDA
Info Provided: Litigation/Judgments/Tax Liens
Media: Printed Report and Call-back
Coverage: DE, NJ, NY, PA

Statement of Capabilities:
LIDA's management averages more than 35 years in public record research, investigations and credit/financial reporting. Among their 17 member staff are five licensed and bonded private investigators. They specialize in Metro New York City, including the five boroughs and surrounding counties.

Lloyds Maritime Information Services Inc

1200 Summer St
Stamford, CT 06905
Telephone: **Fax:**
800-423-8672   203-358-0437
203-359-8383
www.lmis.com

Applications: General Business Information, Direct Marketing, Background Info - Business, Asset/Lien Searching/Verification

Proprietary Products:

Name/Desc: SEADATA/MARDATA

Info Provided: Aviation/Vessels
Media: Online Database (available on Genie)
Coverage: US, International

Name/Desc: APEX (Analysis of Petroleum Exports)
Info Provided: Economic/Demographic
Media: Disk
Coverage: US, International

Name/Desc: LSA (Linear Shipping Analysis)
Info Provided: Economic/Demographic
Media: Disk
Coverage: US, International

Name/Desc: AS+ (Analysis Software +)
Info Provided: Economic/Demographic
Media: Disk
Coverage: US, International

Statement of Capabilities:
Lloyd's Maritime Information Services is a joint venture company owned by Lloyd's Register, the world's premier Classification Society and LLP Ltd. Information is maintained on six computer databases, providing coverage of over 85,000 self-propelled seagoing merchant ships of 100 gross tonnage and above, comprising the world merchant fleet plus those on order, together with movements, casualties, charter fixtures, ownership details, all referenced by the unique Lloyd's Register Identity Number. Lloyd's Maritime provides the world's maritime and business community with some of the most comprehensive, up-to-date and validated maritime information available.

Logan Information Services
636-B Piney Forest Rd #172
Danville, VA 24540
Telephone: **Fax:**
888-640-8613   804-836-6709
804-791-0808

LISINC@gamewood.net

Applications: Direct Marketing, Employment Screening, Real Estate Transactions, Tenant Screening, Asset/Lien Searching/Verification

Proprietary Products:

Name/Desc: Driving Records
Info Provided: Driver/Vehicle
Media: Direct Online to Your Computer and Printed Report

Coverage: CA

Name/Desc: LIS 5
Info Provided: Litigation/Judgments/Tax Liens, Tenant History, Uniform Commercial Code, Voter Registration and Education/Employment
Media: Printed Report and Internet
Coverage: NC, VA

Statement of Capabilities:
Logan Information Services is an information retrieval and verification company providing public records research services to some of the country's largest and best known corporations. Their services include criminal, civil and real estate record searches. One of the principals of the organization was a key employee for a major consumer information provider; he has trained his staff to ensure that each report will be accurately prepared and timely received. Turnaround time on searches is 24-48 hours, depending on the type of search requested. "Rush" service is available on all searches.

Logan Registration Service Inc
PO Box 161644
Sacramento, CA 95816
Telephone: **Fax:**
800-524-4111   916-457-5789
916-457-5787

Applications: Asset/Lien Searching/Verification, Background Info - Business, Background Info - Individuals

Statement of Capabilities:
Logan has more than 20 year experience working with California driver and vehicle records. They are an online vendor that allows their DMV authorized clients to retrieve driver and vehicle registration records in seconds with a computer software program that is available free of charge. Clients are also able to access needed records via phone or fax.

Maine Public Record Services
PO Box 514
Moody, ME 04054
Telephone: **Fax:**
207-646-9065   207-646-9065
Applications: Real Estate Transactions, Asset/Lien Searching/Verification,

Filing/Recording Documents, Competitive Intelligence, Background Info - Individuals

Proprietary Products:

Name/Desc: Maine Public Records
Info Provided: Real Estate/Assessor, Litigation/Judgments/Tax Liens
Media: Disk, Printed Report, Lists or Labells and Call-in
Coverage: ME-Cumberland, Knox, Lincoln, Waldo, York

Name/Desc: Mortgage Filings
Info Provided: Addresses/Telephone Numbers
Media: Disk, Magnetic Tape and Lists or labels
Coverage: ME-6 counties

Statement of Capabilities:

Maine Public Records (MPRS) specializes in corporate services and public research at the federal, state and county level. They maintain a database of County Registrar information for nine Maine counties, primarily York and Cumberland. The database contains mortgage and other legal actions such as tax liens and foreclosure, affecting properties in those counties. The MPRS principals have banking, real estate, and investigative backgrounds.

Martindale-Hubbell

121 Chanlon Road
New Providence, NJ 07974
Telephone: **Fax:**
800-526-4902 908-464-3553
908-464-6800

www.martindale.com

info@martindale.com

Applications: Background Info - Business

Proprietary Products:

Name/Desc: Martindale-Hubbell Law Directory (Attorneys and Law Firms)
Info Provided: Addresses/Telphone, Education/Employment
Media: Available on LEXIS, Publication, Printed Reports, CD-ROM and Lists or Laels
Coverage: US,International

Statement of Capabilities:

Martindale-Hubbell's database is now regarded as the primary source for attorney and lawfirm information around the world. Their flagship product, Martindale-Hubbell Law Directory consists of more the 900,000 listings, organized by city, state, county, and province with extensive cross-references and indexes. Products are available in four media: hardbound print, CR-ROM, via LEXIS/NEXIS (a sister company) and Internet via the Martindale-Hubbell Lawyer Locator. Their data includes corporate law departments, legal-related services such as P.I.s, title search companies, law digests.

MDR/Minnesota Driving Records

1710 Douglas Dr. N #103
Golden Valley, MN 55422-4313
Telephone: **Fax:**
800-644-6877 612-595-8079
612-755-1164

Applications: Insurance Underwriting, Risk Management, Background Info - Individuals, Direct Marketing

Proprietary Products:

Name/Desc: MDR
Info Provided: Driver/Vehicle
Media: Automated Telephone Lookup, Printed Report and Lists or Labels
Coverage: US

Statement of Capabilities:

MDR provides an automated touch-tone call-in service for driver information in Minnesota, letting clients retrieve a record with a verbal response in less than one minute, followed by a fax hard copy within minutes. Service available 24 hours a day every day. The service is endorsed by the Minnesota Insurance Agents Assoc.

Merlin Information Services

215 S Complex Dr
Kalispell, MT 59901
Telephone: **Fax:**
800-367-6646 406-755-8568
406-755-8550

www.merlindata.com/redirect.asp

Applications: Locating People/Businesses, Asset/Lien Searching/Verification, Background

Info - Business, Collections, Fraud Prevention/Detection

Proprietary Products:

Name/Desc: California Criminal
Info Provided: Criminal Information
Media: CD-ROM and Internet
Coverage: CA

Name/Desc: CA Brides and Grooms
Info Provided: Vital Records
Media: CD-ROM and Internet
Coverage: CA

Name/Desc: CA Statewide Property
Info Provided: Real Estate/Assessor
Media: CD-ROM and Internet
Coverage: CA

Name/Desc: CA Civil Superior Indexes
Info Provided: Civil Information
Media: CD-ROM and Internet
Coverage: CA

Name/Desc: CA Prof. License
Info Provided: Professional Licenses
Media: CD-Rom and Intenet
Coverage: CA

Name/Desc: UCC Index
Info Provided: UCC Filing Index
Media: CD-Rom and Internet
Coverage: CA

Name/Desc: CA Corp
Info Provided: Corporation & LTD Partnerships
Media: CD-Rom and Internet
Coverage: CA

Name/Desc: National People Finder
Info Provided:
Media: CD-Rom and Internet
Coverage: US

Statement of Capabilities:

Merlin Information Services produces unique search and retrieval systems to search public record and proprietary information databases. Merlin specializes in new technology for combined media search and retrieval using both CD-ROM and the Internet. Merlin's proprietary databases and several national databases are available on the Internet at their web site. They also sell public record related CD-ROM products produced by a number of other publishers, including voter registration records, DMV records, and Social Security death records.

Metromail Corporation

360 East 22nd St
Lombard, IL 60148
Telephone: **Fax:**
800-927-2238 708-916-1336
www.metromail.com

Applications: Locating People/Businesses, Fraud Prevention/Detection, Direct Marketing

Proprietary Products:

Name/Desc: MetroSearch
Info Provided: Addresses/Telephone numbers
Media: CD-ROM
Coverage: US

Name/Desc: Cole Directory
Info Provided: Addresses/Telephone Numbers
Media: CD-ROM, Publication
Coverage: US

Statement of Capabilities:

MetroNet includes direct access to the electronic directory assistance databases of the Regional Bells (RBOC's). Regional editions of the MetroSearch CD-ROM products and call-in services are featured.

MicroPatent USA

250 Dodge Ave
East Haven, CT 06512
Telephone:
800-648-6787
203-466-5055

http://micropat.com
info@micropat.com

Applications: Legal Compliance, Competitive Intelligence

Proprietary Products:

Name/Desc: MarkSearch Pro
Info Provided: Trademarks
Media: Online, CD-ROM
Coverage: US, International

Name/Desc: PatSearch
Info Provided: Patents
Media: Online, CD-ROM

Statement of Capabilities:
Micropatent is a global leader in the production and distribution of patent and trademark information. MicroPatent is committed to developing intellectual property systems with its sophisticated and talented programming staff. MicroPatent Europe is located in London, England.

Military Information Enterprises Inc

PO Box 17118
Spartanburg, SC 29301
Telephone: **Fax:**
800-937-2133   864-595-0813
864-595-0981

www.militaryusa.com
miepub@aol.com

Applications: Background Info - Individuals, Genealogical Research, Locating People/Businesses

Proprietary Products:

Name/Desc: Nationwide Locator Online
Info Provided: Military Files and Military Service
Media: Internet
Coverage: US

Statement of Capabilities:
Military Information Enterprises specializes in current and former military locates and background checks. They also publish books on locating people. The principal served 28 years in the US Army and is a licensed private investigator in South Carolina and Texas.

Motznik Computer Services Inc

8301 Briarwood St #100
Anchorage, AK 99518-3332
Telephone:
907-344-6254
Applications: Asset/Lien Searching/Verification, Locating People/Businesses, Real Estate Transactions, Litigation, Background Info - Business

Proprietary Products:

Name/Desc: Alaska Public Information Access System

Info Provided: Aviation/Vesels, Bankruptcy, Licenses/Registrations/Permits, Litigation/Judgments/Tax Liens, Criminal Information, Corporate/Trade Name, Uniform Commercial Code, Real Estate/Assessor, Voter Registration and Driver/Vehicle
Media: Online Database, Call back
Coverage: AK

Statement of Capabilities:
Motznik Computer Services' product is a comprehensive information research system that provides access to a wide selection of Alaska public files online. Information that can be researched includes: tax liens, UCC, address, real property, Anchorage civil suits, commercial fishing vessels, judgments, motor vehicles, partnerships, bankruptcies, aircraft, permanent fund filing, businesses, Anchorage criminal cases and commercial fishing permits. MV data does not include driver information.

National Credit Information Network NCI

PO Box 31221
Cincinnati, OH 45231-0221
Telephone: **Fax:**
800-374-1400   513-522-1702
513-522-3832

www.wdia.com

Applications: Background Info - Individuals, Locating People/Businesses, Employment Screening, Tenant Screening

Proprietary Products:

Name/Desc: Evictalert
Info Provided: Tenant History
Media: Printed Report, Fax and Call back
Coverage: IN, KY, OH

Name/Desc: NCI Network
Info Provided: Credit Information, Addresses/Telephone, Social Security Numbers, Voter Registration, Driver/Vehicle
Media: Direct Online to Your Computer and Internet
Coverage: US

Statement of Capabilities:
National Credit Information Network (NCI) specializes in interfacing with credit and public record databases for online searches with immediate response time. Online ordering is

available for setup and for searches using a credit card. Access is available through their Internet site. A variety of packages include applicant identity, SSNs, DMVs, education, reference and credential verification, criminal history, bankruptcy and civil history, workers compensation claims, and more.

National Fraud Center

Four Horsham Business Center
300 Welsh Rd #200Horsham, PA 19044

Telephone: **Fax:**
800-999-5658   215-657-7071
215-657-0800

www.nationalfraud.com

Applications: Fraud Prevention/Detection, Risk Management

Proprietary Products:

Name/Desc: NFC Online
Info Provided: Software/Training
Media: CD-ROM, Disk and Call-in
Coverage: US, International

Name/Desc: Bank Fraud Database
Info Provided: Criminal History
Media: Online Database and Call-in
Coverage: US, International

Name/Desc: Insurance Fraud Database
Info Provided: Criminal History
Media: Online Database and Call-in
Coverage: US, International

Name/Desc: Organized Crime Database
Info Provided: Criminal History
Media: Online Database and Call-in
Coverage: US, International

Name/Desc: Government Fraud Database
Info Provided: Criminal History
Media: Online Database and Call-in
Coverage: US, International

Name/Desc: The Fraud Bulletin
Info Provided: Criminal History
Media: Publication
Coverage: US

Name/Desc: Fraud Alert
Info Provided: Criminal History
Media: Publication
Coverage: US

Name/Desc: Cellular Fraud Database
Info Provided: Check Fraud Database

Media: Online Database
Coverage: US

Name/Desc: Check Fraud Database
Info Provided: Criminal History
Media: Online Database

Statement of Capabilities:
National Fraud Center combines its diverse databases into a system: NFConline. They utilize a fraud prevention, an interdiction program, and risk management tools to discover and prevent fraud and risk. They also specialize in pro-active measures such as security policies, training, and installation of security devices to protect corporations from future losses.

National Information Bureau Ltd

14 Washington Rd Bldg 2
Princeton Junction, NJ 08550

Telephone: **Fax:**
609-936-2900   609-936-2859
http://nib.com

Applications: Background Info - Individuals, General Business Information, Lending/Leasing

Proprietary Products:

Name/Desc: BACAS
Info Provided: Credit Information
Media: Online, Software
Coverage: US

Statement of Capabilities:
National Information Bureau (NIB) offers Courier, a combination of accessible multiple databases for public record retrieval. Other state-of-the-art products include Ca$he, RTK, and BACAS.

National Service Information

145 Baker St
Marion, OH 43301

Telephone: **Fax:**
740-387-6806   740-382-1256
www.nsii.net

Applications: Asset/Lien Searching/Verification, Filing/Recording Documents, Background Info - Business, Lending/Leasing, Legal Compliance

Proprietary Products:

Name/Desc: NSI - Online
Info Provided: Corporate/Trade Name, Uniform Commercial Code
Media: Internet
Coverage: IN, OH

Statement of Capabilities:
Founded in 1989, National Service Information is engaged in the search, filing and document retrieval of public record information. Having offices in Marion, OH and Indianapolis, IN, they consider Ohio, Indiana and Kentucky their local market in addition to 4300 different jurisdictions they search nationwide. They recently unveiled a comprehensive database to allow clients to perform public record searches via the Web. Their web site allows you to perform state level UCC lien and corporate detail searches for Ohio, and state level UCCs for Indiana. NSI also provides the option of requesting copies of microfilmed UCC lien images.

Nebrask@ Online

301 South 13th #301
Lincoln, NE 68508
Telephone: **Fax:**
800-747-8177 402-471-7817
402-471-7810
www.nol.org
INFO@NOL.org

Applications: Asset/Lien Searching/Verification, Legal Compliance, Insurance Underwriting, Lending/Leasing, Direct Marketing

Proprietary Products:

Name/Desc: Nebrask@ Online
Info Provided: Driver and/or Vehicle, Corporate/Trade Name and Uniform Commercial Code
Media: Magnetic Tape and Online Database
Coverage: NE

Name/Desc: Nebrask@ Online
Info Provided: Litigation/Judgments/Tax Liens and Addresses and Telephone Numbers
Media: Online Database
Coverage: NE

Statement of Capabilities:
Nebrask@ Online is a State of Nebraska information system that provides electronic access to state, county, local, association and other public information. Some agency and association data is updated daily, weekly or monthly, Subscribers connect via 800 number, local numbers, or the Internet 24-hours per day. There are sign-up and connect fees if not accessing via the Internet.

New Mexico Technet

5921 Jefferson NE
Albuquerque, NM 87109
Telephone: **Fax:**
505-345-6555 505-345-6559
www.technet.nm.org

Proprietary Products:

Name/Desc: New Mexico Technet
Info Provided: Driver and/or Vehicle, Litigation/Judgments/Tax Liens and Corporate/Trade name
Media: Online
Coverage: NM

Statement of Capabilities:
New Mexico Technet is a self-supporting, non-profit corporation operating to provide management of a statewide fiber optic computer network serving the needs of New Mexico, its state universities and statewide research, educational and economic-development interests. Technet serves as the primary connection point to the Internet for other Internet Service Providers, business, government and private users in New Mexico. Technet offers a full range of Internet services from dial-up to direct connections and web page services to co-located services and New Mexico MVR requests.

Northwest Location Services

1416 E Main Ave #E
Puyallup, WA 98372
Telephone: **Fax:**
253-848-7767 253-848-4414
http://search.nwlocation.com/nwmain.htm

Applications: Locating People/Businesses, Asset/Lien Searching/Verification, Collections, Litigation

Proprietary Products:

Name/Desc: Northwest Online

Northwest Online
Info Provided: Corporation/Trade Name,
Media: Direct Online to Your Computer, Call back, Internet, Fax, E-mail
Coverage: WA, ID

Statement of Capabilities:
Serving investigative, legal and business professionals, Northwest Location Services specializes in witness location, skip tracing, asset research and other information services, with an eye on protecting privacy and the public safety. Licensed and bonded in Washington. Allied with Northweat Online and Digital Research Company who produces CD-ROM database products for investigators, attorneys and collection agencies.

Offshore Business News & Research

123 SE 3rd Ave #173
Miami, FL 33131
Telephone: **Fax:**
305-372-6267   305-372-8724
www.offshorebusiness.com
INFOOFFSHOREBUSINESS.com

Applications: Background Info - Business, Background Info - Individuals, Fraud Prevention/Detection, General Business Information, Litigation

Proprietary Products:

Name/Desc: BE Supreme Court
Info Provided: Litigation/Judgments/Tax Liens and Bankruptcy
Media: Internet
Coverage: BE/Fix

Name/Desc: Grand Court of the CI
Info Provided: Litigation/Judgments/Tax Liens and Bankruptcy
Media: Internet
Coverage: CI/Fix

Name/Desc: BE Business
Info Provided: Corporate/Trade Name Data, Legislation/Regulation and Real Estate/Assessor
Media: Internet
Coverage: BE/Fix

Name/Desc: Cayman Business

Info Provided: Corporate/Trade Name Data and Bankruptcy
Media: Internet
Coverage: CI/Fix

Name/Desc: BA Business
Info Provided: Corporate/Trade Name Data
Media: Internet
Coverage: BA/Fix

Statement of Capabilities:
Offshore owns litigation databases covering Bermuda and the Cayman Islands. They offer 24-7 access, year around via the Internet. They publish investigative newsletters covering Bermuda and the Caribbean.

OPEN (Online Professional Electronic Network)

PO Box 549
Columbus, OH 43216-0549
Telephone: **Fax:**
888-381-5656   614-481-6980
614-481-6999

www.openonline.com

Applications: Background Info - Business, Locating People/Businesses, Employment Screening, Background Info - Individuals, Litigation

Proprietary Products:

Name/Desc: OPEN
OPEN
Info Provided: Real Estate/Assessor, Bankruptcy, Uniform Commercial Code, Corporate/Trade Name Data, Addresses/Telephone Numbers, Social Security Numbers, Workers' Compensation, Education/Employment, Credit Information, Criminal Information, Driver and/or Vehicle
Media: Direct Online to Your Computer
Coverage: US

Name/Desc: Arrest Records
Info Provided: Arrest Records
Media: Direct Online
Coverage: OH,IN,MN,AL,MI

Statement of Capabilities:
OPEN provides a wide range of access to nationwide public records and proprietary information such as driver records, commercial and consumer credit reports, and bankruptcies,

liens and judgments. The service is subscription-based and is available to professionals for a variety of applications including background checks, skip-traces, verification of information such as addresses, phone numbers, SSNs, employment-/educational background. OPEN provides free software and account start-up, toll-free technical support and no monthly minimum.

OSHA DATA

12 Hoffman St
Maplewood, NJ 07040-1114
Telephone:
973-378-8011
www.oshadata.com
mcarmel@oshadata.com

Applications: Litigation, Legal Compliance, Direct Marketing, Background Info - Business, Government Document Retrieval

Proprietary Products:

Name/Desc: OSHA Data Gateway
Info Provided: Regulation and Legislation
Media: Printed Report, Fax
Coverage: US

Statement of Capabilities:

OSHA DATA's database contains corporate regulator violation records for every business inspected since July 1972. Information includes not only OSHA data, but also wage and hour, EEOC, insurance, NLRB asbestos and other regulatory types. The database is updated quarterly. Consultation and software for the utilization of the data are available.

Owens Online Inc

251 Lyndhurst St
Dunedin, FL 34698-7577
Telephone:　　**Fax:**
800-745-4656　　813-738-8275
813-738-1245
www.owens.com
mark@owens.com

Applications: Background Info - Business, Background Info - Individuals, General Business Information, Locating People/Businesses

Statement of Capabilities:

Owens Online specializes in international credit reports on businesses and individuals. They provide worldwide coverage, with nine million foreign credit reports online. Single orders are welcomed and there are no complex unit contracts.

Pallorium Inc

PO Box 155-Midwood Station
Brooklyn, NY 11230
Telephone:　　**Fax:**
212-969-0286　　800-275-4329
www.pallorium.com

Applications: Asset/Lien Searching/Verification, Locating People/Businesses, Employment Screening, Risk Management, Litigation

Proprietary Products:

Name/Desc: Skiptrace America
Info Provided: Aviation/Vessels, Driver and/or Vehicle, Vital Records and Voter Registration
Media: Direct Online to Your Computer
Coverage: US

Name/Desc: People Finder California
Info Provided: Aviation/Vessels, Driver and/or Vehicle, Vital Records and Voter Registration
Media: Direct Online to Your Computer
Coverage: CA

Name/Desc: People Finder Texas
Info Provided: Aviation/Vessels, Driver and/or Vehicle, Vital Records and Voter Registration
Media: Direct Online to Your Computer
Coverage: TX

Name/Desc: People Finder Tri-State
Info Provided: Aviation/Vessels, Driver and/or Vehicle, Vital Records and Voter Registration
Media: Direct Online to Your Computer
Coverage: CT, NJ, NY

Name/Desc: People Finder Florida
Info Provided: Aviation/Vessels, Driver and/or Vehicle, Vital Records and Voter Registration
Media: Direct Online to Your Computer
Coverage: FL

Name/Desc: People Finder Gulf Coast
Info Provided: Aviation/Vessels, Driver and/or Vehicle, Vital Records and Voter Registration
Media: Direct Online to Your Computer
Coverage: AL, GA, LA, MS

Name/Desc: People Finder West I & II
Info Provided: Aviation/Vessels, Driver and/or Vehicle, Vital Records and Voter Registration
Media: Direct Online to Your Computer
Coverage: AZ, CO, NM, OR, UT, WA

Name/Desc: People Finder Great Lakes
Info Provided: People Finder New England
Media: Direct Online to Your Computer
Coverage: ID, IL, MI, OH

Statement of Capabilities:
Pallorium (PallTech Online) services are divided into three areas: the electronic mail system, which links all users (800 investigative/security professionals); the bulletin board system, which provides a forum for the free exchange of information among all approved subscribers (public or private law enforcement only); and the investigative support system, which provides investigative support to approved users. PallTech's searches include aircraft record locator, national financial asset tracker, bankruptcy filings locator, business credit reports, consumer credit reports, NCOA trace, criminal records, national vehicle records, current employment locator, NYC registered voters by address, court and governmental jurisdiction identifier, ZIP Code locator and more searches in the US, Canada, Israel and Hong Kong. New products are CD-ROMs of addresses and personal information for a number of states, totaling more than one billion records.

Paragon Document Research

PO Box 65216
St Paul, MN 55165
Telephone: **Fax:**
800-892-4235   800-847-7369
651-222-6844   651-222-2281
www.banc.com
Applications: Asset/Lien Searching/Verification, Background Info -

Business, Competitive Intelligence, Employment Screening, Litigation
Proprietary Products:
Name/Desc: Pdrlog
Info Provided: Uniform Commercial Code
Media: Lists or Labels
Coverage: US

Statement of Capabilities:
Paragon Document Research's services include searches throughout state and county levels of Minnesota, Montana, North Dakota and South Dakota covering UCC, Tax Liens, Bankruptcy filings, past and present litigation, searches for ownership of, and liens on DMV reports, assumed name searches, name reservations and corporate agents. There are no correspondent fees applied.

Plat System Services Inc

12450 Wayzata Blvd #108
Minnetonka, MN 55305-1926
Telephone: **Fax:**
612-544-0012   612-544-0617
www.platsystems.com
Proprietary Products:

Name/Desc: System90
Info Provided: Property Sales
Media: Disk, Lists or labels, Direct Online to Your Computer and Printed Report
Coverage: MN- Minneapolis, St. Paul

Name/Desc: CompUmap
Info Provided: Addresses/Telephone Numbers and Real Estate/Assessor
Media: Direct Online to Your Computer
Coverage: MN-Minneapolis and St Paul

Name/Desc: PID Directory
Info Provided: Real Estate/Assessor
Media: Reports, Lists or Labels, Publiction and Disk
Coverage: MN-Minneapolis, St. Paul

Statement of Capabilities:
Plat System Services has a variety of services available including online services updated weekly, PID directories published annually, commercial sold reports monthly, residential sold reports monthly, custom reports updated weekly, and other monthly reports such as contract for deeds, and commercial buyers and sellers reports. They also offer mailing lists and

labels, diskettes updated weekly, and PLAT books updated semi-annually. They provide computerized county plat maps.

Professional Services Bureau

315 S College #245
Lafayette, LA 70503
Telephone: **Fax:**
800-960-2214   318-235-5318
318-234-9933

casey@casepi.com

Applications: Asset/Lien Searching/Verification, Real Estate Transactions, Filing/Recording Documents, Lending/Leasing, Document Retrieval

Proprietary Products:

Name/Desc: PSB Database
Info Provided: Addresses, Credit, Social Security, Criminal
Media: Online, Print, Disk, Magnetic Tape
Coverage: LA

Statement of Capabilities:
Professional Services Bureau is a full service investigation agency covering Louisiana and Mississippi. They offer background, criminal, employment, insurance, financial, activity checks, fraud, and missing person investigations, also surveillance and process service. They perform courthouse research, document filing and retrieval at all municipal, state and federal courts. Other services are title abstracting, notary services and claims adjusting. Their firm has proprietary sources of background information in South Louisiana. All 64 Louisiana parishes can be researched in about 48 hours; about 72 hours for Mississippi.

Progenitor

PO Box 345
Paradise, UT 84328
Telephone:
435-245-9386
Applications: Locating People/Businesses, Genealogical Research, Direct Marketing, Competitive Intelligence, General Business Information

Proprietary Products:

Name/Desc: North American Surname Folder Index

Info Provided: Genealogical Information
Media: CD-ROM, 609, Lists or labels, Magnetic Tape, Microfilm/Microfiche and Printed Report
Coverage: US, Canada

Name/Desc: World Source Index
Info Provided: Genealogical Information
Media: CD-ROM, Lists or labels, Magnetic Tape, Microfilm/Microfiche and Printed Report
Coverage: US, Intl

Statement of Capabilities:
Progenitor specializes in surname databases, source databases, pedigree analysis, surname surveys, ethnic information, denominational information, and specific record location services. Other services include family records located, manuscripts located, maiden names determined, obituary locator, cemeteries located/searched, immigration and naturalization sources, locating ancestral villages, contacting collateral cousins, and burned courthouse equivalents.

Property Data Center Inc

7100 E Bellevue #110
Greenwood Village, CO 80111
Telephone: **Fax:**
303-850-9586   303-850-9637
www.pdclane.net

Applications: Real Estate Transactions, Asset/Lien Searching/Verification, Direct Marketing, Lending/Leasing, Insurance Underwriting

Proprietary Products:

Name/Desc: Real Property Assessments
Info Provided: Real Estate/Assessor
Media: Direct Online to Your Computer, Disk, Lists or labels, Magnetic Tape and Printed Report
Coverage: CO

Name/Desc: Real Property Taxes
Info Provided: Real Estate/Assessor
Coverage: CO

Name/Desc: Owner Phone Numbers
Info Provided: Addresses/Telephone Numbers
Coverage: CO

Name/Desc: PDC

Info Provided: Real Estate/Assessor
Media: Online Database, Disk, Magnetic
Tape, Printed Reports and Lists or Labels
Coverage: CO

Statement of Capabilities:
Property Data Center's PDC database includes
three million real property ownership and deed
transfer records for the metro Denver area, plus
counties of Adams, Arapahoe, Boulder,
Denver, Douglas, El Paso, Eagle, Elbert,
Jefferson, Larimer, Mesa, Pitkin, Pueblo,
Summit, Weld. Data is accessible by owner,
location, and indicators such as property value.
They specialize in lender marketing data, new
owners, sold comparables, mapping data and
direct mail lists.

PROTEC
PO Box 54866
Cincinnati, OH 45254
Telephone: **Fax:**
800-543-7651   513-528-4402
513-528-4400

procaq007@fuse.net

Applications: Asset/Lien
Searching/Verification, Background Info -
Business, Background Info - Individuals,
Employment Screening, Fraud
Prevention/Detection

Proprietary Products:

Name/Desc: Consta-Trac
Info Provided: Identifiers-DOB, SSN,
Addresses
Media: Printed Report
Coverage: US

Statement of Capabilities:
PROTEC has 35 years of concurrent exposure
to the information highway, beginning its
database system in 1979 using its own
information. Since that beginning they have
remained unique in responsible information
gathering, being useful in fraud detection and
factual data gathering. Their newest and most
successful database is "CONSTRA-TRAC" - a
master compilation of over 700 record systems
and special use cross-check histories from
individuals, businesses, societies, and public
record data.

Public Data Corporation
38 East 29th St
New York, NY 10016
Telephone: **Fax:**
212-519-3063   212-519-3065
www.pdcny.com

Applications: General Business Information,
Legal Compliance, Locating
People/Businesses, Asset/Lien
Searching/Verification, Background Info -
Business/Individuals

Proprietary Products:

Name/Desc: Public Data
Info Provided: Real Estate/Assessor,
Environmental, Litigation/Judgments/Tax
Liens and Uniform Commercial Code
Media: Call-in, Disk, Magnetic Tape and
Online Database
Coverage: NY

Statement of Capabilities:
Public Data Corporation's 24 million records
database includes real estate, lien, bankruptcy,
environmental and other records for the
boroughs of Manhattan, Bronx, Brooklyn,
Queens. Information is updated daily.

Public Record Research Library
4653 S Lakeshore #3
Tempe, AZ 85282
Telephone: **Fax:**
800-939-2811   800-929-3810
602-838-8909   602-838-8324

http://brbpub.com
brb@brbpub.com

Applications: General Business Information,
Government Document Retrieval, Risk
Management, Locating People/Businesses,
Competitive Intelligence

Proprietary Products:

Name/Desc: PRRS
Info Provided: Addresses,
Legislation/Regulations
Media: CD-ROM, Disk, Publication
Coverage: US

Statement of Capabilities:
The Public Record Research Library is a series
of in-depth databases formatted into books,
CDs and soon to be online. BRB is recognized

as the nation's leading research and reference publisher of public record related information. The principals of the parent company are directors of the Public Record Retriever Network, the nation's largest organization of public record professionals. Over 26,000 government and private enterprises are analyzed in-depth regarding regulations and access of public records and public information. The Public Record Reseach System (PRRS) is available on CD, loose-leaf print, and as a customized database.

RC Information brokers

PO Box 1114
Framingham, MA 01701-0206
Telephone: **Fax:**
508-651-1126 508-657-2414
psconnor@gis.net

Applications: Background Info - Business, Background Info - Individuals, Collections, Genealogical Research, Litigation

Proprietary Products:

Name/Desc: Massdata
Info Provided: Addresses/Telephone Numbers and Vital Records
Media: Disk, Call-in Only and Internet
Coverage: MA

Statement of Capabilities:

RC Information Brokers provide "critical information support" to attorneys, licensed private investigators and other professionals. RCIB specializes in supporting attorneys seeking information on individuals for litigation, credit checks, internal financial investigations and background checks. Information support is also available for major financial centers outside the US, especially London. Specific proprietary databases include "MassData" compiled from various databases archived over the past 22 years on current and previous residents of Massachusetts. Turnaround time depends on specific needs and caseload. Locating Massachusetts individuals past and present including adoption cases is their specialty.

Real Estate Guide Inc, The

PO Box 338
Ravena, NY 12143
Telephone: **Fax:**
800-345-3822 800-252-0906
www.equides.com

Applications: Real Estate Transactions, Lending/Leasing

Proprietary Products:

Name/Desc: Real Estate Filing Guide
Info Provided: Real Estate/Assessor
Media: Print and CD-ROM
Coverage: US

Statement of Capabilities:

The Real Estate Filing Guide is a 4,400 page, 6 volume quarterly-updated service used by real estate documentation specialists for the purpose of accurately recording those documents in any of the 3,600 county recording offices nationwide. It is available in print and CD-ROM. Firms wishing to integrate this information with internal documentation systems may license the underlying databases.

Record Information Services Inc

Box 1183
St Charles, IL 60174
Telephone: **Fax:**
630-365-6490 630-365-6524
http://wwww.public-record.com
metcalf@elnet.com

Applications: Collections, Direct Marketing, Real Estate Transactions

Proprietary Products:

Name/Desc: Foreclosures
Info Provided: Litigation/Judgments/Tax Liens
Media: Disk, Fax-on-Demand, Internet, Lists or labels and Printed Report
Coverage: IL

Name/Desc: Bankruptcies
Info Provided: Bankruptcy
Media: Disk, Fax-on-Demand, Internet, Lists or labels and Printed Report
Coverage: IL

Info Provided: Litigation/Judgments/Tax Liens
Media: Disk, Direct Online to Your Computer, Fax-on-Demand, Printed Report and Software
Coverage: IL

Name/Desc: State & Federal Tax Liens
Info Provided: Litigation/Judgments/Tax Liens
Media: Disk, Direct Online to Your Computer, Fax-on-Demand, Printed Report and Software
Coverage: IL

Name/Desc: Business Licenses
Info Provided: Licenses/Registrations/Permits
Media: Disk, Direct Online to Your Computer, Fax-on-Demand, Printed Report and Software
Coverage: IL

Name/Desc: News Incorporations
Info Provided: Licenses/Registrations/Permits
Media: Disk, Direct Online to Your Computer, Fax-on-Demand, Printed Report and Software
Coverage: IL

Name/Desc: New Homeowners
Info Provided: Real Estate/Assessor
Media: Disk, Direct Online to Your Computer, Fax-on-Demand, Printed Report and Software
Coverage: IL

Name/Desc: Mortgage Recordings
Media: Disk, Direct Online to Your Computer, Fax-on-Demand, Printed Report and Software
Coverage: IL

Name/Desc: Divorces
Media: Disk, Direct Online to Your Computer, Fax-on-Demand, Printed Report and Software
Coverage: IL **Name/Desc:** Judgments

Statement of Capabilities:
Record Information Services provides complete and timely public record data that is delivered through state-of-the-art technology. Custom reports are available upon request.

Richland County Abstract Co
POB 910
Wahpeton, ND 58074-0910
Telephone: **Fax:**
701-642-3781 701-642-3852
Applications: Real Estate Transactions, Filing/Recording Documents, Asset/Lien Searching/Verification

Proprietary Products:

Name/Desc: Judgment & Tax Liens
Info Provided: Litigation/Judgments/Tax Liens
Media: Disk and Printed Report
Coverage: MN, ND

Statement of Capabilities:
Richland County Abstract specializes in providing real estate information for the states of Minnesota and North Dakota.

San Diego Daily Transcript/San Diego Source
2131 Third Ave
San Diego, CA 92101
Telephone:
800-697-6397
619-232-4381

www.sddt.com
editor@sddt.com

Applications: Filing/Recording Documents, Real Estate Transactions, Background Info - Business

Proprietary Products:

Name/Desc: San Diego Source
Info Provided: Tax Liens and Uniform Commercial Code
Media: Internet
Coverage: CA

Name/Desc: US Bankruptcy Court Filings
Info Provided: Bankruptcy
Media: Internet
Coverage: US

Statement of Capabilities:
The San Diego Source is a leading CA web site for public record information and business data. Site visitors can perform customized searches on one or more than fifteen databases. Links with Transcripts Online.

SEAFAX Inc

PO Box 15340
Portland, ME 04112-5340

Telephone: **Fax:**
800-777-3533   800-876-3533
207-773-3533   207-773-9564

www.seafax.com

Applications: Background Info - Business, General Business Information, Lending/Leasing

Proprietary Products:

Name/Desc: Business Reports
Info Provided: Credit Information
Media: Fax-on-Demand and Internet
Coverage: US

Statement of Capabilities:
Seafax is an information provider for the seafood industry, offering complete credit monitoring services, accounts receivable discounting, customized marketing data, contingent collections services, outsourcing, receivables management, and consulting services. Seafax provides one central location for the information for conducting business in the seafood industry.

Search Company of North Dakota LLC

1008 E Capitol Ave
Bismarck, ND 58501-1930

Telephone: **Fax:**
701-258-5375   701-258-5375
mkautzma@btigate.com

Applications: Current Events, Filing/Recording Documents, Asset/Lien Searching/Verification, Background Info - Business, Employment Screening

Proprietary Products:

Name/Desc: North Dakota Records
Info Provided: Addresses/Telephone Numbers, Social Security Numbers, Litigation/Judgments/Tax Liens, Licenses/Registrations/Permits, Driver and/or Vehicle, Criminal Information and Bankruptcy
Media: Printed Report, Fax-on-Demand and Lists or labels
Coverage: ND

Name/Desc: ND UCC
Info Provided: Uniform Commercial Code, Tax Liens
Media: Printed Report, Fax-on-Demand and Lists or labels
Coverage: ND

Statement of Capabilities:
Michael Kautzman, the owner of The Search Company of North Dakota, has ten years of public record searching and filing experience. He concentrates in North Dakota, including 24-48 hour access to all state agencies and to local offices in any of the 53 counties.

Search Network Ltd

Two Corporate Place #210
1501 42nd StWest Des Moines, IA 50266-1005

Telephone: **Fax:**
800-383-5050   800-383-5060
515-223-1153   515-223-2814

Applications: Lending/Leasing, Filing/Recording Documents, Asset/Lien Searching/Verification

Proprietary Products:

Name/Desc: Search Network
Info Provided: Uniform Commercial Code
Media: Online Database, Printed Reports, Lists or Labels, Publication and Microfilm
Coverage: IA, KS

Statement of Capabilities:
In business for over 30 years, Search Network provides full service public record search information. The company maintains an on-site UCC database for Iowa and Kansas. Same day searches and copies are available as well as personal filing service for UCC and corporate documents. Since 1980, they have offered direct online access to their databases of UCC filing/records information in Iowa and Kansas.

Security Search & Abstract Co

926 Pine St
Philadelphia, PA 19107

Telephone: **Fax:**
800-345-9494   800-343-4294
215-592-0660   215-592-0998

Applications: Real Estate Transactions, Legal Compliance, Asset/Lien

Searching/Verification, Filing/Recording Documents

Proprietary Products:

Name/Desc: Security Search
Info Provided: Real Estate/Assessor
Media: Call-in
Coverage: PA

Silver Plume

4775 Walnut St #2B
Boulder, CO 80301

Telephone: **Fax:**
800-677-4442   303-449-1199
303-444-0695

www.silverplume.iix.com

Applications: Insurance Underwriting

Proprietary Products:

Name/Desc: Insurance Industry Rates, Forms and Manuals
Info Provided: Legislation/Regulations
Media: CD-ROM, Magnetic Tape
Coverage: US

Statement of Capabilities:
Silver Plume supplies most of the widely-used manuals in the property and casualty insurance industry in electronic format. All manuals are updated monthly and distributed to subscribing agencies and companies to provide convenient access to vital information without the hassles.

SKLD Information Services LLC

4647 E Evans Ave
Denver, CO 80222-5111

Telephone: **Fax:**
800-727-6358   303-758-6847
303-758-6358

Applications: Real Estate Transactions, Asset/Lien Searching/Verification, Direct Marketing, Filing/Recording Documents

Proprietary Products:

Name/Desc: New Homeowners List
Info Provided: Real Estate/Assessor
Media: Disk, Magnetic Tape, Call-back, and Labels
Coverage: CO

Statement of Capabilities:
SKLD Information Services maintains a complete database of public record information keyed from documents recorded in County Recorder offices since 1990. Information is available to enhance existing databases, create new homeowner mailing lists, report on real estate loan transaction information, and as mortgage marketing data. With archived county recorded documents in their in-house microfilm library, SKLD can provide quick turnaround times. Reports available include: real estate loan activity reports, warranty deed/trust deed match, trust deed report, owner carry 1 and 2 reports, notice of election and demand, and new homeowners list.

Southwest InfoNet

2252 N 44th St #1007
Phoenix, AZ 85008-7201

Telephone: **Fax:**
800-579-1892   800-549-1925
602-286-6804   602-286-6712

www.unisearch.com

paulstr24@aol.com

Applications: Asset/Lien Searching/Verification, Filing/Recording Documents, Government Document Retrieval, Lending/Leasing, Litigation

Proprietary Products:

Name/Desc: WALDO
Info Provided: Uniform Commercial Code
Media: Internet and Direct Online to Your Computer
Coverage: CA, IL, WA

Statement of Capabilities:
Southwest InfoNet's normal turnaround time is 24-48 hours. Projects are generally billed by the number of names searched or records located. Copy costs and disbursements are added to the search charge. Their large microfilm library allows immediate copy retrieval for many states. Their web site includes news, jurisdiction updates and online ordering.

Specialty Services

8491 Hospital Dr #151
Douglasville, GA 30134

Telephone: **Fax:**
770-942-8264   770-942-5355

Applications: Asset/Lien
Searching/Verification, Background Info -
Business, Background Info - Individuals,
Employment Screening, Litigation

Proprietary Products:

Name/Desc: Fulco
Info Provided: Criminal Information and
Litigation/Judgments/Tax Liens
Media: Fax-on-Demand
Coverage: US

Statement of Capabilities:
Speciality Services specializes in record
retrieval from county, state and federal courts
as well as criminal/civil backgrounds for pre-
employment screening, litigation support,
insurance fraud investigation assistance, asset
reports, UCC searches, title work, etc.

Superior Information Services LLC

PO Box 8787
Trenton, NJ 08650-0787

Telephone: **Fax:**
800-848-0489   800-883-0677
609-883-7000   609-883-0677

www.cji.com

Applications: Litigation, Lending/Leasing,
Legal Compliance, Asset/Lien
Searching/Verification

Proprietary Products:

Name/Desc: Superior Online
Info Provided: Litigation/Judgments/Tax
Liens and Bankruptcy
Media: Online Database
Coverage: DC, DE, MD, NC, NJ, NY, PA,
VA

Name/Desc: Superior Online
Info Provided: Corporate/Trade Name
Media: Online Database
Coverage: NY, PA

Name/Desc: Superior Online
Info Provided: Uniform Commercial Code
Media: Online Database
Coverage: NY, PA

Statement of Capabilities:
Superior maintains the most comprehensive
civil public records database in the Mid-
Atlantic states. Court data can be searched by
either defendant or plaintiff. As a primary
source supplier of public records to major
credit repositories in the Mid-Atlantic states,
their databases are accurate and up-to-date.
Data includes federal suits and foreclosure
actions in New Jersey.

Tax Analysts

6830 N Fairfax Dr
Arlington, VA 22213

Telephone: **Fax:**
703-533-4600   705-533-4444
www.tax.org

Applications: Current Events, Litigation, Legal
Compliance, Background Info - Business,
General Business Information

Proprietary Products:

Name/Desc: Exempt Organization Master List
Info Provided: Corporate/Trade Name
Media: CD-ROM and Disk
Coverage: US

Name/Desc: The Tax Directory
Info Provided: Addresses/Telephone
Media: Publication, CD-ROM and Available
on DIALOG & LEXIS
Coverage: US, International

Name/Desc: The OneDisc
Info Provided: Legislation/Regulations
Media: CD-ROM
Coverage: US

Name/Desc: TAXBASE
Info Provided: Legislation/Regulations
Media: Internet
Coverage: US, International

Statement of Capabilities:
Tax Analysts is a nonprofit organization
dedicated to providing timely, comprehensive
information to tax professionals at a reasonable
cost. They are the leading electronic publisher
of tax information. The Exempt Organization
Master List contains information about more
than 1.1 million not-for-profit organizations
registered with the federal government. The
Tax Directory contains information about
14,000 federal tax officials, 9000 private tax

professionals and 8000 corporate tax professionals. Online databases include daily federal, state and international tax information as well as complete research libraries.

The Search Company Inc

1410-439 University Ave
Toronto, ON M5G 1Y8

Telephone:	Fax:
800-396-8241	800-396-8219
416-979-5858	416-979-5857

www.thesearchcompany.com

info@thesearchcompany.com

Applications: Asset/Lien Searching/Verification, Background Info - Business, Background Info - Individuals, Government Document Retrieval, Litigation

Proprietary Products:

Name/Desc: Property Ownership & Tenant Data
Info Provided: Real Estate/Assessor
Media: Direct Online to Your Computer, Internet, Printed Report and Software
Coverage: CD

Statement of Capabilities:
The Search Company covers two distinct markets: 1) Canada wide public record retrieval; 2) Litigation related asset and corporate background reporting with or without a full narrative report, with analysis and opinion regarding the advisability of litigation.

Thomson & Thomson

500 Victory Rd
North Quincy, MA 02171-3145

Telephone:	Fax:
800-692-8833	800-543-1983
617-479-1600	617-786-8273

www.thomson-thomson.com

Applications: Legal Compliance, Direct Marketing, Competitive Intelligence, Background Info - Business, Background Info - Individuals

Proprietary Products:

Name/Desc: TRADEMARKSCAN
Info Provided: Trademarks/Patents and Foreign Country Information

Media: CD-ROM, Direct Online to Your Computer and Internet
Coverage: US, International

Name/Desc: Worldwide Domain
Info Provided: Foreign Country Information
Media: Internet
Coverage: US, International

Name/Desc: Site Comber
Info Provided: Trademarks/Patents
Media: Internet and Printed Report
Coverage: US

Name/Desc: US Full Trademark Search
Info Provided: Trademarks/Patents
Media: Internet and Printed Report
Coverage: US

Name/Desc: US Full Copyright Search
Info Provided: Licenses/Registrations/Permits
Media: Printed Report
Coverage: US

Name/Desc: US Title Availability Search
Info Provided: Vital Records
Media: Printed Report
Coverage: US

Name/Desc: The deForest Report for Script Clearance
Info Provided: Vital Records
Media: Fax-on-Demand
Coverage: US

Statement of Capabilities:
Thomson & Thomson is a world leader in trademark, copyright and script clearance services, with over 75 years of experience and offices in the US, Canada, Europe and Japan. Accessing trademark records from more than 200 countries, T&T analysts provide reports to help clients determine if their proposed trademarks are available for use. Clients can perform their own trademark searches via Thomson & Thomson's TRADEMARKSCAN online databases. Thomson & Thomson also provides a complete offering of equally impressive copyright, title and script clearance services, allowing you to manage and protect your intellectual property assets.

TML Information Services Inc

116-55 Queens Blvd
Forest Hills, NY 11375

Telephone:	Fax:
800-743-7891	718-544-2853
718-793-3737	

www.tml.com

Applications: Insurance Underwriting, Employment Screening, Driver Screening for Auto Rental

Proprietary Products:

Name/Desc: Auto-Search
Info Provided: Driver/Vehicle
Media: Online Database, Internet, Call-back, and Fax
Coverage: AL, AZ, CT, DC, FL, ID, IN, KS, KY, LA, MA, MI, MN, MS, NC, ND, NE, NH, NJ, NY, OH, SC, VA, WI, WV

Name/Desc: Title File
Info Provided: Driver/Vehicle
Media: Online Database, Call-back and Fax
Coverage: AL, FL, SD

Name/Desc: Driver Check
Info Provided: Driver/Vehicle
Media: Online Database and Automated Telephone Lookup
Coverage: AL, AZ, CA, CT, FL, ID, KS, LA, MD, MI, MN, NE, NH, NY, NC, OH, PA, SC, VA, WV

Statement of Capabilities:

TML Information Services specializes in providing access to motor vehicle information in an online, real-time environment. Their standardization format enables TML to offer several unique automated applications for instant access to multiple states' driver and vehicle information, including a touch-tone fax-on-demand service and a rule-based decision processing service for driver qualification for car rental. TML has online access to more than 200 million driver and vehicle records in more than 30 states and expects to add several more states soon.

Todd Wiegele Research Co Inc

1345 16th Ave #6
Grafton, WI 53024

Telephone:	Fax:
800-754-7800	717-276-3395
717-276-3393	

www.execpc.com/~research/

Applications: Real Estate Transactions, Asset/Lien Searching/Verification, Background Info - Individuals, Employment Screening, Litigation

Proprietary Products:

Name/Desc: FASTRACT
Info Provided: Real Estate/Assessor
Media: Disk, Magnetic Tape and Microfiche
Coverage: WI

Statement of Capabilities:

The Todd Wiegele Research Co specializes in Milwaukee County records, but also provides nationwide services utilizing online databases and correspondents. Records specialties include title searches, criminal background checks, asset investigations, civil background checks and database consulting. They offer a database, FASTRACT, to track real estate information in Milwaukee County, WI.

Trans Union

555 W Adams
Chicago, IL 60661-3601

Telephone:
800-899-7132
312-258-1717

www.transunion.com

Applications: Collections, Lending/Leasing, Insurance Underwriting, Real Estate Transactions, General Business Information

Proprietary Products:

Name/Desc: CRONUS
Info Provided: Credit Information, Addresses, Litigation/Judgments/Tax Liens
Media: Online, Paper
Coverage: US

Name/Desc: Real Estate Services
Info Provided: Real Estate
Media: Online, Printed Report, Disks
Coverage: US

Name/Desc: Business Information

Info Provided: Credit Information, Corporate/Trade Name Data
Media: Online, Printed Report
Coverage: US

Name/Desc: Insurance Services
Info Provided: Driver and/or Vehicle
Media: Online, Printed Report
Coverage: US

Statement of Capabilities:
Trans Union, best known for its national consumer credit information file, provides a number of information services. Their TRACE product, based on Social Security Numbers, expands searching facilities to locate people who have changed names or moved without a forwarding address.

Tyler-McLennon Inc
707 W 7th St
Austin, TX 78701
Telephone: **Fax:**
512-482-0808   512-482-8727
www.tyler-mclennon.com
tylermclennon@worldnet.att.net

Applications: Asset/Lien Searching/Verification, Employment Screening, Filing/Recording Documents, Insurance Underwriting, Lending/Leasing

Proprietary Products:
Name/Desc: Crimspree
Info Provided: Criminal Information
Media: Call-back Only
Coverage: TX

Name/Desc: Cook County UCCs
Info Provided: Uniform Commercial Code
Media: Call-back Only
Coverage: IL

Statement of Capabilities:
Tyler-McLennon specializes in public records searches in Texas both at the county and federal level. Located in Austin, they have access to all state offices. They perform court record searches, real estate, property ownership, bankruptcies, asset/lien, UCC searches, also motor vehicle ownership and driving record searches. They utilize database hook-ups with Texas counties and physically do the searches in many. They have employees in Dallas/Ft. Worth, Houston, Austin, Corpus Christi and Tyler, and representatives elsewhere. Larger clients may choose to order and receive records online.

UCC Guide Inc, The
PO Box 338
Ravena, NY 12143
Telephone: **Fax:**
800-345-3822   800-252-0906
www.equides.com

Applications: Legal Compliance, Lending/Leasing

Proprietary Products:
Name/Desc: Uniform Commercial Code Filing Guide
Info Provided: Uniform Commercial Code filing criteria
Media: Print, Disk and CD-ROM
Coverage: US

Statement of Capabilities:
The UCC Filing Guide is a unique 5 volume, 6000 page quarterly updated service used by multi-state UCC filers to prepare UCC financing statements accurately. All 4300 UCC filing offices in the US are covered. Monthly newsletter is included with the annual subscription. The service includes UCC searching information. The disk media includes a database for automatic fee determination and address label/cover letter preparation. An affiliated company now publishes the Real Estate Recording Guide, designed to assist real estate documentation specialists.

UCC Retrievals Inc
7288-A Hanover Green Dr
Mechanicsville, VA 23111
Telephone: **Fax:**
804-559-5919   804-559-5920
Applications: Asset/Lien Searching/Verification, Legal Compliance, Litigation, Filing/Recording Documents

Proprietary Products:
Name/Desc: Federal Tax Liens and UCCs
Info Provided: Litigation/judgments/Tax Liens and Uniform Commercial Code
Media: Printed Reports, Lists or Labels and Online Database

Coverage: VA

Statement of Capabilities:
UCC Retrievals specializes in searching UCC and federal tax liens in Virginia. They also file motor vehicle records, do corporate filings and retrievals, and assist with pending litigation. Their turnaround time is 24-48 hours.

UMI Company
PO Box 1346
Ann Arbor, MI 48106-1346

Telephone:	Fax:
734-761-4700	734-975-6486
800-521-0600	

www.umi.com

business service@umi.com

Applications: General Business Information, Background Info - Business, Competitive Intelligence, Current Events

Statement of Capabilities:
UMI formerly operated DataTimes, now offers a number of useful electronic and print services with information on business, current events, technology innovations, including graphics, charts, photos. Their products are useful to libraries, researchers, scientists, schools, and competitive intelligence gathering. Products include ProQuest packages (includes newspapers) and IntellX.

Unisearch Inc
PO Box 11940
Olympia, WA 98508-1940

Telephone:	Fax:
800-722-0708	800-531-1717
360-956-9500	360-956-9504

www.unisearch.com

Applications: Asset/Lien Searching/Verification, Lending/Leasing, Legal Compliance, Real Estate Transactions, Corporate Registered Agent Service

Proprietary Products:

Name/Desc: WALDO
Info Provided: Uniform Commerical Code
Media: Direct Online to Your Computer, Internet and Printed Report
Coverage: CA, IL, WA

Statement of Capabilities:
Unisearch is online with over 30 states and British Columbia, providing instant access to the most current information available. They maintain a film library of UCC documents for WA, OR, AK, UT, CA, IL, MT, NV, WI, MN. In areas where computer access is not yet available, Unisearch employs a network of correspondents to provide service.

US Corporate Services
200 Minnesota Bldg, 46 E Fourth St
St Paul, MN 55101

Telephone:	Fax:
800-327-1886	800-603-0266
651-227-7575	651-225-9244

www.uscorpserv.com

info@uscorpserv.com

Applications: Asset/Lien Searching/Verification, Competitive Intelligence, Filing/Recording Documents, Lending/Leasing, Real Estate Transactions

Proprietary Products:

Name/Desc: MN Secretary of State Records
Info Provided: Corporation Records
Media: Online, Print
Coverage: MN

Name/Desc: WI UCCs
Info Provided: Uniform Commerical Code
Media: Online, Print
Coverage: WI

Statement of Capabilities:
US Corporate Services is a full service UCC, tax lien, judgment, litigation and corporate search and filing firm. Their optical image library of Minnesota enables them to provide custom reports to their clients. They have nationwide correspondent relationships. Their turnaround time is 24-72 hours. They will invoice monthly; projects are generally billed by the number of names searched.

US Document Services Inc

PO Box 50486
Columbia, SC 29250

Telephone: **Fax:**
803-254-9193   803-771-9905
www.us-doc-services.com
info@us-doc-services.com

Applications: Asset/Lien
Searching/Verification, Background Info -
Business, Filing/Recording Documents,
Government Document Retrieval

Proprietary Products:

Name/Desc: Secretary of State Info
Media: Printed Report
Coverage: NC, SC

Statement of Capabilities:

US Document Services is a nationwide public
record search and document retrieval company
specializing in North Carolina and South
Carolina. They offer UCC, tax lien, suit and
judgment, bankruptcy and asset searches, and
provide legal, financial and commercial clients
with a wide variety of services including
formation, qualification and registrations of
corporations, etc. With an in-house South
Carolina and North Carolina microfilm and
online database, they provide up-to-date
results, with 48-hour turnarounds

Virginia Information Providers Network

1111 East Main Street
Richmond, VA 23219

Telephone:
804-786-4718
www.vipnet.org
webmaster@vipnet.org

Applications: Employment Screening,
Litigation, Insurance Underwriting

Proprietary Products:

Name/Desc: VIPNet
Info Provided: Driver and/or Vehicle
Media: Internet
Coverage: VA

Statement of Capabilities:

The Virginia Information Providers Network
was created by the state of Virginia to
streamline and enhance the ways in which
citizens and businesses access government
information. VIPNet premium services
includes access to state motor vehicle records.

VISTA Information Solutions

5060 Shoreham Place
San Diego, CA 92122

Telephone: **Fax:**
800-767-0403   619-450-6195
619-450-6100
www.vistainfo.com

Applications: Risk Management, Insurance
Underwriting, Legal Compliance,
Lending/Leasing

Proprietary Products:

Name/Desc: VISTACheck
Info Provided: Environmental,
Corporation/Trade Name
Media: Online, Software, Lists
Coverage: US

Statement of Capabilities:

VISTA is a premier provider of environmental
risk information software and services and has
exclusive endorsements by the American
Bankers Association. Their myriad of products
provide information to the environmental and
insurance underwriting industries to assist with
risk management. The VISTA environmental
database includes environmental record
information form more than 500 state and
federal sources, and contains over 10 million
records which are geo-coded.

VitalChek Network

4512 Central Pike
Hermitage, TN 37076

Telephone:
800-255-2414
www.vitalchek.com
webcomment@vitalchek.com

Applications: Genealogical Research,
Background Info - Individuals

Proprietary Products:

Name/Desc: VitalChek
Info Provided: Vital Records
Coverage: US

Statement of Capabilities:

VitalChek Network has a sophisticated voice and fax network setup to help people get certified copies of birth, death and marriage certificates and other vital records. VitalCheck provides a direct access gateway to participating agencies at the state and local level.

West Publishing

620 Opperman Dr
Eagan, MN 55123

Telephone: **Fax:**
800-328-9352   612-687-7302
612-687-7000

www.westgroup.com

Applications: Legal Compliance, Current Events, General Business Information, Competitive Intelligence, Government Document Retrieval

Proprietary Products:

Name/Desc: West CD-ROM Libraries
Info Provided: Legislation/Regulations
Media: CD-ROM
Coverage: US

Name/Desc: Westlaw
Info Provided: Environmental, Legislation/Regulations
Media: Online Database
Coverage: US

Name/Desc: Westlaw
Info Provided: Corporate/Trade name, Uniform Commercial Code
Media: Online Database
Coverage: US

Statement of Capabilities:

West Publishing, now called West Group after its 1996 merger with Thompson Legal Publishing, is one of the largest providers of information to US legal professionals. West Group includes renowned names such as Barclays, Bancroft Whitney, Clark Boardman Callaghan, Counterpoint, Lawyers Cooperative Publishing, West Publishing and Westlaw. Westlaw is a computer-assisted research service consisting of more than 9,500 legal, financial and news databases, including Dow Jones News/Retrieval. West Group produces a total of more than 3,800 products including 300 CD-ROMs.

Western Regional Data Inc

PO Box 20520
Reno, NV 89515

Telephone: **Fax:**
702-329-9544   702-345-1652
www.wrdi.com

Applications: Direct Marketing, Asset/Lien Searching/Verification, Legal Compliance, Locating People/Businesses, Real Estate Transactions

Proprietary Products:

Name/Desc: WRDI's Lead Focus
Info Provided: Real Estate/Assessor and Vital Records
Media: Fax-on-Demand, Lists or labels, Disk, Internet and Microfilm/Microfiche
Coverage: NV

Statement of Capabilities:

Western Regional Data (WDRI) gathers public record information from all 17 counties in Nevada and state agencies, making it available in one online system. The information includes property tax data, building permits, business licenses and other less well-known types of public records. They have a new program called "Lead Focus" that makes available targeted mailing list data with more than 35 ways to pinpoint your market.

WinStar Telebase Inc

435 Devon Park Dr #600
Wayne, PA 19087

Telephone: **Fax:**
800-220-4664   610-341-9447
610-254-2420

www.telebase.com

Applications: General Business Information, Background Info - Business, Direct Marketing, Competitive Intelligence, Collections

Proprietary Products:

Name/Desc: Brainwave
Info Provided: SEC/Other Financial, Corporate/Trade Name
Media: Online Database and Available on Compuserve

Coverage: US

Name/Desc: Iquest
Info Provided: Corporate Records, Names
and Addresses, news, credit, trademarks, SEC
Media: Online
Coverage: US

Name/Desc: Caselaw
Info Provided: Legislation and Regulations
Media: Online
Coverage: US

Name/Desc: Dun & Bradstreet at AOL
Info Provided: Credit, Names and Addresses
Coverage: US

Statement of Capabilities:

Winstar Telebase's Information Services are
designed for people with little or no online
searching experience. Brainwave provides easy
online access to business information for sales
prospecting, market analysis, competitive
intelligence, product development, and other
research. Several thousand sources, from over
450 databases, are available including credit
reports, financial reports, company directories,
magazines, newspapers, newswires, industry
newsletters, etc. Subscribers can connect to
Corporate EasyNet by using a modem-
equipped computer. The service is currently
accessible through the public communications
networks and the Internet.

Web Site Profiles

What follows are detailed profiles of web sites. They are arranged by category. The information includes each site's title, its URL and a brief description. Unless otherwise noted, the content of the site profiled is available for free.

Not all of the sites listed here were mentioned within the main text of this book. Quite a few sites have been included here as "extra" resources. Also, all the sites in this section have been divided by and listed under the following headings:

Accuracy (Chapter 11)
Business (Chapter 9)
Employment
Filters & Filtering (Chapter 10)
Government Records (Chapter 6)
Miscellaneous
News (Chapter 8)
People Finders (Chapter 4)
Privacy (Chapter 13)
Public Records (Chapter 7)
Saving & Downloading (Chapter 5)
Search Engines (Chapter 3)
Specialized Tools (Chapter 4)
Subject Directories (Chapter 3)

Accuracy

America On Hold

http://members.aol.com/
elmothecow/aoh/index.html

Parody of the America Online home page

America Online (AOL)

www.aol.com

America Online home page

America Outtaline

www.bobsfridge.com/
aologon.htm

Parody of the America Online home page

Amnesi - The Internet Name Search Engine

www.amnesi.com

Lets you search for Internet server names (DNS names). You can type your best guess. The engine will try to match names to its extensive database and will give you a list of similar names.

CataLaw: Metaindex of Law & Government

www.catalaw.com

Catalog of law resources online.

CMP Media Inc

www.cmp.com

Extensive computer resources and articles including evaluation sites, advice and how-tos.

CNET

www.cnet.com

Extensive computer resources and articles including evaluation sites, advice and how-tos

El Dorado County Library's What's Hot on the Internet This Week

www.el-dorado.ca.us/~lib-
pl/thisweek.htm

Information rich sources from the El Dorado County, CA Library.

Evaluating Information Found on the Internet

http://milton.mse.jhu.edu:8001/
research/education/net.html

Tools for evaluating web sites.

Evaluating Quality on the 'Net

www.tiac.net/users/hope/
findqual.html

Hope Tillman's guidance on tools for evaluating quality on the Web.

Evaluating Web Resources

www.science.widener.edu/
~withers/webeval.htm

Tools for evaluating web sites.

Evaluating World Wide Web Information

http://thorplus.lib.purdue.edu/
research/classes/qs175/3qs175/
evaluation.html

Tools for evaluating web sites.

Finding Information on the Internet: A Tutorial

www.lib.berkeley.edu/TeachingLi
b/Guides/Internet/FindInfo.html

Superb introduction to and tutorial on searching on the Web.

Go To.Com

www.goto.com

Allows web site owners to pay for placement in a search engine.

Higher Source

www.highersource.com

Actual Higher Source page.

HigherSource.org

www.highersource.org

Satire page of Higher Source page (*see* previous)

ICANN

www.icann.net

ICANN will assign domain names after 1999.

ICYouSee

www.ithaca.edu/library/Training
/ICYouSee.html

Another excellent tutorial on using the Web.

IDG.net

www.idg.net

Extensive computer resources and articles including evaluation sites, advice and how-tos.

iNet: Whois Gateway

www.inet.net/cgi-bin/whoisgw

Regulates the registration of domain names.

International Salary Calculator

http://www2.homefair.com/calc/
salcalc.html

Calculator which helps people determine how much it will cost to relocate to another city.

Internet Corporation for Assigned Names & Numbers (ICANN)

www.icann.org

Newly-designated regulator of Internet Domain names.

Internet Detective

http://sosig.ac.uk/desire/
internet-detective.html

Quizzes and puzzles that provide an introduction to the issues of information quality on the Internet and teach critical evaluation skills.

InterNIC

http://rs.internic.net

Regulates the registration of domain names. Includes WHOIS database

Lycos TOP 5% Best of the Web

http://point.lycos.com/
categories

Rates multiple categories of sites as the top 5% Lycos reviews.

National Abortion & Reproductive Rights Action League

www.naral.org

Women's reproductive issues.

National Right to Life Committee

www.nrlc.org

Women's reproductive issues.

Oswald.jpg

www.aimnet.com/~carroll/
oswald.jpg

Lee Harvey Oswald photo which stresses the idea that Internet and accuracy are not synomous.

Paranoidal Home Page

www.saucers.com

Spoof on flying saucers.

Scout Report

www.cs.wisc.edu/scout/report

Weekly roundup of new findings on the Web, geared to researchers and education. A must.

Search Language Help

www.dejanews.com.help.help_lang
.shtml

Deja News' guide to properly writing newsgroup searches.

SilverPlatter

www.silverplatter.com

Proprietary site with organization and special business listings.

Fee-Based Site

The End of the Internet

http://opaldata.com/the_end/
index.html

The End of the Internet as we know it.

Thinking Critically About Web Information

www.ala.org/rusa/mars/
ets98.html

Evaluative tool for focusing web research.

Top 100 Computer Magazines

www.internetvalley.com/
top100mag.html

Links to online magazines about the Web and computers.

US News Archives on the Web

http://metalab.unc.edu/slanews/
Internet/archives.html

Univ. of NC's listings of newspapers offering access to archives.

Wharton Faculty Research Index

www.wharton.upenn.edu/wharton/
fac_resc.html

Sample of a university authorities list, by subject

White House.com

www.whitehouse.com

An x-rated site – this shows what adults will do to secure domain names close to popular ones, in this case like Whitehouse.gov.

White House.net

www.whitehouse.net

White House satire page.

Wired News

www.wired.com

Extensive computer resources and articles including evaluation sites, advice and how-tos.

ZDNet

www.zdnet.com

Extensive computer resources and articles including evaluation sites, advice and how-tos.

Business

Acxiom Direct Media

www.directmedia.com

Sells mailing lists.

Fee-Based Site

Alex Brown's Equity Research Universe

www.alexbrown.com/
cgi-bin/research.pl

Resource for finding analysts/brokers reports.

Fees for Some Content

American City Business Journals

www.amcity.com

More than 35 local business publications pooled together. Includes in-depth details about companies headquartered by region. Searchable either all at once, or one by one.

American Demographics / Marketing Tools

www.demographics.com

The nationally-reknowned magazine company offers access to the magazine's archives and also its sister publication Marketing Tools.

American Demographics Marketing

www.marketingtools.com

Valuable free article from American Demographics

American Real Estate Exchange, The (Amrex)

www.amrex.com

Real estate information site with extensive resources including property data

Fee-Based Site

American Society of Association Executives

www.asaenet.org

The central clearinghouse of the thousands of trade associations based in Washington, D.C. Links more than 1700 associations searchable by name of association.

ANYwhere Online's Market Research Center

www.anywhereonline.com

Solid links to marketing tools

ASI Market Research Center

www.asiresearch.com

ASI Market Research, a firm that specializes in television advertising research has a lot of free market-oriented information on its web site.

Association of Independent Information Professionals (AIIP)

www.aiip.org

Source for finding professional researchers.

AT&T Business Network

www.bnet.att.com

This free site has links to more than 1000 business sites and offers reviews of several market research sites.

Bank Rate Monitor

www.bankrate.com

Banking site with international information, newsletters includes calculators for mortgage rates and other things to help you customize to your needs.

Barron's

www.barrons.com

Published weekly by Dow Jones. Provides investment information and analysis to both individuals and institutional investors.

BizTravel.com

www.biztravel.com

Travel site geared to the business person.

BizWiz

www.clickit.com/touch/bizwiz.htm

A business supersite.

Bloomberg Online

www.bloomberg.com

Latest stock quotes and business information from one of the largest business wires.

Briefings.com

www.briefings.com

Business newsletters and magazines.

Fees for Some Content

Brill's Mutual Funds Interactive

www.brill.com

A magazine for investors and other business resources.

Business Advisor - Deloitte & Touche

www.dtonline.com/ba/ba.htm

Deloitte & Touche business adviser.

Business Wire

www.businesswire.com

PR wire for business announcements – great for locating what information a company wants the public to know.

BusinessWeek Online

www.businessweek.com

Publishes its entire text online as well as many value-added features including tables, graphics and photos, a topical article library, current stock market information and hourly market news updates in Real Audio format.

Fees for Some Content

CardWeb (RAM Research Group)

www.ramresearch.com

Concerns smart card technology.

CARL Corporation

www.carl.org

Click on Search CARL or Search UnCover. CARL provides an article delivery service with a table of contents database and an index to nearly 18,000 periodicals.

Fee-Based Site

CBS MarketWatch

www.cbsmarketwatch.com

Excellent site for breaking news on business issues.

CBS MarketWatch - Market Data

http://cbs.marketwatch.com/data/marketdata.htx

Extensive market data pages and set of links.

Centigram Home

www.centigram.com

Provides revenue-generating, integrated and enhanced services to service providers in emerging markets.

Fee-Based Site

Centrus Online

www.centrusonline.com

Sells mailing lists.

Fee-Based Site

Cents Financial Journal

http://lp-llc.com/cents/current/home.htm

A financial journal for online business traders.

CEO Express

www.ceoexpress.com

Collection of business news tools.

Charles Schwab & Co.

www.schwab.com

Investors' resource center for business info.

CIT Group

www.citgroup.com/insi.htm

CIT Group's resources page.

CNET's News.Com

www.news.com

CNET's news site for high tech issues.

CNNfn - the financial network

www.cnnfn.com

Provides a continuous "snapshot" of how various markets are doing each day.

CompaniesOnline

www.companiesonline.com

Short company capsule profiles from Dun and Bradstreet and Lycos.

Fees for Some Content

Company News On Call

www.prnewswire.com/cnoc/cnoc.html

PR Newswire's company research database, allows you to search for news or PR stories about specific companies

Cornell University

www.ilr.cornell.edu

Resources for workplace issues.

Corporate Information

www.corporateinformation.com

Information on private and international companies.

Corporate Watch: Researching Corporations

www.corpwatch.org/trac/resrch/resrch.html

Corporate Watch's "How to Research a Transnational Company." Contains valuable tips.

CorpTech

www.corptech.com

Background on private companies, geared to high tech companies.

Crain's New York Business

www.crainsny.com

Another good regional business site.

Daily Stocks

www.dailystocks.com

One of the best sites online for iinformation on investing.

Datamonitor

www.datamonitor.com

A business research tool for marketing.

Derwent information

www.derwent.com

Patent and scientific information.

Fee-Based Site

DIALOG Web

www.dialog.com

Among the largest fee-based services; offers people finders, business, credit, legal, public records and other databases.

Direct Channel Inc.

www.directchannel.com

Brokers and managers of mailing lists.

Fee-Based Site

Direct Marketing Association

www.the-dma.org

Trade association for direct marketing industry.

Disclosure SEC Site

www.disclosure-investor.com

Disclosure Inc's SEC site, loaded with resources.

Fee-Based Site

Dow Jones Interactive

www.dowjones.com

Among the largest fee-based services – offers people finders, business, credit, legal, public records and other databases.

E*TRADE

www.etrade.com

E-trade's online resource center.

EBN Interactive

http://gretel.econ.surrey.ac.uk/~ivan/WebDoc/ebn-inde.htm

European business resource.

EDGAR Access

http://edgar.disclosure.com/ea

Inexpensive way to track companies. Reports can be full-text EDGAR filings or short summaries.

Fee-Based Site

Edward Lowe Foundation

www.lowe.org

Extensive Small Business Resource Center.

Entrepreneur Magazine's BizSquare

www.entrepreneurmag.com

Enterpreneur Magazine and links.

Export@ll.net

www.exportall.net

Site with strong international links for export-related and country-specific info.

Family Business

www.smartbiz.com/sbs/
cats/family.htm

Small Business Supersite from Smart Biz.

Fidelity

www.fidelity.com

Fidelity Investments resource center.

Financenter

www.financenter.com

Personal finance site with tools.

Financial Web

www.financialweb.com

Thorough business resource site.

FIND/SVP

www.findsvp.com

Major market research firm with their own web site. Reports can be bought through their commercial online services. Also host of excellent Information Adviser newsletter.

Fees for Some Content

First Call Corporation

www.firstcall.com

Provides corporate and industry research to the desktop via the Internet using Adobe Acrobat.

Fee-Based Site

FreeEDGAR

www.freeedgar.com

E-mail notification of SEC filings.

Frost & Sullivan

www.frost.com

International marketing, consulting and training company with their own web site. Reports must be purchased through online providers or a client. Expensive.

Fees for Some Content

Fuld & Company Inc

www.fuld.com

Competitive intelligence web site.

Fuld & Company Inc: CI Strategies & Tools

www.fuld.com/i3

Competitive intelligence tools.

Gale Group

www.gale.com

Provides easy access to brand and manufacturing information and Gale's Business Resources database, which has detailed information on more than 400,000 American and foreign companies.

Fee-Based Site

Gomez Advisors

www.gomez.com

Independent rating of top online stockbrokers.

Green Book, The

www.greenbook.org

The New York Chapter of the American Marketing Association publishes a free directory of market research firms. This is a valuable free source to identify companies in specific industries.

GT Online

www.gt.com/gtonline/
ind_tc_main.html

GT Online resources page.

Hoover's Online

www.hoovers.com

Hoover's has a free site with company capsules. These include a company description, information on key competitors, rankings and subsidiaries as well as current news related to the company.

Fees for Some Content

IAC InSite

www.iac-insite.com

An excellent collection of news related resources in an easily searchable database.

Fee-Based Site

IBM Infomarket

www.infomarket.ibm.com

A web based research service that lets you search both the Internet and private databases simultaneously. Priced on a per document basis.

Fee-Based Site

IBM Patent Server Home Page

www.patents.ibm.com

Searched patent and trademark records.

IDS: Market Research

www.csa.com/findexsh.html

Summaries of market research reports and related publications from over 900 publishers worldwide.

IDS: The Internet Database Service

www.csa.com/ijs-desc.html

Cambridge Information Group publishes the Worldwide Directory of Market Research Reports, Studies and Surveys, which can be located on Dialog and also at Cambridge Scientific Abstracts Internet Database Service.

iMarket Inc

www.imarketinc.com

This site requires registration, features New Business Leads Online, which can help you identify business prospects and generate mailing lists.

Fees for Some Content

Inc.'s Resources for Growing Small Business

www.inc.com

Inc Magazine's online resources

Infobel: International Directories

www.infobel.be/infobel/infobelworld.html

International business resources.

Internet Public Library's Associations on the Net (AON)

www.ipl.org/ref/AON

Another great collection of association sites.

INTERNET.ORG!

www.internet.org

This site offers a lookup site for companies and domains.

Investext Group, The

www.investext.com

High-end business tool, offers market research reports from more than 60 firms.

Fee-Based Site

Investment FAQ

www.invest-faq.com

Excellent starting point for FAQ's on investing.

INVESTools

www.investools.com

Tools for helping investors.

Invest-o-rama!

www.investorama.com

Exhaustive directory of investment sites online.

IPO Central

www.ipocentral.com

Current list of initial public offerings. This site also has a comprehensive list of all US IPOs filed since mid-1996. It also provides some news and analysis on a weekly basis.

Jupiter Communications

www.jup.com

Major market research firm with their own web site. Reports must be purchased can be bought through their commercial online services.

justquotes.com

www.justQuotes.com

An excellent source for investment information. Enter a company name or ticker symbol and go to a page that links to current stock quotes, historical quotes, charts, news items, earnings estimates, SEC filings, company profiles, etc.

Larry Chase's Web Digest for Marketers

http://wdfm.com

Good collection of business sites from Larry Chase. Regularly updated with fresh links regularly with marketing tools.

Larry Chase's Web Digest for Marketing

www.mwt.com/may95art.html

Web digest for marketing newsletter and resources.

LEXIS-NEXIS

www.lexis-nexis.com

Among the largest fee-based services; offers peoplefinders, business, credit, legal, public records and other databases.

Lucent Technologies - Octel Messaging Division

www.octel.com

Messaging company software.

Fee-Based Site

Marketdata Enterprises Inc

www.mkt-data-ent.com

Market research reports available for purchase.

Fee-Based Site

Merrill Lynch Financial News & Research Center

www.merrill-lynch.ml.com/financial/index.html

Resource for finding analysts/brokers reports.

Fees for Some Content

MicroPatent

www.micropat.com

Patent information.

Fee-Based Site

Microsoft Expedia Travel

http://expedia.msn.com

Another extensive travel site, geared to business.

Mining Company, The: Business

www.miningcompany.com/business

Gathers and packages business information for users.

Mining Company: Stocks

http://stocks.miningco.com

Subject directory for stocks and finance.

Money Page

www.moneypage.com

Comprehensive guide to banking and finance; has resource lists on bank technology, electronic money, news, regulations and others.

Money.com (*Money Magazine*)

www.money.com

The magazine, plus links for specific companies and discussion groups on investment topics.

Montague Institute

www.montague.com

Competitive intelligence web site.

Motley Fool

www.fool.com

A high profile business resource center.

MSN Money Center Investor

http://investor.msn.com

A business-oriented resource collection.

Multex

www.multexnet.com

Resource for finding analysts/brokers reports.

Fees for Some Content

NASD Regulation

www.nasdr.com

This is the regulatory arm of the National Association of Securities Deadlers, the organization that separately runs the Nasdaq Stock Market. It's public disclosure program helps investors to select brokers or securities firms.

National Association for the Self Employed

www.membership.com/nase

National Association for the Self-Employed's resource list.

NetPartners Internet Solutions: Company Locator

www.netpartners.com/resources/search.html

Searches a database of web addresses from InterNIC, an organization that provides Internet registration services. The database primarily contains American companies.

Newsbytes News Network

www.nbnn.com

Telecommunications business resource from Post-Newsweek.

Fee-Based Site

NewsEdge Company Lookup

www.companylink.com

From NewsPage. It provides contact information, ticker symbol (if public) state and industry. This site also links you to press releases from the company's themselves, stock quotes, news articles and financial filings. Registration also entitles you to information about competitors.

NVST Private Equity Network

www.nvst.com

Venture capitol, mergers and acquisition resources.

OneSource Information Services

www.OneSource.com

Company and industry information.

Fee-Based Site

Online Resources' Online Banking & Financial Services Directory

www.orcc.com/banking.htm

Regional economic information for consumers or bankers.

Open Source Solutions

www.oss.net

Competitive intelligence web site.

PAWWS Financial Network

www.pawws.com

Brokerage and business resources

PR Newswire

www.prnewswire.com

PR news wire for business.

Pressline

www.pressline.com

A German business site that allows you to find information from trade shows from several countries and is available in three languages.

Fees for Some Content

Princeton University Survey Research Center

www.princeton.edu/~abelson/index.html

Links to a lot of survey and polling information, including the Gallup and Pew Research Centers.

Profound

www.profound.com

Database of over 20 million articles, reports and studies.

Fee-Based Site

Proquest Direct

www.umi.com

Extensive business-news database.

Fee-Based Site

Public Register's Annual Report Service, The (PRARS)

www.prars.com

An annual report service.

QPAT-US

www.qpat.com

Patent information.

Fee-Based Site

Quicken FN (formerly NETworth)

http://auth.quicken.com/login/http,3A,2F,2Fquotes,2Equicken,2Ecom,2Finvestments,2Fportfolio,2F

A comprehensive investment web site that is now a part of Quicken – includes database of mutual funds and corresponding morningstar reports.

Fees for Some Content

Quicken Investments

www.quicken.com/investments/quotes/?symbol=indv

An investments resources page.

Quicken.com

www.quicken.com

Business-rich site, including search tool.

Red Chip Review

www.redchip.com

A magazine on small cap stocks.

Fees for Some Content

Responsive Database Services

www.rdsinc.com

Database of several business resources, including Table Base, a collection of graphs and charts on business resources

Fee-Based Site

Reuters Business Information

www.bizinfo.reuters.com

One of many Reuters' tailored services, this one is just business briefing resources – this one goes back 10 years with more than 2000 publications.

SBFocus.com: Small Business Information Search Engine

www.sbfocus.com

Searches through thousands of business web sites, finds resources relevant to the needs of small businesses, and indexes only those sites.

Silicon Investor

www.techstocks.com

Financial information, stock quotes, financial data, technical charts and message boards for discussions.

Fees for Some Content

SilverPlatter

www.silverplatter.com

Proprietary site with organization and special business listings.

Fee-Based Site

Small Business Administration

www.sbaonline.sba.gov

Government clearinghouse on small business.

Small Business Journal

www.tsbj.com

Small Business Journal magazine.

Society of Competitive Intelligence Professionals

www.scip.org

Association of competitive intell folks

System for Electronic Document Analysis & Retrieval (SEDAR)

www.sedar.com

Searches Canada's electronic securities documentation filing system. Also in French.

The Street.Com

www.thestreet.com

A news wire for Wall Street related issues.

Thomas Register of American Manufacturers

www.thomasregister.com

Catalog of manufacturers and products covering 155,000 companies in the US, Canada and Mexico.

Thomson & Thomson

www.thomson-thomson.com

The ultimate trademark site.

Trade Show Central

www2.tscentral.com

A clearinghouse of trade shows – good for finding background info on companies.

Trade Show Channel, The

www.tschannel.com

Information on current tradeshows, venues and other tradeshow related information.

Transium Corporation

www.transium.com

An extensive database of business information.

Fees for Some Content

TSCentral

http://www2.tscentral.com/
index.jhtml

Service providing information on Trade Shows, Conferences & Seminars.

US Patent & Trademark Office

www.uspto.gov

The Federal Government's patent information center.

USADATA

www.usadata.com/usadata/market

Market data by community and region.

Verity

www.verity.com

Verity provides business software for Intranets including searching and indexing capability.

Wall Street Access

www.stockcenter.com

This site connects you to real time (20-minute delayed) stockmarket quotes; look up your favorite stocks or indexes; track them all day.

Wall Street Journal Interactive Edition

www.wsj.com

News and information services from the Dow Jones Company net.

Fees for Some Content

Washington Researchers

www.researchers.com/
freefact.html

A factsheet for CI researchers.

WavePhore Newscast

www.newscast.com

WavePhore Newscast is a high-end news provider customized for businesses.

WorldOpinion

www.worldopinion.com/wo

International market research, this site has all kinds of interesting links as well.

Yahoo! Business

www.yahoo.com/headlines/
business

A business resource.

Yahoo! Finance

http://quote.yahoo.com

Yahoo!'s strong business resources site, which is a subject directory for stocks and finance.

Your Company - Site for Small Business Owners

www.pathfinder.com/@@wdXrLQYAMy
*eOo2a/money/yourco/index.html

Articles geared to small business.

Zacks Investment Research Inc

www.zacks.com

An extensive collection of business market information.

Fees for Some Content

Employment

Academic Employment Network

www.academploy.com

Online job classifieds for US teachers from K-University, indexed by subject, geographic area and position level

America's Employers

www.americasemployers.com

Comprehensive job search site for professionals, managers and executives

Best Jobs USA

www.bestjobsusa.com

Searchable employment ads database from *USA Today*.

Career Find-O-Rama (from Princeton Review Online)

www.review.com/career/find/index.cfm

A keyword searchable database with career profiles.

Career Hotspots - The Best Career Sites on the World Wide Web

www.bev.net/education/schools/admin/career-hot-spots.html

Extensive list of career information sources.

Career Resource Center

www.careers.org

Excellent starting point to begin your job search, including prepping tips.

CareerMosaic

www.careermosaic.com

Search by keyword - choose a company and check their available positions. Includes an index of Usenet jobs newsgroups.

CareerPath.com

www.careerpath.com

Huge collection of job ads from over 50 of the leading newspapers in the country.

careers.wsj.com

http://careers.wsj.com

Wall Street Journal and *National Business Employment Weekly's* deep career info and searchable database.

E-Span's Job Options

www.joboptions.com/esp/plsql/espan_enter.espan_home

Post a resume and look through their extensive directory of job listings.

HeadHunter.NET

www.HeadHunter.NET

Excellent database and resume postings site.

Jobs In Government

http://jobsingovernment.com

Collection of government-related jobs, by geographic region.

JobSmart

www.jobsmart.org

Absolutely the best place to begin a job search. A library-sponsored guide to job-search resouces on the Web. Geared to California, but has excellent national info as well.

JobWeb

www.jobweb.org/textonly.htm

Good site if you're a college student, recent graduate or alumnus and looking for work.

Monster Board

www.monster.com/home.html

All purpose job seekers' site. More than 50,000 free searchable job listings around the world.

Online Career Center

www.occ.com

A database of job listings, searchable by geographic location, industry and keyword.

The Riley Guide: Employment Opportunities & Job Resources on the Internet

www.dbm.com/jobguide

Directory of excellent employment sites compiled by librarian Margaret F. (Riley) Dikel.

Top 100 Electronic Recruiters

www.interbiznet.com/eeri

Thousands of sites were reviewed and these are the top 100.

USAJOBS

www.usajobs.opm.gov/tindex.htm

Every job available from the federal government.

What Color is Your Parachute

www.tenspeedpress.com/parachute/front.htm

Directory listings, resumes and career counseling by author Richard Bolles from his job-hunting book, *What Color is Your Parachute?*

Filters & Filtering

Agent Appendices Pages

www.opensesame.com/agents/
agent_makers_agnt.html

Directory of commercial-agent tools, software applications.

Alexa

www.alexa.com

Web-surfing device that provides a list of sites related to the current page displayed on a browser.

Barnes & Noble.com

www.barnesandnoble.com

Ranks books you like based on what others with similar tastes suggest

BotSpot

http://botspot.com

A clearinghouse for bot-related items. It also has links to different kinds of bots,with examples like shopping and chatter bots.

ChatTimes: "Filmfinder"

www.chattimes.com/cityscape/
diversions/filmfinder/
filmfinderMAIN.html

Search for current films in your community.

Cinemax

www.cinemax.com

All about movies and catering to your tastes.

Clarinet Communications Corp. Home Page

www.clarinet.com

Customized filtering tool.

CNN Custom News

http://customnews.cnn.com

CNN allows you to customize the news to suit your interests.

CNN QuickNews

www.cnn.com/QUICKNEWS/mail

A morning e-mail from CNN Interactive. CNN also has a personalized news tool now that caters to your selections when you visit their pages.

Copernic

www.copernic.com

Excellent tool for searching simultaneous searching of multiple engines.

Fee-Based Site

CRAYON

www.eg.bucknell.edu/~boulter/
crayon

This site will let you create your own personalized newspaper, which only you can visit online.

Cyber Patrol

www.cyberpatrol.com

Content-filtering tool to screen out material not suitable for kids.

CYBERsitter

www.cybersitter.com

Kid content-filtering tool.

CyBot

www.TheArtMachine.com/cybot.htm

A personalized web filtering tool

Daily Briefing

http://grief.dailybriefing.com/home

Top headline stories with sound and video

DigiPhone

www.digiphone.com

Internet telephone technology site.

Digital Persona

www.digitalpersona.com

Makers of UareU fingerprint technology.

Direct Hit

www.directhit.com

Direct Hit offers technology that lets you know where the most people have gone when researching the subject you put in as the keyword. Available on HotBot, Netscape and others.

DOWNLOAD.COM

www.download.com

CNet's software downloading site.

Fees for Some Content

Enfish Tracker

www.enfish.com

Information tracking software – tool to organize your computer.

Fee-Based Site

Excite's NewsTracker

http://nt.excite.com

The Excite search engine also includes a "personal new home page" service that allows you to highly-customize your own news page.

FerretSoft

www.ferretsoft.com

New technology that has the ability to send queries to multiple search engines.

Firefly

www.firefly.com/studio/applications/studio_customers.fly

For customers using customized tools for filtering.

GlobalBrain.net Inc

www.globalbrain.net

Like its competitor, Direct Hit, Global Brain offers profile-based searching systems, allowing marketers to locate you. Worth looking at this cutting edge technology site.

IBM's Intelligence Agent Center of Competence

www.raleigh.ibm.com/iag.iaghome.html

Bot site and intelligence Agents information.

Imagination Engine Inc. (IEI)

www.imagination-engines.com

Databots use ordinary spreadsheet technology to make independent judgments in finding and understanding complex databases.

infoGIST

www.infogist.com

Technology applications for filtering.

InfoJunkie

www.infojunkie.com

News filtering tool, for business, tech and other resources.

Infophile - Intelligent Web Agent, Engine, Bot & Filter List

www.starsite.com/starsite/
botlst11.htm

Various filtering agents and bots.

Informant, The

http://informant.dartmouth.edu

A personalized agent will identify web sites relevant to your keywords and then track them and inform you by e-mail of changes.

Information Filtering Resources

www.ee.umd.edu/medlab/filter

Information Filtering Resources project by Doug Oard, University of Maryland library science assistant professor, which connects you to all kinds of information filters.

Infoscan

www.machinasapiens.com/english/
products/infoscan/
infoscanang.html

Filtering tool for personalizing your e-mail and other information sources.

Infoseek

www.infoseek.com

Both a search directory and a search engine.

InfoTicker

www.panix.com/~erik/
InfoTicker.cgi

A web-watching robot with filtering capability, used to alert you to changes in subjects you regularly monitor. You need Netscape Navigator or MS-IE 4.0 versions or higher to run this.

InGenius Technologies for Page Change Monitoring

www.ingetech.com

Web monitoring services to track the latest technical, business and competitive data.

Inquisit!

www.inquisit.com

Pay service. Allows you to set up a filtering tool from about 600 sources including newswires, newspapers and newsletters.

Fee-Based Site

Intelliseek's BullsEye

www.intelliseek.com

New technology that has the ability to send queries to multiple search engines.

Internet Research News

www.coppersky.com/ongir/news

Excellent filter that brings you the latest info on sites, technology and software on the Internet.

iVillage.com: the women's network

www.ivillage.com

Advice on parenting, health, career, etc.

JavElink

www.javelink.com

This site helps you monitor thousands of sites for changes.

LawRunner: Global Index

www.lawrunner.com

Intelligent agent software used for legal research.

Mata Hari

www.thewebtools.com

New technology that has the ability to send queries to multiple search engines.

MediaFinder

www.mediafinder.com/index.cfm

A centralized site of magazine subscriptions.

Mind-it NetMind

http://mindit.netmind.com

Track changes in other web pages automatically.

MIT Media Lab "Filtering Technology" Contents

http://agents.www.media.mit.edu
/groups/agents/papers/newt-
thesis/tableofcontents2_1.html

Filtering agent technology explanation.

MSNBC Toolkit: Personal News Alert

www.msnbc.com/tools/alert/
alermain.asp

MSNBC will flash an alert icon on your desktop when news breaks. Requires Windows '95 or Windows NT 4.0.

My Yahoo!

http://my.yahoo.com

News that can be personalized to the issues you care about.

MyLaunch

www.myLAUNCH.com

News and resources on music issues, all filtered based on your preferences.

Nando News Watcher

www.nando.net/nt/newswatcher

Posts current headlines on your desktop from Nando's news services.

Need to Know Information Solutions

www.needtoknow.com/what.html

Information consulting firm that develops filtering tools and solutions for business.

Net Nanny

www.netnanny.com

A kid content-filtering tool.

Net News Hound

www.TheArtMachine.com/NNH.htm

News filtering.

Netscape

www.netscape.com

Netscape has developed In-Brief Direct, a free subscription service by e-mail. It provides daily news summaries from the *New York Times*, CNN, Reuters and ABC News.

New York Times Direct

www.nytimes.com/info/contents/
services.html

Get the *Times* or specific sections delivered to you daily electronically.

New York Times on the Web, The

www.nytimes.com

The *New York Times* has a hallowed place in journalism. The web site is superb, easily searchable and top quality.

News.com Dispatch

www.news.com/Push/index.html

CNET's News.com sends an e-mail every business day with headlines.

NewsClip

www.clarinet.com/newsclip.html

Filters Usenet newsgroups.

NewsEdge NewsPage

www.newspage.com

News tool with deep resources.

Fees for Some Content

NewsHound

www.newshound.com

Searches and reports news stories found on the web.

Projects

http://ruby.ils.unc.edu/gants/
projects.htm

Information filters.

QBIC Home Page

www.qbic.almaden.ibm.com

Allows queries of large image databases based on visual image content.

Recreational Software Advisory Council on the Internet (RSACi)

www.rsac.org

Advises on web protections; offers ratings.

SafeSurf

www.safesurf.com

Filters out what you don't want, or shouldn't want.

Services

http://photo.net/philg/services
.html

Notification and other alert services.

Speak Freely for Windows

www.fourmilab.ch/speakfree/
windows

Phone capability on the Internet.

Stanford Information Filtering Tool

ftp://db.stanford.edu/pub/sift/
sift-1.1-netnews.tar.Z

Includes two services, one for tech reports and one for Usenet articles. You must download software

TipWorld

www.tipworld.com

Customized news, tips and gossip.

TotalNEWS

www.totalnews.com

Personalized filtering and searching from news-related resources.

UMBC Agent Web

www.cs.umbc.edu/agents

Information and resources about intelligent information agents.

Washington Post "Keep Me Posted" Service

www.washingtonpost.com/
wp-srv/contents/guide/howto.htm

The *Washington Post's* "Keep Me Posted," a weekly announcement of special reports.

WebWatcher Project

www.cs.cmu.edu/afs/cs.cmu.edu/
project/theo-6/web-
agent/www/project-home.html

WebWatcher is a World Wide Web filtering system developed at the Carnegie Mellon University Learning Lab which learns your preferences and highlights interesting links on web pages that you visit.

WiseWire Corporation

www.wisewire.com

A web news filtering tool, now part of Lycos family.

WorldKids Network Internet Safety Tips

www.worldkids.net/school/
safety/Internet/Internet.htm

World Kids Network's online safety tips for young minds.

ZDNet's Personal View

http://members.zdnet.com/pview/
login.cgi

ZDnet's collection of tech information resources, including email notification and other alert services.

Government Records

Bureau of Economic Analysis in the Commerce Department

www.bea.doc.gov

Statistical analysis and information from the Commerce Department's site for business & investments.

Bureau of Justice Statistics

www.ojp.usdoj.gov/bjs

Justice Department statistics collection, includes crime numbers.

Bureau of Labor Statistics

www.bls.gov

One of the top statistical collections, from the Federal government's Labor Department.

Bureau of Transportation Statistics

www.bts.gov

US Department of Transportation stats, an extensive list.

Campaigns & Elections Magazine

www.camelect.com

Nuts and bolts magazine for campaign strategy from *Congressional Quarterly*.

Fee-Based Site

Center for Public Integrity

www.publicintegrity.org

Chuck Lewis' excellent site for tracking where money and politics collide.

Center for Responsive Politics

www.crp.org

Excellent advocacy site for tracking campaign information.

CIA World Factbook

www.cia.gov/cia/publications/factbook/index.html

Reference tool for background information on countries.

CNN/Time All Politics

http://allpolitics.com/1997/index.html

CNN/CQ's combined site – best place for political news online.

Commerce Business Daily

http://cbdnet.gpo.gov

Commerce Business Daily is the government's list of all bids and contracts and announcement awards. Essential reading for anyone wanting to do business with the government. Available free from the government or for pay on many sources.

Commonly Requested Federal Services

www.whitehouse.gov/WH/Services

Central resource for federal sites.

Congressional Quarterly

www.cq.com

News magazine covering US Congress.

Congressional Quarterly's VoteWatch

http://pathfinder.com/CQ/#search

Search for congressional lawmakers voting records.

Counsel Connect

www.counsel.com/lawlinks/lawlinks.html

An excellent legal resource site, but membership is required.

CourtLink

www.courtlink.com

Federal court records plus some from NY, OR, TX, WA – includes charges as well as convictions.

Fee-Based Site

DEA Drug Data

www.usdoj.gov/dea/drugdata/stats.htm

Drug use statistics.

Defense LINK - US Department of Defense (DOD)

www.defenselink.mil

Main Pentagon site.

Defense Technical Information Center (DTIC)

www.dtic.mil

Pentagon's thorough site for technology-related military things.

Department of Education: Topics A to Z

http://ed.gov/topicsaz.html

US Education Department's links to the best starting points on a variety of educational topics.

Documents Center

www.lib.umich.edu/libhome/Documents.center/index.html

University of Michigan's superb document clearinghouse.

EDGAR Database

www.sec.gov/edgarhp.htm

A searchable database of publicly held companies, which are required by law to file information with the SEC.

EDGAR Online People

http://people.edgar-online.com/people

Allows users to search the SEC filings for information about executives by name. Indexes are free, details cost money. Information is available from the last six months of proxy statements.

Fees for Some Content

Emergency Response Notification System Data & Documentation

www.epa.gov/ERNS/docs/data.html

Environmental Protection Agency Emergency Response reports

Endangered Species Database: US Fish & Wildlife Service

www.fws.gov/r9endspp/
listdata.html

Lists of endangered species compiled by the US Government.

EPA's Toxic Release Inventory TRI Query Form

www.epa.gov/enviro/html/
tris/tris_query_java.html

Environmental Protection Agency's database of company toxic filings.

Establishment Search in Occupational Safety & Health Administration (OSHA)

www.osha.gov/cgi-bin/est/est1

Database of health inspection reports.

European Patent Office

www.european-patent-office.org

European patent and trademark information.

FAA Office of System Safety, Safety Data

http://nasdac.faa.gov/
safety_data

Federal Aviation Administration safety data site, including "Excel" and Bureau of Transportation statistics.

FDIC (Federal Deposit Insurance Corporation) Institutions

http://www2.fdic.gov/structur/
search

US government's database of banks and other institution ownership.

FECInfo

www.tray.com/FECINFO

Former Federal Election Commission staffer Tony Raymond's excellent site for researching political contributions and campaign info.

Federal Court Locator, The

www.law.vill.edu/
Fed-Ct/fedcourt.html

Federal court locator.

Federal Election Commission (FEC)

www.fec.gov

Official site to track campaign-related information.

Federal Web Locator, The

www.law.vill.edu/
Fed-Agency/fedwebloc.html

Links to thousands of government agencies and departments.

FedLaw

http://fedlaw.gsa.gov

Resource for federal legal and regulatory research. It has more than 1600 links to legal-related information and is operated by the General Services Organization.

Fedstats

www.fedstats.gov

Central clearinghouse for government statistical sites.

FedWorld

www.fedworld.gov

Collection of 14,000 government sites, including bulletin boards so you can reach government employees with expertise on many subjects.

FindLaw

www.findlaw.com

Well-organized directory of Internet legal sites.

FindLaw: Law Crawler

www.lawcrawler.com/index.html

Search engine for legal resources.

Foreign Government Resources on the Web

www.lib.umich.edu/libhome/Documents.center/frames/forfr.html

Excellent list of foreign government resources.

Free *Congressional Quarterly* Sites: American Voter

http://voter.cq.com

Search for Congressional lawmaker's voting records.

Geneva International Forum

http://geneva.intl.ch/geneva-intl/gi/egimain/edir.htm

International resources for business.

Global Computing

www.globalcomputing.com/states.html

State-by-state resources.

Global Securities Information's LIVEDGAR

www.gsionline.com

Searches across the entire EDGAR database by key words, SIC (standard industry code) or form type.
Fee-Based Site

GOVBOT - Government Search Engine

http://ciir2.cs.umass.edu/Govbot

Finding agent for government sites.

Governing Magazine

www.governing.com

Congressional Quarterly's magazine for state and local political campaign information.
Fee-Based Site

Government Information Sharing Project

http://govinfo.kerr.orst.edu

Oregon State's resource for regional government information.

Governments on the WWWW

www.gksoft.com/govt

A great collection of international and local government related servers.

Healthfinder

www.healthfinder.org

Great starting point for health resources.

IBM Intellectual Property Network

http://patent.womplex.ibm.com

Searches US Patent and Trademark files.

IGnet: Internet for Federal IG Community

www.ignet.gov

Collection of reports and information from the Inspector General of as many as 60 federal agency departments.

International Agencies & Information on the Web

www.lib.umich.edu/libhome/Docum
ents.Center/frames/intlfr.html

International and inter-governmental web sites lists.

International Documents Task Force (IDTF)

www.library.nwu.edu/govpub/
idtf/home.html

Documents from international organizations and governents, with links.

Internet Law Library

http://law.house.gov

Congressional resources for lawyers.

Inter-Parliamentary Union

www.ipu.org

Links to parliamentary web sites around the world – elections information.

Law Library of Congress

http://lcweb2.loc.gov/glin/
lawhome.html

Law library of the Library of Congress.

Legal Information Institute

www.law.cornell.edu

One of the best legal libraries online. (Cornell's law school page).

LEGI-SLATE

http://legiweb.legislate.com

A subsidiary of the *Washington Post*, it is an online news service geared to federal government issues.

Fee-Based Site

Library of Congress

www.loc.gov

The main site for the Library of Congress.

Meta-Index for US Legal Research

http://gsulaw.gsu.edu/metaindex

Central clearinghouse for circuit court opinions.

Monthly Estimates of the US Population

www.census.gov/population/
estimates/nation/intfile1-1.txt

Downloadable text files of population estimate information.

NASIRE: National Association of State Information Resource Executivies (NASIRE)

www.nasire.org

State-specific information on state government innovations.

National Archives & Records Administration

www.nara.gov

Presidential libraries of all past American presidents.

National Atlas of the United States of America

www-atlas.usgs.gov

Official maps.

National Center for Health Statistics

www.cdc.gov/nchswww

Center for Disease Control statistics collection.

National Council of State Legislators

www.ncsl.org/public/sitesleg.htm

Search for state legislation.

National Journal's Cloakroom

www.cloakroom.com

Extensive coverage of congress and politics.

Fee-Based Site

National Science Foundation

www.nsf.gov

This site is focused mainly on the bureaucratic structure of this government agency; but on the interior pages you'll find a wealth of scientific information. Recommended visit: the external links page to National Science Foundation-funded sites – here you'll find the research, supercomputing, and engineering centers that do the work.

National Technical Information Service (NTIS)

www.ntis.gov

Federal government reports related to technology and science.

NTSB (National Traffic Safety Board) Aviation Accident/Incident Database

http://nasdac.faa.gov/asp/asy_ntsb.asp

Transportation Safety Board's database of aircraft accidents.

NYU EDGAR Development Site

http://edgar.stern.nyu.edu

SEC filings found on EDGAR are also found here, but it allows you to search with some added features like by Zacks Industry Code, which is not available on the SEC site.

Oyez Oyez Oyez

http://oyez.nwu.edu/

Information about Supreme Court cases, including some actual proceedings in Real Audio format.

PACER - Directory of Electronic Public Access Services

www.uscourts.gov/PubAccess.html

Federal court's electronic bulletin board of docket numbers, case summaries and opinions.

Regions & Countries Information

www.ita.doc.gov/ita_home/itacnreg.html

US Dept. of Commerce International Trade Administration's country and regional resource site, good for trade-related issues.

Right Site, The

www.easidemographics.com

This site takes Census data and repackages it into regional information and is a great resource for numbers and info about communities.

Social Law Library

www.socialaw.com

A great legal research site including international law sites.

State & Local Government on the 'Net

www.piperinfo.com/state/states.html

State government resources as well as local ones.

State Court Locator, The

www.law.vill.edu/State-Ct

State court locator.

State Poverty Rates

www.census.gov/hhes/poverty/poverty96/pv96state.html

HTML tables of US Census information.

State Web Locator, The

www.law.vill.edu/State-Agency/index.html

State web locator.

StateLaw: State & Local Government - Executive, Legislative & Judicial Information

http://lawlib.wuacc.edu/washlaw/uslaw/statelaw.html

State Internet resoruces, legislation, courts, statutes, etc.

Stateline.Org

www.stateline.org

The Pew Center on the States, tracking policy developments on a state-by-state basis.

StateSearch - Sponsored by NASIRE

www.nasire.org/ss

The state government search site.

Statistical Abstract of the US

www.census.gov:80/stat_abstract.

US Government's statistical resource.

STAT-USA

www.stat-usa.gov

Comprehensive collection of federal statistics from all agencies.

Fee-Based Site

Superintendant of Documents Home Page (Government Printing Office)

www.access.gpo.gov/su_docs/index.html

The Government Printing Office.

System for Electronic Document Analysis & Retrieval (SEDAR)

www.sedar.com

Searches Canada's electronic securities documentation filing system. Also in French.

TaxWeb

www.taxweb.com

Consumer-oriented directory for federal and state information.

Thomas - US Congress on the Internet

http://thomas.loc.gov

Search for federal legislation.

United Nations System

www.unsystem.org

Foreign government resources.

US Census Bureau

www.census.gov

Clearinghouse for statistics, includes the current edition of the Statistical Abstracts, a great reference book. Search by city, state, ZIP Code or specific industries.

US Federal Government Agencies Directory

www.lib.lsu.edu/gov/fedgov.html

Links to hundreds of federal government Internet sites.

US Government Information

www-libraries.colorado.edu/ps/gov/us/federal.htm

A clearinghouse of government sites

US Postal Service ZIP Code Lookup

www.usps.gov/ncsc

US Postal Services's ZIP Code lookup service.

US Securities & Exchange Commission (SEC)

www.sec.gov

One of the top government sites, let's you track information about publicly held companies.

US State Department: Regions

www.state.gov/www/regions.html

Information and news from around the world.

USADATA

www.usadata.com/usadata/market

Market data by community and region.

USGS National Mapping Information

http://mapping.usgs.gov

The federal government's site with global land information, online data, and map ordering.

VitalChek - State Map

www.vitalchek.com/states.asp

Vital records by state.

Fee-Based Site

Web sites on National Parliaments

www.soc.umn.edu/~sssmith/
Parliaments.html

Resource of foreign government sites.

Welcome To The White House

www.whitehouse.gov

The White House's site.

White House - Economic Statistics Briefing Room

WWW.whitehouse.gov/fsbr/
esbr.html

White House's statistical clearinghouse.

White House: The Economic Statistics Briefing Room

www.whitehouse.gov/fsbr/
esbr.html

Clearinghouses of statistical resources hosted by the White House.

WWW Virtual Library: Law: State Government

www.law.indiana.edu/
law/v-lib/states.html

A collection of state government resources.

Yahoo! Government: Countries

www.yahoo.com/Government/
Countries

A collection of foreign government resources reports and information from the Inspector General of as many as 60 federal agency departments.

Yahoo! Government: US Government: US States

www.yahoo.com/Government/
U_S_Government/State_Government

A collection of US government resources.

Miscellaneous

Bartlett's Familiar Quotations
www.cc.columbia.edu/acis/
bartleby

Ready reference listing. Pre-twentieth century quotations.

Best Information on the 'Net - Statistical Sources & Calculation Tools
www.sau.edu/cwis/internet/wild/
refdesk/stats/staindex.htm

Directory of statistical sources.

Federal Reserve Banks (FBR) Maps with Links
www.bog.frb.fed.us/otherfrb.htm

Lists sites and information on banks in the FRB system.

FindLaw Supreme Court Decisions
www.findlaw.com/casecode/
supreme.html

Search for a specific high court decisions.

Internet FAQ Consortium
www.faqs.org

All about frequently asked questions (FAQ).

Internet Gurus Central
http://net.gurus.com

Introduction to the internet. From authors of *The Internet for Dummies.*

Internet Public Library: Ready Reference Collection
http://ipl.si.umich.edu/ref/RR

Ready reference listing. Categories include Almanacs, Biographies, Census Data & Demographics, Dictionaries, Encyclopedias, Genealogy, Geography, News, Quotations and Telephone numbers.

ProDomains.Com
www.agriculture.org

Public forum.

Quotations Listserver
http://pubweb.ucdavis.edu/Docum
ents/Quotations/homepage.html

Ready reference listing. Quotations.

Ready Reference Using the Internet
http://k12.oit.umass.edu/
rref.html

Ready referrence listing. These files are alphabetical by subject -like a vertical file of pamphlets, and organized by reference librarians at the Winsor School in Boston.

Virtual Reference Desk, The
http://thorplus.lib.
purdue.edu/reference/index.html

Ready referrence listing. Pulled together by Purdue University, well-organized, well-researched.

Yahoo! Reference: Quotations

www.yahoo.com/reference/
quotations

Ready reference listing. Quotations.

News

7@m International News Wires

www.7am.com/worldwires

Posts updated headlines from Nando Times, CNN, Fox News, Reuters/Yahoo, and AP.

A Journalist's Guide to the Internet.

http://reporter.umd.edu

Excellent starting point for journalists, the site is maintained by Chris Callahan, assistant dean at the University of Maryland College of Journalism and author of a book of the same title.

ABC NEWS.com

www.abcnews.com

Cutting edge web site, rich with content including allowing you to search for news and video clips from the multi-media archives.

Advertising Age Magazine

www.adage.com

Advertising Age magazine online services and archives.

Fees for Some Content

AJR/NewsLink

www.newslink.org

Compilation site for thousands of newspapers, magazines and TV and Radio stations, pulled together by Newslink. Perhaps the most thorough collection of journalism sites online

Alpha Complete News Index from Select Ware

www.select-ware.com/news

Excellent source of news publications, pimarily those from outside the US

Artigen Newswire: Information Technology

www.artigen.com/newswire/infotech.html

Info-tech filtering tool for tech news

Barbara's News Researcher's Page.

www.gate.net/~barbara/index.html

Barbara Gellis Shapiro's collection of internet resources.

BiblioData's Full-Text Sources Online (FTSO)

www.bibliodata.com

Offers lists of full-text newspapers or magazines online; however, a subscription is required to access site details.

Fee-Based Site

Canada Newswire

www.newswire.ca

Canadian news resources.

CANOE

www.canoe.com

Canadian wire services.

Casper Wyoming Tribune

www.trib.com

Casper Wyoming Tribune newspaper – also offers the top 20 stories of the day from the lead wire subject areas, like foreign, general, finance, politics, etc.

CBS News

www.cbs.com

Site asks you to type in your ZIP Code, and then it provides local news for you everytime you go to the main page.

Chicago Tribune

www.chicago.tribune.com

They often offer web specials, which include video clips, sound clips and photographs. The newspaper also offers an archive back to 1985 with full-text archives available at inexpensive price.

Fees for Some Content

Christian Science Monitor

www.csmonitor.com

One of the few national newspapers with a free full-text archive going back decades.

CJR Journalism Resources

www.cjr.org/html/resources.html

Columbia Journalism Review Magazine has compiled a page of good links , valuable resource guides and source lists on subjects like covering mental health issues, crime, tobacco and AIDS.

CNN Interactive

www.cnn.com

Offers recent stories, as well as easy-to-download video clips. You can also set up a personalized page for things you care about.

CNN QuickNews

www.cnn.com/QUICKNEWS/mail

A morning e-mail from CNN Interactive. CNN also has a personalized news tool now that caters to your selections when you visit their pages.

Columbia Missourian Newsroom Web Resources

www.missouri.edu/~jschool/missourian

Collection of journalism links compiled by *Missourian* editor Stan Ketterer.

C-SPAN

www.cspan.org

C-SPAN is unvarnished coverage of Congress. The web site has news, video and sound clips and is terrific.

CyberSkeptic's Guide to Internet Research

www.bibliodata.com/skeptic/skepdata.html

Ruth Orenstein's newsletter, *CyberSkeptic*, which is geared to professional researchers of all stripes.

Fee-Based Site

DeadlineOnline

www.deadlineonline.com

Author's own webpages with extensive resource links.

Drew Sullivan's Homepage

www.reporter.org/~drew

Excellent resource of databases on the Web.

Editor & Publisher

www.mediainfo.com

Links to most of the newspapers, television, radio stations and magazines online. From *Editor & Publisher* magazine

E-Journal

www.edoc.com/ejournal

Academic-oriented list of magazines, journals, etc.

Electronic Library

www.elibrary.com

Great collection of more than a million newspaper articles, and hundreds of thousands of magazine articles and book chapters. It also includes TV and Radio Transcripts. Free for 30 days.

Fees for Some Content

ESPN.com

http://ESPN.SportsZone.com

One-stop shopping for sports of all kinds.

Essential Links

www.el.com

A collection of news links.

European Journalism Page

www.demon.co.uk/eurojournalism

Resources of interest to journalists covering Europe.

E-Zine list

www.meer.net/~johnl/e-zine-list

Collection of E-Zines from John Labovitz.

FACSNET

www.facsnet.org

This site, funded by the Foundation for American Communications, has a tremendous set of resources including a top-notch experts list and background material on a wide range of public policy issues.

Guide to Electronic & Print Resources

www.cio.com/central/journalism.html

Good list of tools for writers compiled by Anne Stuart, editor of *CIO Magazine*.

InfoBeat

www.infobeat.com

This service allows you to select customized news summaries and headline reports.

Integrated NewsWire

www.artigen.com/newswire/index.html

Lists current headlines from various sources in these categories: Information Technology, World, Far East, Mideast, SciTech, Health, Biz, Music, Humor and Cool Sites.

Internet Archive, The

www.archive.org

A kind of digital warehouse that has been trolling the Web and hoarding everything if finds, including texts, sounds and images. It stores results on its virtual shelves and preserves long-expired sites. May well have useful pages no longer available.

Internet Hourly News - ABC

www.realaudio.com/contentp/abc.html

Plays audio feeds from ABC News live on your computer.

Internet Newsroom

www.editors-service.com

Internet Newsroom's Tim Maloy's list of reference tools.

Fee-Based Site

Internet Resources for Journalism

www.moorhead.msus.edu/ ~gunarat/ijr

Mississippi State Journalism professor Shelton Gunaratne's list of resources and tools for journalism researchers.

Izvestia

www.online.ru/mlists/izvestia/ izvestia-izvestia

Russia's Izvestia news service.

JournalismNet

www.journalismnet.com

Julian Sher's excellent site, geared to investigative reporters, with special sites for Canadian journalists.

Journalistic Resources Page

www.it-kompetens.com/journ.html

Excellent site for European publications.

Kiosk

www.online-journalist.com/ resources2.html

Good collection of web-published zines, somewhat out of date, however.

Los Angeles Times

www.latimes.com

Has a fee-based archive, but that day's paper is full-text and free.

Fees for Some Content

Magazine CyberCenter

www.magamall.com

This Canadian-based site is a very good place to locate magazines online, but you will have to buy subscriptions.

Fee-Based Site

Mario's Cybserspace Station

http://mprofaca.cro.net

A very deep site of primarily European news resources, but has considerably more than that.

MediaFinder

www.mediafinder.com/index.cfm

A centralized site of magazine subscriptions.

Megasources

www.ryerson.ca/journal/ megasources.html

Online resources compiled by Ryerson Polytech professor Dean Tudor. It is especially good on Canadian resources but still valuable for anyone.

Mercury Center

www.mercurycenter.com

Journalism resource.

Mercury Center: Passport

www.sjmercury.com

One of the top news resources online – especially silicon valley coverage.

MSNBC News

www.nbcnews.com

A news site that has ties to all its local affiliates, enabling you to get regional news as well.

MSNBC Toolkit: Personal News Alert

www.msnbc.com/tools/alert/
alermain.asp

MSNBC will flash an alert icon on your desktop when news breaks. Requires Windows '95 or Windows NT 4.0.

My Yahoo!

http://my.yahoo.com

News that can be personalized to the issues you care about.

Nando News Watcher

www.nando.net/nt/newswatcher

Posts current headlines on your desktop from Nando's news services.

Nando Times

www.nando.net/nt/nando.cgi

Published by the Raleigh News and Observer contains that newspaper and a collection of wires including AP, Reuters and NY Times News Service.

Navigator

www.nytimes.com/library/cyber/
reference/cynavi.html

Rich Meislin maintains this reference home page for reporters at the *New York Times*. Good for anyone, though.

Net Journal Directory

www.nasw.org/users/larryk/
njdn.htm

Will tell you if the full-text of a newspaper or magazine is online. Plan is to have site online. Now just shows that the book is available.

Fee-Based Site

New York Times Direct

www.nytimes.com/info/contents/
services.html

Get the *Times* or specific sections delivered to you daily electronically.

New York Times on the Web

www.nytimes.com

The *New York Times* has a hallowed place in journalism. The web site is superb, easily searchable and top quality.

New York Times: Books

www.nytimes.com/books/home

New York Times' book review.

News Hour

www.pbs.org/newshour

Transcripts of past and current *News Hour* programs available.

News Hunt

www.newshunt.com

Collection of free archives of newspapers.

News Index

www.newsindex.com

Combines a compilation of news headlines and a search capability.

News Resources

http://pw2.netcom.com/~ktvu/resources.html

Collection of sites by Bob Hirschfeld of KTVU in California.

News.com Dispatch

www.news.com/Push/index.html

CNET's News.com sends an e-mail every business day with headlines.

NewsBank, Inc.

www.newsbank.com

A news tool, geared toward schools and academics.

NewsBot

www.newsbot.com

Updates headlines in your areas of interest. From *Wired* Magazine. Also provides special software that will allow you to regularly repeat searches.

NewsCenter

http://qwis2.circ.qwu.edu/~gprice/newscenter.htm

Up to the minute news resources.

NewsDirectory.Com

www.ecola.com

Covers newspapers, magazines and TV stations – extensive magazine collection of links.

NewsEdge NewsPage

www.newspage.com

News tool with deep resources.

Fees for Some Content

Newshub

www.newshub.com

Updated every fifteen minutes with headlines in these areas: Technical, Financial, World, US, Science, Health and Entertainment.

NewsLibrary

www.newslibrary.com

Access to a good collection of full-text newspapers including many from Knight Ridder and Gannett.

Fee-Based Site

NewsLinx Headlines

www.newslinx.com

Offers a daily compilation of headlines, with links to articles, mostly on Internet and computer-related subjects.

NewspaperLinks

www.newspaperlinks.com

The Newspaper Association of America's site has links to many newspapers and newspaper industry news.

Newspapers Online!

www.well.com/user/mmcadams/online.newspapers.html

Mindy McAdams page about news online. Good historical page

Newspapers Online!

www.newspapers.com

Megasite developing links to newspaper sites inside and outside the US.

NewsPlace for News & Sources

www.niu.edu/newsplace

Professor Avi Bass from Northern Illinois University maintains this collection of news research tools and sources. It is especially strong if you are looking for political resources.

NewsTrawler

www.newstrawler.com

An excellent news tool, geared to international news.

NPR Online - National Public Radio

www.npr.org

National Public Radio's site, sound files and reports available.

Power Reporting Resources for Journalists

http://home.att.net/~bdedman

Collection of web tools, by Bill Dedman, now working for the *New York Times* in the Chicago bureau.

Poynter Institute's Hot News/Hot Research

www.poynter.org/research/reshotres.htm

Compiles valuable web resources on current and news topics.

reporter.org

http://reporter.org

One of several sites maintained by Investigative Reporters and Editors and the National Institute of Computer Assisted Reporting.

Reporter's Desktop

www.seanet.com/~duff

Excellent starting point to get quickly to valuable news resources. From *Seattle Times'* Duff Wilson

Reuters News

www.yahoo.com/text/headlines/newsw/summary.html

Key headlines and the top stories from Reuters.

SCOOP Cybersleuth's Guide

http://scoop.evansville.net

Collection of journalism resources by James Derk, computer whiz of the *Evansville Courier-Journal.*

SLA News Division.

http://sunsite.unc.edu/slanews

The Special Libraries Association News Division is an international organization for news librarians and researchers.

Society of Professional Journalists

www.spj.org/index.htm

One of journalism's advocacy groups, it does have some helpful links.

Sources & Experts

http://metalab.unc.edu/slanews/internet/experts.html

Collection of experts lists, compiled by *St. Petersburg Times* news researcher Kitty Bennett and posted on the Special Libraries News Division web site.

Special Libraries Association's News Division

http://sunsite.unc.edu/slanews/
internet/archives.html

Premier collection of news archives on the Internet. Pulled together by librarians and organized well.

Speech & Transcript Center

http://gwis2.circ.gwu.edu/
~gprice/speech.htm

Speech and transcript clearinghouse.

The Onion

www.theonion.com

Excellent satire of news, just in case you need a laugh.

The WIRE - Breaking News from the Associated Press

http://wire.ap.org

Access to the regional AP wires and also the national wires.

Time-Warner's Pathfinder!

www.pathfinder.com

Offers a large portion of the material it puts out in print.

TotalNEWS

www.totalnews.com

Personalized filtering and searching from news-related resources.

TRIBweb, the *Tacoma News Tribune*

www.tribnet.com

Tacoma News Tribune and access to wires.

Ultimate Collection of News Links

http://pppp.net/links/news

International collection of links to newspapers around the world, grouped by region.

US News Online

www.usnews.com

Offers its contents online and has several other non-print sections, like a college and careers section, an email newsletter and discussion forums.

USA CityLink Home Page

www.usacitylink.com

Collection of links ito regional cities with travel, tourism and relocation information.

USA Today

www.usatoday.com

Loaded with all of the newspapers' contents and much more developed just for the web site. It's interactive with chat groups and shopping deals.

Washington Post

www.washingtonpost.com

Offers that day's newspaper, plus two weeks back issues of the paper and the entire AP national wire.

Washington Post "Keep Me Posted" Service

www.washingtonpost.com/wp-
srv/contents/guide/howto.htm

Washington Post's "Keep Me Posted," a weekly announcement of special reports.

Weather Channel

www.weather.com

Storms, hurricanes and earthquakes details as well as allows you to program it to give you your local weather whenever you log on.

WebWatcher Project

www.cs.cmu.edu/afs/cs.cmu.edu/ project/theo-6/web- agent/www/project-home.html

WebWatcher is a World Wide Web filtering system developed at the Carnegie Mellon University Learning Lab learns your preferences and highlights interesting links on web pages you visit.

WWW Virtual Library: Journalism

www.cais.com/makulow/vlj.html

Formerly known as the Awesome list, organized by John Makulowich.

People Finders

Acxiom DataQuick

www.dataquick.com

Commercial service indexing real estate & assessor information.

Ancestry.com

www.ancestry.com

Geneology company; offers SSN's death index free.

Fees for Some Content

Black Book Online

www.crimetime.come/online.html

Robert Scott's excellent site geared to investigators includes links to sites for reverse directories and other phone books, state and federal records online, non-profit sites, verdict and settlement sites, and some pay databases.

BRB Publications

www.brbpub.com

Public records research resources and retrievers.

California Sex Offenders

www.sexoffenders.net

Site that tracks sex offenders who have been released into communities.

CompData

www.compdatagovtedi.com

EDEX data about Workers' Compensation claims.

Church Family History Library

www.lds.org/en/2-
Family_History/
Family_History_Main.html

Good starting place for genealogical research. Find search strategies, forms, and directions to access LDS's reasonably priced Family Searcher and Personal Ancestral File databases, available from the Church or its local Family History Centers..

Deep Data Investigative Sources

www.deepdata.com

Public Record Search Center.

Fee-Based Site

Government Records.com

www.governmentrecords.com

Aristotle Industries' new web site with extensive voter records and other public records-oriented databases for sale.

Harris County Appraisal District

www.hcad.org

Example of property records on the Web.

Information & Privacy, The Office of

www.usdoj.gov.oip

Various filtering agents and bots.

International Association of Assessing Officers (IAAO)

www.iaao.org

Education and trade arm for tax assessors worldwide; also, web site links.

IQ DATA Systems

www.iqdata.com

Commercial service indexing real estate & assessor information.

KnowX.com

www.knowx.com

Real estate assessor and recorder information.

Montgomery Central Appraisal District

www.mcad-tx.org

Example of property records on the Web.

New York State Education Dept. Online License Verification

www.nysed.gov/dpls.opnme.html

Online database of NY's professional license lists.

Online Athens: Police Blotter

www.onlineathens.com/
blotter.html

Athens (GA) Daily News police blotter.

Public Interest Research Groups (PIRG)

www.pirg.org/reports/consumer

Consumer protection information, environmental concerns, dangerous toys, tobacco, etc.

Public Interest Research Groups Credit Bureaus

www.pirg.org/reports/consumer/
credti

PIRG carries issues about credit bureaus.

Public Record Retriever Network

www.brbpub.com/prrn

Record retrieval companies and public record news.

Superior Information Services LLC

www.superiorinfo.com

Mid-Atlantic states regional provider of public records data .

US Bankruptcy Court for the Western District of North Carolina

www.ncbankruptcy.org

North Carolina bankruptcy court.

Utah Dept. of Commerce Div. of Occupational & Professional Licensing

www.commerce.state.ut.us/web/
commerce/dopl/dopl1/htm

Online database of Utah's professional license listings.

Vital Records Information, United States

http://vitalrec.com/index.html

Vital records for the United States.

VitalChek

www.vitalchek.com

A site that allows you to get copies of actual vital records.

West Deptford, NJ, Police Blotter Report

www.westdeptford.com/
blotter.htm

West Deptford, NJ, Police Blotter Report.

Privacy

Anonymizer

www.anonymizer.com

Tool for anonymous remailing.

Fees for Some Content

CDT | Internet Family Empowerment White Paper

www.cdt.org/speech/empower.html

A white paper on Internet Parental Empowerment Tools by the Center for Democracy and Technology.

Center for Democracy & Technology

www.cdt.org

Center for Democracy and Technology's excellent privacy site, which allows you to find out what people know about you when you visit their site.

CyberAngels.org Home Page

www.cyberangels.org

Safety and educational programing.

Electronic Privacy Information Center

www.epic.org

Privacy activist group.

HNC Software Inc.

www.hncs.com

Check fraud detection system software and other products.

Fee-Based Site

Junkbusters

www.junkbusters.com/ht/en/cookies.html

Explanation of cookie technology and privacy ramifications.

KidsCom: Play Smart, Stay Safe & Have Fun!

www.kidscom.com

Children's resources and entertainment.

National Fraud Information Center (NFIC)

www.fraud.org

Fights telemarketing fraud.

Pretty Good Privacy (PGP)

www.pgp.com/products/pgpfreeware.cgi

An encryption tool to protect your privacy.

Privacy Rights Clearinghouse

www.privacyrights.org

An activist site with excellent backgrounders on privacy issues.

Privacy Times

www.privacytimes.com

Privacy newsletter.

Fee-Based Site

Project OPEN/Protecting Your Privacy When You Go Online

www.isa.net/project-open/
priv-broch.html

Privacy protection on the Internet.

QSpace Inc

www.qspace.com

An Oakland, CA company, allows you to fill out a form and within minutes you get your credit file on screen.

Fee-Based Site

Robert Brooks' Cookie Taste Test

www.geocities.com/SoHo/
4535/cookie.html

Expanation of "cookies."

The Lucent Personalized Web Assistant: Proxy Home Page

http://lpwa.com:8000

Let's you surf anonymously, protecting your privacy while you are on the Web.

Welcome to Engage Technologies | Accipiter

www.engagetech.com

A sophisticated marketing technology used by advertisers.

Public Records

Acxiom DataQuick

www.dataquick.com

Commercial service indexing real estate & assessor information.

Fee-Based Site

Ancestry.com

www.ancestry.com

Geneology company; offers SSN's death index free.

BRB Publications

www.brbpub.com

Public records research resources and retrievers.

California Sex Offenders

www.sexoffenders.net

Site that tracks sex offenders who have been released into communities.

CompData

www.compdatagovtedi.com

EDEX information about Workers' Compensation claims.

Fee-Based Site

Deep Data Investigative Sources

www.deepdata.com

Public Record Search Center.

Government Records.com

www.governmentrecords.com

Aristotle Industries' new website with extensive voter records and other public records-oriented databases for sale.

Harris County Appraisal District

www.hcad.org

Example of property records on the Web.

Information & Privacy, The Office of

www.usdoj.gov.oip

various filtering agents and bots.

International Association of Assessing Officers (IAAO)

www.iaao.org

Education and trade arm for tax assessors worldwide; also, web site links.

IQ DATA Systems

www.iqdata.com

Commercial service indexing real estate & assessor information.

Fee-Based Site

KnowX.com

www.knowx.com

Real estate assessor and recorder information.

Fee-Based Site

Montgomery Central Appraisal District

www.mcad-tx.org

Example of property records on the Web.

New York State Education Dept. Online License Verification

www.nysed.gov/dpls.opnme.html

Online database of New Yorks's professional license listings.

Online Athens: Police Blotter

www.onlineathens.com/blotter.html

Athens (GA) Daily News police blotter.

Public Interest Research Groups (PIRG)

www.pirg.org/reports/consumer

Consumer protection information, environmental concerns, dangerous toys, tobacco, etc.

Public Interest Research Groups (PIRG) Credit Bureaus

www.pirg.org/reports/consumer/credti

PIRG carries issues about credit bureaus.

Public Record Retriever Network

www.brbpub.com/prrn

Record retrieval companies and public record news updates.

Superior Information Services LLC

www.superiorinfo.com

Mid-atlantic states regional provider of public records data .

Tracers

www.tracersinfo.com

They offer access to county, state and federal public records information.

Fee-Based Site

US Bankruptcy Court for the Western District of North Carolina

www.ncbankruptcy.org

North Carolina bankruptcy court.

Utah Dept. of Commerce Div. of Occupational & Professional Licensing

www.commerce.state.ut.us/web/commerce/dopl/dopl1/htm

Online database of Utah's professional license listings.

Vital Records Information, United States

http://vitalrec.com/index.html

Vital records for the United States.

VitalChek

www.vitalchek.com

A site that allows you to get copies of actual vital records.

Fee-Based Site

West Deptford, NJ, Police Blotter Report

www.westdeptford.com/blotter.htm

West Deptford, NJ, Police Blotter Report.

Saving & Downloading

Adobe Systems Inc: Acrobat Reader

www.adobe.com/prodindex/
acrobat/readstep.html

Adobe's Acrobat Reader is freeware; it's becoming predominant.

CNET Software Library

www.cnet.com

Software source for downloadable programs.
Fees for Some Content

Copyright Clearance Center Online

www.copyright.com

A site that explains rules of copyrights.
Fee-Based Site

ESC Marketing Group

www.gotubs.com/alice.html

Free downloadable children's stories coupled on a commercial site.

FilePile

www.filepile.com

Files of software for downloading.
Fees for Some Content

Finding Data on the Internet: A Journalist's Guide

www.nilesonline.com/data/
index.shtml

Reporters' guide to finding stats and sources of data.

Jasc's Paintshop Pro

www.jasc.com

Allows you to control what part of a screen you want to capture.

Jumbo! Download Network

www.jumbo.com

Source for downloading software.

SHAREWARE.COM

www.shareware.com

Source for downloading shareware software. Try now, pay later.
Fees for Some Content

ZDNet Software Library

www.hotfiles.com

Library of software programs, many can be doawloaded.
Fees for Some Content

Search Engines

All-in-One Search Page

www.albany.net/allinone

Allows you to stay on their search page and conduct your search using various search engines.

AlphaSearch: Gateway to the "Academic" Web

www.calvin.edu/library/as

Gateway to the Academic Web links to internet "gateway" sites, all relevant sites related to a discipline, subject, or idea; instant access to hundreds of sites by entering just one gateway site.

AltaVista

www.altavista.com

One of the lbest search engines on the net. Easy to use.

Beaucoup!

www.beaucoup.com

perhaps the best collection of other search engines. Sort of a directory of search tools.

CIT Information Resource Guides

www.unc.edu/cit/guides/
subjects.html

Excellent guide to finding information on the Internet, particularly on education and technology.

Copernic

www.copernic.com

Excellent tool for searching simultaneous searching of multiple engines.

Fee-Based Site

Cyber 411

www.cyber411.com

Sixteen search engines, advanced queries, yellow pages, maps, directories, white pages and e-mail.

Disney's Internet Guide (DIG)

www.disney.com/dig/today

Disney's Internet Guide is a subject directory that has numerous categories to search.

Dogpile

www.dogpile.com

The most complex, but easily the most thorough of all the meta-tools. It allows you to run your query in as many as 25 search engines at once. For some reason, however, it does not include Northern Light. It's customized features allows you to pick which engines and directories you want to look in.

Excite

www.excite.com

A strong search engine – this also has some good evaluative channels when you know what you are looking for.

FACSNET: Sources Online

www.facsnet.org/sources_online/
main.htm

Maintained by the Foundation for American Communications, a journalism group, tool for finding experts on a variety of subjects quickly.

Free Internet Encyclopedia

http://clever.net/cam/
encyclopedia.html

Solid subject directory, categorized into macro and micro topic areas.

GO Network

www.go.com

New search tool by Infoseek and Disney folks – will also include material from Starwave properties including ESPN and ABC News. Not expected to be functioning until spring 1999.

Google!

www.google.com

The latest new search engine developed at Stanford (Yahoo!, Excite) is pushing to be the most accurate of the engines. It is so bold it dares you to go to its number one result, and does a pretty good job at it. Watch for this star to rise.

Greg Notess'

www.imt.net/~notess

Shows how search engines rank pages.

HotBot

www.hotbot.com

HotBot is one of the more complex search engines, but that's because it offers you so many options to focus your search. It lets you do several kinds of specific research at the very beginning of your search, like narrowing for photos or images.

Inference Find

www.infind.com

One of the easiest search tools to use, it goes out to half a dozen of the search engines, submits your request and brings back the results, removing the duplicates – something all search tools should do – and groups the items from the site they came from.

Infoseek

www.infoseek.com

Both a search directory and a search engine.

Internet EZ

www.ezin.net/search

New meta-tool search engine, searches several engines simultaneously. This is free version. A more extensive pay version also exists.

Internet Sleuth - Quick Reference Chart to Search Operators

www.isleuth.com/hts-chart.html

This meta-tool allows you to combine different variations of search tools. Use the quick reference chart information to find sites quickly.

Internet Sleuth, The

www.isleuth

The Internet Sleuth, or iSleuth, is a meta-tool that runs as many as six other search tools at once. It also allows Top, Reviewed, New, and Best of Web searches.

Lycos

www.lycos.com

A search engine, a subject directory and an evaluative site all rolled into one.

Mamma: Mother of All Search Engines

www.mamma.com

Searches up to 7 search engines at once. However, the results do not identify which engine they came from. Includes a directory of annotated and rated "Top 1 %" sites.

Manning & Napier's Information Services

www.mnis.com

Home of Dr. Link, Dr. Elizabeth Liddy's Natural Language Search Engine.

Fee-Based Site

Mansfield University Library Home Page

www.mnsfld.edu/~library

Cornell University's guide to sources on the Internet, arranged by librarians with access to good list of federal government sites.

MetaCrawler

www.metacrawler.com

A meta-search tool – it allows you to search multiple Internet directories simultaneously.

MSN Web Search

http://search.msn.com

Microsoft's entry into the search engine world. This was too new to evaluate as of this writing. But with corporate backing, it should be worth watching.

Netsurfer Digest

www.netsurf.com/nsd

Netsurfer reviews web sites and evaluates them. Subscribe and get electronic newsletter or browse the URL.

Northern Light

www.northernlight.com

A rising star search engine. Northern Light is organized by librarians and it shows.

Fees for Some Content

Open Directory Project

www.newhoo.com

Web subject directory with extensive list of volunteer experts on particular topics.

Principles of Web Searching

http://mann77.mannlib.cornell.edu/reference/workshops/WebSearching/index.html

An excellent resource on explaining nuances of search tools and how they work.

ProFusion

www.profusion.com

While this meta-tool works with most of the major search engines, the unique feature is the ability to automatically update subjects you are interested in.

Fees for Some Content

Reference.Com

www.reference.com

Search newsgroups and mailing lists.

SavvySearch

www.savvysearch.com/search

This meta-search tool is particularly good for looking up international sites, allowing searches in many languages. You can limit your search to people finders, reference tools and images. You can also vary the way the results are presented, getting one continuous list or separate lists, by different search engines. Leaving the integrate results box unchecked allows you to see which search engine is helping most.

Search Engine Showdown

http://imt.net/~notess/search

A comparison site of search tools.

Search Engine Watch

http://searchenginewatch.com

Extensive news about search tools from expert Danny Sullivan.

Fees for Some Content

Search Engine Watch's Search Engine Features Chart

http://searchenginewatch.com/
webmasters/features.html

Shows how search engines rank pages – one of the best sites for details on search engines and how they work.

SEARCH.COM

www.search.com

Good for finding specialized search engines, more than 400 that find all kinds of information.

Searchopolis

www.searchopolis.com

Filtered search engine geared to kids with content restrictions, from N2H2, a Seattle-based company that's other product, Bess, is used in schools all over the country to filter sites for kids.

searchUK

www.searchuk.com

British-based search engine.

Tradeways Galaxy

www.einet.net

A subject-oriented site. It's deep, but spotty organization.

webtaxi.com

www.webtaxi.com

Quick access to several major search tools and specialized directories.

Yahoo! - Search Engines

www.yahoo.com/Computers_and_Int
ernet/Internet/World_Wide_Web/S
earching_the_Web/Search_Engines

A comprehensive list of search engines.

Yahoo! Local Events

http://localevents.yahoo.com

List of local events, searchable by subject or region.

Specialized Tools

1001 Sites.com - The Arab Internet Directory

www.1001sites.com

Arab World Online's site is more than a searchable index to information on the Arab world. It is one of many specialized directories available by region of the world.

555-1212.com

www.555-1212.com

Phone books online. Better than many others because you can search several of the other web telephone services from this site.

A Web of Online Dictionaries

www.facstaff.bucknell.edu/rbeard/diction.html

Searchable versions of a comprehensive set of English and multilingual dictionaries

AcqWeb's Directory of Book Reviews on the Web

www.library.vanderbilt.edu/law/acqs/bookrev.html

Part of the AcqWeb site, maintained by librarians, has great resources for book review sites on the Web.

Acronym Dictionary

www.vs.afrl.af.mil/dictionary.html

An acronym dictionary.

AlphaSearch

www.calvin.edu/Lib_Resources/as

A directory of subject directories to Internet resources considered suitable for college-level research.

AltaVista Photo Finder

http://image.altavista.com

Currently the most comprehensive database of images on the Internet, with the best searching capability. AltaVista has combined the Corbis photo database with indexed images from the Web to provide millions of images. Images not limited just to photos.

Ask Jeeves for Kids!

www.ajkids.com

A subject directory that allows the user to enter a question in plain English. Jeeves searches its knowledge base of already researched questions, returns several possible question matches and then runs your question through WebCrawler. This version of Ask Jeeves is geared toward children.

Awesome Library

www.neat-schoolhouse.org

A comprehensive database of educational materials. Includes only sites that have been reviewed and judged to be of high quality by educators.

Beginner's Guide to Effective E-mail

www.webfoot.com/advice/email.top.html

A resource for how to use e-mail more effectively.

Berit's Best Sites for Children

http://db.cochran.com/
li_toc:theoPage.db

One of the best sites online for kids. Created by the Canadian Broadcasting Company.

Best Information on the 'Net

www.sau.edu/CWIS/Internet/Wild/
index.htm

A librarian's guide to the best info on the Internet.

Best Information on the 'Net: Statistical Sources and Calculation Tools on the Net

www.sau.edu/cwis/Internet/wild/
Refdesk/Stats/staindex.htm

St. Ambrose University site with solid links to statistics. Add #useful to URL for "useful tools."

Best of Asia Pacific

www.bestofasiapacific.com

Comprehensive directory for Asian-related sites.

Bigfoot

www.bigfoot.com

This e-mail search tool is one of the best. Includes e-mail listings by state and white page information by state and city.

BigYellow

www.bigyellow.com

National business listings - searchable by name and type of business. Also has a good e-mail finder and phone lookup.

Black's LawPage

www.tfs.net/~dlblack/
lawpage.html

A nice collection of legal-related sites.

Bookmark Central

www.onlineinc.com/bookmark/
marklist.html

A collection of carefully selected, reviewed and annotated sites on specific topics, pulled together by readers of two of the top online research magazines, *Online* and *Database*.

Bookmarks2Go - Starting Points

www.sideclick.com

Interesting web directory from Switchboard is a "discovery tool" that finds sites related to a topic of interest or related to other sites. Enter a URL and SideClick will show you other sites they've categorized under the same topic.

Canada411

http://canada411.sympatico.ca

A Canadian phone book for almost all provinces and territories.

Canadian Information by Subject

www.nlc-bnc.ca/
caninfo/ecaninfo.htm

Extensive subject listings from Canada by the National Library of Canada.

Carroll's Government Directories & Charts

www.carrollpub.com

Government phone books and directories.

Chronicle of Higher Education

http://chronicle.com

Academe This Week is the Chronicle's online news service.

Classroom Connect

www.classroom.net

Excellent K-12 resource. It's easily searchable and browsable.

College & University (ALL) Web Site Links

www.mit.edu:8001/people/
cdemello/univ.html

Searches through college/university affiliations.

Commonplace Book, The

http://metalab.unc.edu/ibic/
Commonplace-Book.html

Internet Book Information Center provides a comprehensive, opinionated source for information about books.

Compleat Internet Researcher

www.aallnet.org/products/
crab/index.html

Legal research site with strategy tips and resources.

Confering Software for the Web

http://thinkofit.com/webconf

David Woolley's excellent resource for learning about text-based online conferencing.

Contacts Directory, The

www.dir.org

Phone, fax and e-mail contact information for companies and individuals.

Cornell's CU-SeeMe

http://rocketcharged.com/
mac/cu-seeme.html

Video-conferencing program and details.

Cornell's CU-SeeMe FAQ page

http://support.wpine.com/
cuseeme

Details about CU-SeeMe videoconferencing from Frequently Asked Questions.

Cybertown - 3DVR Community of the Future

www.cybertown.com

Cutting-edge 3-D technology with chat in a virtual environment.

Dictionary of Phrase and Fable

www.bibliomania.com/Reference/
PhraseAndFable/index.html

Full text of E. Cobham Brewer's classic reference, which explains the origins of English phrases and characters from myths and fables

Directorio Global Net en Español

www.dirglobal.net

Spanish language subject directory.

Disinformation

www.disinfo.com

Calling itself the "subculture search engine," you will find things here on current affairs, politics and other subjects that you won't find elsewhere.

Dr Felix's Free MEDLINE Page

www.beaker.iupui.edu/drfelix

A list of all the places on the 'net that offer free Medline, the federal government's health-medical index

Edcuation Week on the Web

www.edweek.org

Education news and resources.

EDUCAUSE

www.educause.edu

The latest trends in education and technology

Encyclopedia Smithsonian FAQs

www.si.edu/resource/faq/start.htm

Ready reference resources – includes lots of FAQ files.

Encyclopedia.Com

www.encyclopedia.com

Electric Library's free encyclopedia.

ETAK SkyMap

www.etak.com/skymap

Attaches a small homing device to your laptop, uses global positioning satellites and helps guide you home if you are lost.

FAQ Finder

http://ps.superb.net/FAQ

A collection of FAQs on all kinds of subjects

Forté Free Agent Newsreader

www.forteinc.com/forte/agent/freagent.htm

Tools for regularly using the Usenet.

Fee-Based Site

Good Stuff

www.netins.net/showcase/trhalvorson/g-stuff/index.html

TR Halvorson's collection of links to legal and business sites.

Healthatoz

www.healthatoz.com

Quick access to medical information on the Web.

Highway 61

www.highway61.com

Another of the many meta-tools.

Hypertext Webster Gateway at UCSD

http://c.gp.cs.cmu.edu:5103/prog/webster?

The folks at Carnegie Mellon offer an interface that allows you to put in a word and get a definition or a thesaurus reference from Webster's online.

ICQ: World's Largest Internet Online Communication Network

www.mirabilis.com

A chat service tool – allows you to know when others are online

InterCat WebZ Server

http://orc.rsch.oclc.org:6990

Searchable database of bibliographic records for Internet resources, selected and cataloged by libraries worldwide.

International Research Center

www.researchedge.com

Mark Goldstein's nice collection of research links.

Jump City

www.jumpcity.com/start.shtml

Another great collection of specialized search engines.

KidsClick!

http://sunsite.berkeley.edu/KidsClick!

KidsClick! is a searchable and browsable directory of close to 4000 Web resources of use to kids and those who work with them.

Learn the Net: An Internet Guide & Tutorial

www.learnthenet.com/english/index.html

Excellent primer on the 'Net and how it works.

List of Usenet FAQs

www.cis.ohio-state.edu/hypertext/faq/usenet/top.html

Lets you search for FAQs on Usenet newsgroups by subject or keyword.

Lists of Mailing Lists

www.duke.edu/~mg/usenet/mailing-lists.html

Mailing list information.

Maple Square

http://maplesquare.com

Searchable and browsable Canadian Internet subject directory.

MG's House of News Knowledge

www.duke.edu/~mg/usenet

Directory of Usenet tools.

NetGuide

www.netguide.com

Deep site with reviewed web sites.

NetGuide: Women's Guide

www.netguide.com/women

Directory of reviewed sites of interest to women.

Netiquette Home Page

www.fau.edu/rinaldi/netiquette.html

Etiquette on the Internet.

NIC 0Top - Top Level Heritage

http://sunsite.unc.edu/usenet-i/hier-s/top.html

Description of various Usenet newsgroups.

Nua - Online Relationship Management

www.nua.ie

Another great resource for tracking stats about web usage.

Odden's Bookmarks - The Fascinating World of Maps & Mapping.

http://kartoserver.frw.ruu.nl/ html/staff/oddens/oddens.htm

Extensive collection of links to maps, geographical societies and everything cartographic.

OneLook Dictionaries

www.onelook.com

Access to more than 80 specialized dictionaries on business, medicine, science, etc.

Open Market - The Internet Index

www.openmarket.com/intindex/ index.cfm

Monthly set of Internet stats and strange facts about online usage.

Parent Soup

www.parentsoup.com

Parental resources.

Perry-Castaneda Library Map Collection

www.lib.utexas.edu/Libs/PCL/Map _collection/Map_collection.html

Includes more than 230,000 maps.

Policy.com

http://policy.com

Comprehensive, non-partisan treatment of today's political arena.

Purely Academic

www.netsoc.tcd.ie/Background

Good academic starting point from Dublin University Internet Society. Emphasis on actual research sources.

Quotations Page, The

www.starlingtech.com/quotes

Eclectic collection of modern quotations.

Research-It!

WWW.iTools.COM/research-it

Ready referrence listing. This is a very useful collection of reference material, including dictionaries, thesauri as well as translations, acryonyms, biographies and maps.

Researchpaper.com

www.researchpaper.com

Huge collection of school-related research papers. Once in a while you may find something you need.

Roget's Thesaurus

www.thesaurus.com/thesaurus

Complete thesaurus online. Type in your word and get a group of alternative words.

Scour.Net

www.scour.net

A "guide to multimedia on the Internet."

Sources Select Online

www.sources.com

Need an expert in Canada. The long-trusted Canadian directory is online and searchable. People pay to be listed here, however.

Starting-Point

www.stpt.com

A well organized set of links on business, computing, education, news, etc.

Telephone Directories On the Web

www.contractjobs.com/tel

A great site for finding telephone directories for countries other than the US. Includes links to online telephone, fax and business directories from around the world.

Top of the Web

www.december.com/web/top.html

An excellent collection of links on a variety of subjects. Including searchable indexes and directories. From Internet guru John December.

Transactional Records Access Clearinghouse (TRAC)

http://trac.syr.edu

Amazing collection of law enforcement related information that can be localized to your region.

Ultimate White Pages

www.theultimates.com/white

The white pages online.

Usenet - Welcome from The Mining Co.

http://usenet.miningco.com/index.htm

A good Usenet primer.

Usenet FAQ Archive

www.faqs.org/faqs

Full-text search of actual FAQ contents.

UT Austin Search: Searching for People

www.utexas.edu/search/email.html

Good collection of e-mail address finders.

Videoconferencing

http://disc.cba.uh.edu/~rhirsch/spring97/rappold1.htm

Scholarly site for videoconferencing information.

Virtual Search Engines

www.dreamscape.com/frankvad/search.html

Excellent guide to specialized search engines.

webCATS

http://library.usask.ca/hywebcat

A research tool for locating library catalogs on the Web, searchable geographically.

Webgator - Investigative Resources on the Web

www.inil.com/users/dguss/wgator.htm

Investigative resources for tracking courts, parole boards, records, licensing, etc.

WebRing
www.webring.com

A searchable catalog of web rings, which are related groups of sites.

WorldPages Global Find
www.worldpages.com/global

International phone book with access to more than 60 countries.

Yahoo! Computers & Internet: Internet: World Wide Web: Chat
http://dir.yahoo.com/
Computers_and_Internet/
Internet/World_Wide_Web/Chat

Current Chat Room listing on Yahoo.

Subject Directories

Amazon.com

www.amazon.com

Online book store

Argus Clearinghouse

www.clearinghouse.net

Breaks its material into fourteen categories and hundreds of subcategories.

Argus Clearinghouse: Environmental

www.clearinghouse.net/
cgi-bin/chadmin/viewcat/
Environment?kywd++

Argus Clearinghouse's environmental site. Good example of a topic-specific page

Best Environmental Resources Directory

www.ulb.ac.be/ceese/meta/
cds.html

Subject directory focusing on the Environment and pulled together by the Belgian government's Office of Scientific, Technical and Cultural Affairs.

Cyndi's List of Genealogical Sites on the Internet

www.CyndisList.com

One of the best sites online for genealogy information.

Direct Search

http://gwis2.circ.gwu.edu/
~gprice/direct.htm

This is a superb directory of subject-oriented directories, pulled together by Gary Price at George Washington University.

Dow Jones Business Directory

www.bd.dowjones.com

Dow Jones, owners of the *Wall Street Journal* have made a tremendous business subject directory.

eBLAST: Britannica's Internet Guide

www.eblast.com

Encyclopedia Britannica's web site based on its encyclopedias which have been around since 1768. The company waited a long time to move to the Web, and this site is excellent.

Forum One

www.forumone.com

Discussion group locator.

Fractal Cow Studio

www.fractalcow.com

Outrageous humor site.

INFOMINE: Scholarly Internet Resource Collections

http://lib-www.ucr.edu

Contains scholarly Internet resources pulled together by librarians for the University of California campuses and Stanford University.

LANDINGS

www.landings.com

A subject-specific directory on aviation and related transportation matters .

Librarians' Index to the Internet

http://sunsite.berkeley.edu/
InternetIndex

Geared to academic resources. Collected and categorized by public librarians to help answer reference questions. Relatively small database, so search terms should be broad in scope. Everything is evaluated, annotated and selected for content and reliability.

LookSmart

www.looksmart.com

Offers 12 main categories and over 24,000 subcategories.

Magellan Internet Guide

www.mckinley.com

Both a search directory and a search engine. Owned by the Excite company.

Mining Company, The

www.miningcompany.com

Evaluative guides on over 500 subject areas. A top quality subject directory.

Prices's List of Lists

http://qwis2.circ.qwu.edu/
~qprice/listof.htm

Clearinghouse for best lists of things on the Internet.

Snap

www.snap.com

Sixteen major topics, plus chat, free e-mail, message boards, yellow pages, maps, classifieds, downloads, stock quotes horoscopes and searching.

Statistical Resources on the Web

www.lib.umich.edu/libhome/
Documents.center/stats.html

Valuable statistics, mostly from federal government sources. Also has other resources and other subject directories of value.

University Law Review Project

www.lawreview.org

Excellent site for finding law review articles.

WebCrawler

www.webcrawler.com

Both a search directory and a search engine. Owned by the Excite company.

Yahoo!

www.yahoo.com

Categorizes subjects into 14 topics and hundreds of subtopics, one of the most thorough of the subject directories.

Contributors

Stephanie C. Ardito is President of Ardito Information & Research, Inc., an information firm specializing in pharmaceutical, medical and business information research, as well as intellectual property and copyright matters. Stephanie is a past president of The Association of Independent Information Professionals. Address: sardito@ardito.com

Kitty Bennett is a news researcher for the *St. Petersburg Times.*

Susan M. Detwiler is president of The Detwiler Group, an information consulting firm that has long specialized in the business side of medicine and health. Since 1992, Susan has produced *Detwiler's Directory of Health and Medical Resources.* Address: sdetwiler@detwiler.com or www.detwiler.com.

Dr. Susan Feldman was the coordinator of The Internet Search-Off for *Searcher Magazine*, February 1998. She is President of Data Search and teaches at Cornell University.

Jennifer Kaplan is president of JKreative Solutions Inc., an international management consultancy. Address: Jennifer@JKreative.com.

Carole A. Lane is the author of *Naked In Cyberspace: How To Find Personal Information Online.* Internet Address: calane@technosearch.com.

Eva M. Lang is an authority on electronic research for business and litigation support services. Eva is also technology columnist for *CPA Expert* Newsletter. Eva's e-mail address is: lemay_lang@csi.com

John E. Levis is president of John E. Levis Associates, a longtime specialist in primary and secondary market research in healthcare and medicine, and a past president of the Association of Independent Information Professionals (AIIP). Address: john@jelevisassoc.com or www.jelevisassoc.com.

Greg R. Notess is author of *Government Information on the Internet*), a reference librarian at Montana State University and a columnist for

Online and *Database* magazines.
Address: notess@imt.net and http://imt.net/~notess.

Nora Paul is the Library Director of The Poynter Institute, a former *Miami Herald* librarian, a nationally-recognized lecturer and co-author, with Margot Williams, of the upcoming *Great Scouts! Cyberguides for Subject Searching on the Web*.

Lynn Peterson, President of PFC Information Services Inc in Oakland, CA, is a well-known expert in public record research and retrieval. Address: lpeterson@pfcinformation.com or www.pfcinformation.com.

Barbara Quint is editor of *Searcher Magazine*. Barbara's e-mail address is bquint@netcom.com

Don Ray is a multi-media investigative reporter/producer/author and frequent lecturer. Don's books include *The California Investigator's Handbook, Checking Out Lawyers, Diggin' Up Gold on the Old Paper Trail: a Guide for Investigatin' Folks* and *Don Ray's 104 Privacy Tips*. Don Ray's web site is www.donray.com/donray; Don's e-mail is donray@donray.com.

Drew Sullivan is a reporter for the *Nashville Tennessean* and former systems director for the National Institute for Computer Assisted Reporting. Address: drew@nicar.org and www.nicar.org/~drew.

Dave Wickham is creator of the Public Servant's Internet Abuse Page. Address: davew@inlandnet.com

Robbin Zeff, PhD is president of The Zeff Group, a research and training firm specializing Internet advertising and marketing. Robbin is author of the best-selling *Advertising on the Internet* and *The Nonprofit Guide to the Internet*. Address: robbin@zeff.com or www.zeff.com

Glossary

Terms & Definitions

Attachment Any file that is attached to an e-mail message.

Back Slash Slash mark on your keyboard that goes from top left down to bottom right (\).

Boolean Method of searching a database or text in which Boolean operators (like AND, OR and NOT) are used to limit and specify the search criterion.

Browser Software that looks at various types of Internet resources. Browsers can search for documents and obtain them from other sources. A browser allows you to look at the World Wide Web. Common browsers include Netscape Navigator, Microsoft Internet Explorer, Internet Chameleon and Internet-in-a-Box. Browsers are also called Web Browsers.

Chat Room Chat is the synchronous line-by-line communication (happening in real time, like a phone conversation but unlike an e-mail exchange) with another user (or users) over a network. Chat rooms are the places wherein people conduct these online conversations.

Cyberspace A term coined by science fiction author William Gibson to describe the whole range of information resources available through computer networks.

Database A structured format for organizing and maintaining information that can be easily retrieved. A simple example of a database is a table or a spreadsheet.

DNS (Domain Name Service) An online distributed database responsible for mapping host names to their respective IP addresses. Also refers to Domain Name Server.

Domain The unique name that identifies an Internet site. The Internet is made up of hundreds of thousands of computers and networks, all with their own domain name or unique address. Domain names always have two or more parts separated by dots. For example, "whitehouse.gov" is the domain name belonging to the White House computer system. Domain names typically consist of some form of the organization's name and a suffix that describes the type of organization.

Download The method by which users access and save or "pull down" software or other files to their own computers from a remote computer, usually via a modem.

E-mail Short for electronic mail, e-mail consists of messages, often just text, sent from one user to another via a network. E-mail can also be sent automatically to a number of addresses.

FAQ Acronym for Frequently Asked Questions. FAQs are online documents that list and answer the most common questions on a particular subject. FAQs were developed by people who got tired of answering the same questions over and over again.

Filter Is a program that allows certain messages or certain kinds of material to reach the user while eliminating other messages. Email filters, separate email into categories. Other filters are used to pull out racy material so kids don't see it, and still other filters allow you to get just news on specific subjects you want, eliminating other non-relevant material.

Firewall Security measure of the Internet that prevents users from doing any harm to underlying systems by protecting information and preventing access.

Forward Slash Slash mark on your keyboard that goes from bottom left to top right (/).

Frames Area of the screen of some graphical web browsers (such as Netscape Navigator and Microsoft Internet Explorer) that can be updated independently and may also scroll separately.

Freeware Software distributed for free with no fee required.

Gateway A computer that interconnects and performs the protocol conversion between two different types of networks, bridging the gap between two otherwise incompatible applications or networks so that data can be transferred different computers. This is common with e-mail that gets sent back and forth between Internet sites and commercial online services (like America Online) which has its own internal e-mail systems. It can also be an online company that offers access to the Net as well as other online services.

Hits Refers to the number of files that are downloaded from a web server. It's a way of measuring traffic to a web site that can be misleading. The number of hits a site receives is usually much greater than the number of visitors it gets. That's because a web page can contain more than one file.

HTML Stands for Hyper-Text Markup Language. It is the basic language that web pages are created in. It is designed such that the basics are easy to learn. There are several good books about programming HTML, as well as a large selection of programs that generate it automatically for you.

Intranet Think of an intranet as an internal Internet, or "network," designed to be used within the confines of a company, university or organization. What distinguishes an intranet from the Internet, is that intranets are private.

IP Address Numeric code that uniquely identifies a particular computer on the Internet. Like your home address, every computer on the Internet has a unique address, too. Internet addresses are assigned to you by an organization called ICANN, formerly assigned by Internic. When you register an address, you get both a domain name like (whitehouse.gov), and a number (198.38.240.10), which is generally referred to as the IP address or IP number. Because the numeric addresses are difficult to understand or remember, most people use names instead.

ISP Acronym for Internet Service Provider; the company you get an account from in order to get access to the Internet.

Java An object-oriented programming language developed by Sun Microsystems, Inc. to create executable content (i.e self-running applications) that can be easily distributed through networks like the Web. Developers use Java to create special programs called applets that can be incorporated in a web page to make it interactive. When you see pages moving and jumping and dogs walking across pages on the Web, chances are good that it is a Java applet. Like a gateway (CGI) script, a special HTML tag on a web page activates Java.

Mailing List A way of having a group discussion by electronic mail. Also used to distribute announcements to a large number of people. A mailing list is very much like a conference on a bulletin board system, except the conversation comes to you by email. Each time you or any member of the list posts a reply to the conversation, it is distributed to the e-mail box of every member of the list. All of this traffic is automated and managed by programs called mailing list managers or mail servers. The two most frequently used programs are Listserv and Majordomo.

Meta-Tools Meta-tools are hybrids of search engines and subject directories that allow you to search several sites at once.

Portal Portal sites combine specialized content, free e-mail, chat services and a variety of retail and consumer offers to draw users into making the site their starting point and principal destination on the Web. They make their money by getting huge amounts of web traffic and through ad revenue and commercial transactions.

Proxy Server Security measure that enables users behind a firewall to browse the web. Viisited resources are actually downloaded by the proxy server and then viewed internally from there without exposing the contents of the material to public scrutiny.

Push Technology A method of distributing information over the Web, by which updates are scheduled and then automatically sent to the user's screen or window, as if the content were being "broadcast" to a receiver.

Real Time The time used for synchronous communication, in which both participants must be available (as in a telephone conversation). It also means taking place at the present time, live, not delayed or recorded.

Search Tools These are the tools you use to search around on the Internet. They include search engines, which are a type of software that creates indexes of databases of Internet sites and allows you to type in what you are looking for and it then gives you a list of results of your search. Other tools include subject directories, which are catalogues of resources, pulled together and ranked by human being s and meta-tools, which allow you to search several search tools at once.

Searching The effort to find specific things online using a series of search tools to help you locate whatever it is you are interested in. Usually it is done by specifying key words to match.

Server A network application or computer that supplies information or other resources to client applications that connect to it. In conventional networking, server usually refers to a computer; for Internet client/server applications, server usually refers to a program.

Shareware Computer programs that are available for a free trial with the understanding that, if you decide to keep the program, you will send the requested payment to the shareware provider specified in the program. You are on the honor system with the understanding that if you like the software and want to keep the inventor in business, you will pay for the software's continued development. Payment may also buy you manuals, support and updates.

Signature Text automatically included at the bottom of an e-mail message or newsgroup posting to personalize it. This can be anything from a snappy quote to some additional information about the sender, like their title, company name and additional e-mail addresses they may have.

Snail Mail Internet slang for US Postal Service mail, so called for its relative slowness compared to the speed of electronic mail.

Truncation Shortening or cutting off of words, where search engines automatically use shortened versions of words in searching.

Upload Often confused with download, uploading a file means loading it from your computer onto a remote one. Most people do a lot more downloading than uploading.

URL Acronym for Uniform Resource Locator. URL is the address for a resource or web site. It is the convention that web browsers use for locating files and other remote services.

Usenet Usenet is the collection of newsgroups and a set of agreed-upon rules for distributing and maintaining them.

Web Browser A program used to navigate and access information on the World Wide Web. Web browsers turn HTML coding into a graphical display.

Web Page A web page is a document created with HTML (HyperText Markup Language) that is part of a group of hypertext documents or resources available on the World Wide Web. It usually contains hyptertext links to other documents on the Web. Collectively, these documents and resources form what is known as a web site.

Web Site A collection of World Wide Web pages, usually consisting of a home page and several other linked pages.

Webmaster Person in charge of maintaining a web site. This can include writing HTML files, setting up more complex programs, and responding to e-mail.

Wildcard These are special characters used to represent either any single character or any number of characters. Usual wildcard characters are ? (for single characters) and * (for any number of characters). Using wildcards allows you to search when you do not have entire phrases or are missing a specific piece of your search criteria.

Page Index

1

*100 Most Common Questions That Pet
 Owners Ask the Vet* 229
13-F Form 163
13-G Form 163

3

3D chatting 77

A

ABC News 152
academic records 140
accuracy 195
Acxiom DataQuick 127
Acxiom Direct Media 170
ADA .... *See* Americans with Disabilities Act
Adobe 53
Adobe Acrobat 89, 91, 167
Adrem Profiles 139
advanced search feature 30-31, 174
Adventures of Tom Sawyer 102
Advertising Age 151
agency functions 126
age-related rooms 76
AIDS 67
aiff or au 88
AIIP .... *See* Association of Independent
 .... Information Professionals
airfares, bargain 183
AJR/Newslink 145
Akroyd, Dan 219
Alabama 139
Alaska 132
Alexa 191
Alice in Wonderland 102
All Things Considered 153
Allen, Tim 220

All-in-One 48
AlphaSearch 44
alt, alternative 78
AltaVista 30, 32, 33, 34, 39, 44,
 ...... 51-52, 56, 79, 174, 175-176, 217, 238
 news 144
Amazon.com 183, 193
Ameche, Don 234
America Online .... *See* AOL
American Cancer Society 67
American Dental Association 67
American Journalism Magazine 145
American Library Association 205
American Marketing Association 56
American Medical Association ....
 .... 56, 62, 67, 69
American Real Estate Exchange ....
 .... *See* Amrex
American Society of Association Executives
 .... *See* ASAE
American Voter 122
Americans with Disabilities Act 140
Amrex 127
Ancestry.com 129
animal testing 226
Annan, Kofi 143
Anonymizer 254
anonymous re-mailers 254
AnyWho 59, 220
AOL 48, 58, 69, 75-76, 147,
 .... 161, 165, 178, 207, 246-47
AP .... *See* Associated Press
archives 144, 156, 201
 foreign 156
 government 105
 messages 69, 254
 news 144-45, 148, 155, 241
 periodicals 203, 241
 presidential 111

self-extracting 94
Ardito, Stephanie C. 94
Argus Clearinghouse 42, 45, 63, 206
ARISTOTLE 126
Arizona 139
arrest records 132
ASAE 166, 169, 197
ASCII 88-89, 99
Ask Jeeves 239
assets 125, 128, 130, 136-37, 163
Associated Press 146, 147, 150, 165, 187
Association of Independent Information
    Professionals 66, 178
AT&T 59
au or aiff 88
audio conferencing 76, 77
authority 195, 196-97, 232
AVERT 139
avi 88
aviation 42, 45
accidents/incidents 97

B

backgrounding 23, 73, 129
    a company 159, 180
    a government 116
    a person 82, 202, 209, 258
    tools 57, 73, 171
Baltimore Sun 221
BANK Rate Monitor Infobank 178
banking account records 58, 137
bankruptcy court records 122, 130
bankruptcy listings 131, 136
Barnes & Noble 193
Bartlett's Familiar Quotations 72
Beaucoup! 47-48
Bennett, Kitty 63, 149
Berinstein, Paula 117
Berne Convention 94
Best Environmental Resources Directory . 45
BiblioData 145
BigBook 71, 171
BigYellow 72
bill summaries 110
Billboard 153
BinHex 101
Biographical Dictionary 62

bionet 78
BIOS 253
birth certificates 128
bit 78
Bixby, Bill 234
biz 78
Biztravel.com 174
bmp 89
bookmarks 182
BookWord Press 229
Boolean 26
    operators 26-27, 33, 35, 39
    searching 37, 47, 49, 145
Boston Globe 143
Boston Herald 143
bots 191
BotSpot 191
Breeze FTP 102
Brenda Starr 143
Brooklyn Eagle 210
browser 9, 99
    preferences 99
bulletin boards 106, 246
Bureau of Economic Analysis . 115, 166, 170
Bureau of Justice Statistics 116
Bureau of Labor Statistics 53, 116, 166
Bureau of Transportation Statistics 111
business 45, 159
    & economic statistics 116
    appraisers 169
    directories 161, 171
    records 131, 137
Business Wire 164

C

cable TV 250
cache 245, 248, 249, 253, 255
California 132, 134, 136, 139, 213-14,
                    220, 222, 226-27, 229, 252
Campaigns & Elections 124
Canada 59, 61, 95, 164
card catalog 29
catalog .... *See* index
CBS 152
CDB Infotek 58, 82, 131, 137, 140, 165
census 55, 71, 109, 117, 166
Center for Democracy & Technology 255

Center for Media Education 250
Centers for Disease Control & Prevention....
.... 68
Centerwatch 68
Centrus Online 170
channels 35
chat discussion sessions 76
chat groups 77, 246
chat rooms 69, 73, 75-76
Chicago 165
Chicago Tribune 143, 147, 148
children 132, 185, 250–51, 258
Children's Online Protection Act 258
China 146
Christian Science Monitor 155
CI .... *See* competitive intelligence
CIA World Factbook 71, 116
civil court records 129, 139-40
ClassMates Online 61
Cleveland 165
Cleveland Plain Dealer 81
Clinton, President Bill 14
Cloakroom 124
CNET 102, 190, 246
CNN 152-53, 189
   CNNfn 178
   Custom News 189
   Interactive 153
Colorado 139
Columbia University 72
commercial tools 58
Commonly Requested Federal Services .. 106
comp 77
CompaniesOnline 161
company directories 161
Company Link 161, 227
CompData 141
competitive intelligence 171-75, 180
compressing 93
CompuServe ....
.... 69, 84, 88, 147, 165, 178, 202, 247
Computer Assisted Reporting 57
concept searching 35
conference coverage
   finding 236
Conference Plus 193
conferencing 76

Congress 110, 122-23, 258
Congressional
   action 110
   committee votes 122
   Directory 110
   floor speeches 122
   information 123
   member profiles 122
   news highlights 122
   voting records 110, 148
Congressional Quarterly 122-24
Congressional Record 110, 123-24
Connery, Sean 219
contact information 240
content-screening 185
Cookie Taste Test 248
cookies 248–49, 253, 255-56
COPA . *See* Children's Online Protection Act
Copernic 98 186
copyright 92, 94-96, 105, 145
   laws 94-95
   violations 94-95
Copyright Act of 1976 94
Corbis 34
corporate information 150, 161, 164, 171
corporate records 131
Counsel Connect 123
court records 129-30, 137
CourtLink 121, 129, 131
Crain's Business Publications 165
crawler .... *See* Spider
credibility 69, 195-97, 200-01, 203, 205
credibility test 33, 205
credit
   agencies 58
   agency 138
   headers 58, 82, 138
   reports 137-38, 140, 259
credit card transactions 12
criminal court records 129, 139
csv 99
Curie Inc 229
current events 42
CU-SeeMe 76
Cyber Patrol 185
cybergeek speak 9
CYBERsitter 185

CyberTimes *149*
Cybertown 77
CyBot 192
Cyndi's List of Genealogical Sites on the
   Internet 45

D

Daily Diffs 187
Database Magazine 54
databases 29, 52, 97, 98, 100
   commercial ....
      .... 12, 52, 54, 82, 131, 144, 169, 234
   downloading 96
   medical 235
   news 145, 212
   search directory 40
   search engine 56, 98
   searchable 41, 97-98
   specialty 41
Databots with Imagination 192
Datamonitor 167
dbf 99
DBT Autotrack 58, 82, 131, 165, 229
Dead Sea Scrolls 110
DeadlineOnline 156
death certificates 128, 129
decompressing 93
Defense LINK 111
Defense Technical Information Center ... 111
Deja News ....
   48, 63, 74, 78, 79, 80, 81, 200, 246, 247,
   254
DeLorme 64
demographic data 17, 116
Denver Post 155
Department of Social & Health Services .. 81
Derwent 177
Detroit 165
Detroit News 81, 155
Detwiler, Susan M. 66, 232
DIALOG 82-84, 86, 117, 143, 165,
   ..... 167-71, 196, 202, 224, 227-30, 234-35
DigiPhone 77
Dilbert 219
Direct Channel 170
Direct Marketing Association 257
Direct Search 44

directories
   professional 57, 63
   staff 54
   subject .... *See* subject directories
   telephone .... *See* telephone numbers
Disclosure SEC Site 163
discussion groups 73-74, 246
   feature 77
   lists 77
divorce records 128-30
doc 89
doctoral theses 82
document
   access & retrieval 136
   conferencing 77
   finders 65
Documents Center 107
Dodgers 210-15, 217-18, 222
Dogpile 47-48, 52, 225
Dole, Bob 234
domain name 174, 197-98, 240
Don Ray's 104 Privacy Tips 14
Dow Jones 45, 82-86, 147, 149,
   .... 165, 167-69, 224, 228, 235
Download Butler 183
Download.com 183
downloading 87, 90-91, 96, 98, 183
   databases 100
driver & motor vehicle records 133, 140
driver's license 105, 133
drug-related information 68
Dun & Bradstreet 161, 164, 168,
   .... 171, 228, 230

E

eBLAST 40, 42, 70
EDEX 141
EDGAR ... 109, 137, 162, 163, 164, 172, 180
EDGAR Online People 163
Editor & Publisher 146
Editor & Publisher Interactive 145
edu 55
EFOIA .... *See* Electronic Freedom
   .... of Information Act
E-Journal 154
electronic conferencing 77
Electronic Data Systems 258

Electronic Freedom of Information Act .. 105
Electronic Library 151, 187
e-mail 9, 14, 74, 79, 87, 181-184,
.... 192, 238, 245-47, 254-55
   attachments 101
   definition of 9
   managing 181
   privacy 74, 247, 251, 252-57
   reminders 183
   unsolicited 171, 182, 254
e-mail address finders 57, 63
e-mail addresses .. 58, 63, 200, 237, 248, 256
employee monitoring 251
employer's computer 247
encryption 255, 256
Encyclopedia Britannica Company 70
Encyclopedia.Com 70
Enfish Tracker Pro 184
Engage Technologies 13
Entertainment Weekly 151
environment 45, 68, 78, 83, 98
Epicurious Gourmet Online Cookbook 41
Epson America Inc. 251
Equifax 12, 257
ETAK SkyMap 64
eTRUST 259
Eudora Pro 182, 183
European Patent Office 177
European Union 258
evaluative tools 206
Excite 30, 32, 35, 41, 43, 46, 51-54,
.... 189, 191, 225, 238
exe 89
Experian 12, 257
expert finders 63
experts 63, 157, 199-200, 242
E-Zine list 154
E-Zines 153, 154

F

FACSNET 63
FAQ 69, 70, 73, 76, 80
FAQ archives 70, 80
favorites 182
FBI 139
FDA .... *See* Food & Drug Administration

FDIC .... *See* Federal Deposit
.... Insurance Corporation
federal agencies 105, 107, 116
Federal Aviation Administration 98, 137
Federal Deposit Insurance Corporation 98
Federal Electronic Privacy Act 247
Federal Register 123
Federal Trade Commission .... *See* FTC
Federal Web Locator 108
FedLaw 107
Fedstats 106, 116
FedWorld Information Network 107
fee-based services 58, 65, 69, 82-83,
.... 133, 165, 236
   vs. the Web 236
fee-based tools 82, 236, 237
   legal 121
   people finders 58
Feldman, Susan 235, 237-38
fictitious business name statements. 132, 137
Fidelity Management 193
field searching 50, 145
file extension 88, 89
file transfer protocol .... *See* FTP
FilePile 103
filter 182
filtering 181-84, 186
   collaborative 17
   commericial tools 188
   for kids 185
   news 146, 188
Financenter 178
FIND/SVP 167, 172
finding business information 165, 209
Finding Statistics Online 117
FindLaw 45, 123
fingering 256
firewall 254
First Call 167
flames 75, 171
Florida 105, 132, 139
Florida Atlantic University 80
Flowers Jr., James R. 7
FOIA 126
Food & Drug Administration 68
Ford 258
foreign

companies 119
governments 118
languages 32, 34, 238
newspapers 155
parliamentary bodies 120
sites 32, 107, 238
foreign archives .... *See* archives, foreign
formulas 71, 116
Forté Free Agent 80, 182-83
Fortune 151
forum name 79
Forum One 73
forums 69, 73-74, 80, 246
privacy 245
forward slash 10, 32
Four11 59
FOX 152
FoxPro 99
Franklin, Ben 239
Free Legal Resources on the Internet 122
free news reader 80
Freedom of Information Act .... *See* FOIA
Frequently Asked Questions .... *See* FAQ
Frost & Sullivan 167
FTC 250, 257
FTP 48, 52, 91, 98, 102-03
Fuld & Company Inc. 172, 173
Full Text Sources Online (FTSO) 145

G

Gannett News Service 150
genealogy 45, 129
Geneva International Forum 119
Georgia 134
Georgia State University 124
gif 88-90, 101
Glamour 16
Global Computing 112
Gould, Cheryl 30
gov 55
GOVBOT 107
government
boards 130
gateways 106–8
records 126
statistical resources 115-16
Government Information on the Internet .. 54

Government Information Sharing Project .....
.... 52, 112
Government Resource Guides 106
Governments on the Web 118
Grantor/Grantee Indexes 128
graphic interchange format .... *See* gif
Great Universal Stores 259
Greek.Com 60
Greenspun, Phil 183
Greg R. Notess 113, 118
Gretsky, Wayne 219
Gulf War 111
Gumby 220

H

Harding, Tonya 78
Hawaii 139
health screenings 257
Healthfinder 106, 232
Healthgate 67
help screens 30
Hilton International 258
historical documents 110, 122
historical figures
finding 236
hits 21, 31, 233
hlp 89
home page 63, 196, 204
Hoover's....37, 150, 16162, 168-69, 171, 227
HotBot 27, 30, 32-33, 36-37, 43-44,
..51, 54, 77, 79, 98, 156, 217, 219-20, 238
Hotmail 237
HTML 39, 53, 91, 93, 100
HTTP 9
Hussein, King 234
hyperlinks 9
definition of 9
Hypertext Markup Language .... *See* HTML
hyptertext links .... *See* hyperlinks

I

IAAO 127
IAC Insite 165
IBM 188
IBM Patent Server 177
ICANN 162
ICQ 75

identifying file types 88
identifying information, personal.............. 58
identity fraud 249–50
Identity Theft Law 258
IGnet... 110
images 92
   finding 236
   saving.. 92
   scanned 53
index..31, 56
   death 129
   governmental web sites 107
   legal subjects 46
   UN Organizations............................. 119
Indiana... 132
Inference Find 49
Infobel International Directories 72
Infogist 192
INFOMINE 40, 108
Information America... 58, 82, 131, 140, 165
information supermarkets.......................... 82
Informus 141
Infoseek..........27, 30, 32, 37, 51-52, 54, 189
InfoSpace.com.....................59, 61, 130, 220
Inquisit! 187
insurance policies 137
InteliHealth.. 69
intelligent agent............................. 188, 192
Intelliseek 192
intergovernmental organizations..... 118, 119
Internal Revenue Service 135, 169
international
   news wires 146
   resources 117
   yellow pages 72
International Association of Assessing
   Officers.....................................*See* IAAO
International Documents Task Force 119
International Trade Administration......... 117
Internet address .... *See* URL
Internet Address Finder............................ 63
Internet advertising................. 16, 17, 15–18
Internet Explorer ....
   ....9, 47, 55, 80, 182, 249, 256
Internet Public Library 70
Internet Search-Off, The 238
Internet Sleuth 41, 49, 63

INTERNET.ORG!................................... 162
InterNIC 162
Inter-Parliamentary Union...................... 120
interrupts... 193
Investext 230
Investext Group 167
investment research................. 116, 179, 180
INVESTools..179
IQ DATA Systems 127
IRSC 131, 165
ISP 245–46, 256
iVillage...193

J

Java..90
JavaScript 248
JavElink...186
JKreative Solutions Inc. 174
Johns Hopkins University 68, 204
Journal of the American Dental Assoc......67
Journal of the American Medical Assoc....67
Journalism Net.......................................154
jpe..89
jpeg..88, 89
jpg...89-90, 92, 101
JT Research 164
Jumbo! Download Network 102
Junkbusters 255
Jupiter Communications..........................168

K

k12..78
Kansas 132
Kardashian, Robert.............................134
Kassler, Helene....................................173
Kerrigan, Nancy 78
keywords 26, 31-32, 44, 50, 53-54, 176
   unique...50
Kiosk 154
Knight-Ridder.............................147, 187
KnowX 82, 127, 134, 140

L

Lachmann, Rene....................................222
LaFleur, Jennifer 109
LANDINGS 42, 45

Lane, Carole A. 234, 252
Lang, Eva M. 169
Late Show with David Letterman 54
Law Library of Congress 123
LawRunner 120
Legal Information Institute 123
legal resources 113, 122-23
legal/legislative resources 121
Levis, John E. 66
Lewinsky, Monica 14
LEXIS-NEXIS 82-83, 85, 86, 121,
.......................128-29, 131, 140, 143, 168,
.............................214, 221, 224, 228, 234
liabilities 128, 136
Libby, Elizabeth 39
Librarian's Index to the Internet 44
library catalogs 54
Library of Congress 69, 106, 109, 123
Link feature 174, 176, 205
Link Search feature 33-34, 36, 38
listserv administrator 74
listservs 200
Liszt 75
LIVEDGAR 164
log files 17
   analyzing 17
LookSmart 43, 56
Los Angeles Daily News 229
Los Angeles Times 16, 84, 147-49, 222-23
Lotus 1-2-3 99
Louisiana State University 107
lurking 75
Lycos 30, 37, 48, 51-52, 144, 161, 189

M

m1v 89
Macintosh users 9, 77, 88, 93
magazines 95, 144, 149, 150, 153-54
Magellan Internet Guide 43
mail forwarding orders 82
mailing lists 74-75, 77, 80, 170-71, 246
managing incoming information 181
MapBlast! 65
mapping tools 64–65
MapQuest 64
Maps On Us 64
market reports 166, 168

finding 236
market research 84-85, 165-66, 168, 172
   data vendors 167
   free sources 166
market studies 82, 85, 159, 168
Marketing Intelligence Service 228
marriage certificates 128
Martindale-Hubbell
   Lawyer Locator 62, 220
Maryland 139
Massachusetts Institute of Technology ...143
mdb 99
MedGate 67
Media Finder 151
Medical Information Bureau 250
medical records 250, 258
medical statistics
   finding 236
medicine 66, 68, 70, 83
Medline 66-67, 69
Medscape 67
Megasources 154
Melrose Place 171
mental health 202
Mercury Center Passport 189
Merlin ...82, 129, 132, 134-36, 214, 221, 229
MetaCrawler 47
meta-search engines 238
meta-tag 53-54, 176
   stacking 54
meta-tools 29, 47–49, 50
   advantages of 47
   definition of 29
   disadvantages of 47
Metromail 12
Mexico 146
Miami Herald 81, 147, 187
Micropatent 178
Microsoft 184, 252, 258
Microsoft Access 99
Microsoft Excel 89
Microsoft Expedia Travel 175
Microsoft Internet Explorer ....
......................................*See* Internet Explorer
Microsoft Network 247
Microsoft Outlook 182-83
Microsoft Word 88-89

Midnight Download 183
mil 55
militarycity.com Databases 62
MIME... 101
Mining Company 43, 178, 201, 206, 234
Mirabilis 75
misc 78
missing children information 132
Mississippi 139
Money Magazine 151
Montague Institute 172
Montgomery, Sandra.............................249
Morning Edition 153
Morningstar 179
mortgage relocation cost estimators........ 116
mov.. 88
mpe.. 89
mpeg...89-90
mpg... 89
MSNBC...152-53, 190
multimedia conferencing.......................... 76
Murray, Bill...219
Mutilate 256
Mutual Funds Interactive 179

N

Nando News Watcher 190
Nando Times 76, 147
Nashville Tennessean 96
NASIRE 112, 114
National Agricultural Library 106
National Archives & Records
    Administration.................................. 111
National Association of State Information
    Resource Executives.............. *See* NASIRE
National Atlas, The United States of
    America 65
National Cancer Institute 67, 69
National Crime Information Center 139
National Health Council........................... 69
National Institute for Computer
    Assisted Reporting.............................. 96
National Institutes of Health 67, 69
National Journal 124
National Library of Education 106
National Library of Medicine........... 66, 106
national news wires................................. 146

National Technical Information Service
    (NTIS)..110
National Traffic Safety Board 97
natural language search engines................39
naturalization court records.................129-30
Navigator......9, 47, 55, 80, 202, 248-49, 255
NCIC ....
    ....*See* National Crime Information Center
Net Meeting..77
Net Nanny 185
netiquette...80
NetMind 186, 188
NetPartner...162
Netscape 47, 55, 182, 248-49, 255
Netscape Navigator .... *See* Navigator
NETworth...179
New Guinea...230
New York 133, 165
New York Times.............. 17, 52, 84, 149, 190
New York University 164
News Hour..144
News Index...187
News Reader 80
News Tracker 53, 191
News Wires 146
NewsBot............................156, 186, 191
newsgroup
    members...74
    news..78
    rules..78, 80
    subject categories............................77, 79
newsgroups...
    ....73-75, 77, 80, 200, 247, 254
    searching..78, 80
    searching by key phrase.........................80
NewsHound.......................................187, 191
Newshunt...155
Newsindex.Com..156
newsletters...150-51
Newslink...148
Newspage 187
newspaper archives ....*See* archives, news
newspapers 53, 144, 148-49, 155-56, 186
    foreign...155-56
Newspapers Online 146, 148
NewsTrawler 155
newusers (of newsgroups)...........................78

Nightline................................. 143
Northern Light............ 30, 32-33, 38, 51-52,
.... 156, 210, 215, 225, 238
Notess, Greg R. 54
Notimex.. 147

O

Occupational Safety & Health
   Administration.................................... 97
Odden's Bookmarks 65
Office of Information & Privacy............. 126
O'Harrow, Robert................................... 249
Online Magazine 54
Online Professional Electronic Network. 139
online searching 22, 26
OPEN .... *See* Online Professional
..................................Electronic Network
Open Source Solutions........................... 173
Oregon.. 139
Oregon State University Library............. 112
org 55

P

PACER..............................121-22, 131, 139
Paintshop Pro 93
Pankove, Melissa 171
Papau.. 230
parliaments................................... 118, 120
   women in 120
PARLINE.. 120
PARLIT... 120
password-protected files 255
passwords 144, 246, 248, 253
patent... 177
   documents.. 95
   research................................... 177, 178
   searchers 177
Pathfinder.................................... 123, 151
Paul, Nora...............22-23, 25, 57, 211, 223
Pauling, Dr. Linus 234
PAWWS Financial Network................... 179
PC411.. 60
pcx.. 89
PDAs..............*See* personal digital assistants
pdf 53, 89, 91, 100
PEBES.................. *See* Personal Earnings &
.....................Benefits Estimate Statement

Pegasus Mail 182
Pennysavers.. 146
Pentagon.. 111
people finders 57, 59, 60, 79, 210
   specialty... 60
People for the Ethical Treatment of Animals
.... 226
People Magazine 143, 151
people search...............................59, 82, 97
Perry-Castaneda Library Map Collection..65
personal digital assistants 183-84
Personal Earnings & Benefits ....
   Estimate Statement 257
personal finance calculators 71, 116
personal financial information.....................
.... 159, 178, 180, 259
personal information managers 183, 184
personalization tools.............................. 190
PETA... 226
Peterson, Lynn............................... 136, 138
Peterson's.. 61
PFC Information Services 136
Philadelphia Inquirer 147, 187
phone numbers .... *See* telephone numbers
photo-finding tool.................................... 34
phrase searching 32, 56, 60
Physician Select....................................... 62
PIMs ......*See* personal information managers
PKZIP..................................... 89, 93, 94
portals.............................46, 58, 206
   definition of 29, 46
Portland Oregonian 81
postings.........................63, 74, 80, 246
   by organization 80
   chat room 75
   news 81, 148
   newsgroup & listserv 200
   newsgroup and listserv 74, 78
   searches... 79
   Usenet.. 247
   your own messages 75
Poynter Institute 22, 26, 57, 157
PR Newswire.................................164-65
PRARS 162
pre-employment background checks.......138
preferences 248
   browser 99, 249, 253, 255-56

personal 17, 185, 193
privacy.......................11, 13, 19, 245-49
    e-mail.......................*See* e-mail privacy
    in the workplace 247, 251
    protecting online........................252, 255
Privacy International 258
Privacy Journal.................................251
Privacy Rights Clearinghouse.........250, 255
probate court 128, 130
Prodigy 148
product information..........40-41, 54, 56, 236
professional licenses 140
Professional Searchers 242
ProFusion 47, 49
Pronto...256
property records 82, 127
proprietary services 82, 83
Public Interest Research Groups 138
public opinion data................................ 116
public record providers 214
Public Record Retriever Network 136
public records...................... 18, 82, 105, 125,
    .... 126, 134, 137-38, 141, 256
    criminal.. 139
    types of 126, 128
    versus government records.................. 126
PubMed 66
Purdue University 204
push technology 192-93

Q

qt 88
QuackWatch.......................................69
Quattro Pro.......................................99
Quicken 178
Quicken FN....................................... 179
Quint, Barbara..................21, 195, 231, 239
quotation finders 72

R

ra or ram...89
RAM Research Group............................ 179
ranking formulas 31, 54
Ray, Don 14, 134
ready reference tools 69, 70
Real Audio 88, 152
real property 136, 137

real-time
    audio 88
    data...35, 188
rec 77
Recreational Software Advisory
    Council on the Internet 185
Reference.Com..................80, 201, 247
regional information..............................117
registrar
    college or university 140
    voting..126
Remind Me.. 183
reQUESTer..............................85, 221
Reuters.................67, 146-47, 165, 179, 187
reverse directories 57, 59, 63
Rich Text Format 89
Robert Ellis Smith 251
robot ....*See* Spider
ROCKRGRL Magazine 154
Ross, Steven 234
rtf................................*See* Rich Text Format
Rule of Concentric Circles 224

S

SafeSurf...185
sales prospecting 170
sales research.......................12, 85, 170, 174
San Francisco Chronicle........................155
San Francisco Examiner.........................228
San Jose...229
San Jose Mercury News 109, 148, 187
saving 87, 101
    documents & text.................................90
    files 90, 92, 101
    images & sounds....................................92
    links 93
    programs 90
SavvySearch 47, 49, 52
Schmich, Mary 143
scholarly journals 44, 82, 202, 236, 241
Schwartz, John 249
sci 77
Science..21
scientific information 66, 68, 119, 236
scientific reports 54, 177
screen captures 92-93
screen-sharing..76

sea 88-89
Search Engine Showdown 50
Search Engine Watch 50, 54
search engines 29, 30–39, 56, 201, 238
     comparison of 50-52, 239
     definition 30
     natural language.................................... 39
search results 48, 54, 96, 239
     number of 239
search strategy 7, 21-22, 26
search string 233
search tools.......................... 21, 29, 50, 191
     enhanced 46
     results.................................... 22, 31, 32
Searcher Magazine 21, 195, 235, 238-39
Searching Smart on the World Wide Web....
     30
Seattle Times 157
SEC 109, 162, 219, 225, 227
SEC Filings 85, 109, 137,
     .... 160, 162-64, 170, 172, 180
Securities & Exchange Commission .... *See* SEC
SEDAR.. 164
sending or transferring files 101
sexual predator databases 132
SHAREWARE.COM 102
Shatner, William 219
Shedden, David 157
Shoars, Alana 251
SIC Code 163, 164, 170, 171
Simpson, Nicole Brown 135
Simpson, O. J. 134-35
single mailbox .... *See* unifiers
site clustering 36
skip-tracing tools.................................... 58
SLA News Division 155, 157
Slate.. 153
small claims court 129
Smith, Robert Ellis................................ 251
Snap.. 56
soc 78
Social Security Numbers................. 12, 126,
     .... 129, 138, 249, 253, 257
Society of Competitive Intelligence
     Professionals................................. 173
sounds 92
     saving.. 92

South Park 220
spam 182, 254
spamming 54
Speak Freely for Windows 77
Special Libraries Association.......63, 156-57
Speech & Transcript Center 108
spider...31, 52-53, 191
Sports Illustrated 151
spreadsheets......................89, 97, 99, 100
     downloading 96, 97
St. Ambrose University 71
Starr, Ken 14
State & Local Government on the 'Net ...113
State Court Locator 108, 114
State Web Locator 108, 114
StateLaw...113
StateSearch... 114
Statistical Abstract of the US 109
Statistical Resources on the Web 46, 117
statistical sources...............................71, 116
statistics 46, 68, 71, 115, 117, 166
     best government.................................115
     crime & law enforcement 116
     employment & economy......116, 117, 166
     health 68
     international 116
     transportation 111
STAT-USA...................................117, 166
Statute of Anne...94
stocks 137
Strawberry, Darryl....................................234
Stuffit..93
subject directories...................29, 39, 41-42,
     .... 46, 50-51, 56, 75
     links 56
     specialized 44, 63
     topic-specific 45
     when to use 40
Sullivan, Danny 50, 54
Sullivan, Drew...96
Superior Online 131, 136, 140
Supreme Court........................45, 95, 250
Supreme Court opinions.........................124
surfing the Internet 22
     for health information 69
     under another identity 254
Switchboard...59

Sysop..69

T

targeting 12, 16-18, 66, 174
  based on behavior 18
Tate, Leroy B. 134
tax assessor web sites...................... 128
tax court records...........................129-30
tax liens 131, 138
Teeth.com..62
telemarketing............................. 12, 257
telephone numbers 57-58, 197
  unlisted 58
Telnet...............................52, 101-02
Tesh, Arnold..............................210-223
Texas 139
Thematic Mapping System 109
thesaurus...........................35, 69, 70
Thomas.............................. 109, 123
Thomas Register of American
  Manufacturers................................53
Thomas, Bill.......................... 227, 230
Thomas, Dawn Curie 227, 228, 229
tif file 89
Tillman, Hope 204
Time Magazine 151
Time-Warner.............................. 151, 234
Tow Zone 183
Trade Show Central 173
Trade Show Channel........................... 173
trademarks.................................... 177
TradStat....................................... 117
Trans Union................................. 12, 257
transcripts 145, 155
  news...........................144-45, 148, 151
  of speeches 108
transferring. See sending or transferring files
Transium 173
translation feature..................32, 34, 238
translations 197
Tripp, Linda 14
truncation 51, 55, 201
Tudor, Dean 154
Tudor, Jan Davis 164
txt 88-90

U

Ultimate White Pages...............................60
UN organizations.................................120
unifiers...184
Uniform Commercial Code 131
Uniform Resource Locator............. See URL
United Airlines 258
United Kingdom.............................59, 95
United Nations..........................119, 259
United Nations System.....................119
Universities.com................................61
University Law Review Project 46
University of Colorado......................108
University of Michigan 68
University of Texas 68
UNIX..88
uploading.......................................87
URL........9, 33-34, 51, 55, 71, 215, 239, 240
  definition of 9
  difficult to find..............................55
  how to read 9
US Census Bureau..................55, 71, 100,
  ....109, 117, 166, 170
US Datalink................................141
US Department of Defense.....................111
US Department of Transportation 111
US Federal Government Agencies
  Directory...................................107
US Geological Survey........................65
US Government Information...................107
US House of Representatives.................114
US News Online 152
US Patent & Trade Office 177
US President.................................111
US State Department.........................117
USA Today...................................150
USADATA....................................112
USDA...69
Usenet..................74, 78, 81, 183, 247
  beginners....................................78
  filtering 183
Usenet Cookbook............................41
Usenet newsgroups................77, 247, 254
Utah..133
uuencoding 101

V

vegan 226
vehicles, boats & aircraft........................ 136
Veterinarian's Best 223-230
VetSearch................................... 63
videoconferencing..............................76-77
virtual community 73
Virtual Meeting.............................. 77
Virtual Reference Desk........................... 71
vital records......................................128-29
   certified copies.................................. 128
VitalChek 128
Vogue 16
Vonnegut, Kurt.................... 143, 144
voter registration records.................. 82, 126
VoteWatch 123

W

Wall Street Journal 84, 149, 168-69
Warhol, Andy.. 215
Washington 81, 139
Washington Post ....
.........................84, 147-148, 150, 156, 249
wav 88, 89, 90
Wavephore's Newscast.......................... 188
web browser ....*See* browser
web chat ....*See* chat rooms
Web Track.................................. 251
Web TV.................................... 256
Webchat 75
Webmaster 13, 243
Wells Fargo Bank........................... 229
West Legal Directory 62, 220
Westlaw......................62, 121, 129, 220
White House............................... 110, 116
WhoWhere? 60

Widener University 204
wildcard characters............................33, 81
Williams, Margot 156
WINZIP......................................94
Wired Magazine 156
Woodland Hills 229
WordPad.....................................89
WordPerfect 88, 89
Workers' Compensation records.........140-41
World Alumni Net..............................60
World Wide Web 9, 21
   definition of 9
WorldPages Global Find 60
worm.............................*See* Spider
wpd.......................................89
Wright, Frank Lloyd.............................110
WWW ....*See* World Wide Web
WWW Virtual Library 115, 154

X

Xerox......................................251
Xinhua 146
xls 89, 99

Y

Yahoo!............. 30, 40, 41, 43-44, 46, 51-53,
.....56, 59, 72, 76, 115, 118, 146, 190, 234
Yahooligans...................................46
Yellow Page Finders 71

Z

Zacks 163, 168, 179
ZDNet......................................103, 190
Zeff, Robin 16
zip..89, 93, 94
ZIP Code 17, 148, 152

Notes

Notes

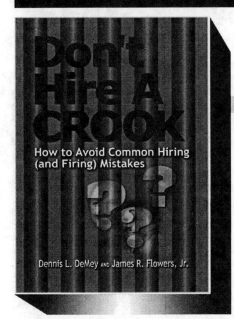
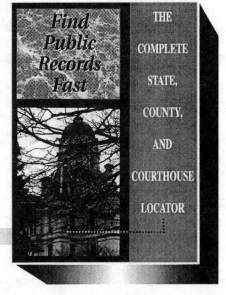

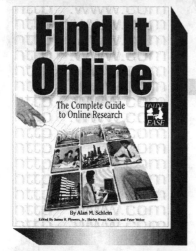